Intelligent
Multimedia
Interfaces

Intelligent Multimedia Interfaces

Edited by

Mark T. Maybury

MENLO PARK, CALIFORNIA
CAMBRIDGE, MASSACHUSETTS
LONDON, ENGLAND

AAAI Press / The MIT Press

Contents

Section 3: Architectural and Theoretical Issues / 277

Preface

This collection is an outgrowth of the American Association for Artificial Intelligence (AAAI) Workshop on Intelligent Multimedia Interfaces which took place at Anaheim, California in August of 1991. Multimedia interfaces are computer interfaces that communicate with users using multiple media (e.g., language, graphics, animations, video, non-speech audio) in multiple modalities (e.g., written text versus spoken language). *Intelligent* multimedia interfaces go beyond traditional hypermedia or hypertext environments to both process input and generate output in an intelligent or knowledge-based manner.

The purpose of the AAAI workshop was threefold: (1) to bring together researchers and practitioners to report on current advances in intelligent multimedia interface systems and their underlying theories, (2) to encourage scientific interchange among these individuals, and (3) to evaluate current efforts and make recommendations for future investigations. The workshop addressed a broad range of issues spanning the disciplines of artificial intelligence, computational linguistics, computer graphics, cognitive science, education/intelligent tutoring, software design, and information retrieval.

In addition to the many previous workshops on individual media (e.g., text generation, graphics generation), related workshops and collections have focused on intelligent user interfaces in general [Sullivan and Tyler 1991; Gray et al. 1993], multimedia interface design [Blattner and Dannenberg 1992], and multimedia communication [Taylor and Bouwhuis 1989]. This collection focuses specifically on those intelligent interfaces that exploit multiple media and modes to facilitate human-computer communication. As a consequence, this collection will be of interest to researchers and practitioners in computer science, artificial intelligence, computer-human interaction, cognitive science, and graphics design.

The book is organized into three sections: Automated Presentation Design; Intelligent Multimedia Interfaces; and Architectural and Theoretical Issues. The chapters in the first section focus on methods for the automatic design of multimedia presentations. Multimedia design involves a number of complex issues addressed by these papers including temporal coordination of multiple media, the relationship of textual and graphical generation, automatic design of graphics, and modality selection (e.g., realizing language as text or speech.) The chapters in the second section report on several investigations into systems that integrate multimedia input and generate coordinated multimedia output. These prototypes point the way to possible future systems that will enhance human-computer interaction. A final section considers knowledge sources and processes required for processing multiple media. These include the need to represent and reason about models of tasks and information, media, the user, and the discourse context. While research in this entire area is still in its formative stages, the individual contributors and I hope that this initial collection will help foster the scientific interchange and motivate necessary research to solve many of the remaining fundamental problems.

Acknowledgments

I would like to thank the American Association for Artificial Intelligence and MIT Press, in particular Mike Hamilton and Bob Prior, as well as The MITRE Corporation, for their support and cooperation. I thank the authors and reviewers who worked hard to interrelate their chapters. This book would not have been possible without the administrative support of Susan Hanlon who spent endless hours typing, faxing, mailing, and proofing the many versions of the book. Finally and most importantly, for her continuous support while I edited the book on weekends and nights, I dedicate this collection to my wife, Michelle.

Mark Maybury
Bedford, Massachusetts
March, 1993

Intelligent Multimedia Interfaces

Introduction

Mark T. Maybury

Abstract

Multimedia communication is ubiquitous in daily life. When humans converse with one another, we utilize a wide array of media to interact including spoken language, gestures, and drawings. We exploit multiple human sensory systems or modes of communication including vision, audition, and taction. Some media and modes of communication are more efficient or effective than others for certain tasks, users, or contexts (e.g., the use of speech to control devices in hand and eyes-busy contexts, the use of maps to convey terrain and cartographic information). Whereas humans have a natural facility for managing and exploiting multiple input and output media, computers do not. The ability of machines to interpret multimedia input and generate multimedia output would be a valuable facility for a number of key applications such as information retrieval and analysis, training, and decision support. This chapter introduces the need for intelligent multimedia interfaces, defines key terms and concepts, outlines the current state of the art, and describes the structure of this collection which addresses some remaining fundamental problems.

1. Need

Human abilities should be amplified, not impeded, by using computers, and the synergistic utilization of multiple media can support this amplification. If appropriate media are utilized for human computer interaction, there is the potential to (1) increase the bandwidth of information flow between human and machine (that is, the raw number of bits of information being communicated), and (2) improve the signal-to-noise ratio of this information (that is, the amount of useful bits conveyed). To achieve these potential gains, however, requires a better understanding of information characteristics, how they relate to characteristics of media, and how they relate to models of tasks, users, and environments. This goal is exacerbated by the proliferation of new interactive devices (datagloves and bodysuits, head mounted displays, three dimensional sound), the lack of standards, and a poor or at least ill-applied knowledge of human cognitive and physical capabilities with respect to multimedia devices. For example, some empirical studies [Krause, this volume] provide evidence that even well accepted applications of multimedia (e.g., the use of check marks and greying out in menus) can exacerbate rather than improve user performance. This motivates the need to understand the principles underlying multimedia communication. Understanding these principles will not only result in better models and interactive devices, but also lead to new tools for context-sensitive multimedia help, automated and semi-automated multimedia interface construction, and intelligent agents for multimedia information retrieval, processing, presentation, and authoring.

2. Definitions

We begin with a clarification of the terms multimedia and multimodal. By mode or modality we refer primarily to the human senses employed to process incoming information, e.g., vision, audition, taction, olfaction. We do not mean mode in the sense of purpose, e.g., word processing mode versus spread sheet mode. Additionally, we recognize medium, in its conventional definition, to refer both to the material object (e.g., paper, video) as well as the means by which information is conveyed (e.g., a sheet of paper with text on it). We would elaborate these definitions to include the possibility of layering so that a natural language mode might use written text or speech as media even though those media themselves rely on other modes.

Media and mode are related non-trivially. First, a single medium may support several modalities. For example, a piece of paper may support both language and graphics just as a visual display may support text, images, and video. Likewise, a single modality may be supported by many media. For example, the language modality can be supported visually (i.e., written language) and aurally (i.e., spoken language) – in fact spoken language can have a visual component (e.g., lip reading). Just as a single medium may support several modalities and a single modality may be supported by many media, many media may support many modalities, and likewise. For example, a multimedia document which includes text, graphics, speech, video, effects several modalities, e.g., visual and auditory perception of natural language, visual perception of images (still and moving), and auditory perception of sounds. Finally, this multimedia and multimodal interaction occurs over time. Therefore, it is necessary to account for the processing of discourse, context shifts, and changes in agent states over time.

Multimedia interfaces are computer interfaces that communicate with users using multiple media (e.g., language, graphics, animations, video, non-speech audio), sometimes using multiple modes, such as written text together with spoken language. "Intelligent" multimedia interfaces go beyond traditional hypertext or hypermedia environments in that they process input and generate output in an intelligent or knowledge-based manner. This area is multidisciplinary by nature, spanning the disciplines of at least artificial intelligence, computational linguistics, computer graphics, cognitive science, education/intelligent tutoring, software design, and information retrieval.

3. State of the Art

The state of the art in intelligent multimedia interfaces is exemplified by limited prototypes in narrow domains that are able to interpret a few kinds of input and generate limited forms of output. These systems often integrate or build upon single-media components that perform tasks such as spoken language recognition and generation or graphical design. For example, the state of the art includes the ability to interpret typed or spoken natural language utterances together with deictic mouse or dataglove gestures to resolve ambiguous references (e.g., "put that there") [Bolt 1980; Neal et al. 1989].

On the output side, the majority of work has investigated automated generation of single output media. In recent years a number of advances have been made in the area of linguistic realization (e.g., PENMAN [Mann 1983], MUMBLE [McDonald and Pustejovsky 1985], FUF [Elhadad et al. 1993]) and text planning (e.g., [McKeown 1985; Hovy 1988a; Moore 1989; Maybury 1990]). At the same time, others have made progress in graphical design. For example, mechanisms have been developed to design tables and charts [Mackinlay 1986b], network diagrams [Marks 1991ab], business graphics displays [Roth and Mattis 1991], and three dimensional explanatory graphics [Feiner 1985].

In addition, several laboratory prototypes have been developed that automatically generate coordinated multimedia presentations. For example, André et al. [this volume] describe WIP which presents and understands combinations of graphics, text, and pointing gestures (e.g., it can generate captioned visual instructions on how to operate an espresso machine). COMET (Columbia Operations and Maintenance Explanation Testbed) [Feiner and McKeown, this volume] automatically designs integrated textual and three dimensional graphical presentations to explain the operation and maintenance of an Army field radio. The integrated interfaces project is able to display Navy briefing information using maps, text, and tables [Arens et al. 1991] and SAGE automatically creates business graphics displays [Roth and Mattis 1991]. Finally, TEXPLAN [Maybury, this volume] provides narrated animations of directions over an object-oriented map using a collection of multimedia actions (e.g., speech acts, graphical acts) for media integration and control.

Other prototypes integrate multimedia input and output. For example, Burger and Marshall [this volume] describe an intelligent multimedia interface (AIMI) which can engage a user in a multimedia dialogue, for example, responding to a natural language query by automatically designing business-like graphics, which the user can then interact with or refer to. AIMI is able to choose alternative media to express information in an underlying KL-ONE-like knowledge base, for example, using non-speech audio to convey the speed, stage, or duration of an otherwise invisible process.

Despite the exciting possibilities suggested by these early prototypes, many fundamental questions remain only partially answered. This collection both reports on these early prototypes and begins to address some of these questions.

4. Key Remaining Problems: An Overview of the Book

From a system's standpoint, the key areas which require further investigation include the integration of multimedia input, the selection and coordination of multimedia output, and fuller knowledge of and better models for representing and reasoning about media and modes. From an architectual standpoint, we need to understand the infrastructure required to support and encourage progress in the field as well as fundamental questions such as: What are they key components?, What functionality do they need to support?, What is the proper flow of control?, and How should they interact? (e.g., serially, interleaved, co-constraining). Finally, we need to better understand from an empirical standpoint how well our integrated multimedia interfaces will function. This entails designing metrics and conducting evaluations. The book is organized around these issues into three sections: Section 1: Automated Presentation Design, Section 2: Intelligent Multimedia Interfaces, and Section 3: Architectural and Theoretical Issues.

4.1. Intelligent Multimedia Input and Output

The chapters in the first section of the book address the automatic generation of multimedia presentations, beginning with a survey by Roth and Hefley. Those in the second section of the book address interfaces which not only present but also interpret multimedia information.

At the most basic level, more investigation is needed in representing and reasoning about media. For input, current display-device technology remains cumbersome and low fidelity. Development and experimentation with new interactive devices (e.g., those replicating force feedback) and the integration of their multiple inputs (e.g., spoken language, gestures, and eye-trackers) is required. The integration of these must be done carefully to ensure synergistic coupling among multiple media. This is perhaps one of the least investigated areas, despite the widespread use of two input devices (i.e., keyboard and mouse). Koons et al. [this volume] describe an innovative approach to integrating speech, gaze, and gesture.

Multimedia output also requires further investigation. Many of the articles in the first and second sections of this book directly address this problem. Multimedia generation can be divided into the processes of content selection (i.e., choosing what to say), media allocation (choosing which media to say what in), media realization (choosing how to say items in a particular media), and media coordination. The design, realization, and coordination of text and speech, graphs, tables, pictures, maps, and forms offers a number of challenges. Key problems include the temporal coordination of multiple media, the relationship of textual and graphical generation, automatic design of graphics, and modality selection (e.g., realizing language as text or speech). The generation of multimedia presentations requires knowledge about the kind of information to display, the goal of the producer, the characteristics of the addressee, and the nature of the media (e.g., text versus graphics). Another issue concerns the degree of automation versus mixed initiative. Other issues concern whether or not systems save the history or structure of a presentation and if and how animations were connected to representations of abstract knowledge. The need for deep knowledge of designed graphics depends upon the intended use of the multimedia presentation (e.g., for teaching versus manual generation) and the environment in which it is used (e.g., interactive, static).

There are several common problems in allocating and coordinating media. These include the need for presentation balance, mutual reference and the interaction between text and graphics, and the relationship between the characteristics of the information to be presented and the devices available for presentation. More sophisticated architectures may be required to control the design process (e.g., André et al.'s WIP [this volume] exploits two feedback loops, one after presentation design and one after realization, to help resolve inter- and intra-media synthesis problems). Related to the need to dynamically plan presentations is the choice between plan reuse, refinement, or replanning after a failed presentation. And when multiple choices among presentations are possible, one problem is the need for "goodness" metrics that, for example, measure the consistency and coherency of multimedia presentations.

A related issue concerns when, how, and why media are chosen to convey different types of information. Whereas some researchers take a practical approach to this problem, building systems that are based on reverse engineering of naturally-occuring presentations, others argue that media selection should be a machine-learned activity based on interaction with users, and still others argue that it requires empirical validation through observation of man-machine interactions. Related to this focus on empiricism is the need to provide statistical evidence that the additional machinery required to design and render more complex multimedia presentations is warranted by some pedagogic benefit, increase in efficiency, or increase in the effectiveness of accomplishing some task.

In summary, the capabilities of intelligent multimedia systems go beyond hypermedia to include the ability to interpret (possibly multimedia) questions and automatically design multimedia answers (e.g., WIP, COMET, AIMI), to deal with follow-up questions and make backward references (e.g., AIMI), and to post-edit presentations (e.g., COMET). Other areas which require further research include incorporating dialogue (e.g., context and turn-taking) into multimedia interfaces, more complex models of pedagogue, and a capability to provide diagnosis and advice giving as a user designs a presentation. A final possibility is tailoring multimedia presentations to individual user's psychological state, knowledge, abilities, attitudes and preferences, goals, and plans. The research results on reader adaptation in technical documentation, on user modeling in interactive computer systems, and on computer-aided tutoring systems, might also be relevant to this endeavor.

4.2. Architectural and Theoretical Issues

The last section of the book addresses issues concerning the architectures and empirical evaluation of intelligent multimedia interfaces. One of the primary concerns is what kinds of information and knowledge must be represented to support these systems, and how we should represent and reason about it. Necessary models include: (1) models of media (e.g., the characteristics, strengths and weaknesses), (2) models of the user (e.g., the ability to acquire, represent, and maintain useful data about user abilities (physical and cognitive), preferences, attention, and intentions from interactions with the interface), (3) modeling of dialogue history (e.g., the ability to automatically assimilate information from user interactions with the interface, and (4) modeling of the situation (e.g., the ability to automatically track system parameters such as load and available media, which can be used to influence interface decisions on input and output).

Questions remain as to how to acquire, represent, maintain, and exploit the models. Equally unspecified is the architectural relation of intelligent multimedia interface components – What is flow of control? Finally, there remains a need for facilities to integrate canned media with dynamically generated media.

Other issues are introduced in this collection by Roth and Hefley [this volume], Krause [this volume], and others, concerning metrics and methods for evaluating progress and capabilities in this area. First, it is necessary to more fully understand existing media. This includes representing media strengths and weaknessess in a standard manner, including the protocols that describe the kind of information these systems can use. This will demand standard terms, units of measurement, levels of performance, techniques of use, and so on. Equally important, however, is the need to match media to human (physical and cognitive) capabilities such as memory and attention. We will need to formulate metrics for time/quality tradeoff among media, and use these to judge among possible input and output facilities. Finally, we will require metrics for both glass box and black box evaluation of interface functionality to measure individual component effectiveness (e.g., timeliness and fidelity of generated media) as well as measuring overall interface effectiveness.

5. Conclusion

If successful, intelligent multimedia interfaces promise to enable systems and people to use media to their best advantage, in several ways. First, they can increase the raw bit rate of information flow between human and machine (for example, by using the most appropriate medium for information exchange). Second, they can facilitate human interpretation of information by helping to focus user attention on the most meaningful or relevant information. Third, they can use multiple media to more effectively allocate information across media during presentation. Finally, these investigations can provide explicit models of media to facilitate interface design so, for example, future interfaces can benefit from additional aspects of human communication that are currently ignored by current interfaces (e.g., speech inflections or hand gestures).

The goal of achieving context sensitivity will be limited only by the richness of models that can be created. In short, this area has the potential to improve the quality and effectiveness of interaction for everyone who communicates with a machine in the future. To achieve these benefits, however, we must overcome the remaining fundamental problems outlined above. The contributions in this book aspire to provide initial solutions.

6. Acknowledgments

I would like to thank all the workshop participants and authors for their ideas, many of which have been adopted above, especially Ed Hovy, Yigal Arens, Brad Goodman, John Burger, and Ralph Marshall. Finally, I thank Marc Vilain for the original inspiration for the workshop.

Automated Presentation Design

The papers in this first section raise in a concrete manner issues central to multimedia presentation design including: How can a system represent and reason about heterogeneous media in an integrated fashion? How should we select and apportion content to different media during design? How do we coordinate media? How can we ensure that given communicative goals are achieved by the resulting artifact? What is the relation between canned presentations and those that are dynamically designed and realized? authoring.

In the first chapter, Steven Roth and William Hefley place in historical and technical perspective the many investigations into intelligent multimedia presentation. They first consider the purposes of multimedia presentation systems and key functional requirements (e.g., content selection and presentation design, media apportionment and coordination). This leads to a consideration of their architectural structure and function, flow of control, and so on. They then consider the nature of the information contained in these systems. This is followed by a discussion of the range of functions of presentations and the implications this has on their underlying architectures, be they based on rules, constraints, rhetorical schema, plan operators, etc. They then consider various classes of presentation design knowledge associated with functions such as content selection, media and presentation technique selection, and presentation coordination. They conclude by providing a Human Computer Interaction (HCI) view of intelligent multimedia presentations which include concerns for evaluation metrics (e.g., usability as well as design complexity). A final section argues for the requirement for mechanisms to support interactive design, which entails defining vocabularies for specifying goals or tasks, methods for selecting among design alternatives, and possibilities for controlling rendering choices (e.g., color, fonts, orientation) or critiquing user designs.

The remaining chapters describe four systems which automatically design multimedia presentations, an extended TEXPLAN, WIP, COMET, and a visual repair prototype.

Chapter two describes an extension of a communicative act theory of multisentential text to multimedia presentations. In particular, building on the action-based view of communication advocated by Austin and Searle, the chapter defines linguistic, graphical, and physical actions as all being different methods of performing various communicative acts. These media-specific actions are abstracted into media-independent actions, called rhetorical actions, such as describe, compare, or explain. The chapter illustrates how a computational implementation of these ideas is able to represent and reason about multimedia actions in an integrated framework. This is exemplified by multimedia plans which were used in a object-oriented cartographic system for coordinated multimedia location identification and route exposition.

Immediately following this paper are two papers that detail the WIP system, which plans coordinated linguistic (English or German) and three-dimensional graphical displays (e.g., illustrated instructions for the operation of an espresso machine). The first chapter by Elisabeth André, Wolfgang Finkler, Winfried Graf, Thomas Rist, Anne Schauder, and Wolfgang Wahlster provides an architectural overview of WIP. Similar to TEXPLAN, WIP approaches multimedia design from a plan-based paradigm. Whereas TEXPLAN designs narrated animations of routes, WIP generates three dimensional graphics and embodies a constraint-based layout manager that is able to reject designs that do not fulfill layout constraints. Architecturally, WIP consists of two parallel processing cascades that enable the incremental design and realization of text (using tree adjoining grammars) and graphics. Further, individual media design and realization are interdependent processes that allow (graphical or textual) realization constraints to guide (graphical or textual) design goals, which in turn can constrain overall presentation or layout goals. This can be both within and across media, exemplified by the generation of a cross-modal referring expression (e.g., "The on/off switch is located *in the upper left corner of the picture*").

The second WIP paper by Elisabeth André and Thomas Rist argues that traditional hierarchical planners are inadequate to handle complex interdependence of content determination, mode selection, and realization. They suggest that what is required are interleaved components which allow for revision and communication among one another. They outline mode preferences for information types such as: 1) prefer graphics for concrete information such as visual properties of objects or events involving physical objects, 2) prefer graphics for spatial information such as the location, orientation, composition, or movement of objects unless the emphasis is on minimizing errors in which case text is preferred, and 3) prefer text for quantification, negation, conditional, and causal relations if there is potential ambiguity. They also detail how mode decisions depend on the communicative goal. For example, a comparison might dictate using similar presentation modes to emphasize differences, a request might be best conveyed linguistically, and because pictures increase authenticity, they may be preferred over text if the goal is to provide evidence for a claim. The remainder of the article details the formalization and use of presentation knowledge as plans such as request-enable-motivate, describe-orientation, and depict-object.

The next chapter contains two contributions which describe COMET (COordinated Multimedia Explanation Testbed) and proposed extensions to it. The first by Steven Feiner and Kathleen McKeown details how COMET uses rhetorical schemas [McKeown 1985] to select content independent of media and then apportions this to text and three-dimensional graphics to design coordinated multimedia presentations concerning the operation and maintenance of an Army field radio. While COMET designs illustrated instructions like WIP, they are architecturally quite different. COMET differs from the previous two systems because 1) it uses (media independent) schemas rather than plans for content selection and 2) media allocation occurs after not during content selection. That is, after logical forms are selected by a schema, a media coordinator annotates logical forms to be realized as text or graphics. The media coordinator uses media allocation rules such as use: 1) graphics alone for locational and physical attributes, 2) text for abstract acts and relations, and 3) text and graphics for simple and compound actions. COMET allows for two types of coordination between media. First, the media coordinator attempts to coordinate sentence breaks with picture breaks. Second, COMET allows for media cross-references both to structure (e.g., a picture) or to content (e.g., the location of an entity in a picture). Like TEXPLAN and WIP, COMET reasons about both domain knowledge as well as knowledge of the user and previous discourse to make content and mode allocation decisions. Further, it allows text and graphics to influence one another via the logical form and separates communicative goals from the media used to carry them out.

The second contribution from Steven Feiner, Diane Litman, Kathleen McKeown, and Rebecca Passonneau proposes extensions to COMET to enable explicit reasoning about temporal media (e.g., animation and speech) and temporal information associated with (domain or communicative) events (e.g., points in time, durations, ordering relations). They describe using Allen's temporal logic to construct temporal plans to move beyond COMET's current reliance on solely sequential relations of actions. This would enable the generation of certain kinds of linguistic phenomena (e.g., temporal adverbials such as "before" or "simultaneously") which can be used to signal temporal relations if these are not indirectly expressed by the linear order of language. Further, these temporal relations can be used to guide graphical generation. For example, a dissolve from one scene to another can be used to convey elapsed time. In addition to this temporal editing effect, spatial editing effects are possible (e.g., a split screen can be used to depict simultaneous actions or multiple views of the same action). Access to underlying temporal relations may even suggest media choices (e.g., simultaneous actions can be more effectively presented graphically than in linear speech). Finally, the authors point out the difficulty of coordinating temporal media (e.g., synchronizing the start and duration of communicative acts so that the reference in a voice-over identifying a highlighted object occurs precisely at the same time and duration as the corresponding visual display), an issue addressed in part by the next chapter.

The final chapter in this first section is by Brad Goodman and reports on a presentation planner that composes pre-recorded video clips and annotates them with speech, text labels, and graphical overlays based on an underlying repair plan for a Macintosh IIcx. Unlike the design graphics of WIP and COMET, this visual repair application re-uses previous canned media, splicing it and augmenting it with narration on the fly. A user is able to graphically describe a repair plan which can be critiqued or played-back to promote learning. Analogous to the work described in the first chapter on multimedia communicative acts, this chapter illustrates how graphical, spoken, and written communication can be expressed in an underlying action-based formalism (e.g., displaying video of a power supply, annotating objects in the video with labels, and narrating the action being performed in speech). This chapter raises the possibility of reusing and editing previously produced media (e.g., using overlays to focus attention on a pre-recorded video) and integrating this with media generated on the fly.

Chapter 1

Intelligent Multimedia Presentation Systems: Research and Principles

Steven F. Roth and William E. Hefley

1. Introduction

Rapid progress in computer technology is bringing enormous potential to our desktops for accessing vast amounts of new information. Progress includes faster information processing, greater storage capabilities, better networking infrastructure for high-speed information transfer, and higher quality video, audio and graphics display capabilities. Accompanying this progress is a greater collective expectation that people will be more able to solve problems if we can provide them access to more kinds of information than they have ever obtained before. Information is becoming a commodity.

While the infrastructure for storing, transferring and displaying information is developing rapidly [Fox 1991], we still need technology that enables people to effectively make use of this information. Users need technology which communicates information when they need it, and in formats they can use to support the tasks they are performing. These needs are representative of those of any user – regardless if their tasks are seeking treasures in a video game, rescheduling factory operations or planning a travel itinerary. Systems must be developed which retrieve, construct and present relevant information by automatically selecting and integrating effective combinations of multimedia communication techniques.

A growing research area is addressing this problem through the application of knowledge-based techniques for creating Intelligent Multimedia Presentation Systems (IMMPS). This paper discusses the research problems and approaches that are central in this area, drawing upon lessons learned from automated presentation of information graphics, and proposes some guiding principles for building such systems. As these systems expand to deal with increasing amounts of information and multimedia communication techniques, these principles must provide a rich synthesis of computational and interface design perspectives.

What does an intelligent multimedia presentation system do? In understanding multimedia communication, our perspective acknowledges that IMMPS are indeed artifacts situated in the user's world, and that these artifacts serve as mediators betweem them and the world [Norman 1991]. As an artifact, an IMMPS provides a rich means of communicating information to users through its multimedia presentations. As input, an IMMPS takes a collection of information to be communicated and a set of communicative goals (i.e., purposes or intentions for communicating information or the tasks to be performed by the user of the information); an IMMPS has available a set of alternative media and presentation methods (i.e., communicative techniques). The function of an IMMPS is to design a presentation which expresses this information using a combination of the available presentation techniques and media in a way which achieves the communicative purposes and supports users in performing their tasks.

This definition focuses attention on several key research tasks that have been topics of investigation and which form the basis for designing components of an IMMPS architecture. They include:

- Developing mechanisms for determining the appropriate information content to be communicated,
- Representing the essential characteristics of information relevant to creating presentations,
- Representing communicative intent or purpose and the tasks that presentations are designed to support,
- Incorporating knowledge for choosing among presentation media,
- Incorporating design knowledge for selecting and assembling techniques within presentation media,
- Incorporating knowledge for coordinating different media or modalities within a presentation, and
- Developing techniques for interactive exploration of presented information.

Why must a multimedia presentation system be intelligent as well? An *intelligent* multimedia presentation system would automate the process of designing presentations and thereby communicate effectively when the types and combinations of information to be presented are not predictable. It would be most effective in situations when it is not possible for system developers to design presentation software because they cannot anticipate all possible combinations of information that will be requested for display. An IMMPS would be generative – it would flexibly construct presentations honoring constraints posed by variations in the availability of media techniques, information characteristics, user preferences and situational goals. It would also be valuable in exploratory or problem-solving situations requiring manipulation of complex information structures which are difficult to map onto presentation designs. An IMMPS would assume the burden of as much of the presentation design process as is desirable by a user (particularly as many users lack the expertise, time, or interest to design multimedia presentations). Even when users know the display presentation approach they desire, an IMMPS would support the specification of displays by enabling effective communication of design choices. A knowledgeable presentation system would infer gaps in a user's incompletely specified design and augment them with its own design choices when appropriate.

The purpose of this paper is to outline the central findings from research on intelligent graphics presentation and point out some unanswered questions in research on intelligent multimedia presentation. Our focus is intentionally narrowed to problems of designing presentations, rather than two-way communication (i.e., both presenting and receiving information) in a dialogue between a user and a computer system. While still in its infancy, a growing body of research has emerged which addresses the presentation aspects of intelligent interfaces, at least for a subset of information and media. However, because it is still in its infancy, it is not obvious how to integrate the diverse work even on this portion of the problem, due to different perspectives, vocabulary, and emphases. Nonetheless, we see important principles and research strategies emerging which, if properly characterized, can provide guidance for generalizing to broader classes of information, media, and other aspects of intelligent multimedia interfaces.

The next section characterizes interface concepts useful in understanding multimedia communication. Key topics that will be addressed in subsequent sections include:

- A conceptual architecture typical of intelligent multimedia presentation systems, addressing both the processing that occurs within the architecture and the relevant knowledge sources,
- Properties of application systems and the data sources which provide the input to intelligent multimedia presentation systems,
- Characterizing application data,

- Characterizing presenter's and recipient's goals, tasks, and cognitive processes, and
- Knowledge and mechanisms for designing presentations, including representation of presentation technique syntax, semantics, and pragmatics.

2. Interface Concepts

The terms *multimedia, multimodal, media, modes,* and *modality* have often been defined and used differently throughout the literature. From the perspective of a user, a *multimodal* interface is an interface that causes one to utilize more than one sensory channel (or *modality*) to perceive the information being presented or to interact with a system. From the perspective of a system, such an interface may also be a *multimedia* interface using different information carriers (i.e., *media*) to express and communicate the information.

This distinction between perspectives is reflected in the field's confusion between the terms *multimedia* and *multimodal*. From the system designer's perspective, the term *multimedia* is typically applied to the use of some sort of interaction across *media* (or carriers) and concerns are focused on integrating carriers and time-based media, such as video, sound, or animation. As a result, many of the critical research issues here address the computational problems of the synchronization of the time-based media with respect to absolute time scales (e.g., making sure that presentations don't run faster when executed on a faster machine) and relative time scales (e.g., making sure that the sound annotations of a video start and end at the proper points in the video), as well as the more general design and usability problems of providing effective techniques for searching, browsing, and interacting with the information held within such a system.

From a user perspective, *modality* distinctions can be made along human sensory channels, technology used to store or present the information, or even computational techniques used to present the information (i.e., speech output is different from written text on the screen). So far, we have discussed modality as "the manner in which a human being communicates or acquires information" [Coutaz 1992]. This manner of communication is concerned not only with the type of communication (or sensory channel) used, but also affects the expression of the information on the communication channel. This accounts for part of the confusion over the term *modality*, because it has been used to refer to both the sensory channel by which information is expressed (i.e., visual) and the form of the expression (i.e., information graphics). To complicate matters further, *multimodal* also means multiple modes, the latter a more general term used to differentiate muliple forms of expression (whether different media, sensory channels or presentation techniques within media).

In order to avoid confusion, we will consider *modality* to be a "single mechanism by which to express information" [Arens and Hovy 1990a] regardless of whether it reflects different sensory channels. Examples include the many styles of written text, each a different modality with its own text layout, structure, and conventions, or the many styles of information graphics (e.g., charts, network diagrams and tables), each a different modality of expression. These distinctions can be viewed at different levels of detail. For example, information graphics include chart and network modalities, the chart (i.e., dual axis) modality can be further differentiated based on the alternative graphical objects and attributes from which different chart styles are defined.

Recognizing these levels of description, and with some arbitrariness, we use the term *media* to emphasize the differences among broader classes of expression (e.g., natural language text, information graphics, maps, realistic graphical depictions, photographs, music, etc). We use *modality* to refer to classes of presentation techniques within media (e.g., barcharts, plotcharts, tables). As a result, we frequently refer to modalities as intra-media presentation techniques.

Whatever the dividing line between media, modalities and techniques, it is possible to define their syntax and semantics at a level of precision that allows them to be understood in presentation generation [Hovy and Arens 1991], and in doing so, support apportionment and coordination of the information content in the resulting presentation. For further discussion of these terms, see [Dannenberg and Blattner 1992] and [Coutaz 1992].

3. An Intelligent Multimedia Presentation Architecture

3.1. Architectural Drivers

An intelligent multimedia presentation system must not only *present* information, but it must also *design* presentations that communicate information using a combination of the available presentation techniques and media in a way which achieves the communicative purposes and supports users in performing their tasks. In designing presentations, whether by hand or by an automated presentation generator, Norman's **appropriateness principle** [Norman 1991] should hold:

> The surface representation used by the artifact should allow the person to work with exactly the information acceptable to the task: neither more nor less.

A conceptual architecture that builds on existing efforts, and associated issues, can be generalized to a number of key processes. The processes, shown in Figure 1, include:

- Content planning – determining what information should be presented and selecting the content needed to support the user's tasks,
- Technique selection – apportioning information to media and modalities, selecting appropriate media or modalities which will be used for realization, and coordinating the selections for specific information content,
- Presentation design – determining how media or modalities will be used to communicate their selected information content, and
- Coordination – composing, organizing, resolving conflicts and maintaining presentation consistency.

These processes are general, and provide an applicable framework for understanding a number of high-level design issues. In fact, most occur at multiple levels, for example in processes which consider either media or intra-media (i.e., modality) design decisions. These issues include problems of apportionment, coordination, feedback to content selection from subsequent stages, consideration of task, user and data characteristics in selecting techniques, and related design decisions. Thus, decisions about how to apportion information between natural language and graphics should be made using similar principles as decisions about apportioning information within the graphics medium (e.g., choosing appropriate charts, as well as selecting alternative graphical objects within charts).

3.2. Conceptual Architecture

Many view the architecture of an IMMPS as consisting of a mostly sequential flow of these general processes, or a hierarchical planning process leading to a fully-instantiated and articulable plan for multimedia presentation. However, an effective presentation design process must involve processes which are parallel and interacting (e.g,. [Wahlster 1989; Seligmann and Feiner 1991]). This suggests extensive feedback between components making decisions about media and modalities, rather than a strictly hierarchical, sequential decision-making process. In the architecture shown in Figure 1, these processes are indeed inter-related and are all driven by concern for data and task characteristics, situational context and the state of the discourse (these concerns are represented as parallel inputs to all processes).

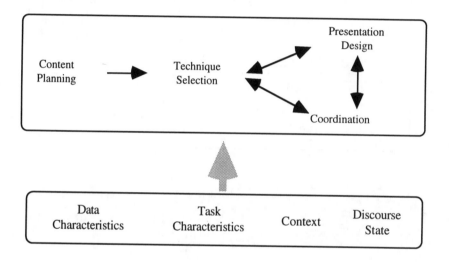

Figure 1. Feedback and Multiple Knowledge Sources Among IMMPS Processes

Figure 1, in its description of the relations among key processes for intelligent design of presentations, provides a starting point for understanding the larger issues of a conceptual architecture for intelligent multimedia presentation. However, to develop an appropriate presentation, an IMMPS must address a number of higher-level concerns, many of which are inadequately represented in Figure 1. These include the goals and focus of the dialogue, the user's context and their current task, and media selection to represent this information in a way that maps to these concerns. As with multi-modal input [Koons et al., this volume], although one mode may present a significant portion of the information, many messages are presented and interpreted by the user using information from other modes, the context of the presentation, and the user's current goal structures.

Figure 2 summarizes a high-level conceptual architecture for IMMPS, building on and extending previous efforts in intelligent interfaces and intelligent multimedia presentation systems [Feiner 1991; Roth and Mattis 1990a; Roth and Mattis 1991, Roth et al. 1991; Edwards and Mason 1989; Hefley 1990; Hefley and Murray 1993; Wahlster et al., this volume].

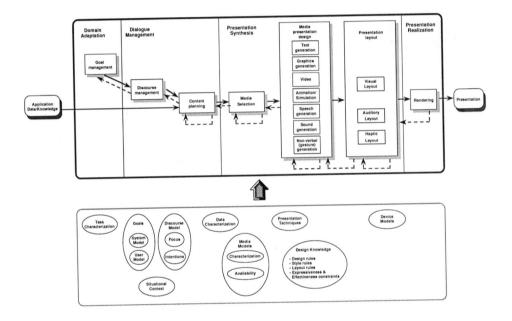

Figure 2. Conceptual Architecture and Knowledge Sources Used by an IMMPS

Figure 2 shows a primarily sequential processing flow using bold arrows. The dotted arrows indicate feedback or backtracking and coordination between and within processes. Even this conceptual architecture, which suggests extensive feedback between and within media and modalities, may not adequately emphasize the role of feedback and coordination, because a hierarchical, sequential decision-making process for selection and design decisions between and within media may not be appropriate.

Some information is communicated better, in the context of a user's situation and tasks, by a combination of media (i.e., some situationally-dependent combination of written text, static graphics, dynamic graphics or animation, video, speech, sound, and touch or gestures). In developing its output, an IMMPS must consider not only the characterization of the data provided by the underlying application, but also take into account a characterization of the system's and user's goals, user's tasks and cognitive processes, as well as the current state of the discourse. [Kobsa and Wahlster 1989] provides more in-depth discussions of the possible roles of user models in dialogue systems. These knowledge sources (shown at the bottom of Figure 2) may be drawn upon at each step in the IMMPS' processes. They not only provide information needed at each step, but provide valuable constraints for resolving conflicts and coordinating the results of subsequent processes.

Nonetheless, there is likely to be a large hierarchical/recursive nature to media and presentation technique selection as well as for coordination. This is independent of media; it is equally true of graphics design, textual design, or design in another media. For example, Maybury's [1990, 1992b] textual explanations are planned using a similar high-level to low-level refinement from communicative acts to presented text. The recursive nature of selection, refinement and coordination (within media), often serves as a stimulus for improvements in how components handling different media communicate. Among the interactions among media that can be addressed include conflicts (perceptual or task-related, as well as in mapping of information to techniques), references to other portions of the presentation, or consistency within the presentation. Similar coordination effects can be seen both within and across media as part of the layout process [Arens et al., this volume].

Using the conceptual architecture presented here as a common framework, the remaining sections of this paper each cover a different area of concern, followed by a discussion of broader implications for the architecture from a perspective of effective human-computer interaction.

4. Domains, Applications, and Information

Before considering the methods by which intelligent systems design presentations, it is worthwhile to consider the form of application data sources that constitute the inputs to these systems as well as assumptions about the way applications and presentation systems interact. In particular, research approaches can be considered in terms of (1) the types of data with which they are concerned and the data modeling paradigms they employ, and (2) the degree of integration or independence between presentation system and application system components, including the extent to which the processes of content selection and content expression are functionally segregated across the application/IMMPS boundary.

4.1. Information Types and Modeling Approaches

IMMPS research programs differ in the types of information on which they focus and, consequently, the types of presentation design problems they address:

- Quantitative and relational facts have been expressed using charts, tables, and networks augmented with shape, color, size, texture and related properties of multi-dimensional graphical objects [Gnanamgari 1981; Beach 1985; Mackinlay 1986b; Gargan et al. 1988; Binot et al. 1990; Westfold et al. 1990; Roth et al. 1991; Casner 1991; Marks 1991a; Senay 1991],

- Three-dimensional objects have been depicted with realistic three-dimensional graphical displays [Feiner and Seligmann 1991],

- Procedural instructions have been expressed with combinations of natural language and realistic graphics or maps [Feiner and McKeown 1991; André et al., this volume; Maybury 1991b; Sukaviriya and Foley 1990],

- Summaries of the causal relationships among data changes in quantitative models have been expressed with combinations of natural language and charts, tables and networks [Roth 1991c],

- Geographically related situations have been expressed using iconic and map techniques [Neal and Shapiro 1991; Arens et al. 1991], and

- Business forms have been expressed using a graphical representation of the form [Wahlster 1991]

Previous IMMPS research efforts have been grounded in numerous applications domains. Numerous efforts have addressed information graphics in several domains, including two-dimensional tables [Beach 1985; Westfold et al. 1990], two-dimensional diagrams [Westfold et al. 1990], two-dimensional presentation graphics [Gnanamgari 1981], chart graphics [Mackinlay 1986], and network diagrams [Marks 1991b, Binot et al. 1990]. Other applications domains which IMMPS work has addressed include:

- Animation [Karp and Feiner 1990; Sukaviriya and Foley 1990],
- Architecture [Flemming 1989],
- Business forms [Wahlster 1991],
- Cartographic information systems [Maybury 1991b; Wahlster 1988a],
- Context-sensitive animated help [Sukaviriya and Foley 1990; Sukaviriya et al. 1992],
- Electronic equipment maintenance and repair [Feiner and McKeown 1991; Seligmann and Feiner 1991],
- Emergency crisis management [Tyler et al. 1991a],
- Exploratory data analysis [Smith et al. 1992],
- Factory management [Roth and Mattis 1990b; Gargan et al. 1988],
- Financial models [Marks 1991c],
- Instruction manuals [André and Rist 1990b; Arens and Hovy 1991; Hovy and Arens 1991; Arens et al., this volume],
- Intelligent training [Goodman, this volume],
- Machine maintenance [Koller 1992],
- Marketing analysis [Anand and Kahn 1992],
- Military situation monitoring and planning [Friedell 1983; Neal and Shapiro 1991; Arens et al. 1991; Burger and Marshall, this volume],
- Musical instrument instruction [Dannenberg and Joseph 1992],
- Process control [Bory 1990],
- Project management [Roth and Hendrickson 1991b],
- Travel schedule information [Casner 1991; Burger and Marshall, this volume],
- Scientific data visualization [Senay 1991; Mezrich 1984],
- Virtual worlds [Feiner et al. 1992],
- Visual speech presentations [Brooke 1989],
- Visualization of planning system behavior [Roth and Mattis 1991], and
- Weather reports [Kerpedjiev 1992].

An equally important dimension to consider, besides the type of data, is the data modeling paradigm with which applications encode domain concepts for input to an IMMPS.

Ultimately, a fully-coordinated multimedia system must have a vocabulary or inter-lingua for communicating with applications and among IMMPS components. Currently, even systems which design presentations for similar types of information have adopted different data modeling paradigms. For example, quantitative and relational facts, serving as input to information graphics design systems, have been expressed as relational database tuples [Mackinlay 1986b], logical assertions implemented in prolog or lisp [Gargan et al. 1988; Casner 1991], object-attribute/frame notations [Roth and Mattis 1991], and data-graph structures [Marks 1991a].

To some extent, these data modeling paradigms are syntactic variations with equivalent expressive power. Differences among them should not pose conceptual difficulties for each IMMPS approach nor for attempts to integrate an IMMPS with other applications. However, adopting a general and commonly used data modeling method that is useful in many domains can ultimately simplify integration with new applications without necessarily sacrificing application-independence. For example, an IMMPS which uses a relational database approach for representing its inputs should be integrated easily with a natural language or conventional query language interface to a database and thereby provide automatic presentation capabilities for any application using the database. An implementation approach like this is also valuable for research purposes if usability studies are performed which provide opportunities to collect a corpus of user-defined database queries and manipulations (e.g., joins, projections). The latter can vary in interesting, unexpected ways which can be more complex than researcher-generated test cases.

There are, however, some negative consequences associated with linking automatic presentation research with assumptions rooted in a particular data modeling paradigm. Paradigms differ in the ease with which they enable us to encode different types of information. Having chosen a paradigm, researchers tend to focus on information which can be encoded more naturally in it and treat other types less thoroughly. For example, a relational database approach is very effective at expressing assertions about elements of a set (e.g., *population*, *area*, and *national budget* can be viewed as relations mapping between a set of countries and various quantities). An IMMPS adopting a relational database paradigm can express assertions about a set of twenty countries in a straightforward manner (perhaps as graphical attributes of a set of objects in a chart or in cells of a text table). However, a single assertion about the *total population* or *total area* or the *range of national-budgets* for the set cannot be expressed easily in the data model (unless some artificial total or range relation is constructed with just one element). Similar problems exist when attributes of elements of sets are represented using frame-based approaches.

As a result, most of the information graphics-oriented IMMPS research has not addressed these *singular* assertions, partly because the data modeling approaches do not lend themselves to encoding them. Consequently, these systems lack presentation design mechanisms for displaying this summarative information in a manner which is integrated with displays of entire sets of data (although in some cases, parallel summaritive natural language expressions are appropriately generated.)

This IMMPS deficiency is particularly noticeable for systems specializing in information graphics because the latter are commonly used to express both sets of values as well as set summary information (e.g., hierarchical budget totals). It is ironic that electronic spreadsheets directly support the encoding of these types of relationships and represent the most common sources of data for commercial presentation systems. Yet, there are no research approaches which explicitly use spreadsheet styles of representation for expressing variables and arithmetic relationships (while the SAGE system [Roth et al. 1991] generated displays of spreadsheet models, it did so by converting individual cells and their contents to a schema-attribute form, with an explicit attribute to indicate the directed graph relationship between variables contained in formulae).

In contrast, singular assertions like these are addressed directly in natural language generation systems, which typically use propositional expressions (e.g., [Maybury 1990, Wahlster 1988b]). Similarly, in their overview of information characterization for intelligent multimedia presentation, [Arens et al., this volume] were able to consider a broad range of information types partly because they did not attempt to commit to any data modeling paradigm for expressing the information.

Similar difficulties arise from a tendency of presentation design mechanisms to be overly influenced by syntactic or structural idiosyncrasies of a particular data modeling paradigm. Gray [1991] discusses this type of limitation arising in some approaches to interactive presentation systems. Their early implementation within the Smalltalk paradigm assumed a one-to-one correspondence between data objects and graphical objects, where each data attribute is encoded by an attribute of a single graphical object (e.g., color, size, shape). Relations among data objects cannot be encoded in the data model or visualized by their system. For example, indented tables cannot be used to represent hierarchical budgets or organizational tree structures and node-link techniques cannot be used for directed graph relationships (like inter-city airline connections, precedence constraints among activities in project management, and prerequisite relations among college courses).

In contrast, these relationships are easily encoded using a graph theory notation which also provides a straightforward communication protocol between application and IMMPS, and a convenient structure for mapping information to presentation designs. Marks' ANDD system [Marks 1991b] encodes relational data to be presented as two distinct sets: a set of vertices and a set of edges. As a result, an application can then easily request that a presentation system visualize both vertices and edges. If appropriate to a user's goals, these can then be mapped to a set of graphical nodes and links, respectively. By distinguishing between the encoding of vertices and edges, it is possible for *orphan* vertices (those which do not have edges) to be visualized as linkless nodes in the same display as the linked nodes in a network. This is appropriate, because it is often important to view nodes with no connections. The data graph paradigm also provides some convenient ways of expressing pragmatic network design directives, to be discussed in later sections.

Presentations of this type of information are more awkwardly supported in systems using a relational database paradigm. The latter typically encodes a data graph of vertices and edges as a single relation (e.g., the *prerequisite* relation between pairs of courses). In communicating its presentation needs to an IMMPS, a relational database application need only convey the relation name. However, a relation is defined and implemented as a list of tuples, each of which defines a link between a pair of vertices (i.e., a pair of courses which have a prerequisite ordering). Orphan vertices (i.e., courses which do not have prerequisites and do not serve as prerequisites for other courses) would not be included as tuples in the relation and therefore would not occur in a presentation without an additional complicating mechanism. In general, it is not easy to capture these "orphan" vertices using a single relation in a relational database notation. More generally, difficulties exist in relational databases for all situations when it is necessary to express the fact that an element of a data set does not have a value (e.g., for Boolean properties, like the *critical* status of resources).

In contrast, a relational database paradigm, more so than other modeling paradigms, encourages one to think about multi-domain facts (e.g., a weather database might have a regional temperature relation which maps a longitude, latitude and date to a temperature). This property, referred to as the arity of a relation, is discussed in the next section.

The important point here is not that there is a best data modeling paradigm, but rather that all paradigms have both constraining and enhancing effects on the IMPS research which employ them. Whatever approach is selected, an IMMPS must be able to provide mechanisms for addressing the complete set of data presentation possibilities raised by all approaches. Indeed, the multimedia presentation problem necessarily presumes the ability to consider a variety of types of information, each potentially represented in a different paradigm.

4.2.   The Relationship Between Application and IMMPS

As the application examples discussed above imply, the task of modeling a domain and creating mechanisms for selecting relevant information to present is often assumed to be the responsibility of other system components and/or application developers or users. A similar division was made in the APEX and COMET systems [Feiner 1991; Feiner and McKeown 1991], in which a diagnostic system generated instructions for manipulating electronic equipment while an independent presentation system expressed this information. For all these systems, the main reason for this separation is the need for extensive content selection knowledge, which must change for each domain and possibly each application. Separating the task of content selection simplifies the task of maintaining application independence.

Ultimately, however, it will be a mistake to strictly isolate application content selection from IMMPS components. Decisions about the type, quantity, level of detail, combinations and distribution of information within a single, or across a sequence of discourse segments should be coordinated with and strongly influenced by presentation design considerations. Decisions about what to present must be influenced by display space limitations, hardware capabilities (monochrome, text vs. graphics displays, screen resolution, etc.), design commitments made for previously conveyed information (possibly by user-imposed design choices or domain conventions), and by a consideration of the cognitive complexity resulting from attempts to convey different content alternatives. Sometimes, two alternative sets of information can be equally suitable substantively, but result in presentations that differ greatly in complexity. None of these considerations are possible without feedback or other mechanisms for coordinating content selection and expression components. Similar concerns have been raised in research on natural language generation systems (e.g., [Appelt 1981]).

Some initial ideas for providing feedback from design components were considered by

Roth et al. [1991] to determine appropriate content for each of a series of dialogue segments in the presentation of causal explanations. The entire set of facts and relationships that needed to be conveyed was generated by a separate application program. A discourse processor ordered these assertions prior to consideration by a graphics presentation design component. Using this sequencing, the graphics design component determined the point at which the addition of more information to a display altered the cohesiveness of assertions already included in that display (e.g., using layout heuristics reflecting inter-node distances in network trees, where each node represented an assertion). The graphics component notified the discourse segment of the assertions that could be included in the next display segment and remaining assertions were then postponed until subsequent displays.

Generalization and extension of this type of coordination will be necessary for an IMMPS to be able to design presentations for large sets of information. Current systems are not capable of designing displays appropriate to the tasks one performs with large data sets, nor are they able to interact with content selection components to determine how to abstract or partition information across multiple presentations. Ironically, applications involving large, diverse data sets are the ones that are most in need of the capabilities which IMMPS research has promised. Future research in this area must address these needs for this area to begin to have any significant impact. We discuss some of the IMMPS mechanisms required for large data display in later sections.

Finally, there have been several attempts to address the content selection/expression coordination problem in systems which integrate or merge these functionalities within single domains in application-specific ways. Integrated Interfaces [Arens et al. 1991] and CUBRICON [Neal and Shapiro 1991] are systems which make extensive use of the underlying cartographic representations for their military situation monitoring applications. Thus, these systems are more tightly coupled with their underlying applications than other IMMPS systems. Decisions about information presentation are not based upon general heuristics of design or tasks, but on the specifics of the applications. This is an important distinction in these systems, as they map data onto predefined display objects [Arens et al. 1991], rather than generating display objects based on general data characteristics and expressiveness definitions. Such an approach may be appropriate for a limited set of tasks in a well-understood domain; however, it also places limits on flexibility, as the resulting IMMPS is not extensible to automatically deal with new combinations of information.

In summary, this section focused on the types of information considered in IMMPS research and the data modeling paradigms researchers have adopted to support conceptualization and system development. We pointed out that each modeling approach encourages researchers to focus on different properties and types of information and that excessive reliance on the syntactic properties of data representation can alter the generality of presentation design mechanisms. Finally, we discussed several issues related to the interaction of processes of content selection (typically isolated to an application system in most IMMPS architectures) and content expression, including approaches which perform both within a single application. We pointed out that current systems have not addressed the problem of designing presentations of large data sets. Presenting information from large data sets will require several new mechanisms; but, in particular, will require an architecture that coordinates content selection and presentation. Some approaches to coordination have been suggested (e.g., [Maybury, this volume; André et al., this volume; André and Rist, this volume]).

The next section considers the essential characteristics of information to which IMMPS's must be sensitive in order to design effectively.

5. Characterizing Information to be Presented

As we pointed out earlier, progress on IMMPS research has depended on the development of a language for describing the characteristics of information that are most relevant to presentation design. A complete set of information characteristics makes the knowledge definition and representation process a tractable one because it focuses attention on an appropriate level of reasoning for mapping between information and presentation techniques. A complete, but probably small set of information characteristics will reduce the magnitude of the otherwise impossible task of providing design knowledge which maps between all possible communication media/modalities to all possible domains and applications. It guides us to extract media-independent presentation characteristics and mapping rules which can then bridge between media and information.

John McDermott, in his paper entitled "On Talking to Eskimos About Snow" [McDermott 1990], makes an analogous point about the process of automating software design. His claim is that Artificial Intelligence (AI) research could contribute to software design by developing a vocabulary for talking about the tasks that people perform in their work and a related vocabulary for describing software mechanisms which are assembled to create programs to support tasks. Armed with a related pair of vocabularies, the mapping from diverse job tasks to diverse software mechanisms would be straightforward.

All IMMPS approaches have made use of some level of data characterization and developed a vocabulary appropriate to the data models they used and presentation classes they addressed (e.g., [Mackinlay 1986b; Marks 1991a]). Others have attempted to enumerate a comprehensive set of characteristics beyond that implemented in a particular system (e.g., [Arens et al., this volume; Norman 1991; Roth and Mattis 1990a; Kosslyn 1989; Senay 1991]. It is encouraging that there is remarkable consistency among the collection of characteristics that researchers have proposed. Unfortunately, this consistency is often masked by different, but overlapping vocabularies. These often overlap inconsistently with terms used in statistics, database theory, and related fields. A further difficulty is that information characteristics are often structured or classified in relation to an underlying data model used in an IMMPS (e.g., a relational database or graph theory model), making it awkward to communicate terms without describing details of the data model. Lastly, some approaches merge characteristics of information with characteristics of users' tasks or presentation goals (the latter is the topic of the next section).

It is beyond the scope of this chapter to present either a new framework or a comprehensive discussion of information characteristics. Instead, we summarize the main classes of characteristics relevant to quantitative and relational information. We will identify commonalities across systems which are otherwise obscured by different vocabularies, and identify areas which have not been addressed which should be the focus of new research. We include frequent references to direct readers to more detailed discussion of each concept and characteristics of broader classes of information.

5.1. Characteristics of Types, Classes, Domain Sets

All characterization schemes recognize the importance of ordering information. Mackinlay's [1986] system was the first to select different presentation techniques depending on whether domain sets (in relational database terms) were quantitative, ordinal or nominal.

Several researchers have noted the importance of a long understood distinction between two types of ordered data, called coordinates versus amounts [Roth and Mattis 1990a] or interval versus ratio scales [Kosslyn 1989]. A coordinate data type has elements which signify points in time, space, temperature, or other domains and do not possess a magnitude relative to a zero reference value. The terms ratio and interval scales suggest the types of comparisons which are meaningful among elements of coordinate and amount data types, respectively. The only comparisons appropriate for coordinates are differences (i.e., intervals) and not ratios. Thus, it makes sense to think of the difference or interval between two dates or geographic locations, but not the ratio between them. In contrast, it is appropriate to think of either ratios or differences between two amounts (e.g., two weights or budget costs). The term interval has also been used to refer to complex data types (discussed below), referring to ranges containing a beginning, end, and size [Roth and Mattis 1990a]. Intervals may be defined for either coordinate or amount data (e.g., a time interval or a weight range). Cardinal scales [Norman 1991] refer to data types that represent a count or frequency of elements. Finally, quantitative data can be further distinguished as continuous or discrete (or dense versus discrete, [Hovy and Arens 1991]). This is orthogonal to the coordinate-amount distinction.

Another characteristic is the domain of membership [Roth and Mattis 1990a], which communicates whether a data type refers to time, space, mass, temperature, currency, or other domains. These are necessary for grouping similar data types in displays and for honoring conventional preferences (e.g., expressing dates and east-west spatial coordinates on a horizontal rather than a vertical axis). It is surprising that domain types are not considered much in the IMMPS literature, yet it is one of the few data-typing distinctions extensively provided in spreadsheet packages (primarily for presentation formatting purposes in displays).

5.2. Characteristics of Relational Structure

In relational database terms, this group of characteristics refers to the way in which a relation maps among its domain sets. APT [Mackinlay 1986b] distinguished relations having functional-dependency as those for which the relation maps from each element of a domain set to exactly one element of another domain set. In Roth and Mattis' [1990a] terms, this refers to attributes of data objects which have cardinality of exactly one. For example, a salary relation can be a functional dependency if it maps from each element of the employee domain set to one value in the dollar-amount domain set (in other terms, the range of the salary attribute of the employee object is a single dollar amount). Graphical techniques like bar charts can only express relations which are functional dependencies (e.g. because missing bars can be misconstrued as minimal values).

Roth and Mattis [1990a] further distinguished functional dependencies as being either bi- or uni-directional depending on whether or not they map from each element of a domain set to a *unique* element of another domain set (i.e., an attribute whose range has a cardinality of one and is unique is a bi-directional functional dependency). For example, a student- orientation database in a college might contain a mentor-relation which maps from each freshman to one senior uniquely (i.e., unique pairs are defined by the relation). In other words, there are functional dependencies from freshmen to seniors and from seniors to freshmen. Typically, an employee-salary relation would have only one functional dependency, from employee to dollar-amount, because two employees can have the same salary.

Relations which do not have functional dependencies can be characterized further in terms of cardinality (not to be confused with cardinal scales mentioned earlier) and coverage [Roth and Mattis 1990a]. For example, the responsibility relation, which expresses the activities in a company that each department performs in a project, may have variable cardinality (departments perform different numbers of activities) but either coverage or non-coverage (i.e., whether every department is responsible for at least one activity or possibly none). Note also that a complete characterization of this relation would describe similar properties of activities with respect to departments (i.e., whether each activity is associated with at least one, exactly one or more departments).

5.3. Arity, Dimensionality, and Complex Relations

These terms refer to one of the most important information characteristics, which, although noted in several papers, has not been incorporated thoroughly within any presentation system. They refer to the number of domains that define a relation. It defines the complexity of a "fact". This means that a tuple or fact in a relational database is an assertion about N elements, where N is the *arity* (or *dimensionality* in terms used by [Arens et al., this volume]). Examples of unary, binary, ternary and quaternary relations are shown in Table 1.

With a few narrow exceptions, current systems are concerned solely with binary (i.e., two-domain relations), partly because these are more simply characterized and more simply mapped through design mechanisms to presentation techniques. Binary object-attribute tuples are ways of asserting many simple facts about a single object. It is often convenient to represent them with a single primitive property of a single graphical object (i.e., in an information-graphics medium). Combining primitive presentations of individual objects can be accomplished through alignment and merge compositions, to be discussed in later sections.

Table 1. Examples of Information Relations

Arity	Relation (domain)	Sample Fact/Tuple
unary	critical(machine)	critical(drill-press)
binary	budget(project, dollar-amount)	budget(Acme Building, $20,000,000)
ternary	reservation(hotel, date, name)	reservation(HOJO, January 4, Weiss)
quaternary	inventory(store, date, product, count)	inventory(A&P, January 4, Ajax, 200)

In contrast, the presentation design process is more complex with multi-domain relations because domains can be distributed across (1) multiple attributes of a single object set (e.g., the positions, colors, shapes, and/or sizes of a set of objects in a chart), (2) multiple object sets (e.g., a cluster of text and graphical symbols on a map or within nodes of a network), and (3) multiple displays (e.g., an alignment of charts and tables, each of which conveys a single domain). Similarly, expressing relations involving three or more domains requires data characterizations of all the relationships described above (e.g., functional dependency, cardinality, and coverage), but for all combinations of the domains within a relation. For example, to present the *inventory* relation, it is necessary to know that each *store* has information for every *date*, but for only a subset of all *products*. Each *product* is associated with only one *count* for a particular *store* and *date*.

5.4.   Characteristics of Large Data Sets

Most approaches to IMMPS have addressed the presentation of small amounts of information. Realistically, the value of an IMMPS will be for situations involving far greater amounts of information. We are not just referring to large numbers of single variable observations (e.g., as shown in dense scientific visualizations). We are also referring to numerous attributes of collections of heterogeneous objects (e.g., presentations of semantic networks, databases with numerous object types and attributes, technical documentation for large systems, etc.).

These situations will require:

- Characterizations of the relations among data elements (e.g., the algebraic dependencies in large budget models),

- Characterizations of the relations among attributes of data elements that enable a system to partition or aggregate along some dimensions rather than others, and
- Characterization of information that enables greater coordination with content selection components in order to support user directed exploration of additional information based on currently viewed displays.

5.5. Conclusions about Data Characterization

Successful research on automatic presentation has been built on clear definitions of the characteristics of information that are critical for presentation design. Careful information characterization has been a prerequisite to defining the expressiveness of presentation techniques and automating the process of technique selection. This has been true for design of presentations consisting of a *single* medium (e.g., for selecting among graphical properties of objects within charts). It has also proved true for automating selection among more divergent presentation techniques (e.g., choosing among tabular, network, and chart-based techniques). Similar conclusions have been made for presentation techniques that are most clearly different media: the coordination of natural language and map displays or realistic three dimensional graphics ([Arens et al. 1991; Feiner and McKeown 1991; Wahlster 1988a; Maybury 1991a]).

As we discuss later, our claim is that to solve the problem of choosing among and apportioning information to very different media, it will be necessary to articulate a set of characteristics that distinguish media by the information for which they are most appropriate. Such a clear information characterization will also be necessary to support media coordination. For example, it will certainly be desirable for an IMMPS to coordinate video presentations of actions with animated information graphics presentations of quantitative measurements associated with those actions - perhaps for correlating biological measurements and views of animal behavior or meteorological measurements and views of storm-cloud behavior. In both these cases, a precise temporal characterization is necessary for a system to select and coordinate views which can express and synchronize temporally-varying presentations. (See [Davis 1991]) for a description of a "videogram": a spatially and temporally aligned graphical display of audio and video content that is based on such a representation).

There are three areas which should be addressed by future research. The first is the problem of characterizing more-completely all information that can be presented to users across many media. The intent is to describe, with a single language and in an application- and media-independent manner, the characteristics of information that will be the focus of media selection and other presentation design mechanisms. Some preliminary suggestions have been offered by Arens et al. [this volume]. Davis [1991] points out the need to develop semantics to represent the content and context of video presentations (including objects, characters, spatial location, temporal location, actions, relative spatial positions, etc.). We propose that this vocabulary would lead to characterizations necessary to automatically design presentations of this information.

Second, and more specifically, it will be necessary to express more complex information structures than that considered thus far, at least for relational and quantitative information. As we pointed out earlier in this chapter, most of the work in this area has focused on characteristics of *binary relations* or *attributes* associated with sets of homogeneous sets of information, rather than singular propositions or the complex assertions embedded in video images.

Third, IMMPS data characterization research must address the problems of presenting large information sets. This includes describing the arithmetic, hierarchical, and other semantic relationships among elements of large sets. We must also understand the relationship between the characteristics of sets of information and the data objects which aggregate, abstract, or otherwise summarize these sets.

While this section focused on characteristics of the informational content of presentations, the next section considers research on characteristics of the users' information processing tasks that presentations are designed to support.

6. Characteristics of the Function of Presentations: Information-Seeking Goals, Cognitive Task Analysis, and Pragmatics

As Jarvenpaa and Dickson [1988] pointed out, there have been contradictory results from a large number of studies of human performance that compared the effectiveness of information graphics to tabular and textual presentations of information. A primary reason for the apparent inconsistency is that empirical studies have varied greatly in the types of tasks which users were required to perform with informational displays. These results, together with studies which explicitly explore the interaction of task characteristics and visual representations (e.g., [Larkin and Simon 1987]) argue strongly for the need for IMMPS research to attend to the cognitive implications of design decisions.

Fortunately, attempts to consider these issues in the IMMPS community have started to occur in several research areas:

- Characterization of users' cognitive tasks and information seeking goals in the design of informational graphics [Casner 1991; Norman 1991; Roth and Mattis 1991; Kosslyn 1985],
- The role of pragmatic directives, the perceptual organization of displays, and concern for shared rhetorical assumptions between message presenter and recipient in the design and layout of network diagrams [Marks 1991ab],
- Representations of communicative intent in the generation of natural language and graphical presentations (e.g., [Maybury 1992ab; Feiner and McKeown 1991; Seligmann and Feiner 1989; Wahlster et al. 1991b; Whittaker and Walker 1991; André and Rist 1990b], and
- Models of discourse and focus of attention in the generation of natural language and multimedia presentations (e.g., [Burger and Marshall, this volume; Feiner and McKeown 1991; Neal and Shapiro 1991; Wahlster 1991; Maybury 1991b; Reichman 1989; Grosz and Sidner 1986; McKeown 1985].

All of these approaches recognize the need to represent the function or intent of a presentation distinct from its form or style or the information it conveys. Approaches differ in their perspective on the function of presentations: whether the research effort focuses on modeling the communicative intent of the presenter or the information processing tasks facing the user. Consequently, they also differ in their views of presentations as messages to be conveyed versus interfaces through which users can explore information.

Our goal in this section is to define and contrast these different but complementary approaches and describe the need to integrate them within a single characterization taxonomy of presentation function. Our discussion is meant to convey the main problem areas rather than provide a comprehensive review of the literature. We also intentionally postpone discussion of the computational mechanisms for reasoning about these characteristics until later. We suggest some areas that have not been addressed that should be the focus of new research.

6.1. Considering Cognitive Task Characteristics in Presentation Design

The first work on the automatic design of information graphics [Mackinlay 1986b] placed major emphasis on characteristics of information that can be used to construct definitions of graphical language expressiveness. Graphical languages or styles consist of graphical techniques, which are primitive properties of graphical objects used to encode information (e.g., horizontal and vertical position, length, area, saturation, color, shape, etc.). During design, technique selection was primarily based on the ability of languages to express characteristics of data.

No distinctions were made between different tasks or presentation functions, although graphical designs were constructed to support the single task of reading values accurately from a display. Based on this assumption, graphical techniques could be ordered in terms of the ease and precision with which users could extract data values encoded with them (based on empirical work by Cleveland and McGill [1984]). For example, quantitative data encoded along an axis was read more precisely than when it was encoded using the area or level of saturation (i.e., gray-scale) of a circle.

The SAGE system [Roth and Mattis 1990a; Roth and Mattis 1991] contained one of the first attempts to differentiate a set of *information-seeking goals* to represent differences in the ways people need to obtain information from presentations to serve different purposes. Goals or purposes for viewing quantitative and relational information include:

- Accurate value-lookup (e.g., looking up a price in a catalog),
- Value-scanning (expressing the need to view a data set to perform approximate computations - like estimating the mean, range, or sum of a set),
- Counting (expressing the need to determine the frequency of different values in a set),
- N-wise comparing (expressing the need to compare two or more values, as in comparing last year's and this year's sales for each element of a set of products),
- Judging correlation (i.e., estimating the degree of covariance of two or more variables), and
- Locating-data (expressing the need to index or search a presentation by the values of one or more attributes, e.g., the start-dates versus the names of a set of activities).

In this approach, a presentation request to SAGE consisted of a list of data sets, a list of data attributes to be displayed for each set, and one or more goals to be achieved for each attribute. Therefore, goals could be combined to express composite presentation purposes.

In his work on the BOZ system, Casner [1990, 1991] further differentiated a set of primitive cognitive tasks and created a *logical task description language*. The language can be used to construct *logical procedures* for characterizing sequences of operations that a presentation is designed to support. There were two groups of operations: search operations and computation operations. These reflected the assumption that the relative effectiveness of different displays can be judged by their ability to streamline the search for information and their ability to enable a user to substitute simple perceptual operations for more complex logical ones (e.g., substituting judgments of distance and size in a display for logical operations of mental arithmetic or numerical comparisons). Computation operations include arithmetic or logical predicates (+, -, *, /, AND, OR, and NOT). Search operations consist of: retrieving a value for an object's attribute (e.g., looking up the presidential candidate who won in Utah) or retrieving all objects with a particular attribute value (e.g., finding all the states that a particular presidential candidate won).

By assembling these operations into a logical procedure, it is possible to define the information-seeking task that a display must support. A typical task for a flight reservation system might be:

> "Find a pair of connecting flights that travel from Pittsburgh to Mexico City. You are free to choose any intermediate city as long as the layover in that city is no more than 4 hours. Both flights that you choose must be available. The combined cost of the flights cannot exceed $500. Find an available seat on the flight." [Casner 1991]

Casner represents this verbal statement as a logical description by constructing a PASCAL-like program of functions whose inputs are database objects and relations. Each function is cross-referenced with the logical operations that must be performed on them. Stepping through the logical operation sequence guarantees a solution to the information-processing task. Substituting graphical objects for data objects and corresponding perceptual operations for logical ones generates a perceptual procedure which serves as a model of the cognitive processes needed to perform a task with a particular presentation. The latter can then be the subject of empirical validation.

The value of this description is that it decomposes a complex task into a *sequence* of primitive operations that can be used to guide design of the structure of presentations. In the airline example, the search operations of finding flight connections and performing computations on cost and time attributes are explicitly defined logically to occur prior to (i.e., orthogonally to) that of checking the status of seats once an acceptable pair of flights has been found. This characteristic of task structure is valuable because it enables a system to separate the flight and seating information into separate displays, perhaps hiding the seating until a user interactively selects an individual flight.

A shortcoming of this approach is the need to model all perceptual tasks as sequential operations (i.e., operations performed serially). For this reason, it is difficult to express tasks that are more likely to be performed using parallel processes which seem very sensitive to perceptual grouping properties. For example, it is awkward to construct a logical task description that corresponds to the perceptual tasks of identifying the functional relationship between two variables in a chart (perhaps by visually fitting a curve), identifying clusters of symbols with similar attribute values on a map, or more generally identifying patterns or trends among points in displays. Similarly, the sequential relationship among all the nodes of a path in a network is probably not perceived in a serial fashion. Recognizing this point, [Marks 1991a] has encoded layout knowledge for emphasizing these network relationships by addressing the perceptual cohesiveness of groups of objects rather than considering sequential operations.

The complexity and procedural flavor of an approach using logical task descriptions illustrates the point made earlier - that the purpose of the presentation design system is to construct interfaces that enable users to perform well-specified data exploration and analysis tasks. A somewhat different perspective on characterizing the purpose of a presentation is one shared by several research groups whose work is rooted in natural language planning approaches.

6.2. Communicative Act Approaches

An example of a taxonomy of acts is provided by Maybury [1990; this volume], who articulated a hierarchical representation of media-independent presentation goals derived from a plan-based theory of communication (see also [Elhadad 1989; André and Rist 1990; Ostler 1989]). At the highest level, communication is viewed as a process of acting to influence the beliefs, knowledge, goals, and plans of an addressee. These communicative goals can be realized by rhetorical acts, which are collections of media-independent communicative acts. These in turn can be realized by the selection of media-specific linguistic and visual acts. For example, the rhetorical act of *compare* can be achieved by the selection of one or more linguistic acts (e.g., several verbal *assert* acts) or visual acts (e.g., drawing graphical objects, depicting complex images, highlighting, etc.).

Decisions about which acts to choose, as well as much of the other knowledge of presentation design would presumably be based on evaluation of preconditions and constraints stored with plan operators. Eventually, however, plan operators must be expressed in sufficient detail to lead to presentation design choices (e.g., the types of graphical objects and encoding techniques). An important question is how to integrate or make the transition between the planning of communicative acts and the analysis of task characteristics.

To give a more detailed comparison of these different perspectives on characterizing the purpose of a presentation (i.e., task analytic versus communicative act views), we describe a very focused example from Marks' [1991a] approach to automating the design of network diagrams. Previous approaches to network layout were based solely on aesthetic considerations (e.g., minimizing inter-node distances and link crossings). In contrast, the ANND system performs layout based partly on *pragmatic directives* provided to the system. Directives convey the communicative intent to *emphasize* one or more structural properties. We can view *emphasize* as a rhetorical act that can be achieved by visual layout acts.

A small number of directives were implemented in ANDD to specify the need to *emphasize* the following different structural properties of networks:

- A particular path (source-to-sink) or loop through a network,
- The nodes which are inputs relative to a specified node
  (in a directed graph),
- The nodes which are outputs relative to a specified node
  (in a directed graph),
- The hub-like properties of a node
  (i.e., emphasis of both inputs and outputs).

The purpose of this research was to explore network design and layout techniques which influence the perceptual organization of displays to achieve the communicative intent of *emphasizing* these structural properties of a network. The intent is provided as input by a message creator (i.e., a user or system which also provides data to be presented). As a vehicle for expressing the purpose of a presentation, pragmatic directives have some similarities to logical operations. They are both form-independent: neither specifies the presentation design techniques or layout conventions that should be used to achieve the purpose. Both constrain the structural properties of displays.

The important but subtle difference between pragmatic directives and logical operations is that a pragmatic directive is a more abstract statement of the purpose of a display. It describes the intended effect that a presenter requires a display to have on a viewer. In Marks' work, as in Maybury's detailed characterizations of communicative intent, no commitment is made at this level to a particular set of operations that should be performed by a viewer to achieve the communicative intent. In fact, no attempt to model these was attempted. In contrast, a logical task description represents a commitment to a sequence of conceptual operations (although not to specific perceptual ones).

In principle, there may be many logical procedures which can achieve the communicative intent of a presentation (just as there are many programs that can achieve a desired functional relationship between input and output). In the airline example, the goal of finding an acceptable pair of flights might be achieved by presenting only those flights which satisfy all constraints, rather than providing a display to enable a user to perform the search and computation themselves. Without some representation of the goal of a display, there is no way a system can understand the functional equivalence of these different methods (particularly if they lead to differentially-complex presentations).

These should probably be viewed as different but complementary stages in the specification of the function of a presentation. Remaining at the level of abstract pragmatic directives will not be sufficient if an IMMPS must be able to explicitly reason about the cognitive complexity of presentations, because the latter depends on the perceptual operations that must be performed. Conversely, it would be useful for a system to be able to reason about alternative logical procedures to automatically create or select from among them as an intermediate task in the design of displays.

The need for this integration is illustrated in the ANDD system, which both lays out networks in response to pragmatic directives and encodes quantitative and nominal attributes of vertices and edges of network models using graphical properties of nodes and links. No attempt was made to define pragmatic directives or logical operations relevant to attribute encodings, so these presentation decisions were based solely on data characteristics. It will be necessary to integrate these levels of analysis to describe complex network analysis tasks involving both structural properties and graphical attributes of nodes and links.

6.3.   Conclusions and Future Directions

The goal of this section was to convey current approaches to characterizing the purposes of presentations so that they can be considered during automatic design. We described a task analytic approach which attempts to model the actions, perceptual and other cognitive operations performed by the recipient of a presentation. We contrasted this with a plan-based communicative act view of presentation, which emphasizes a presenter's goals (or intents). More generally, these approaches emphasize the importance of characterizing the full interactive context within which a presentation is considered (i.e., system and available media, user, tasks, and discourse). Following are several areas for future work.

6.3.1.   Characteristics of a User's Prior Experience

An IMMPS must characterize a user's experience with alternative presentation media and techniques. Unique graphics displays which integrate many kinds of information must be evaluated for consistency with those used elsewhere in users' environments.

For example, the Graphic StoryWriter [Steiner and Moher 1992] is a system that allows young users to author stories in a direct manipulation environment. This environment was modeled after an item familiar to the target audience of young, sometimes pre-literate, users — a storybook. The Graphic StoryWriter storybook presents the user's story as written and spoken text, graphics, animation, and sound effects.

Presentation design must also be sensitive to clarity. While it is true that the complexity of a display is a function of the perceptual operations required to use it, this presumes a viewer is able to interpret it in the first place. There is nothing in the task analysis approach that considers one's ability to determine how to use a presentation -- determining how information is encoded or how to use the presentation to perform the perceptual operations it was designed to support. Work is needed to define the complexity of a presentation from this perspective: perhaps the first time a viewer must interpret it [Marks and Reiter 1990] as well as after having viewed similar displays with different uses of the same encoding techniques. Evaluating complexity will also require consideration of users' knowledge of the information being presented. A complete model of these processes will require integrating a task-analytic approach with a communicative model of presentation.

6.3.2.   Prior Discourse and Focus of Attention

There has been much work considering the discourse context within which human-computer interaction occurs, especially in natural language processing systems [Allen et al. 1989; McKeown 1985; Grosz and Sidner 1986]. The complexity and coherence of discourse has been shown to reflect the extent to which presentations maintain a consistent focus of attention and provide smooth focus transitions [Grosz and Sidner 1986; McKeown 1985]. Focus of attention has been shown to depend on syntactic, semantic, and pragmatic/domain characteristics which determine the structure of natural language discourse. Likewise, a multimedia theory of focus is needed to consider the appropriateness of a new presentation in the context of prior presentation media and styles, prior informational content, and tasks being performed (see Burger and Marshall [this volume] for a discussion of this topic).

Much of the previous IMMPS work has been concerned with design of individual presentations or planned sequences of presentations, as opposed to the introduction of unanticipated new information introduced in the context of an existing presentation. The latter case is a more realistic need that would be an especially valuable role for an IMMPS. Theories of presentation and task complexity are needed to determine how to introduce new information, whether by folding it into the existing presentation (i.e., holding media and design choices constant) or constructing a new presentation, either integrating or maintaining the independence of previous and new information (i.e., optimizing presentation effectiveness at the expense of consistency).

6.3.3.   Generalizing Task Analytic Models

An important element of a task analytic approach is the emphasis on modeling the cognitive and perceptual processes of human-computer interaction. This emphasis suggests several potential areas of new research. They include:

- Extending the consideration of presentation efficiency and complexity to include the motor and cognitive aspects of *interactive* presentations (e.g., applying GOMS (goals, operators, methods and selection rules) or other techniques for specifying tasks and interactive interfaces [Card 1983; Casner 1990; Diaper 1989; Tauber 1990; Bösser and Melchior 1992]),

- Applying these techniques to characterizing the unique tasks involved in users' interaction with intelligent interfaces, including the user's interaction with presentations of large amounts of information,

- Developing characterizations of the broader tasks that users perform within which computer-based presentations occur, including communicating with others, problem solving, accessing non-computer sources of information, and manipulating objects (e.g., tools or machines), and

- Developing models of the cognitive processes relevant to *multimedia* presentations. While the task analytic approach described here was applied to analysis tasks performed on informational graphics, it is clearly appropriate for comparing these with verbal, propositional encodings as well as diagrams [Larkin and Simon 1987]. Therefore, it is plausible that these techniques can be applied to study the cognitive processes involved in natural language and other presentation media.

7. Presentation Design Knowledge

Previous sections have focused on characterizing the information and purposes to which intelligent presentation systems must be sensitive. This section briefly outlines the types of knowledge and design mechanisms which are used to consider this information to create presentations. Each section refers to a different component of the conceptual architecture shown in Figure 2.

7.1. Content Selection

The process of content selection and its interaction with other components has not been well developed in current IMMPS systems. As we pointed out in the section on domains, applications and information, many systems assume that selection of relevant information to present is the responsibility of other application-specific components or users and has been kept independent of other presentation components. Ultimately, however, it will be necessary for IMMPS components to be better coordinated with those for content selection because the latter can be influenced by constraints imposed by (1) the size and complexity of presentations, (2) the quantity of information, (3) the limitations of the display hardware (e.g., resolution, color, number, and size of displays), and (4) the need for presentation completeness and coherence. There are several systems that perform some aspects of content selection automatically.

Natural language generation components have integrated aspects of content selection with presentation design by using rhetorical models (e.g., [McKeown 1985; Roth et al. 1991; Moore 1989; Moore and Paris 1989; Hovy 1988a; Hovy et al. 1992; Maybury 1992ab]). As we discussed in the previous sections, rhetorical models are sequences of communicative acts which define the types and organization of concepts in a domain which must be expressed for a particular purpose. Examples are rhetorical models for: expository discourse (e.g., describing the structure of a database, identifying a particular database object, and comparing and contrasting two database objects), procedural instruction (e.g., for repairing a device or navigating a route), and explanation (e.g., of causal relationships among quantitative facts or justification of expert system conclusions). Rhetorical models provide the knowledge for a discourse planner both to select a relevant partition of a potentially larger content set and to sequence that information coherently.

McKeown et al. [1992] describes some ways in which the COMET system's presentation design components might invoke processes of content selection to obtain additional information to support identification of unfamiliar terms. In the COMET architecture, a model of a user's familiarity with individual terms is accessed by lexical components within a natural language generator. When the lexical component must refer to an unfamiliar term, it communicates this back to a content selection component which then selects additional identifying or locating information to be included in the presentation. Wahlster et al. [1991a] and [André et al. [this volume] illustrated by means of several examples (annotations, cross-modal references) why a strictly sequential approach in which information (and the resulting output) flowing only from content selection to presentation design is inaappropriate.

Similar bi-directional communication between content selection and presentation components will be needed for an IMMPS to support a user's need to interactively direct the expansion and change of information content in a presentation. A natural way for this to occur is through direct manipulation of presentation objects (e.g., to support database navigation or query). As we'll discuss later, most automatically designed presentations are non-interactive, a shortcoming that will have to be addressed to support presentation and exploration of large amounts of information.

7.2.   Media and Presentation Technique Selection

In contrast to the problem of content selection, there has been much more research on knowledge and mechanisms for choosing among alternative presentation methods. Knowledge of media selection is defined partly in terms of the information characteristics described in an earlier section. For example, Kovacevic [1992] has enumerated characteristics which apply to the selection and coordination of media and presentation technique selection, and the mapping of information to techniques. These include: content, channel, temporal, granularity or level of abstraction sequencing, and coordination.

Most systems encode selection knowledge as rules which define the expressiveness of alternative media as well as alternative encoding techniques within each medium. The idea of viewing selection rules from the perspective of presentation language expressiveness originated in work on automatic design of informational graphics [Mackinlay 1986b].

Expressiveness rules define the data characteristics which can be expressed by each presentation medium (e.g., natural language, informational or realistic graphics, cartographic representations, and video) and by each alternative encoding technique within a medium (e.g., within information graphics: horizontal position, shape, size, link thickness, etc.).

Often these rules have theoretical justification. For example, there must be a correspondence between the nature of a graphical property and the ordering characteristic of a data attribute which it can express. Failure to maintain isomorphism in this way can result in spurious inferences [Marks and Reiter 1990]. For example, non-quantitative attributes should not be encoded using properties of graphical objects which vary quantitatively (e.g., using the lengths of bars in a chart to encode the departments in which a set of employees work). Conversely, quantitative data attributes (length of employment for employees) must be encoded using quantitatively varying graphical properties (i.e., not color or shape). A comprehensive set of expressiveness principles has been emerging along with the progressing differentiation of data characteristics was discussed in an earlier section.

Creating a theoretical basis for defining the expressiveness of media alternatives is more difficult than for alternative graphical techniques. As a result, many systems use do-main- appropriate heuristics. For example, in an application of SAGE [Roth et al. 1991] for presenting explanations of quantitative modeling systems using combinations of nat-ural language and informational graphics, the assignment of content to medium was done using a set of heuristics. Natural language was selected when explanation content contained either (1) statements of causality, process, conclusion, and other abstract con-cepts (e.g., the increase in the total budget was *counteracted* by an increase in revenue) or (2) relational attributes for a small number of data objects (e.g., the total budget is $2,000,000). Informational graphics were selected when explanation content contained large numbers of quantitative or relational facts (e.g., to enumerate all the costs in a pro-ject or to show the derivational structure among the variables in a quantitative model).

Similarly, COMET [Feiner and McKeown 1991] uses heuristics for choosing either or both three dimensional realistic graphics and natural language to convey radio repair in-structions:

- Location information, physical attributes - graphics only,
- Simple and compound actions - both,
- Conditionals - text for connectives, both for actions, and
- Abstract actions - text.

Whether theoretically based or ad hoc, expressiveness criteria based on information characteristics still only provide a partial pruning of presentation alternatives. There are often many methods for presenting each type of information. Therefore, alternatives must be further distinguished with IMMPS knowledge of the effectiveness with which each medium or intra-medium encoding technique realizes the purpose of a presentation. Technique selection criteria are based on preferences implied by (1) perceptual operators [Casner 1990], (2) information-seeking goals [Roth and Mattis 1991], (3) communica-tive acts or intentions [André et al., this volume; Arens et al., this volume; Feiner and McKeown 1991; Elhadad 1989], and (4) pragmatic directives [Marks 1991a].

For example, rules for selecting methods for supporting a user's ability to locate one of many facts in a presentation may express preferences for graphical techniques which can be processed preattentively.[1]

It is important to emphasize again that selection processes, whether for choosing among media or presentation techniques within a medium, do not occur independent of other design processes. Previously, we mentioned the need to provide feedback to content selection mechanisms when it is not possible to express all information or when additional information is needed for completeness. It is also necessary for media and technique selection processes to be guided by constraints imposed by the need to coordinate elements of presentations, which we discuss next.

7.3. Presentation Coordination

We purposely generalize the term "coordination" to refer to elements besides information encoded with two different media because it is a process which must occur at multiple levels, as the architecture in Figure 2 suggested. It is also the case that principles used to guide coordination at one level are applicable to other levels as well. Current research on IMMPS has studied mechanisms for supporting coordination among: (1) encoding techniques (e.g., among graphical attributes, sentence forms, audio attributes, or between media), (2) presentation objects that represent facts (e.g., coordination of the spatial and temporal arrangement of points in a chart, nodes in a network, realistic objects in a diagram, and sentences in a text description), and (3) multiple displays (e.g., windows).

7.3.1. Coordination of Encoding Techniques

Coordination can be viewed as a process of composition—as the term is used in automatic design of informational graphics. These systems employ sets of composition operators for merging, aligning, and synthesizing graphical and tabular objects to construct

---

[1]Preattentively processed encoding techniques are those which enable objects to be located in a densely populated display using parallel perceptual processes. Horizontal position (relative to an axis), color and saturation are clear examples of properties which enable an object to be located preattentively (e.g., making it easy to pick out several red circles in a field of many more black ones [Bertin 1983]).

displays that convey multiple attributes of one or more data sets. For example, Figure 3 resulted from the composition of objects encoding attributes using color, position, and size. It also involves the composition of two chart-like displays, which are aligned along a horizontal axis.

Composition must be guided by several concerns. First, it must be sensitive to presentation purpose. The complexity of a display and the resulting efficiency of perceptual processes for performing a task depend on how information is distributed across encoding techniques, but also how these techniques are coordinated, (e.g., whether information is distributed across similar attributes of different object sets or different attributes of the same object set, as illustrated by the double bar chart (used to compare two variables) and the scatter plot (used to view correlations between two variables) in Figure 4.

Coordination must be concerned with ambiguity. Attempts to compose two sets of objects, each of which uses color to encode a property must either reject these choices and require selection mechanisms to change them, or find a way to impose constraints so that two sets of colors can be constructed by rendering modules that can be clearly perceived as distinct groups. Coordination must also be sensitive to the perceptual impact of synthesizing multiple objects and techniques, including concern for clutter (e.g., when too many objects are integrated within a single display) and scale choices when two attributes are integrated against a common axis or key (e.g., consider the effects of merging two attributes with widely different ranges using the same axis).

Achieving coordination which supports a particular task or purpose and which does so in an unambiguous, perceptually-effective way usually requires feedback to selection mechanisms that provide alternative encoding techniques. In other words, coordination attempts often fail for a given set of technique selections. The need to iterate between coordination and selection operations can result in a search problem to select techniques which satisfy both selection and coordination criteria.

Coordination of techniques across multiple media has some properties in common with those described above. Composition of objects across multiple media can also occur based on a common dimension, e.g., aligning textual descriptions with graphics figures which refer to the same objects or actions (e.g., map directions, procedural instructions, explanations [Feiner and McKeown 1991; Wahlster et al. 1991a; Roth et al. 1991; André and Rist 1990b] or synchronization of temporally varying properties of audio, video and graphics (e.g., [Davis 1991; Goodman, this volume]). Coordination of multimedia also

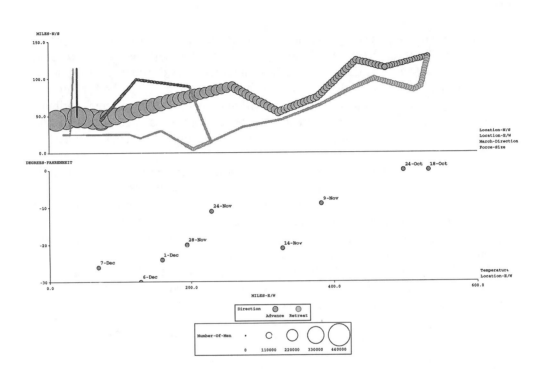

Figure 3.
A display, automatically generated by the SAGE system, showing troop strengths as a function of location during Napolean's advance and retreat from Russia (after [Tufte 1983]). The lower display shows temperatures at selected locations and dates during the retreat from Russia. These illustrate the potential of technique composition for integrating diverse information.

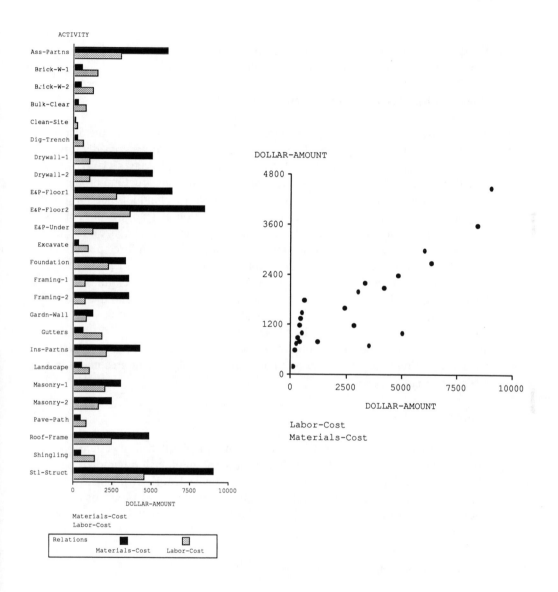

Figure 4.
Alternative displays of the same data set supporting tasks of value comparison (bar chart) and judging correlation (scatter plot)

requires addressing the problem of cross-reference and raises similar questions about feedback mechanisms between selection and coordination processes.

7.3.2.   Coordination of Objects Within Presentations

As was true for coordinating media and techniques, the coordination of multiple display objects within a presentation is governed by many of the same cognitive considerations. Presentations must support the tasks for which they are designed. Marks [1991b] has demonstrated that spatial layout can be used to emphasize important structural properties of networks. His ANDD system also coordinates layout with technique selection processes. Layout mechanisms attempt to reinforce the perception of graphical properties by grouping nodes sharing common graphical values (e.g., shape, color, size). Similar layout strategies are applied to produce sequential orderings which reinforce perception of quantitative values associated with nodes. Roth, Mattis and Mesnard [1991] have discussed the concept of structural compatibility, which describes the relationship between the sequence in which objects are referenced in natural language and their corresponding spatial location and sequence in graphical displays. It was necessary to coordinate natural language descriptions and graphics so that viewers can efficiently locate and perform perceptual operations on objects in an efficient fashion. Roth and Mattis [1991] have also explored the use of sorting to organize chart objects and tree nodes in a way that supports search.

7.3.3.   Display Coordination

Finally, the distribution of information across multiple displays requires attention to additional issues of coordination. These include supporting the transition among multiple displays, determining how to provide cross reference [McKeown et al. 1992; Wahlster et al. 1991a], and achieving spatial as well as embedding relationships among displays which support user's tasks efficiently [Casner and Larkin 1989; Prevost and Banda 1990].

7.4.   Summary and Needs for New Research

The goal of this section was to characterize types of presentation design knowledge. These uses emphasize the importance of characterizing the full interactive context within which a presentation will be used. Several areas of future work hold promise:

- Design knowledge for creating interactive presentations for handling large data sets,
- Knowledge to support animation and synchronization of time-based media,
- Knowledge for updating presentations dynamically and a reactive approach to presentation design and management which will utilize this knowledge,
- The role of domain-specific knowledge and the related issues of: how to effectively acquire, integrate and make use of this knowledge, and capturing appropriate levels of detail in this knowledge,
- Gaining better understandings of how to use rendering knowledge.

8. Effective Human-Computer Interaction Using IMMPS

This section emphasizes a number of human-computer interaction issues that provide opportunities for future extensions to IMMPS efforts. The first issues focus on the psychological aspects of the use of IMMPS – that is the need to consider the broader work tasks within which people use presentations, including approaches for modeling the cognitive operations of users.

8.1. Context

Several aspects of the knowledge sources shown in Figure 2 deal with context. These include certain key linkages to the user's world – the current situation, as well as the goal space and discourse state. These aspects of context provide valuable linkages to the user's world to ensure that usable presentations are generated.

8.2. Linkages to the World Beyond the Presentation Display

Static knowledge of a domain and user's tasks, and dynamic knowledge of the goals, both user's and system, and discourse need to be considered in presentation design. Situational context will also play an important role, as it is difficult to distinguish between a single task's context and the total context possessed by the user [Maskery and Meads 1992]. As shown in Figure 5, the user's context encompasses not only the current task, but also their knowledge of the system and their environment. This context is indeed larger than the shared common ground between the system and the user; however, the use of situational context should be to maintain a common focus of attention between the user and the system which helps keep the user focused on their task [Maskery et al. 1992].

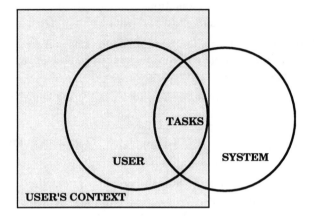

Figure 5. User's Context

The view of context in Figure 5 reinforces another important aspect of understanding the user's context. Throughout this paper, the common ground between user and system has been referred to as "presentation," while in Figure 5, it is labeled "tasks." This congruence between *presentations* and *tasks* is, in part, an artifact of the perspective one adopts – a user-centered view of tasks to be performed or a system-centric view of presentations generated. However, a more important understanding of this relationship is as part of a function for the evaluation of intelligent multimedia presentation systems.

8.3. Evaluation

Evaluation of intelligent multimedia presentation systems should ultimately be based on the same criteria used to evaluate other types of human-computer interfaces. That is, the greater the congruence between the results of the system's use (in this case, the presentations generated) and the user's needs (i.e., their tasks), the better the evaluation of the system should be. Thus far, however, most systems have either not been tested for usability or they have been developed solely to support basic research issues. In the latter case, they have not reached a level of focus or maturity to make usability testing feasible.

For example, the goal of work on automatic design of informational graphics has been to develop representations of graphical techniques and design knowledge. Mechanisms are developed to test whether these are sufficient to account for most naturally occurring graphical presentations or produce new ones which are more effective. Empirical work has focused on confirming the theoretical assumptions about design and complexity, rather than addressing usability of these systems for producing presentations.

It will be necessary for these systems to be conceptualized from the perspective of particular uses before they can be judged as effective interfaces. Evaluation efforts must not only address the issues of efficient presentation design and layout, but must also address issues of effectiveness in supporting users in performing their tasks. Doing so will not only provide an opportunity to perform evaluation. More importantly, consideration of the uses for this technology will change the basic research questions that must be addressed and probably the underlying mechanisms for performing intelligent design. To be effective, an IMMPS must: be situated in the user's context, be consistent with ongoing discourse, and provide appropriate information tailored to the user's tasks and presented to minimize user effort. Effectiveness will depend on interactive capabilities as well.

8.4. Interactive Capabilities

There are at least three types of interactive capabilities which IMMPS's must have, that will be needed for most potential applications.

8.4.1. Mechanisms for Interactive Design

The potential of research which has encoded knowledge of presentation design will be realized when systems can provide many levels of assistance to users in the design process. The levels differ in terms of the degree and nature of design specifications which users elect to create themselves, leaving the rest for a system to complete or offer alternatives. Users can specify designs at three levels:

Specifying goals or tasks. A vocabulary and set of interface constructs will be needed to enable users to communicate the information-seeking goals for a display. One rationale for these systems is that it is difficult for users to interact with interfaces to existing systems to fully specify their presentation design choices. The assumption is that it is more natural for users to learn a vocabulary for describing the tasks they need to perform or their goals in viewing a display than to learn vocabularies for describing graphical techniques and their components. Thus far, however, there has not been any research to provide effective interfaces which make the specification of goals a natural design task.

Selecting techniques and coordination methods. Often, users of these systems will either strongly prefer particular design choices in advance of display generation or wish to alter design choices for displays already created. Design choices may be alternative encoding techniques or methods for coordinating them. Research is needed to develop flexible interfaces to support interactive design. This view suggests an intelligent design assistant role for IMMPS technology, in which users make one or more design choices and an IMMPS completes the design process or offers design alternatives that are compatible with existing design choices. A related suggestion [Kochhar 1991; Marks 1991a] is to allow computers to act as design critics which can evaluate and suggest alternatives to user decisions.

Making rendering choices. Most current commercial presentation software provides users with the ability to control rendering level choices, such as axis scale, color, fonts, the relative spatial position of objects in displays, etc. Similar interactive capabilities will be needed for useful implementations of IMMPS technology. Rendering knowledge has not been an active research area thus far. Systems usually contain ad hoc heuristics at this level.

8.4.2.   Mechanisms for Interactive Modification of Information

While presentations can be used to answer specific questions, there are many situations where the task to be performed requires manipulation of information. At the simplest level, this involves making changes to the values of database facts through direct manipulation of presentation objects. However, a general interface mechanism for making display updates in this manner can be extremely complex, requiring dynamic redesign of displays when the quantity and value ranges of information makes current displays inappropriate. At a more complex level still, interactive mechanisms for combining and modifying large amounts of information may suggest the need for IMMPS's to contain interface as well as presentation design knowledge.

8.4.3. Mechanisms for Interactive Content Selection and Navigation

Finally, the potential of IMMPS technology is greatest for the interactive exploration of large amounts of information. None of the current research efforts have addressed presentation as well as interface design for interacting with large amounts of information. This will require methods for navigating, aggregating, abstracting, partitioning information to be considered during the design process and for interfaces to achieve these to be assembled dynamically.

8.5. Separability

A final issue is the appropriate separation of the user interface (including the IMMPS) from the application. Separation concerns must address the software engineering concerns of coupling and cohesion [Yourdon 1978] while meeting the information needs of the user interface to support the user's task demands within their work context. These concerns of separability and linking user interfaces to application code remains an area of active research [Edmonds 1992]. Of the three logical components of a user interface management system (presentation, dialogue control, and application interface [Green 1985]), we have introduced IMMPS issues dealing with dialogue management and applications interfaces. These concerns will continue to be important in understanding how to best develop user interfaces; especially as interactive user interfaces grow to 50 *per cent* or more of an application's code [Myers and Rasson 1992; Young 1987]. As Hill et al. [1992] point out, application programs are no longer the apparent locus for modality integration; modality cooperation and integration must increasingly be an integral part of the architectures of intelligent multimedia systems. These issues will also be increasingly important as IMMPS systems strive to move from research labs to broader use.

9. Conclusions

This paper presented current approaches to intelligent multimedia presentation, which tend to take a computer-centered view of the process linking human, computer, and task. We have argued that further gains in IMMPS technologies will come as a result of expanding a user-centered view to these efforts, rather than viewing these efforts as interesting basic research in computational techniques.

We have explored issues dealing with IMMPS interfaces to applications, data characterization, task characterization (including characterizing the full interactive context within which a presentation will be used), and the use of presentation design knowledge. It will be necessary to reexplore these areas within a user-centered approach, considering the full context within which these systems will be used. Further advances in IMMPS will not only come as a result of increased focus on pragmatics and user's tasks, but also from increased exploration of the various roles that an IMMPS can play: automated and interactive presentation design; as a critic, tool, assistant or expert for the user; as a tool for interactive exploration and modification of information.

Solutions to apportionment and coordination issues can profit from: lessons learned from technique selection and composition in information graphics work; better integration of the feedback processes linking technique selection, composition and coordination, and greater consideration of pragmatics/task characterization and information characterization

Finally, we have presented a conceptual architecture that emphasizes interaction among components and greater emphasis on pragmatics and meeting user's task-oriented needs through intelligent multimedia interaction.

10.   Acknowledgments

We would like to thank our colleagues and visitors to the Intelligent Interfaces Laboratory, Robotics Institute, Carnegie-Mellon University, for discussions which contributed to extending our understanding of intelligent presentation research. These individuals include: Jake Kolojejchick, Jade Goldstein, and Joe Mattis, and Carolyn Dunmire (U.S. Army Human Engineering Laboratory). We would also like to thank our reviewers for their comments. Financial support for the first author is provided by DARPA Contract #F30602-88-C-0001 and Army Research Office Contract #DAALO3-91-G-0328.

Chapter 2

Planning Multimedia Explanations Using Communicative Acts

Mark T. Maybury

Abstract

A number of researchers have investigated the use of plan-based approaches to generate textual explanations (e.g., [Appelt 1985; Hovy 1988a; Moore 1989; Maybury 1990]). This chapter extends this approach to generate multimedia explanations by defining three types of communicative acts: linguistic acts (illocutionary and locutionary speech acts), graphical acts (e.g., deictic acts), and media-independent rhetorical acts (e.g., identify, describe). This chapter formalizes several of these communicative acts as operators in the library of a hierarchical planner. We illustrate the use of these plan operators to compose route plans in coordinated natural language and graphics in the context of a cartographic information system.

1. Introduction

The notion of communication as an action-based endeavor dates to Austin's [1962] view of language as purposeful behavior. Searle [1969] extended this view with his formalization of speech acts. Bruce's [1975] suggestion of a plan-based model of speech acts was followed by computational investigations into planning speech acts [Cohen 1978], planning referring expressions [Appelt 1985], and planning multisentential text to achieve particular communicative goals (e.g., [Hovy 1988a; Moore 1989; Maybury 1990]). Just as Grosz and Sidner [1986] argued that discourses have purposes and particular discourse segments have purposes, in Maybury [1990, 1992b] we claim that texts (spoken or written) in and of themselves are composed of a hierarchy of communicative acts, each of which are aimed at achieving particular effects on the addressee, independently and in conjunction.

Figure 1 gives a sense of our approach, which was embodied in the text planning system, TEXPLAN (Textual EXplanation PLANner). TEXPLAN reasoned about a

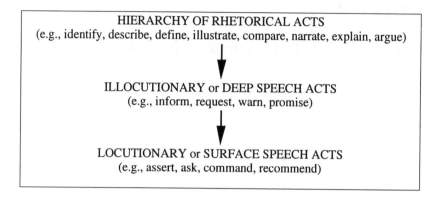

Figure 1. Integrated, Hierarchical Theory of Communicative Acts

hierarchy of communicative actions to accomplish particular discourse goals. Space does not permit the presentation of or support for the broad range of communicative actions that we formalized as plan operators, so we will exemplify them here and define some below. TEXPLAN planned higher level rhetorical actions such as; identify a given entity, compare two entities, or explain a process, in terms of more primitive illocutionary speech acts [Searle 1969] which in turn were further specified as locutionary or surface speech acts [Appelt 1985]. For example, to get a hearer to perform an action (i.e., argue that they do it), the system might plan to first request that they perform the action (which in turn might be accomplished by asking them nicely to do it or commanding them to do it), and subsequently tell them how to do it and/or motivate them to do it. Each communicative act has necessary conditions which must hold before its execution and specific intended effects which are achieved by its execution. Choices among alternative actions could be made guided by a number of factors including (1) the contents of the application knowledge base, (2) a model of the user's knowledge, beliefs, and plans, (3) a model of discourse, (4) the complexity of the actions (e.g., number of items in the decomposition), and so on. Rhetorical acts usually spanned more than one utterance and could be composed of one another (e.g., an explanation might require the narration of a set of events preceded by a description of key parts) or of more primitive speech acts. This enabled a hierarchical and compositional approach to planning multisentential text (for details see Maybury [1990, 1992b]).

In the remainder of this chapter we describe the extension of this approach to incorporate multimedia actions in order to generate coordinated language and graphics. We first define several communicative acts, including linguistic and graphical ones, in a common plan operator language. Next, we use these operators to plan coordinated texts and graphics which identify objects and convey route plans from the Map Display System [Hilton and Anken 1990], a knowledge-based cartographic information system. A final section identifies limitations and areas for further research.

2. Multimedia as Communicative Acts

Just as text can be viewed as consisting of a hierarchy of intentions, similarly, multimedia communication can be viewed as consisting of linguistic and graphical acts that, appropriately coordinated, can perform some communicative goal such as describing an object, narrating a sequence of events, or explaining how a complex process functions. For example, when giving directions on how to get from one place to another, if possible, humans will often utilize maps, gestures, and language to explain a route.

Just as humans communicate using multiple media (i.e., language, graphics, gestures) in multiple modes (i.e., language can be written or spoken), we have implemented an explanation planner that represents and reasons about multimedia *communicative acts* (see Figure 2). Communicative acts include rhetorical, linguistic, and graphical acts as well as non-linguistic auditory acts (e.g., snap, ring) and physical acts (e.g., gestures). A *rhetorical act* [Maybury 1990] is a sequence of linguistic or graphical acts which are used to achieve certain media-independent rhetorical goals such as identifying an entity, describing it, dividing it into its subparts or subtypes, narrating events and situations explaining a complex operation, and arguing to support a conclusion or to persuade someone to act.

In contrast, a *linguistic act* is a speech act [Searle 1969] such as INFORM or REQUEST which characterizes the illocutionary force of a single utterance. These illocutionary speech acts can be accomplished by *locutionary* or *surface speech acts* [Appelt 1985] such as ASSERT, ASK, and COMMAND which are associated with particular grammatical structures (declarative, imperative, and interrogative mood, respectively). While illocutionary speech acts are useful for plan abstraction (e.g., a REQUEST can be achieved by asking, commanding, recommending, etc.), we focus here on locutionary acts.

PHYSICAL ACT		LINGUISTIC ACT		GRAPHICAL ACT
DEICTIC ACT		*REFERENTIAL/ ATTENTIONAL ACT*		*DEICTIC ACT*
point, tap, circle				*highlight, blink, circle etc.*
indicate direction		*ILLOCUTIONARY ACT*		*indicate direction*
		inform		
ATTENTIONAL ACT		*request*		*DISPLAY CONTROL ACT*
pound fist/stomp foot		*warn*		*display-region*
snap/tap fingers, clap hands		*concede*		*zoom (in, out)*
				pan (left, right, up, down)
BODY LANGUAGE ACT		*LOCUTIONARY ACT*		
facial expressions		*assert (declarative)*		*DEPICT ACT*
gestures		*ask (interrogative)*		*depict image*
sign-language		*command (imperative)*		*draw (line, arc, circle)*
		recommend ("should")		*animate-action*
		exclaim (exclamation)		

Figure 2. Communicative Acts: Rhetorical, Linguistic, and Graphical

In contrast to linguistic acts, *graphical acts* include graphical deictic gestures (e.g., pointing, highlighting, blinking, circling), display control (e.g., zooming, panning), and image depiction. In the current implementation deictic gestures are considered primitive acts. In contrast, depiction can include depictions of primitive images (e.g., a point or line), composite images (e.g., a tree with arcs and nodes), and complex images (e.g., a picture of a location). Thus, depiction itself can be viewed as a plan-based endeavor (e.g., composing and rendering a bar graph) [Feiner 1985; Burger 1989]. The next section details several of these communicative acts for identifying locations.

Before doing so, however, we note that communication can occur not only via graphical and linguistic actions, but also via physical ones. For example, pointing to a group of people is a perfectly acceptable response to the request "Which soccer team do you want to be on?" I term this *physical deixis* (in contrast to linguistic deixis, as in "I want the one I just described"). As with other communicative acts, physical deixis might be performed in support of some higher level domain activity, such as selecting members for a soccer team, using a touch screen to select a part from an inventory system, or indicating a heading when giving directions.

In contrast to physical deixis, two other classes of physical communicative actions are *attentional actions* and body *language actions*. Attentional actions include snapping fingers or banging a shoe on a table and are performed with the purpose of managing focus of attention. More complex physical actions include facial expressions, gestures (e.g., a peace sign), and, closely related sign language. Physical actions may have linguistic and non-linguistic correlates, indeed the very name of sign-language suggests a connection not only between physical actions and language but also between physical actions and graphics or pictures. Formalizing "body language" actions would prove useful to virtual interfaces, which often incorporate gesture recognition from data gloves but also include full body suits. Each of these actions have constraints and enablements (e.g., facial expressions are not effective if they cannot be viewed by the addressee) and are performed to achieve particular effects (e.g., to gain attention, to offend). To

illustrate how these kinds of actions can be formalized in plan operators, we next detail graphical, linguistic, and higher level communicative actions for identifying locations.

3. Multimedia Plans for Location Identification

Similar to physical actions, communicative acts (rhetorical, linguistic, and graphical) can be formalized as plans. Communicative acts are represented as operators in the plan library of a hierarchical planner [Sacerdoti 1977]. Each plan operator defines the *constraints* and *preconditions* that must hold before a communicative act applies, its intended *effects* (also known as postconditions), and the refinement or *decomposition* of the act into subacts. Preconditions and constraints encode conditions concerning both physical states (e.g., is an object too large to be displayed) as well as cognitive states (e.g., does the hearer believe some proposition). Constraints, unlike preconditions, cannot be achieved or planned for if they are false. The decomposition of a plan operator defines how higher level communicative acts (e.g., describing an object) are divisible into potentially coordinated lower level actions (e.g., describing it in natural language, depicting an image of it, or both).

For example, the uninstantiated Identify-location-linguistically plan operator shown in Figure 3 is one of several methods of performing the communicative action Identify. As defined in the HEADER of the plan operator, the Identify act takes three arguments, the speaker (S), the hearer (H), and an entity. The English translation of Figure 3 is as follows: Provided the third argument is indeed an entity[1] (CONSTRAINTS) and the speaker wants the hearer to know about it (PRECONDITIONS), the speaker (S) will identify the location of the entity by informing the hearer (H) of its location (DECOMPOSITION), which has the intended effect that the hearer knows about it (EFFECTS).

```
NAME    Identify-location-linguistically
HEADER            Identify(S, H, entity)
CONSTRAINTS    Entity?(entity)
PRECONDITIONS            WANT(S, KNOW(H,
Location(entity)))
EFFECTS            KNOW(H, Location(entity))
DECOMPOSITION            Assert(S, H, Location(entity))
```

Figure 3. Uninstantiated Linguistic Plan Operator

Plan operators are encoded in an extension of first order predicate calculus which allows for optionality within the decomposition. Predicates (which have true/false values (e.g., Entity?)), functions (which return values), and communicative acts (e.g., Identify, Assert, Blink) appear in lower-case type with their initial letter capitalized. Arguments to predicates, functions, and communicative acts include variables and constants. Variables are italicized (e.g., *S*, *H*, and *entity*) and constants appear in upper-case plain type.

Intentional operators, such as WANT, KNOW, and BELIEVE appear in capitals. KNOW details an agent's specific knowledge of the truth-values of propositions (e.g., KNOW(H, Red(ROBIN-1)) or KNOW(H, ¬Yellow(ROBIN-1)))where truth or falsity is defined by the propositions in the knowledge base. That is, KNOW(H, P) implies P ∧ BELIEVE(H, P). Agents can hold an invalid belief (e.g., BELIEVE(JOHN, Yellow(ROBIN-1))). KNOW-ABOUT is a predicate that is an abstraction of a set of epistemic attitudes of some agent toward an individual. An agent can KNOW-ABOUT an object or event (e.g., KNOW-ABOUT(H, ROBIN-1) or KNOW-

---

[1]An entity is an object or event (e.g., a process or an action).

ABOUT(H, EXPLOSION-445)) if they KNOW its characteristics, components, subtypes, or purpose. KNOW-HOW indicates an agent's ability to perform an action.

If the object we are identifying has an associated graphical presentation in the backend cartographic display, we can augment natural language with visual identification. The Identify-location-linguistically-&-visually plan operator in Figure 4 is selected only if its constraints are satisfied (i.e., the given entity is a cartographic entity such as a town, road, lake, etc.). If these constraints are satisfied, the plan operator then ensures that the entity is visible. If the designated entity is out of the currently visible region or too small to be seen, this can be achieved by either panning, jumping, or zooming to the region around the designated entity. For example, Figure 5 illustrates the map display action, Make-entity-visible, which displays the region surrounding a given entity. Note that the precondition of this plan operator will ensure the entity is displayed. If it is not already displayed on the map, this will be planned for.

NAME	Identify-location-linguistically-&-visually
HEADER	Identify(*S, H, entity*)
CONSTRAINTS	Cartographic-Entity?(*entity*)
PRECONDITIONS	Visible(*entity*) ∧
	WANT(*S*, KNOW(*H*, Location(*entity*)))
EFFECTS	KNOW(*H*, Location(*entity*))
DECOMPOSITION	Indicate-Deictically(*S, H, entity*)
	Assert(*S, H*, Location(*entity*))

Figure 4. Plan Operator for Graphical/Textual Display

After the entity is visible, the decomposition of the identify action of Figure 4 deictically indicates the entity and then describes its location in natural language (as above). There are several plan operators for deictic indication available including highlighting (a permanent indication of an entity), blinking (intermittent highlighting), and circling. These forms of visual deixis can be used to indicate individual objects (e.g., roads, towns, dams), groups of objects, or geographical regions. While the current implementation simply defaults to highlighting, the choice among different deictic techniques could be motivated by a number of considerations including the number and kind of entities visible in the region, their visual properties (e.g., size, color, shading) in order to maximize the distinction of the given entity and its background, and the kind of communication being generated (e.g., highlighting may be preferred when communicating route plans so that upon completion the entire route is visible). We next illustrate these plans in action.

NAME	Make-entity-visible
HEADER	Make-Visible(*entity*)
CONSTRAINTS	Cartographic-Entity?(*entity*)
PRECONDITIONS	Displayed(*entity*)
EFFECTS	Visible(*entity*)
DECOMPOSITION	Display-Region(*entity*)

Figure 5. Plan Operator for Map Display Control

4. Multimedia Identification Exemplified

To illustrate these and other communicative acts, we detail the planning of multimedia directions for the Map Display System [Hilton and Anken 1990], a knowledge-based cartographic information system which represents over 600 European towns, 227 airbases, 40 lakes, 14 dams, as well as other objects. The road network in the map includes 233 roads (divided up into 4,607 road segments) and 889 intersections.

If the user queries the system "Where is Chemnitz?," this is simulated by posting the goal Identify(SYSTEM, USER, #<Chemnitz>) to the explanation planner. The planner then uses a unification algorithm to find all operators from the library whose HEADER portion matches the current goal. This includes the identification plan operators in Figures 3 and 4. Next all operators whose header matches this goal are found and instantiated with the bindings of the variables that match the header. Figure 6 shows the plan operator for linguistic and visual identification instantiated with bindings. When the action Identify(SYSTEM, USER, #<Chemnitz>) unifies against the header of the plan operator in Figure 4, the variable *S* is bound to SYSTEM, *H* is bound to USER, and *entity* is bound to the object #<Chemnitz>. These bindings are used to instantiate the entire plan operator to that shown in Figure 6.

Because there may be many methods of achieving a given goal, those operators that satisfy the constraints and essential preconditions are then prioritized using *preference metrics*. For example, operators that utilize both text and graphics are preferred over simply textual operators. Also, those operators with fewer subgoals are preferred (where this does not conflict with the previous preference). The preference metric prefers plan operators with fewer subplans (cognitive economy), with fewer new variables (limiting the introduction of new entities in the focus space of the discourse), those that satisfy all preconditions (to avoid backward chaining for efficiency), and those plan operators that are more common or preferred in naturally-occurring explanations (e.g., certain kinds of communicative acts occur more frequently in human-produced text or are preferred by rhetoricians over other methods). While the first three preferences are explicitly inferred, the last preference is implemented by the sequence in which operators appear in the plan library.

NAME	Identify-location-linguistically-&-visually
HEADER	Identify(SYSTEM, USER, #<Chemnitz>)
CONSTRAINTS	Cartographic-Entity?(#<Chemnitz>)
PRECONDITIONS	Visible(#<Chemnitz>) ∧
	WANT(SYSTEM, KNOW(USER, Location(#<Chemnitz>)))
EFFECTS	KNOW(USER, Location(#<Chemnitz>))
DECOMPOSITION	Indicate-Deictically(SYSTEM, USER, #<Chemnitz>)
	Assert(SYSTEM, USER, Location(#<Chemnitz>))

Figure 6. Instantiated identify *Plan Operator*

Working from this prioritized list of operators, the planner ensures preconditions are satisfied and tries to execute the decomposition of each until one succeeds. This involves processing any special operators (e.g., optionality is allowed in the decomposition) or quantifiers (∀ or ∃) as well as distinguishing between subgoals and primitive acts. For example, if the planner chooses the plan operator in Figure 6 from those that satisfy their constraints, it first ensures its preconditions hold (i.e., by making sure the entity is visible through other graphical acts).

Next, the planner attempts to execute the two subacts in its decomposition, Indicate-Deictically(SYSTEM, USER, #<Chemnitz>) and Assert(SYSTEM, USER, Location(#<Chemnitz>). Assert is a primitive act and so decomposition halts here. In contrast, Indicate-Deictically is not a primitive act and so the planner is reinvoked. As indicated in the previous section, in the current implementation deictic indication defaults to highlighting, which is also a primitive act.

Thus, our original simulated user query, "Where is Chemnitz?", results in the hierarchical decomposition shown in Figure 7. This tree is linearized by a depth-first search and the resulting sequence of linguistic and graphical primitive actions is executed. The surface speech act, Assert, together with the Location predicate and its argument,

#<Chemnitz>, are passed to the linguistic realization component. Using this information, the realizer fills a semantic case role associated with the Location predicate to yield a semantic specification #<Assert location-predicate Chemnitz>, which contains the following information:

```
ACTION:       #<be-copula>
AGENT:        #<Chemnitz>
PATIENT:      #<town>
MODIFIERS:    (location (latitude 50.82) (longitude 12.88))
```

This specification is used to build grammatical relations (subject, object), then syntactic constituents (noun, verb, adverbial, and prepositional phrases), and finally a surface tree which is realized as (see [Maybury 1991b]):

```
Chemnitz is a town located at 50.82°latitude 12.88° longitude.
```

This is uttered after the map displays the region around Chemnitz and highlights its icon.

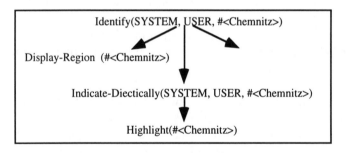

Figure 7. Hierarchical Multimedia Plan to Identify Chemnitz

5. Extended Multimedia Directions

While the above coordinated graphical and linguistic identification of Chemnitz may satisfy the user's query, often a cartographic information system must communicate a route between distant points. This can be accomplished in language alone, or by coordinating language and map displays. The communicative act Explain-Route, formalized in Figure 8, does the latter, the former being a simplification thereof. The constraints of this operator first test if both objects are cartographic ones and that there exists a path between them in the underlying Map Display System [Hilton and Anken 1990]. The function cartographic-path which is used in the plan operator takes as arguments two objects from the cartographic knowledge base and, using a branch and bound search strategy, explores the road network to return the "best" route between the two points (if one exists). The path returned by the function is an ordered list of roads, intersections, and towns indicating the preferred route from one entity to another, as defined by the rewrite rules:

```
path      ->   segment + (path)
segment ->   point + road-segment + point
point    ->   intersection | city | town | bridge
```

where "()" indicates optionality and "|" indicates logical disjunction. For any given segment, the functions source, link, and destination return the source and destination point and the link that connects them (i.e., a road segment).

If the constraints on the Explain-Route action are satisfied, then the planner attempts to achieve its preconditions. The first precondition requires the source location to be visible. If not currently the case, this can be achieved using graphical actions like the make-visible act defined in Figure 5. If the constraints and preconditions can be satisfied, then the decomposition first visually identifies the source of the next segment, next linguistically requests the hearer to move from the source to the destination of that segment, then visually identifies the link of the next segment, and lastly visually indicates the direction of the movement along the link between the two (using an arrow). (The initial source location is not *linguistically* identified because we assume the hearer is traveling from that location and thus is familiar with it.) After repeating this for all

segments, the plan concludes by identifying the ultimate destination using actions like those of Figures 3 and 4. The effect of explaining the route is that the hearer knows how to get from origin to destination and the hearer knows the segments of that route.

For example, assume the user asks "How do I get from Wiesbaden to Frankfurt?", simulated by posting the discourse goal Explain-Route(SYSTEM, USER, #<Wiesbaden>, #<Frankfurt-am-Main>). The planner uses the Explain-Route act of Figure 8 to build the explanation plan shown in Figure 9. This plan is realized as (graphical acts indicated parenthetically in italics):

> *(Display map region around Wiesbaden) (highlight Wiesbaden)* From Wiesbaden take Autobahn A66 Northeast for thirty-one kilometers to Frankfurt-am-Main. *(highlight Autobahn A66) (indicate direction with blinking arrow) (highlight Frankfurt-am-Main)* Frankfurt-am-Main is located at 50.11° latitude and 8.66° longitude.

NAME	Explain-route-linguistically-and-visually
HEADER	Explain-Route(*S, H, from-entity, to-entity*)
CONSTRAINTS	Cartographic-entity?(*from-entity*) $\wedge$
	Cartographic-entity?(*to-entity*) $\wedge$ *path*
PRECONDITIONS	visible(*from-entity*) $\wedge$
	WANT(*S*, KNOW-HOW(*H*, Go(*from-entity, to-entity*)))
EFFECTS	KNOW-HOW(*H*, Go(*from-entity, to-entity*)) $\wedge$
	$\forall$*segment* $\in$ *path*
	KNOW(*H*, Subpath(*segment, path*))
DECOMPOSITION	$\forall$*segment* $\in$ *path*
	Indicate-Deictically(*S, H*, source(*segment*))
	Command(*S, H*, Do(*H*, Go(source(*segment*),
	link(*segment*),
	destination(*segment*))))
	Indicate-Deictically(*S, H*, link(*segment*))
	Indicate-Direction(*S, H*, source(*segment*),
	link(*segment*),
	destination(*segment*))
	Identify(*S, H, to-entity*)
WHERE	*path* = cartographic-path(*from-entity, to-entity*)

Figure 8. Explain-Route *Plan Operator*

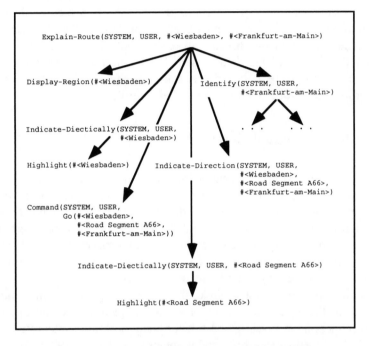

Figure 9. Hierarchical Plan for Locational Instructions

A slightly more complex locational instruction results if the user asks how to get from Mannheim to Heidelberg, initiated by posting the discourse goal Explain-Route(SYSTEM, USER, #<Mannheim>, #<Heidelberg>). The resulting multimedia explanation is realized as:

> (Display map region around Mannheim) (highlight Mannheim) From Mannheim take Route 38 Southeast for four kilometers to the intersection of Route 38 and Autobahn A5. (highlight Route 38) (indicate direction with blinking arrow) (highlight intersection of Route 38 and Autobahn A5) From there take Autobahn A5 Southeast for seven kilometers to Heidelberg. (highlight Autobahn A5) (indicate direction with blinking arrow) (highlight Heidelberg) Heidelberg is located at 49.39° latitude and 6.68° longitude, four kilometers Northwest of Dossenheim, six kilometers Northwest of Edingen, and five kilometers Southwest of Eppelheim.

The linguistic realization component keeps track of the relationship of the current *spatial focus* (the current visited segment) to the previous spatial focus (the previously visited segment). This relationship constrains the choice of surface choices [Maybury 1991b] such as demonstrative pronouns ("this" versus "that"; "here" versus "there") as well as the generation of spatial directionals (e.g., "Southeast", "West") and durationals (e.g., "seven kilometers"). This focus-based choice contrasts with the use of heuristic approaches based on rules (e.g., describe an entity using a demonstrative noun phrase if there is no proper name for that entity [Neal et al. 1989]).

6. Contrast with Related Research

As noted in the introduction, in recent years a number of advances have been made in the area of text planning. At the same time, others have made progress in graphical design. For example, mechanisms have been developed to design graphical presentations of relational information [Mackinlay 1986b], to design network diagrams [Marks 1991b], and to automatically create business graphics displays [Roth and Mattis 1990]. Others began investigating the automatic generation of coordinated multimedia explanations. Some have focused on the knowledge underlying mixed media presentations [Arens et al., this volume], on media-independent representations of intentions [Elhadad et al. 1989], or on the psycho perception of verbal and pictorial elements [Guastello and Traut 1989]. Others have investigated selecting and designing integrated information displays including maps, text, tables, and graphics (e.g., [Arens 1991; Burger and Marshall, this volume]).

Recently, however, there is a move to an even tighter coupling of text and graphics design. For example, COMET [Feiner and McKeown, this volume; Feiner et al., this volume] uses rhetorical schema to select content independent of media and then apportion this to text and three dimensional graphics to design coordinated multimedia presentations concerning the operation and maintenance of an Army field radio. Unlike COMET, mode allocation in our approach occurs during not after content selection so that content selection and mode allocation can co-constrain. More closely related to our approach, WIP [André and Rist, this volume; André et al., this volume] uses plan operators to design presentations. In contrast to WIP, however, our approach is based on a generalization of a set of rhetorical acts used previously for multisentential text planning in the TEXPLAN system [Maybury 1990, 1992b]. This accounts, for example, for the distinction between illocutionary and locutionary acts in TEXPLAN (see Section 2).

WIP, on the other hand, claims roots in rhetorical structure theory-based (RST) text planners [Hovy 1988a; Moore 1989]. See Maybury [1992a] for a contrast of these two approaches and Hovy et al. [1992] for a discussion of a more integrated approach. Another difference is that WIP focuses on the generation of static illustrated instructions (i.e., picture sequences) whereas our multimedia extension to TEXPLAN focuses on the design of dynamic, narrated animation of routes over an object-oriented cartographic information system. Also, WIP includes a fine-grained constraint-based layout mechanism [Graf 1992] whereas our approach controls only coarse-grained layout by way of display control actions (see Figure 2). Also, WIP's tree adjoining grammar approach supports incremental generation below the clause level whereas TEXPLAN can only generate incrementally at the clause level. Finally, WIP and COMET address the challenging problem of cross-modal references. Nevertheless, COMET, WIP, and the extended TEXPLAN all raise issues central to multimedia design such as: how do we select and apportion content to different media, how do we coordinate media, and how do we ensure that our communicative goals are achieved by the resulting artifact?

7. Conclusion and Future Directions

This chapter proposes a number of communicative acts — linguistic, graphical, and rhetorical — that can be exploited to plan and coordinate multimedia explanations. We first formalize several linguistic acts and graphical acts as plan operators. These are abstracted into higher level, media-independent actions called rhetorical acts. A computational implementation is described which identifies locations and composes route plans in coordinated natural language text and graphics in the context of a cartographic information system.

We are currently extending the implementation to incorporate other types of graphical acts. For example, the system is able to divide an entity linguistically in two ways: by detailing its constituents or subparts (e.g., "The United Kingdom contains England, Scotland, Wales, and Northern Ireland.") or if the entity is an abstract concept, by indicating its subtypes or subclasses (e.g., "There are three Baltic languages: Old Prussian, Lithuanian, and Latvian."). Graphically, subpart division can be accomplished, for example, by depicting subcomponents or hierarchical trees.

Similarly, subtype division can be accomplished graphically using trees (which indicate parent/child relations) or Venn diagrams (indicating set relationships). Also, while the system can linguistically characterize an entity (e.g., "The pancreas is a long, soft, irregular shaped gland located behind the stomach."), entities which have visual attributes such as size, shape, color and location can be depicted, perhaps with greater effect than the corresponding linguistic description. Finally, the system can generate paragraph-length comparisons of entities, and we intend to compose tabular comparisons of attributes and values, although this will require planning of more sophisticated composite graphs [Feiner 1985; Burger 1989]. Other composite graphical acts also require further investigation (e.g., circling a group of objects and indicating their movement with an arrow).

There are several issues which require further investigation. These include the relationship of deictic and display control acts to the model of the user's attention (i.e., salient objects, events, and regions). Another important issue concerns coordinating graphical and linguistic acts at the clausal and lexical level (e.g., referring expressions coordinated with deixis). One approach would be to extend paragraph planning below the sentence level [Appelt 1985]. Much more difficult is how to narrate events and situations in multiple media, which requires communication of temporal, spatial, and causal information (i.e., story telling coupled with graphical animation).

Finally, we need to investigate the relation of linguistic and graphical acts to other non-speech audio acts. For example, there are analogs between mediums such as linguistic, graphical, and auditory warnings (exclaiming, flashing, and beeping), graphical and auditory icons (e.g., using sirens to indicate danger), and graphical and auditory motion (e.g., using the perception of Doppler effects to indicate motion). Lastly, we are also investigating the utility of probabilistic media allocation algorithms that might overcome some of the inflexibility of rule-based approaches and also augment the formal plan-based approach we have detailed. These remain interesting avenues for future research.

8. Acknowledgments

I thank the reviewers for their comments and Karen Sparck Jones, John Burger, Sam Bayer, and Marc Vilain for stimulating discussions on related issues.

Chapter 3

WIP: The Automatic Synthesis of Multimodal Presentations

Elizabeth André, Wolfgang Finkler, Winfried Graf, Thomas Rist, Anne Schauder, and Wolfgang Wahlster

Abstract

Due to the growing complexity of information that has to be communicated by current artificial intelligence (AI) systems, there comes an increasing need for building advanced intelligent user interfaces that take advantage of a coordinated combination of different modalities, e.g., natural language, graphics, and animation, to produce situated and user-adaptive presentations. A deeper understanding of the basic principles underlying multimodal communication requires theoretical work on computational models as well as practical work on concrete systems. In this article, we describe the system WIP, which is an implemented prototype of a knowledge-based presentation system that generates illustrated texts that are customized for the intended audience and situation. We present the architecture of WIP and introduce its major components; the presentation planner, the layout manager, and the generators for text and graphics. To achieve a coherent output with an optimal media mix, the single components have to be interleaved. The interplay of the presentation planner, the text and the graphics generator will be demonstrated by means of a system run. In particular, we show how a text-picture combination containing a crossmodal referring expression is generated by the system.

1. Introduction

With increases in the amount and sophistication of information that must be communicated to the users of complex technical systems, comes a corresponding need to find new ways to present that information flexibly and efficiently. Intelligent presentation systems are important building blocks for the next generation of user interfaces, because they translate from the narrow output channels, provided by most of the current application systems, into high-bandwidth communications tailored to the individual user. Since in many situations, this information is only presented efficiently through a particular combination of communication modes[1], the automatic generation of multimodal presentations is one of the tasks of such presentation systems. Multimodal interfaces combining, e.g., natural language and graphics take advantage of both the individual strength of each communication mode and the fact that several modes can be employed in parallel, e.g., in the text-picture combinations of illustrated documents (see also [Sullivan and Tyler 1991; Ortony et al. 1992; Roth and Hefley, this volume]).

It is an important goal of this research not simply to merge the verbalization results of a natural language generator and the visualization results of a knowledge-based graphics generator, but to carefully coordinate graphics and text in such a way that they complement each other (see also [Wahlster et al. 1991ab]).

The automatic design of multimodal presentations has only recently received significant attention in artificial intelligence research. Most systems generate written text and graphics including bar charts (see the system SAGE [Roth et al. 1991], network diagrams [Marks and Reiter 1990], weather maps [Kerpedjiev 1992] and depiction's of three-dimensional objects (see the systems COMET [Feiner and McKeown, this volume] and WIP [Wahlster et al. 1991b; Wahlster et al. 1992]. Maybury [this volume] is concerned with the planning of multimodal directions in a cartographic information system. Badler et al. [1991] focus on the generation of animation from instructions. Further work concentrates on the analysis and representation of relevant design knowledge [Arens et al., this volume] as an important prerequisite for the automatic design of multimodal presentations.

The work closest to our own is done in the COMET project [Feiner and McKeown, this volume]. Both projects share a strong research interest in the coordination of text and graphics. COMET generates directions for the maintenance and repair of a portable radio using text coordinated with three-dimensional graphics. In spite of many similarities, there are major differences between COMET and WIP, e.g., in the systems' architec-

---

[1] Since one of the generation parameters of WIP is the specification of the output device, we use the term 'medium' in the sense of a physical carrier of information. In contrast, the term 'mode' is used throughout this paper to refer to the particular sign system. We are aware of the fact that other authors use these terms differently.

tures, representation languages and processing strategies. While during one of the final processing steps of COMET the media layout component is supposed to combine text and graphics fragments produced by media-specific generators, in WIP layout considerations can influence the early stages of the planning process and constrain the media-specific generators. In WIP, we view layout as an important carrier of meaning. COMET uses a schema-based content planner while WIP uses an operator-based approach to planning. Other distinguishing features of WIP's architecture are that it supports incremental output and that mode selection is done not after, but during content planning.

2. A Functional View of WIP

The task of the knowledge-based presentation system WIP is the generation of a variety of multimodal documents from an input consisting of a formal description of the communicative intent of a planned presentation. The generation process is controlled by a set of generation parameters such as target group, presentation objective, resource limitations, and target language.

The example of a presentation goal in Figure 1 represents the system's assumption about the mutual belief (BMB) of the presenter P and the addressee A that it is P's goal that A carries out a plan denoted by the constant fill-in-128. This is a concrete domain plan specified as part of WIP's application knowledge. In this case, the plan is a fully instantiated sequence of actions represented in the assertional part of the hybrid knowledge representation system RAT (Representation of Actions in Terminological Logics) [Heinsohn et al. 1992]. The terminological part of RAT is used to represent the ontology and abstract plans for a particular application domain (see Figure 1).

In addition to this propositional representation, which includes the relevant information about the structure, function, behavior, and use of the technical device, WIP has access to an analogical representation of the geometry of the machine in the form of a wireframe model (see Figure 1). WIP is a transportable interface based on processing schemes that are independent of any particular back-end system and thus requires only a limited effort to adapt to a new application. Obviously, for a new domain, the application knowledge and the wireframe model must be transformed into WIP's representation schemes. Currently all input for the development and testing of the system is, however, created manually.

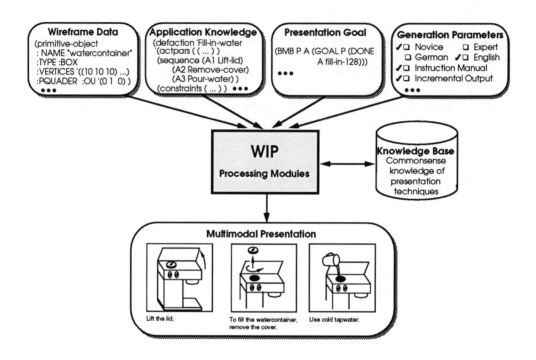

Figure 1. A Functional View of WIP

A good example of the use of a system like WIP is the generation of user-friendly multimodal instructions for technical devices. As a first domain, we have chosen instructions for the use of espresso-machines. Figure 1 shows a typical text-picture sequence that may be used to instruct a user in filling the water container of an espresso-machine.

3. The Architecture of WIP

The design of the WIP system follows a modular approach. WIP includes two parallel processing cascades for the incremental generation of text and graphics. In order to achieve a fine-grained and optimal division of work between the single system components, we allow for various forms of interaction between them. Besides interaction within the cascades, all components also have access to the design record which contains all results generated so far. Figure 2 sketches the architecture of the current WIP prototype system.

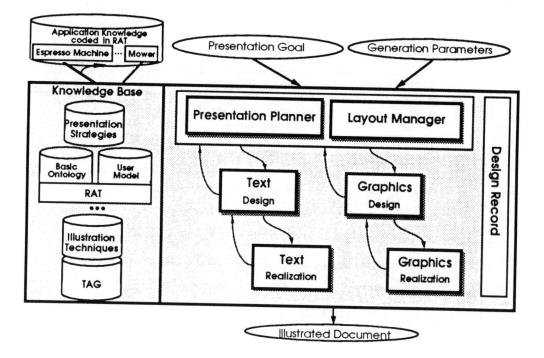

Figure 2. The Architecture of the WIP System

3.1. The Presentation Planner

The presentation planner is responsible for determining the contents and selecting an appropriate mode combination. A basic assumption behind the WIP model is that not only the generation of text and dialog contributions, but also the design of graphics and multimodal documents can be considered as an act sequence that aims to achieve certain goals. Thus, a plan-based approach seems appropriate for the synthesis of multimodal presentations [André and Rist 1990ab]. The result of the planning process is a hierarchically-structured plan of the document to be generated in the form of a directed acyclic graph (DAG). This plan reflects the propositional contents of the potential document parts, the intentional goals behind the parts, as well as rhetorical relationships between them. While the top of the presentation plan is a more or less complex presentation goal

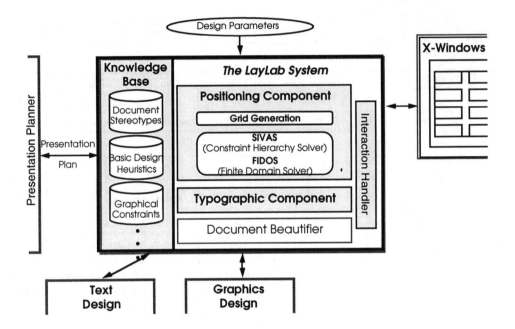

Figure 3. The Various Modules of the Layout Manager

(e.g., explaining how to make coffee), the lowest level is formed by specifications of elementary presentation tasks (e.g., formulating a request or depicting an object) that are directly forwarded to the mode-specific design components. A detailed description of the presentation planner is given in [André and Rist, this volume].

3.2. The Layout Manager

To communicate generated information to the user in an expressive and effective way, a knowledge-based layout component has to be integrated into the presentation design process. In order to achieve a coherent output, a layout manager must be able to reflect certain semantic and pragmatic relations specified by a presentation planner to arrange the visual appearance of a mixture of text and graphics fragments delivered by the mode-specific generators, i.e., to determine the size of the layout objects and the exact coordinates for positioning them on the document page. Therefore, we use a grid-based approach as an ordering system for efficiently designing functional (i.e., uniform, coherent, and consistent) layouts [Müller-Brockmann 1981]. This concept has also been used in the GRIDS system for automatically laying out displays containing text and pictures [Feiner 1988] and by Beach for low-level table layout [Beach 1985]. Figure 3 sketches the architecture of WIP's layout manager including a constraint-based positioning component (CLAY), an intelligent typographer, a document rendering component, and an interaction handler. For the rest of this paragraph we will only talk about the positioning component (see also [Graf and Maaß 1991; Maaß 1992]).

The automatic placement of layout objects in a design space can be viewed as a combinatorial problem. Therefore, we treat layout as a constraint satisfaction problem (*CSP*) in a finite discrete search space [Mackworth 1977]. We encode graphical design knowledge via constraints expressing semantic/pragmatic and geometrical/topological relations. Semantic and pragmatic constraints essentially correspond to coherence relations, such as the rhetorical relations 'sequence' and 'contrast' specified in Rhetorical Structure Theory (RST) by [Mann and Thompson 1988], and can be easily reflected through specific design constraints. They describe perceptual criteria concerning the organization of the visual elements, such as the sequential ordering (horizontal versus vertical layout), alignment, grouping, symmetry, or similarity. Geometrical and topological constraints refer to absolute and relative constraints. Absolute constraints fix geometric parameters to constant values (e.g., coordinates). Relative constraints relate a geometric parameter of one object to another.

CONTRAST $(G1,G2) \leftrightarrow$
$G1 \equiv pkt(x_{G_1}, y_{G_1}, wi_{G_1}, he_{G_1}) \wedge$
$G2 \equiv pkt(x_{G_2}, y_{G_2}, wi_{G_2}, he_{G_2}) \wedge$
$[\textbf{EQUAL}(y_{G_1}, y_{G_2}) \wedge \textbf{BESIDE}(x_{G_1}, wi_{G_1}, x_{G_2})$
$\vee$
$\textbf{EQUAL}(x_{G_1}, x_{G_2}) \wedge \textbf{UNDER}(y_{G_1}, he_{G_1}, y_{G_2})]$

Figure 4. Representation of the Compound-Constraint CONTRAST

To give an example of a typical compound constraint in a predicate logic like notation, let's have a look at the representation of the 'contrast'-constraint (Figure 4) and the illustration through the corresponding constraint network in Figure 5.

When using constraints to represent layout knowledge, one often wants to prioritize the constraints in those which must be required and others which are preferably held

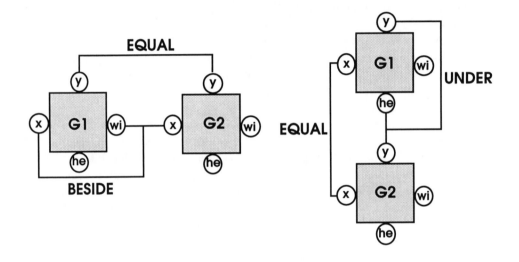

Figure 5. Constraint Network of the Definition Above

[Borning 1987]. A powerful way of expressing this layout feature is to organize the constraints in a hierarchy by assigning a preference scale to the constraint network. We distinguish between *obligatory*, *optional* and *default constraints*. The latter state default values, which remain fixed unless the corresponding constraint is removed by a stronger one. As graphical constraints frequently have only local effects, they are generated by the system on the fly.

For constraint solving, two dedicated incremental solvers are organized hierarchically in CLAY. An incremental constraint hierarchy solver based on the DeltaBlue algorithm by Freeman-Benson et al. [1990] and a domain solver that handles finite domains like the approach in CHIP [Hentenryck 1989] are integrated in a layered model. These solvers are triggered from a common meta level by rules and defaults. For a more detailed description of the layout manager see [Graf 1992].

3.3. The Text Generator

WIP's text generator consists of the text design and the text realization component, which form a cascade. The text design component receives as input from the presentation planner exactly that piece of knowledge that was chosen to be presented as text. It determines in which order the given input elements shall be realized in the text. The structure of a text is worked out at several levels. This comprises, for example, the partition of a paragraph into sentences, the assignment of a perspective or the use of anaphora to obtain a coherent text. Therefore, this component is comparable with the so-called 'Micro-planner', a part of the what-to-say component – while the presentation planner can be seen as 'Macro-planner' [Levelt 1989].

The resulting preverbal message is grammatically encoded, linearized and inflected in the text realization component (How–to–Say component). Thereby, the generation parameters direct the choice of syntactic structures. One difficulty is in defining the boundary between the What–to–Say and the How–to–Say component. We decided to associate the process of lexical choice with the text design component. The valency information of the chosen lemmas form syntactic constraints for the text realization component, e.g., a transitive verb must be combined with two complements, subject and object, before the sentence is syntactically correct and complete. Since these lemmas are chosen relatively independent from each other, they can cause conflicts during verbalization in the text realization component. To be able to report these problems to the text design component we propose a model with feedback between the two modules.

Our main emphasis for the text generator is on an incremental style of processing. Both components of the cascade work incrementally and information is handed over in a piecemeal fashion. This leads to greater flexibility and efficiency, since the realization component can start working before the design component has completed its results. One of the prerequisites for incremental processing in the realization component is the use of a grammar formalism which allows the specification of entities of an adequately small size (see below).

Figure 6 shows the architecture of the text realization component. The input from the text design component is called 'goal of the utterance.' It comprises the content words and indicates their semantic relation. On this basis the 'Interface' component chooses the respective grammar rules. The text realization component is based on the formalism of tree adjoining grammars (TAGs) [Harbusch et al. 1991]. Reasons for the use of TAGs are, e.g., its adequate power [Joshi 1985] and its combination operations that allow the flexible expansion of syntactic trees [Schauder 1992]. For each lemma of the input a grammar rule (a tree of the TAG) is chosen that represents its subcategorization frame. In order to perform this task, we use lexicalized Tree Adjoining Grammars. This formalism restricts the size of trees, so that they describe exactly one lemma as the head of the represented structure which is used as anchor in the lexicon.

The interface is associated with two boxes: 'LD Gram' contains the descriptions of the pure hierarchical structures (without ordering constraints), the 'Syntax Lexicon' relates lemmas with tree families of 'LD Gram'. We use LD/LP TAGs (local dominance/linear precedence TAGs) to divide the grammar rules into a set of mobiles and a set of order restricting constraints. This leads to a more compact representation, because all grammar

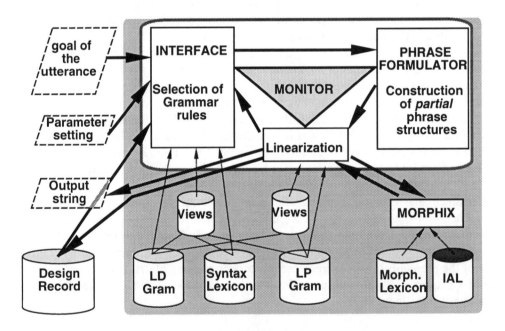

Figure 6. The Architecture of the Syntactic Generator

rules representing the same hierarchical structure with different word order can be expressed within one local dominance structure (a mobile). The 'Views' on the grammar are used, if there are alternative structures. They guide the choice among these alternatives with respect to the given generation parameters (e.g., the style).

The processing inside the Text Realization component takes place within two modules: In the 'Phrase Formulator', syntactic structures are composed without consideration of word order rules. Thereby, the chosen elementary trees are combined by means of the TAG operations adjunction and substitution. The specified semantic relations are mapped to functional relations and guide these combinations. In the 'Linearization' module, the resulting trees are traversed and an adequate and syntactically correct word order is computed.

Incremental processing is supported by parallelism because the expansion of existing structures can be performed simultaneously at several branches of syntactic trees. Therefore, the basis for the text realization component is a distributed parallel model with active cooperating objects. For each given lemma one object is created which is responsible for the further processing of the respective syntactic structure. The dependency relations between the various lemmas define a hierarchy of objects. In the phrase formulator the objects try to build the complete syntactic tree by communicating with one another and exchanging information. If an object fulfills specific completeness constraints, it moves to the linearization level. There it tries to compute its local word order and – again by communication with other objects – to correctly integrate its partial terminal string into the whole sentence. After the computation of word position, the lemmas are inflected using the module MORPHIX (see [Finkler and Neumann 1988]). Then, complete parts are uttered incrementally.

In addition to the incremental inner working, the production of incremental output is one important feature of our system. While there are several other approaches to incremental generation, most of them do not deal with incremental output. If output is delayed until it is complete, the utterances become less natural because of the long initial delay. If the output is generated incrementally, the uttered prefix forms an additional constraint for the further processing because each change becomes visible to the dialogue partner (see [Finkler and Schauder 1992]).

3.4. The Graphics Generator

WIP generates illustrated instructions explaining how to operate technical devices, such as an espresso machine or a lawn mower. Thus, WIP often has to graphically communicate information about physical objects, i.e., information about object properties (such as shape, material surface characteristics, constituent structure and function), static relations to other objects (such as the location, the orientation and the distance of the objects) and dynamic relations that represent changes of object attributes and static relations (e.g., a change in the spatial position of an object).

As with text generation, we distinguish between components for graphics design and graphics realization [Rist and André 1992ab]. The realization component can be considered as an extension of a object-oriented graphics editor that handles both two-dimensional concepts and three-dimensional models of objects and object configurations. Thus, the component has to support three kinds of operations. First, there are operators to create and manipulate three-dimensional object configurations. Examples are: adding an object to a configuration, spatially separating object parts to construct exploded views and cutting away object faces to make opaque parts visible. The second kind of operators constrains mapping functions and viewing specifications and performs the instantiation of images from three-dimensional models. Finally, there are several operators defined on the picture level. E.g., an object depiction may be annotated with a label, or picture parts may be colored in order to emphasize them. Beside these achievement operators that effect either models, mappings or pictures, the functionality of the realization component also encompasses evaluation operators (e.g., to check whether an object as part of an object configuration is visible from a given viewing specification, or to check whether a picture part can be discriminated from other picture components). These evaluators are necessary in order to recognize whether the effect of an achievement operator has been destroyed by the application of subsequent achievement operators. The major modules of the realization component are: a three-dimensional studio, a mapping controller, a two-dimensional clipboard and a module for handling data structures for images and pictures (Figure 7).

The task of the graphics design component is to transform presentation tasks received from the presentation planner into a sequence of operators to be executed by the graphics realization component. Basic knowledge about how to accomplish this transformation is represented by so-called design strategies. Each design strategy consists of a header, an applicability condition and a body. The header may be a presentation task or a graphical constraint. The applicability condition specifies when a strategy may be used and constrains the variables to be instantiated. The body contains a set of graphical constraints that have to be achieved in order to accomplish the goal indicated in the header. Whereas some graphical constraints are directly related to achievement operators, others lead to the application of further design strategies. In addition, graphical constraints are associated with evaluation operators to check whether constraints are already satisfied and whether they are still satisfied after having executed further achievement operators.

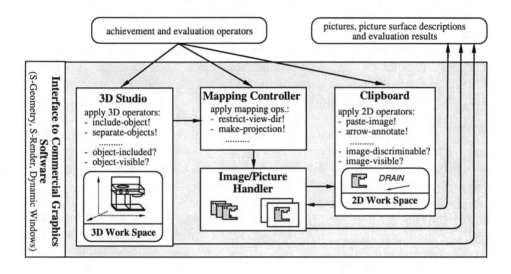

Figure 7. The Graphics Realization Component

4. Interplay of the Various Components

In the following, the interplay of the presentation planner, the text generator, and the graphics generator will be demonstrated by means of an example.

Figure 8 and Figure 9 show snapshots of a system run. The discourse structure built up by the planner is shown in the upper left window of the WIP frame. The results of the text and graphics generators appear in the two lower left windows. The right window displays the verbal trace messages of all system components.

In our example, the presentation planner has decided to explain to the user where the on/off switch of the espresso machine is located. To accomplish this task, one can a) activate a representation of the concept switch-2 that identifies switch-2 as an on/off switch, b) activate a representation of switch-2 that contains information to localize it and c) ensure that a coreferential link between the representations activated in a) and b) can be established. A presentation strategy for achieving this is to name switch-2 as 'on/off switch,' show the location of the switch with respect to a landmark object in a picture and relate the generated name with the corresponding picture object via graphical annotation. Since the switch is part of the espresso machine, the espresso machine is considered a suitable landmark object. After the expansion of this strategy, the graphics generator receives the task of creating a picture with the espresso machine and the switch whereas the text generation component has to find a natural language expression for the switch. In the example, the expression 'on/off switch' is generated and passed as label onto the graphics generator (see the TAG Results Window in Figure 8). Complex nominal phrases for titles or labels are handled in exactly the same way as 'normal' sentences with a verbal predicate. The highest object in the hierarchy realizes the head of the sentence (a verb, a noun, ...) and decides on its completion.

When trying to place this text string within the picture, it turns out that there is not enough space. It is neither possible to place the string inside the corresponding picture object nor close to it. Therefore, the graphics generator sends a message to the presentation planner that it could not accomplish the annotation task. The presentation planner then has to backtrack and try another presentation strategy. This time, it tries to achieve c) by unambiguously describing the location of the picture element corresponding to switch-2.

The top left pane in Figure 8, labeled 'Document Structure', shows the DAG that has been produced by the presentation planner. The presentation goal (Localize P A (Object switch-2) G) has been decomposed into three subgoals: (Elaborate P A ...), (Background P A ...) and (S-Depict P A ...). After the refinement of (Elaborate P A ...), four acts have been posted as new subgoals: three referential acts for specifying the spatial relation, the reference object and the subject, and an elementary speech act (S-Assert P A ...) which is passed on to the text designer.

As mentioned before, the planner passes on a certain piece of information to the respective generator as soon as it has decided which component should encode it. In the example, (S-Assert P A ...) is sent to the text designer although the contents of the assertion are not yet fully specified. Currently, this component is only rudimentarily realized. The computation of the output is done by a simple transformation. The input for the text realization component consists of entities containing content words and functional relations between the entities as can be seen in the trace window of the example of WIP (see Figure 8). These entities and relations may be specified in a piecemeal way. Their order is independent from the word order in the resulting utterance. The resulting structures

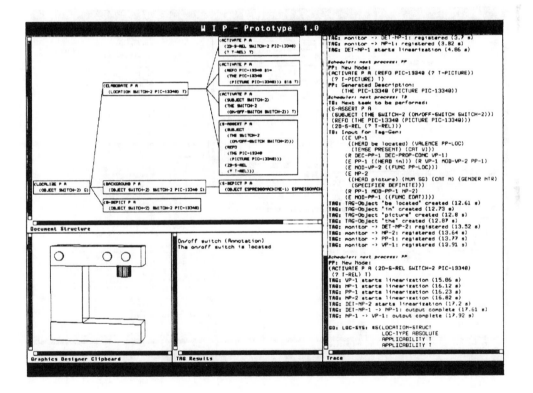

Figure 8. Snapshot 1

generated by the text designer at this state in our example are not sufficient for the TAG generator to start with the utterance. All it can do now is to prepare a small package of syntactic information, which will later be associated with the head of the sentence and lead to the realization of the respective style (assertion clause, ...).

Some time later, the planner has determined the contents for the description of the switch. Thus, the incomplete task specification that has been sent to the text designer is supplemented accordingly. The text design component is now able to provide new input for the TAG generator. The TAG generator then starts computing and generates two objects which together form the noun phrase 'the on/off switch.' Since the verb of the

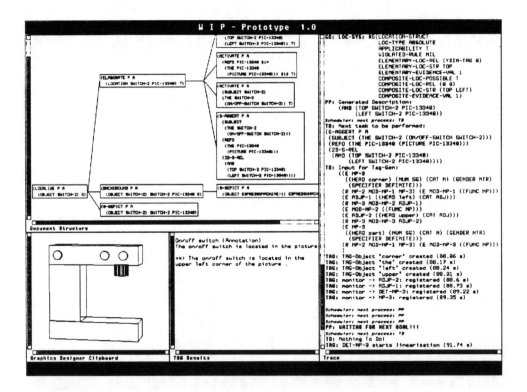

Figure 9. Snapshot 2

sentence is not yet chosen and the relation between the noun 'on/off switch' and the verb is not yet specified, its position in the sentence cannot be computed immediately (unless we use default values as 'first noun is subject'). So the utterance is delayed until the verb is realized. Figure 8 shows a snapshot of the system run shortly after the first part of the sentence has been uttered.

At this time, the planner has also determined the contents of a referring expression for the picture. Since there are no other pictures with which it can be confused, it is sufficient to include the concept 'picture' in the description. After the corresponding structures have been transformed by the text designer, the TAG generator has enough information to build a syntactically correct and complete sentence. Since the utterance should start as soon as possible, all words are uttered that can be added to the right of the previously uttered prefix according to the linearization rules. Since no further input information is known, the TAG generator assumes that the sentence is complete and generates: *The on/off switch is located in the picture.*

After the sentence has been completed, new information about the exact position of the switch in the picture is provided by WIP's localization component [Wazinski 1992]. Since it is not possible to incorporate this information after transformations by the text designer into the already generated sentence in a syntactically correct way, the TAG generator has to revise the utterance. Up to now we have not realized sophisticated strategies for the integration of revised parts in the sentence on the output screen, so the easiest way to make revision visible is to repeat the whole sentence: *The switch is located in the upper left corner of the picture* (see the TAG Results Window in Figure 9).

Now all components have finished their task and no new goals have been posted. Thus, the layout manager is activated that is responsible for the arrangement of the text and the pictures (Figure 10).

5. Conclusions

As a first step towards a computational model for the generation of multimodal presentations we have conceived the knowledge-based presentation system WIP. In this paper, we described the architecture and the main components of the first implemented WIP prototype. The system can be considered as a testbed to examine various forms of interactions which are necessary to tailor textual and pictorial output to each other. The experience we gained from this prototype provides a good basis for a deeper understanding of the interdependencies between text and graphics. In the future, we will not only concentrate on conceptual extensions but also evaluate the performance of the WIP system by adapting it to other domains. WIP is currently able to generate simple German or English explanations for using an espresso machine, assembling a lawn-mower, or installing a modem, demonstrating our claim of language and application independence.

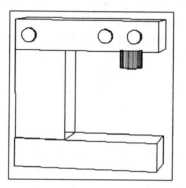

The on/off switch is located in the upper left corner of the picture.

Figure 10. Final Results

6. Implementation of the Prototype

The WIP system has been developed on a Symbolics XL 1200 Lisp machine and several MacIvory workstations. The modules are implemented in Symbolics Common Lisp using CLOS and Flavors for object-oriented programming.

The constraint-based positioning component CLAY of the layout manager has been implemented using ideas from the DeltaBlue algorithm and the forward checking mechanism from the CHIP system. First evaluations of a standalone prototype gained a high runtime efficiency.

The text realization component was conceived as a distributed parallel model in the framework of object-oriented concurrent programming. We use the Ivory boards in our local area network to run the processes in parallel.

The graphics realization component utilizes both facilities of the symbolics window system and the commercial software packages S-Geometry and S-Render. Representations of domain objects comprise wire-frame models which are based on the modeling primitives provided by S-Geometry.

7. Acknowledgments

The development of WIP is an ongoing group effort and has benefited from the contributions of our colleagues Karin Harbusch, Jochen Heinsohn, Bernhard Nebel, and Hans-Jürgen Profitlich as well as our students Andreas Butz, Bernd Herrmann, Antonio Kruger, Daniel Kudenko, Wolfgang Maaß, Peter Poller, George Schneider, Frank Schneiderlöchner, Christoph Schommer, Dudung Soetopo, and Detlev Zimmermann.

Chapter 4

The Design of Illustrated Documents as a Planning Task

Elisabeth André and Thomas Rist

Abstract

Not only the generation of text, but also the generation of multimodal documents can be considered as a sequence of communicative acts which aim to achieve certain goals. For the realization of a system able to automatically generate illustrated documents, a plan-based approach seems adequate. To represent knowledge about how to present information, we have designed presentation strategies which relate to both text and picture production. These strategies are considered as operators of a planning system. However, a conventional hierarchical planner for determining the contents and the rhetorical structure of a document has proven inappropriate to handle the various dependencies between content determination, mode selection and content realization. To overcome these problems, a new planning scheme has been developed that supports data transfer between the content planner and the mode-specific generation components and allows for revising an initial doct.

1. Introduction

Recently, there has been increasing interest in the design of systems generating multimodal output. Research in this area addresses the analysis and representation of presentation knowledge [Arens et al., this volume] as well as computational methods for the automatic synthesis of multimodal presentations [Badler et al. 1991; Feiner and McKeown, this volume; Marks and Reiter 1990; Maybury, this volume; Roth et al. 1991; Wahlster et al. 1991a]. There is general agreement that a multimodal presentation system cannot simply merge the results of the mode-specific generators, but has to carefully tailor them to each other. Such tailoring requires knowledge concerning the functions of textual and pictorial document parts and the relations between them. Furthermore, a presentation system must be able to handle the various dependencies between content planning, mode selection, and content realization.

In the following, we will show that many concepts applied in natural language generation, such as communicative acts and coherence relations, can be adapted in such a way that they become useful for the generation of text-picture combinations. We will present an approach that integrates content planning and mode selection and allows for interaction with mode-specific generators. This approach has been integrated into the multimodal presentation system WIP [André et al., this volume] which generates illustrated instructions for technical devices.

2. The Structure of Illustrated Documents

Our approach is based on the assumption that not only the generation of text, but also the generation of multimodal documents can be considered as an act sequence that aims to achieve certain goals [André and Rist 1990b]. We presume that there is at least one act that is central to the goal of the whole document. This act is referred to as the *main act*. Acts supporting the main act are called *subsidiary acts*.[1] Since main and subsidiary acts can, in turn, be composed of main and subsidiary acts, a hierarchical document structure results. While the root of the hierarchy generally corresponds to a complex communicative act such as describing a process, the leaves are elementary acts, i.e., speech acts [Searle 1969] or pictorial acts [Kjorup 1978].

The structure of a document is, however, not only determined by its hierarchical act structure, but also by the role acts play in relation to other acts. In text linguistic studies, a variety of coherence relations between text segments has been proposed (e.g., see [Grimes 1975] and [Hobbs 1978]). Perhaps the most elaborated set is presented in Rhetorical Structure Theory (RST) [Mann and Thompson 1987]. Examples of RST-relations are *Motivation, Elaboration, Enablement, Interpretation,* and *Summary.* Text-picture researchers have investigated the role a particular picture plays in relation to accompanying text passages. For example, Levin has found five primary functions [Levin et al. 1987]: *Decoration, Representation, Organization, Interpretation* and *Transforma-*

---

[1]This distinction between main and subsidiary acts essentially corresponds to the distinction between *global* and *subsidiary speech acts* in [Searle 1969], *main speech acts* and *subordinate speech acts* in [Van Dijk 1980], *dominierenden Handlungen* and *subsidiären* Handlungen in [Brandt et al. 1983] and between *nucleus* and *satellites* in [Mann and Thompson 1987].

tion. Hunter and colleagues distinguish between: *Embellish, Reinforce, Elaborate, Summarize,* and *Compare* [Hunter et al. 1987]. An attempt at a transfer of the relations proposed by Hobbs to pictures and text-picture combinations has been made in [Bandyopadhyay 1990]. Unfortunately, text-picture researchers only consider the communicative functions of whole pictures, i.e., they do not address the question of how a picture is organized. To get an informative description of the whole document structure, one has to consider relations between picture parts or between picture parts and text passages too. E.g., a portion of a picture can serve as background for the rest of the picture or a text passage can elaborate on a particular section of a picture.

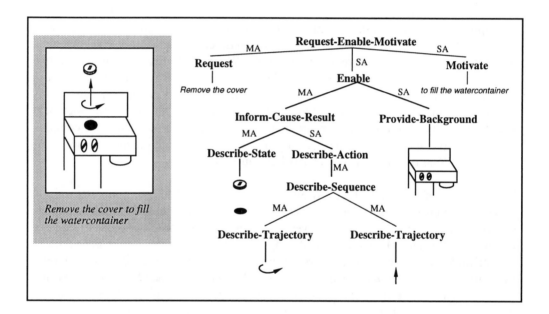

Figure 1. A Document Fragment[2] and its Structure

---

[2]The example is a slightly modified and translated version of instructions for the Philips espresso-machine HD5649.

In Figure 1, an example document fragment and its discourse structure are shown. The goal of this document fragment is to instruct the user in removing the cover of the water container of an espresso machine. The instruction can be considered as a composite goal comprising a request, a motivation and an enablement part. The request is conveyed through text (main act (MA)). To motivate that request, the author has referred to a superordinate goal, namely filling the water container (subsidiary act (SA)). The picture provides additional information which enables the addressee to carry out the request (subsidiary act). The generation of the picture is also subdivided into a main act, which describes the result and the actions to be performed, and a subsidiary act, which provides the background to facilitate orientation.

3. Design Criteria for Text-Picture Combinations

When designing an illustrated document, an author has to decide which mode combination is the most suitable for meeting his goals. The decision-making process for mode selection is influenced by different factors including the kind of information content, the communicative functions that textual and pictorial document parts ought to fill in a presentation, resource limitations (e.g., limitations due to the output medium, or space and time restrictions), user characteristics (e.g., trained or untrained in reading visual displays) and the user's task. Since in the current version of the WIP system the first and second factors have the strongest influence on mode decisions, they are examined in more detail.

3.1. Mode Preferences for Information Types

Given a certain information content, we first have to check in which mode of presentation the information can be expressed. In cases where text as well as graphics may be employed, the question of which mode conveys the information most effectively arises. Although several classifications of information content that are relevant for selecting the mode of presentation have been proposed (e.g., [Bieger and Glock 1984; Roth and Mattis 1990; Feiner and McKeown, this volume; Arens et al. this volume; Whittaker and Walker 1991]), an exhaustive classification has not yet crystallized. In the following, we will present some classification criteria that are of importance in the domain of maintenance and repair instructions for technical devices. Of course, further criteria are necessary, in particular when shifting to another domain.

Concrete information: Information concerning visual properties of concepts (such as shape, color, and texture) is classified as concrete. We regard events and actions as concrete if they involve physical objects and if their occurrence causes visually perceptible changes. Since pictures seem to be superior in teaching perceptual concepts (e.g., see [Molitor et al. 1989]), graphics will be used in preference to text when presenting concrete information.

Spatial information: Since space is conceptualized mainly through objects, the category of spatial information primarily includes information concerning the location, orientation and composition of objects. Furthermore, physical events and actions mostly have a spatial component. Since a movement of a physical object can be characterized by means of spatial concepts (such as the direction of movement or the starting and end position), actions and events also get the attribute *spatial* if they involve movements of physical objects. In deciding how to present spatial information, we can partly fall back on empirical psychological studies. For example, Bieger and Glock [1986] found out that in assembly instructions spatial information is perceived faster if pictures are used; on the other hand, subjects confronted with textual presentations make fewer mistakes when carrying out instructions. Thus, if the emphasis is on speed, pure pictorial presentations of spatial information should be preferred.

Temporal information: In the domain of operating instructions, the temporal relations between states, events or actions play an important part. The sequential order of events can be effectively communicated by arranging pictures from top to bottom or from left to right. In some cases, subsequent events can even be depicted in a single picture (Figure 1). While precedence relations can be easily communicated through pictures, the fact that two events overlap in time is hard to express pictorially. Furthermore, for a number of time specifications, such as *mostly, periodically* or *in the future*, textual presentations should be preferred in order to avoid misconceptions.

Covariant information: Covariant information expresses a semantic relationship between at least two pieces of information that vary together. Such relationships are: *cause/effect, action/result, problem/solution, condition*, and *concession*.[3] Cause/effect and action/result relationships are often expressed through a single picture, a sequence

---

[3]These relations also appear in RST to describe a semantic relation between real world entities.

of pictures or through a text-picture combination. The presenter has, however, to consider that cause/effect and action/goal relationships between (parts of) pictures are often interpreted as pure temporal relationships. If it is not certain whether the addressee recognizes the intended relationship, text should be used in preference to graphics. To ensure that a problem/solution relationship is correctly interpreted, the problem should be presented in text unless a kind of picture language is used (e.g., in [Strothotte and Schmid 1990], a question mark indicates that a picture presents a problem.). The relationships *condition* and *concession* can hardly be expressed by graphics without verbal comments.

Quantification: In general, it is very difficult to graphically depict quantifiers. Even if quantification is to be done over finite sets of physical objects and thus it seems to be straightforward to communicate quantifying information by graphically enumerating instances, a viewer will be confused if he does not recognize whether the picture is meant to show a complete set or most/some/any/exactly-n/etc. instances. Apart from this, such pictorial enumerations tend to be long-winded and waste space in a document.

Negation: Although there is no "natural" way to graphically express negation, some kinds of negation are frequently expressed using conventionalized graphical symbols. Perhaps the most widespread convention is the use of overlaid crossing bars. E.g., think of graphical warnings where a technical device is shown in a particular state and crossing bars indicate that this state must not be achieved. However, a viewer may have difficulties in figuring out the scope of a negation symbol. Furthermore, it is questionable whether already conventionalized negation symbols can be employed for other kinds of negation, e.g., to express the absence of objects or object attributes.

3.2. Achievement of Communicative Goals

As mentioned before, mode decisions depend not only on the kind of information to be communicated, but also on the communicative function of an utterance. There is no doubt that many communicative acts (e.g., *describe*, *inform* or *warn*) can be accomplished with pictures [Novitz 1977]. In this section, we will concentrate on communicative functions that pictures fulfill in relation to text or other pictures. Some of these functions have also been identified by text-picture researchers, most of them correspond to pragmatic relations in RST.

Attract-Attention: The text directs the addressee's attention to special aspects of the picture/text. E.g., directives, such as "Look at ..." can be used to tell the addressee what is important in a picture. Furthermore, a part of a picture can emphasize other document parts, e.g., think of arrows pointing to important objects.[4]

Compare: Two document parts provide a comparison between several concepts. To emphasize the differences or parallels between the concepts, the same presentation modes should be used for describing the concepts.

Elaborate: One part of a document provides further details about another part. Text can elaborate on a picture, e.g., by specifying attributes of an object shown in the picture. On the other hand, a picture can elaborate on text, e.g., by showing an object belonging to a verbally described class. Pictures can also elaborate on other pictures, e.g., think of an inset that shows further details of a depicted object.

Enable: The picture/text provides additional information in order to enable the addressee to perform the requested action. E.g., a request may be accompanied by a picture showing how an action should be carried out. The request is typically conveyed by text.

Elucidate: One document part provides an explanation or interpretation of another part. E.g., text can be used to express the meaning of a picture or to clarify graphical techniques. While text can explain pictures or text passages, pictures can explain text, but normally not other pictures [Muckenhaupt 1986].

Label: A piece of text serves as a label for a portion of the document. Typical examples of the label-relationship are: *headline/paragraph*, *caption/figure* and *name/picture part*.

Motivate: The addressee is to be motivated to comply with a request. This goal can be met by means of pictures or by means of text. Think of an advertisement showing a cup of steaming coffee to motivate people to buy this coffee. Typically, the request implicitly follows from the context or is explicitly conveyed through text.

---

[4]This situation must not be confused with situations where a document part indirectly attracts the addressee's attention because of its visual appearence (e.g., because of its size, position or color).

Evidence: The picture/text produces evidence for a verbal claim. Since pictures increase authenticity [Smith and Smith 1966], they are well suited to support a claim. Typical examples are TV news.

Background: One document part establishes the context for the other. E.g., text may provide the necessary background information for a picture that shows a device from an extraordinary perspective. Background can also be provided by parts of a picture, e.g., a picture of an object may include further objects in order to reduce ambiguities by showing the object's spatial context.

Summarize: The picture/text provides an organized, reduced form of the text structure. E.g., a picture may be presented in advance to show the most important parts of a machine which are described in detail by text. On the other hand, text may be used to summarize the contents of a picture.

4. Representation of Presentation Knowledge

As is the case with a human author, a presentation system should have a set of presentation strategies at its disposal which can be selected and combined according to a particular presentation task. Such strategies reflect general presentation knowledge as indicated in the preceding section, or they embody more specific knowledge of how to present a certain subject.

To represent presentation strategies, we follow the approach proposed by Moore and colleagues [Moore and Paris 1989; Moore and Swartout 1989] to operationalize RST for text planning. The strategies are represented by a name, a header, an effect, a set of applicability conditions and a specification of main and subsidiary acts. Whereas the header of a strategy is a complex communicative act (e.g., to enable an action), its effect refers to an intentional goal (e.g., the user knows a particular object).[5] To represent intentional goals, we use the same notation as in Hovy's RST planner (cf. [Hovy 1988a]). The expression (Goal P x) stands for: The presenter P has x as a goal. (Bel P x) should

---

[5]In [Moore and Paris 1989], this distinction between header and effect is not made because the effect of their strategies may be an intentional goal as well as a rhetorical relation.

be read as: P believes that x is satisfied. (BMB P A x) is an abbreviation for the infinite conjunction: (Bel P x) & (Bel P (Bel A x)) & (Bel P (Bel A (Bel P x))), etc. The applicability conditions specify when a strategy may be used and constrain the variables to be instantiated. The main and subsidiary acts form the kernel of the strategies. Examples of presentation strategies are shown below. The first strategy can be used to request the user to perform an action. Whereas text is used to perform the main acts, the mode for the subsidiary acts is open. In this strategy, three kinds of acts occur: the elementary act S(urface)-Request, three referential acts for specifying the action and the semantic case roles associated with the action (Activate), and two complex communicative acts (Motivate and Enable).

```
[S1] Name:   Request-Enable-Motivate
     Header:  (Request P A ?action T)6
     Effect:  (BMB P A (Goal P (Done A ?action)))
     Applicability Conditions:
              (And
                (Goal P (Done A ?action))
                (Bel P (Complex-Operating-Action ?action))
                (Bel P (Agent ?agent ?action))
                (Bel P (Object ?object ?action)))
     Main Acts:
              (S-Request P A (?action-spec (Agent ?agent-spec)
                                           (Object ?object-spec)))
              (Activate P A (Action ?action) ?action-spec T)
              (Activate P A (Agent ?agent) ?agent-spec T)
              (Activate P A (Object ?object) ?object-spec T)
     Subsidiary Acts:
              (Motivate P A ?action ?mode-1)
              (Enable P A ?action ?mode-2)
```

The second and third strategies may be employed to show the orientation of an object and to enable its identification in a picture (see also [André and Rist 1990a]).

6T stands for text, G for graphics.

```
[S2] Name:          Describe-Orientation
     Header:        (Describe P A (Orientation ?orientation) G)
     Effect:        (BMB P A (Has-Orientation ?orientation ?x))
     Applicability-Conditions: (Bel P (Has-Orientation ?orientation ?x))
     Main Acts:     (S-Depict P A (Orientation ?orientation) ?p-orientation ?pic)
     Subsidiary Acts:
                    (Achieve P (BMB P A (Identifiable A ?x ?px ?pic)) ?mode)
```

```
[S3] Name:          Provide-Background
     Header:        (Background P A ?x ?px ?pic G)
     Effect:        (BMB P A (Identifiable A ?x ?px ?pic))
     Applicability Conditions:
                    (AND
                         (Bel P (Image-of ?px ?x ?pic))
                         (Bel P (Perceptually-Accessible A ?x))
                         (Bel P (Part-of ?x ?z)))
     Main Acts: (S-Depict P A (Object ?z) ?pz ?pic)
     Subsidiary Acts:
         (Achieve P (BMB P A (Identifiable A ?z ?pz ?pic)) ?mode)
```

When defining presentation strategies, one has to decide whether to define relatively specific strategies by anticipating important design decisions, e.g., about mode selection, or whether to define more general presentation strategies, e.g., by leaving mode decisions open. By constraining design decisions, we can avoid situations in which decisions have to be retracted because they are not realizable. However, we have to take care that we do not unnecessarily restrict the set of possible designs. Strategy [S1] can be considered as a compromise between these two approaches. Whereas the mode for the subsidiary acts is left open, the strategy prescribes text for the main acts.

Since there may be several strategies for achieving a certain goal, we need criteria for ranking the effectiveness, the side-effects and costs of executing presentation strategies. To formulate selection criteria, we use meta rules.

```
[M1]  IF (IS-A ?current-attribute-value Spatial-Concept)
      THEN (Dobefore *graphics-strategies* *text-strategies*)
```

E.g., the meta-rule [M1] suggests a preference for graphics over text when presenting spatial information. The studies listed in Section 3 form the theoretical basis of such meta rules.

5. The Presentation Planning Process

To automatically generate documents, one has not only to identify and represent relevant presentation knowledge, but also has to operationalize the synthesis process.

5.1. The Basic Planning Scheme

Presentation strategies are treated as operators of a planning system. The basic idea behind the planning process is as follows: For each presentation goal, try to find strategies which are either specified by the header or whose effect matches the presentation goal. Check for which variable bindings the applicability conditions of the strategies hold. All strategies whose applicability conditions are satisfied become candidates for achieving the presentation goal. If several strategies are applicable, prioritize them employing meta-rules. Then select a strategy, instantiate it and post the main and subsidiary acts as new subgoals or - in the case of elementary acts such as 'S-Depict' or 'S-Assert' - write them into the task queues of the mode-specific generators. In case a subgoal cannot be achieved, backtrack. The planning process terminates if all goals are expanded to elementary acts that can be realized by the text or graphics generator. The result of the planning process is a refinement-style plan in the form of a directed acyclic graph (DAG).

To ensure that document fragments in multiple modalities are smoothly tailored to each other in the document to be generated, one also has to consider various dependencies between content determination, mode selection and content realization. As a consequence, the process sketched above appears to be much more complicated with respect to flow of control and data between the presentation planner and the generators.

5.2. Interleaving Content Planning, Mode Selection and Content Realization

Previous work on natural language generation has shown that content selection and content realization should not be treated independently of each other (see also [Hovy 1987] and [Reithinger 1991]). A strictly sequential model in which data only flow from the "what to present" to the "how to present" part has proven inappropriate because the components responsible for selecting the contents would have to anticipate all decisions of the realization components. This problem is compounded if, as in our case, content realization is done by separate components (currently a text and a graphics generator) of which the content planner has only limited knowledge.

It seems even inappropriate to sequentialize content planning and mode selection although mode selection is only a very rough decision about content realization. Selecting a mode of presentation depends to a large extent on the information to be communicated (Section 3). On the other hand, content planning is strongly influenced by previously selected mode combinations. E.g., to graphically refer to a physical object, we need visual information that may be irrelevant to textual references.

A better solution is to interleave content planning, mode selection and content realization. In the WIP system, we interleave content and mode selection using a uniform planning mechanism. This has become possible since the presentation strategies and meta-rules accessed by the planner contain not only knowledge about what to present, but also knowledge about adequate mode combinations. In contrast to this, presentation planning and content realization are performed by separate components that access disparate knowledge sources. This modularization enables parallel processing, but makes interaction between the single components necessary. As soon as the planner has decided which generator should encode a certain piece of information, this piece should be passed on to the respective generator. Conversely, the planning component should immediately incorporate the results of the generators. Therefore, the processing of all components has to be 'interrupted' at certain decision points to allow other components to react.

However, we cannot presume that the results of the single components are always available at a given time. In some situations, it might happen that the planner is not able to expand a node because it is still waiting for a generator to supply realization results. If this generator, in turn, is also waiting for the planner or another generator to provide new data, a deadlock occurs. To cope with uncertainties concerning the results of other components, WIP's presentation planner maintains partial descriptions of unspecified variables through the use of constraints. Thus, it is able to continue planning without premature commitment. Furthermore, it does not always expand nodes in a depth-first fashion, but flexibly selects the nodes to be expanded. To illustrate this, let's have a look at Figure 2. Assume that the expansion of node B relies on information provided by executing the elementary act A (Figure 2a). To avoid time delays, C is expanded first (Figure 2b). After A has been executed, the required information is available and B can be expanded (Figure 2c).

Since the generators provide information about (partial) results as soon as possible, situations in which information is missing for every plan node to be expanded seldom occur. In such cases, the planner has the possibility to select a node considering selection heuristics, such as the costs of the assumptions to be made.

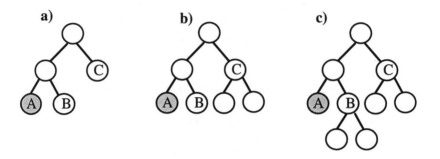

Figure 2. Opportunistic Node Expansion

5.3.   Propagating Data During Presentation Planning

Since every component has only limited knowledge of other components, data have to be passed from one component to the other. E.g., if a generator finds a better solution or is not able to satisfy a task, it has to inform the planner, which has to reorganize its initial plan (see also Section 5.4) or to backtrack. To ensure the consistency of the document, all changes have to be propagated to other branches of the plan structure.

Information flow is not only necessary between the content planner and the generators, data also have to be propagated from one generator to the other. Suppose the text generator has generated a referring expression for an object shown in a picture. If the picture is changed due to graphical constraints, it might happen that the referring expression no longer fits. Thus, the planner will have to create a new object description and pass this description on to the text generator, which will have to replace the initial referring expression by a new one.

Furthermore, the need for propagating data during presentation planning arises when dealing with dependencies between presentation strategies. E.g., a decision about mode selection often depends on earlier decisions. Let's assume the system decides to compare two objects by describing the different values of a common attribute. At this time, the only restriction is that both descriptions should be realized in the same mode. Once the system has decided on the mode for the attribute value of the first object, the result of this decision must be made available for describing the value of the second object. We handle this problem by passing mode information during the planning process both from top to bottom and from bottom to top (Figure 3).

Mode information is propagated via the header of a strategy. Depending on whether the main acts of a strategy are to be realized in text, graphics or both modes, the values T(ext), G(raphics) or M(ixed) are assigned. The mode remains unspecified until mode decisions are made for the main acts of a strategy. By deferring mode decisions for as long as possible, the planner is able to continue planning without making too specific selections.

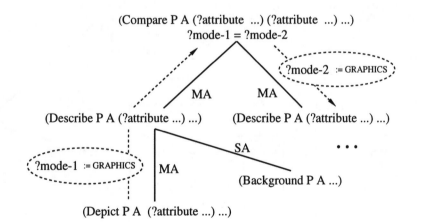

Figure 3. Passing of Information

5.4.   Restructuring after Realization

Since the content planner has no access to realization knowledge of the generators, it cannot consider this knowledge when building up the document structure. As a consequence, it may happen that the results provided by the generators deviate to a certain extent from the initial document plan. Such deviations are reflected in the DAG by output sharing, structure sharing and structure adding. Although in the following examples, restructuring is caused by decisions of the graphics generator, there is no question that restructuring methods are also useful for text generation (e.g., see [Hovy 1990b]).

5.4.1.   Output Sharing

By studying multimodal documents, we found that authors often use one and the same picture or picture part for different purposes. When automatically generating documents, the question arises which component decides when to reuse a picture or picture part. Since the content planner has no knowledge about how information is encoded graphically, the final decision should be left up to the graphics designer. If document parts are reused, this has to be reflected in the document structure.

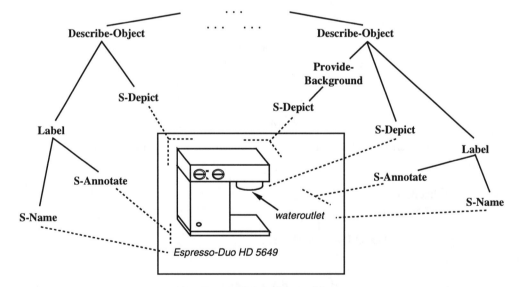

Figure 4. DAG with Output Sharing

To illustrate this, let's look at an example. Suppose the planner decides to introduce an object by showing it in a picture and by annotating the corresponding picture part with the name of the object. Let's further assume that some time later it plans to introduce a part of this object in the same way. The graphics designer, however, doesn't generate a new picture since it recognizes that both tasks can be accomplished with a single picture.[7] The planner registers this by linking the corresponding parts of the generated DAG with each other (Figure 4).

5.4.2. Structure Sharing

In the example above, parts of the generated output have been used for different purposes (as background and as part of a label). However, it might also happen that not only the output, but even a more complex part of the DAG can be shared. As an example, let's assume the presentation planner decides to enable the user to carry out an action by creating two pictures showing the action and its result. To facilitate the user's orientation, it is planned to show background objects in both pictures (Figure 5a). If the graphics designer is able to convey the requested information in a single picture, the background for the actions has to be included only once. Consequently, the structure of the document can be simplified by factoring out the background branch (Figure 5b).

5.4.3. Structure Adding

Whereas structure sharing leads to simplifications of the initial document plan, structure adding results in a more complex plan. It occurs if the graphics generator is expected to integrate information in a single picture, but is not able to do so. Let's suppose the planner decides to show the state of the espresso machine in the picture after it has been switched on. Thus, the graphics designer receives the task of generating a picture showing the current orientation of the on/off switch and the lamp in a burning state. When executing this task, the graphics designer realizes that the labels to the left of the on/off switch are too tiny to be readable if the entire espresso machine is shown (Figure 6a).

---

[7]This is possible because, during the generation process, the graphics designer builds up an explicit representation of the surface aspects of a picture as well as the semantic mapping between graphical means and the information to be conveyed (for details see [Rist and André 1992b]).

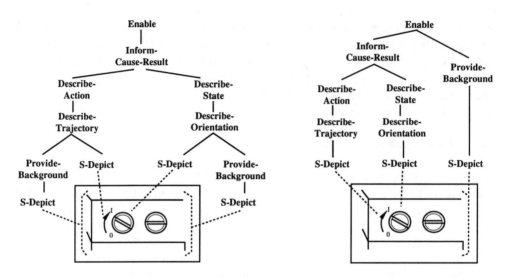

Figure 5a. DAG without Structure Sharing   Figure 5b. After Simplification

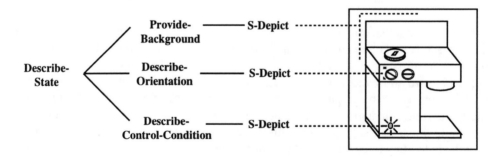

Figure 6a. Initial DAG

If the graphics designer decides to overcome this problem by creating an inset with a different background, the structure of the document has to be modified as in Figure 6b.

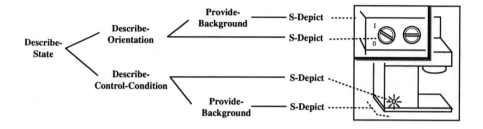

Figure 6b. DAG after Structure Adding

5.5. Architecture of the Presentation Planner

The considerations above led to the architecture for the presentation planner shown in Figure 7. The basic planning module selects operators that match the presentation goal and expands the nodes to generate a refinement-style plan in the form of a DAG. The plan evaluation/revision module is responsible for evaluating and revising plans. To allow for alternating revision and expansion processes, WIP's presentation planner is controlled by a plan monitor that determines the next action and the next nodes to be expanded. All components of the presentation planner have read/write access to the document plan.

In the overall WIP system [André et al. this volume], the presentation planner collaborates with a text generator [Harbusch et al. 1991], a graphics generator [Rist and André 1992a] and a layout manager [Graf 1992]. As shown in Figure 7, the leaves of the document plan are connected to entries in the task queues of the mode-specific generators. Thus, the document plan serves not only as an interface between the planner and the generators, but also enables a two-way exchange of information between the two generators.

6. Planning Example

In the following, we give an example that illustrates opportunistic node expansion and revision after graphics generation. Let's assume the system as the presenter P wants the

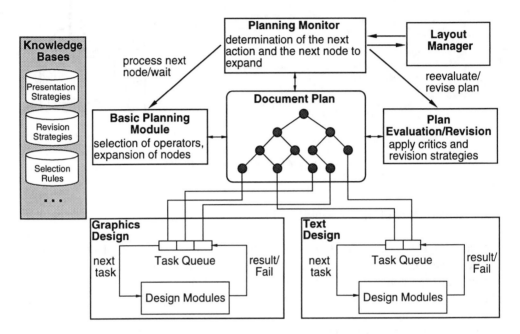

Figure 7. The Architecture of the Presentation Planner

addressee A to switch on an espresso machine. Thus, it attempts to find plan operators which match the goal:

[1]   (BMB P A (Goal P (Done A switch-on-1))).

One plan operator for achieving this goal was shown in Section 4. Suppose this plan operator is selected. Then, the main and subsidiary acts are posted as subgoals. In this operator, three kinds of acts occur: two complex communicative acts (Enable and Motivate) which have to be further expanded, an elementary speech act (S-Request) which is passed on to the text designer and several referential acts (Activate) for filling the semantic case roles associated with the 'switch on' action. Assume that the user knows why the action should be carried out. Thus, it is not necessary to motivate him. The expansion of the 'Enable' act leads to a strategy that informs the user via a picture about the trajectory of the object to be manipulated and the result of the manipulation. After further refinement steps, the following subgoals are posted:

[2] (S-Depict P A (Trajectory trajectory-1) ?p-traj ?pic)

[3] (Achieve P (BMB P A (Identifiable A switch-2 ?px ?pic)) ?mode)

[4] (Describe P A (State state-1) ?mode)

At this point the plan monitor has to decide which of these three goals to expand next, so it inspects each one in turn. The first subgoal is an elementary act which is forwarded to the graphics designer. The second represents an intentional goal which is only expanded if it is not yet satisfied. Therefore, the presentation planner requests the graphics designer to evaluate:

[5] (BMB P A (Identifiable A switch-2 ?px ?pic))

For the purpose of this example, assume that the graphics designer has not yet executed [2] and thus is not able to immediately respond to [5]. As a consequence, the presentation planner cannot refine [3]. Instead of waiting for the response, the presentation planner tries to continue with another goal. It expands [4] and posts

[6] (S-Depict P A (Orientation orientation-1) ?p-orientation ?pic) and

[7] (Achieve P (BMB P A (Identifiable A switch-2 ?px ?pic)) ?mode)

as new subgoals. The first subgoal is passed on to the graphics designer. The discourse plan generated so far is shown in Figure 8.

Note that at this time the mode variable occurring in [4] has already been instantiated by propagating the mode in the header of strategy [S2] bottom up. When trying to satisfy the pictorial acts [2] and [6], the graphics designer finds out that it is possible to accomplish these tasks by means of a single picture (namely pic-4). After the goals in [3] and [7] have been instantiated, the planner recognizes that they are identical. As a consequence, these goals can be achieved with a shared discourse plan. The planner decides to simplify the discourse plan by factoring out the structures corresponding to the goals in [3] and [7]. After switch-2 has been depicted, the graphics designer is able to evaluate

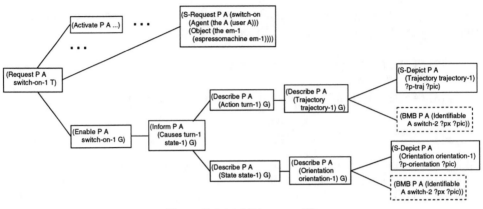

Figure 8. Initial Discourse Plan

[8] (BMB P A (Identifiable A switch-2 p-switch-2 pic-4))

where p-switch-2 is the depiction of switch-2 in the picture pic-4. Since the graphics generator assumes that it is unclear to the user which switch is shown, the presentation planner has to find and instantiate[8] a strategy to achieve [8]. Let's assume, it decides to select strategy [S3] and sends the graphics designer the request to depict the espresso machine as a landmark object. The final discourse plan is shown in Figure 9.

7. Summary

In this paper, we have argued that not only the generation of text, but also the synthesis of multimodal documents can be considered as a communicative act which aims to

---

[8]Note that acts of the form (Achieve P <goal> <mode>) are treated specially. Whereas <goal> has to match the effect of a strategy, <mode> has to match the mode field in the header of a strategy.

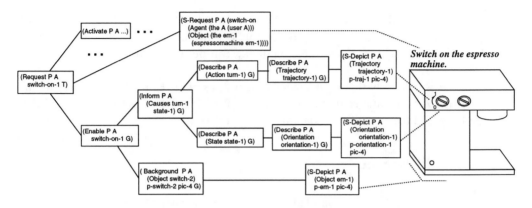

Figure 9. Discourse Plan after Factoring out the Background

achieve certain goals. We have introduced presentation strategies to represent knowledge about presentation techniques. In order to decide between several presentation strategies, we have examined how the kind of information to be conveyed influences mode selection and which communicative functions single document parts play in text-picture combinations. In particular, we have argued that most semantic and pragmatic relationships which have been proposed for describing the structure of texts can be generalized in such a way that they are also appropriate for describing the structure of pictures and text-picture combinations.

For the realization of a system able to automatically generate illustrated documents, we have proposed a plan-based approach that supports data transfer between the content planner and the mode-specific generators and allows for global plan evaluation after each plan step. The modularization of presentation planning and mode-specific generation has led to the problem that the results provided by the generators may deviate from the initial presentation plan. Since such deviations have to be reflected in the presentation plan, the planning scheme also comprises restructuring methods.

8. Implementation

The presentation planner has been implemented in Symbolics Common Lisp under Genera 8.0 running on a Symbolics XL1200 and MacIvory workstations. It has been integrated into the WIP system (cf. [André et al. this volume]). A stand-alone version of the planner is also available. It is embedded in a comfortable test-environment that includes an incremental plan displayer and provides various debugging facilities.

The planner is able to build up document structures as in the examples presented in this paper. However, in some examples we used graphics (e.g., the inset in Figure 6b) that currently exceed the capacities of the implemented version of our graphics generator.

9. Acknowledgments

The work presented here is supported by the German Ministry for Research and Technology (BMFT) under grant ITW8901 8. We would like to thank Wolfgang Wahlster for comments and discussions and the anonymous reviewers for comments.

Chapter 5

Automating the Generation of Coordinated Multimedia Explanations[1]

Steven K. Feiner and Kathleen R. McKeown

Abstract

Explanations, particularly those that refer to objects and actions in the physical world, are much more effective when they include both pictures and text. However, the use of multiple media adds a level of complexity to the *creation* of explanations: Which information should be communicated in which media? How does knowledge about what is communicated in pictures influence the generation of text, and vice versa? How should pictures and text refer to each other? In this chapter, we show how these questions are addressed by COMET (COordinated Multimedia Explanation Testbed), a knowledge-based system that produces coordinated, interactive explanations that combine text and three-dimensional graphics, all of which are generated on the fly. We describe how COMET determines which information is best expressed in text and which in graphics. COMET coordinates both these media using bidirectional interaction between its separate text and graphics generators. We focus on several types of coordination requiring interaction: coordination of sentence breaks with picture breaks to avoid splitting sentences over picture boundaries, the generation of cross references from text to graphics, and the influence of generation in one medium on the other. This interaction is carried out through a content description that is shared and annotated by both generators.

---

[1]Based on "Automating the Generation of Coordinated Multimedia Explanations" by S. K. Feiner and K. R. McKeown which appeared in *IEEE Computer* 24(10):33-41, October, 1991, © 1991 IEEE.

1. Introduction

Sometimes a picture is worth the proverbial one thousand words; sometimes a few well chosen words are far more effective than a picture. Pictures often describe objects or diagram physical actions more clearly than words do. In contrast, language often conveys information about abstract objects, properties, and relations more effectively than pictures can. Pictures and language used together can complement and reinforce each other to enable more effective communication than can either medium alone. In this sense, multimedia information systems may greatly increase effective communications.

Fortunately, technical advances are beginning to reduce the cost of hardware for computer-based multimedia and hypermedia. First-generation authoring facilities let users create presentations that include text, graphics, animation, and video. Regardless of the basic functionality or interface provided, however, multimedia authoring systems require authors to possess even more skills than do single-medium authoring systems. Not only must authors be skilled in the conventions of each medium, but they must also be able to coordinate multiple media in a coherent presentation, determining where and when to use different media, and referencing material in one medium from another. Furthermore, since the presentation must be authored in advance, the ways in which it can be customized for an individual user or situation are limited to those built in by the author.

To overcome the disadvantages of this predesigned authoring approach, we have developed an experimental test bed for the automated generation of multimedia explanations. COMET (COordinated Multimedia Explanation Testbed) [Elhadad et al. 1989; Feiner and McKeown 1990ab] has as its goal the coordinated, interactive generation of explanations that combine text and three-dimensional graphics, all of which is generated on the fly.

In response to a user request for an explanation, COMET dynamically determines the explanation's content using constraints based on the type of request, the information available in a set of underlying knowledge bases, and information about the user's background and goals. Having determined *what* to say, COMET also determines *how* to express it at the time of generation. The pictures and text that it uses are not "canned": COMET does not select from a database of conventionally authored text, preprogrammed graphics, or prerecorded video. Instead, COMET decides which information should be expressed in each medium, which words and syntactic structures best express the portion to be conveyed textually, and which graphical objects, graphical style, and picture structure best express the portion to be conveyed graphically. COMET's text and graphics are created by separate *media generators*, each of which can communicate with the other.

We first provide a brief overview of COMET's domain and architecture. Then we focus on the specific ways in which COMET can coordinate its text and graphics. *Coordination* begins with the choice of media in which specific information is communicated. For example, an object's complex shape may be shown in a picture, rather than described in text, while a sentence may describe a causal relation between several actions involving the object. Coordination also means applying knowledge about what information is expressed in text to influence the generation of graphics, and vice versa. Thus, the graphics generator may use the fact that a causal relation is being communicated in text to determine how it depicts other information, even though the relation itself is not depicted. Finally, coordination means using knowledge about how information is expressed in other media in decision-making. For example, if the graphics generator shows the location of an object by highlighting it, the text generator can refer to "the highlighted object."

2. Overview

Much of our work on COMET has been done in a field maintenance and repair domain for a military radio receiver-transmitter. When provided with a set of symptoms, COMET generates multimedia explanations that instruct the user in how to carry out diagnostic tests. The user interacts with COMET by means of a simple menu and can initially choose to request instructions for a specific procedure or to invoke the diagnostic component. In the latter case, an underlying expert system is called to determine the problems that the radio is experiencing and to identify their causes.

The user selects symptoms from a menu. If the expert system decides that a set of diagnostic tests must be run to determine the cause of the problem, it calls the explanation component to tell the user how to carry out these tests. Explanations consist of one or more steps that are presented in a series of displays. Although our emphasis thus far has been on generating explanations, rather than on navigating through them, COMET's menu interface also provides rudimentary facilities for exploring the explanation by paging forward and backward through its steps. It can also access steps by name.

Figure 1. COMET's Directions for Clearing the Radio Display

Figure 1 shows COMET's explanation for clearing the radio's display. Figure 2 shows the beginning of COMET's multi-step explanation for installing a new "holding battery." (The holding battery provides power for the radio's memory when the main battery has been removed.) In these first two steps, the user is instructed to turn the radio upside down, and remove the cover plate from the battery compartment. Replacing the holding battery is the first of a series of actions that COMET instructs the user to per-

form in the course of troubleshooting loss of radio memory, a symptom that the user selected from COMET's menu.

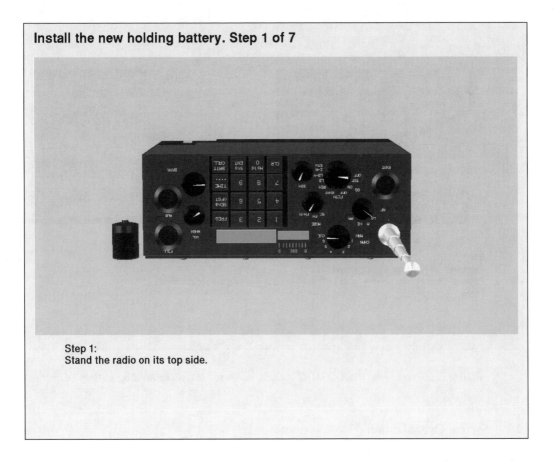

Install the new holding battery. Step 1 of 7

Step 1:
Stand the radio on its top side.

Figure 2a. First step from COMET's explanation for installing holding battery

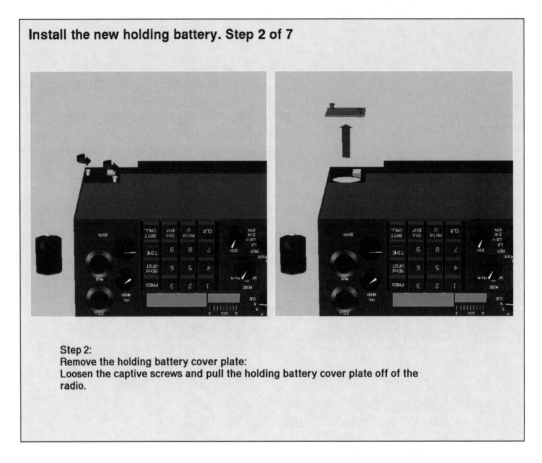

Figure 2b. Second step from COMET's explanation for installing holding battery

2.1. System Organization

COMET consists of a set of parallel processes that cooperate in the design of an explanation, as shown in Figure 3. On receiving a request for an explanation, the content planner uses text plans or *schemas* [McKeown 1985; McKeown et al. 1990] to determine which information from the underlying knowledge sources should be included in the explanation. COMET uses three different domain knowledge sources: a static representation of domain objects and actions encoded in the LOOM knowledge representation language [LOOM 1987], a diagnostic rule-base, and a detailed geometric knowledge base needed for graphics generation. It also maintains a user model and a model of the previous discourse. These knowledge sources are used by all system components to construct the explanation, not just by the content planner. Consequently, they are shown separately at the bottom of the Figure without arrows to each module.

The *content planner* produces the full content for the explanation, represented as a hierarchy of *logical forms* [Allen 1987] (LFs), as explained in the Supplement. The LFs then are passed to the *media coordinator*. This component refines each LF by annotating it with directives that indicate which portions are to be produced by each of the media-specific generation systems.

The *text generator* and *graphics generator* each process the same LFs, producing fragments of text and graphics that are keyed to the LFs they instantiate. The media generators can also interact further with the media coordinator, allowing the generation of cross-references [McKeown et al. 1992]. The output from both generators is processed by the *media layout component*, which formats the final presentation for the low-level *rendering-and-typesetting* software.

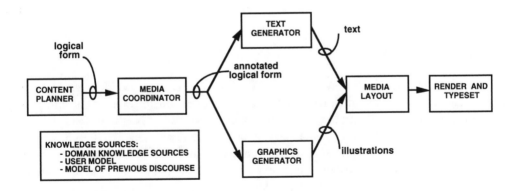

Figure 3. System Architecture

COMET's major components run in parallel on up to five networked workstations. Text and menus are displayed through the X Window System, while three-dimensional shaded graphics are rendered by Hewlett-Packard's Starbase graphics package. Each example shown in the Figures takes approximately 5-10 seconds to generate and display following the initial user request.

One main feature of COMET's architecture is the use of the LF as a type of blackboard facility. (A *blackboard* [Reddy et al. 1973] is a central repository in which a system component can record its intermediate decisions and examine those of other components.) Each component reads and annotates its LF, continually enriching it with further decisions and finer specifications until the explanation is complete. Annotations include directives (like the media coordinator's choice of medium) and details about how a piece of information will be realized in text or graphics (like the proper verb to convey an action). While the annotated LF serves as a blueprint for the final explanation, it also allows for communication between media-specific components. For example, when deciding which expressive possibilities best convey the specified content, a media generator can examine decisions made in other media by reading their annotated LFs and use that to influence its own choices. COMET uses a single mechanism, FUF (Functional Unification Formalism), to make annotations throughout the system. This allows for additional bidirectional interaction between COMET's components through the use of unification, as described in the Supplement. Before describing coordination in more detail, we briefly describe some of COMET's key components, focusing on their individual capabilities.

2.2.   Media Coordinator

This component performs a fine-grained analysis of an input LF to decide whether each portion should be realized in either or both media. After conducting a series of informal experiments and a survey of literature on media effectiveness, we distinguished six different types of information that can appear in an LF. We have categorized each type as to whether it is more appropriately presented in text or graphics. We use graphics alone for location and physical attributes, and text alone for communicating abstract actions and expressing connectives that indicate relationships among actions, such as causality. Both text and graphics represent simple and compound actions. The media coordinator has a FUF grammar that maps these information types to media.

Figure 4 shows a representative portion of the annotated LF produced by the media co-ordinator for Figure 1. The part of the LF in roman font was generated by the content planner, while the annotations added by the media coordinator are in boldface. This LF specifies a single substep and its effect, where the substep is a simple action (c-push) and the effect is also a simple action (c-clear). The c-push substep has one role (the medium, c-button-clr), and it also specifies that the location and size of the button should be included.

Figures 1 and 4 illustrate the fine-grained division of information among media. For example, location information is portrayed in graphics only, while the actions are realized in both text and graphics. In contrast, other information in the LF is communicated only in text, such as the causal relation between pushing the button and clearing the display.

2.3. Text Generator

COMET's text generator [McKeown et al. 1990] realizes the LF segments it has been assigned in text. It must determine both the number of sentences needed to realize the segments and their type (compound, simple, declarative, or imperative). It must select verbs to express LF actions, and nouns and modifiers to refer to LF objects. Finally, it must construct the syntactic structure for each sentence and linearize the resulting tree as a sentence.

```
((cat lf)
(directive-act substeps)
(substeps
[((process-type action)
(process-concept c-push)
(mood non-finite)
(speech-act directive)
(function ((type substeps)
           (media-text yes)
           (media-graphics no)))
(roles
((medium
((object-concept c-button-clr)
        (roles
          ((location ((object-concept c-location)
                      (media-graphics yes)
                      (media-text no)))
           (size ((object-concept c-size)
                  (media-graphics yes)
                  (media-text no))))))
      ...
      ))
(cat lf)
(media-graphics yes)
(media-text yes))])
(effects
[((process-type action)
(process-concept c-clear)
(mood non-finite)
(function ((type effects)
           (media-text yes)
           (media-graphics no)))
(speech-act assertive)
(roles
((agent
((object-concept c-display)
        (roles
          ((location ((object-concept c-location)
                      (media-graphics yes)
                      (media-text no)))
           (size ((object-concept c-size)
                  (media-graphics yes)
                  (media-text no))))))
      ...
      ))
(cat lf)
(media-text yes)
(media-graphics yes))]))
```

Figure 4. Logical form for Figure 1.

The text generator divides into two modules that carry out these functions: the *Lexical Chooser* and the *Sentence Generator*. The Lexical Chooser selects the overall sentence type and the words, while the Sentence Generator produces individual sentences. Both modules are implemented using FUF.

The text generator can select words based on a variety of underlying constraints. This enables it to use a number of different words for the same LF concepts, depending on the context. The result is a wider variety of more appropriate output. COMET can use constraints from the underlying knowledge base, from previous discourse, from a user model, and from syntax. For example, for the knowledge-base concept c-install, the text generator can use "install, "reinstall," or "return." It makes a choice based on previous discourse (that is, what it has already told the user). Thus, after the user has installed the new holding battery, COMET instructs the user to remove the radio's main battery to check the new holding battery's functionality. At this point, COMET uses the previous discourse to select the verbs "reinstall" and "return" when instructing the user to put the main battery back in the radio. If the user had not been previously instructed to remove the battery, COMET would have selected the verb "install."

COMET can also avoid words that the user does not know. For example, it generates "Make sure the plus lines up with the plus" in place of "Check the polarity" when describing how to install a battery to a user not familiar with the word "polarity." The novel use of FUF to represent the lexicon efficiently provides a variety of different interacting constraints on word choice.

2.4.   Graphics Generator

IBIS (Intent-Based Illustration System) [Seligmann and Feiner 1989; Seligmann and Feiner 1991] generates illustrations designed to satisfy the communicative goals specified in the annotated LFs that it receives as input. The communicative goals that IBIS currently supports include showing absolute and relative locations of objects, physical properties (such as size, shape, material, and color), state (such as knob setting), change of state (such as the change in a knob setting), and a variety of actions (such as pushing, pulling, turning, and lifting). In designing an illustration, IBIS controls all aspects of the picture-making process: the objects included and their visual attributes, the lighting specification, the graphical style used in rendering the objects, the viewing specification, and the structure of the picture itself.

IBIS uses a generate-and-test approach. The IBIS rule base contains at least one design rule for each communicative goal that can appear in an input LF. Each design rule invokes a set of stylistic strategies that specify high-level visual effects, such as highlighting an object. These strategies are in turn accomplished by still lower-level rules that realize the strategies. The lower-level rules create and manipulate the graphical depictions of objects included in the illustration, and modify the illustration's lighting specification, viewing specification, and rendering information.

IBIS uses a combination of techniques to portray the location of the button in Figure 1, as requested in the LF of Figure 4. It selects a viewing specification that (1) locates the button panel centrally in the illustration, (2) makes additional, surrounding context visible, and (3) ensures that both the object and context are recognizable. It highlights the button by modifying the intensity of the lights that illuminate the objects in the illustration.

IBIS rules evaluate the success of each task that it performs. This is important because of the complex interactions that can occur in an illustration. Consider object visibility. Each object may be obscured by or obscure other objects. IBIS must determine whether visibility constraints are violated and address these by modifying the illustration. If an IBIS strategy doesn't succeed, it can backtrack and try another one. For example, if illuminating an object doesn't make it brighter than surrounding objects, IBIS can try to decrease the intensity of the lights illuminating the surrounding objects.

3. Media Coordination

A multimedia explanation system must coordinate the use of different media in a single explanation. It must determine how to divide explanation content between different media such as pictures and text. Moreover, once the content has been divided, the system must determine how material can be generated in each medium to complement that of the other media.

A few other researchers are also addressing the automated generation of coordinated multimedia explanations with emphasis on how the media can complement each other. Integrated Interfaces [Arens et al. 1991] produces Navy briefing charts, using rules to map objects in the application domain (a database of information about ships) into objects in the presentation. Several experimental command and control systems [Neal and

Shapiro 1991; Maybury, this volume] generate maps and spoken language. SAGE [Roth et al. 1991] generates graphs and text to explain how and why quantitative models change over time, while WIP [André et al., this volume; André and Rist, this volume] explains physical actions like those of COMET's domain.

With the exception of WIP, all these systems operate in a two-dimensional world of charts, graphs, and maps, and do not address the problems of describing objects and actions in three dimensions. WIP takes a fine-grained incremental approach to media coordination in a three-dimensional domain. Each piece of information to be communicated is assigned sequentially to its generators. Their evaluations of potential success, based on knowledge of what has been generated thus far, are returned to the planner to help determine media assignments. In contrast, COMET provides its media generators with larger chunks of information at a time, in a common LF that describes what the other generators have been assigned. The LF can also be enriched with accomplishments of the other generators. Thus, while media generators in both systems are aware of what other generators have done, COMET gives its media generators more context about the entire explanation within which to make their initial decisions, while still allowing feedback.

Here we focus on two aspects of media coordination in COMET. First, we show how the use of a common content-description language allows for more flexible interaction between media, making it possible for each generator to query and reference other generators. By passing the same annotated description of what is to be described to each generator, we permit each generator to use information about what the other generators present to influence its own presentation. Then, we show how bidirectional interaction between the media-specific generators is necessary for certain kinds of coordination. Bidirectional interaction allows COMET to generate explanations that are structurally coordinated and that contain cross-references between media.

4. Common Content Description

All components in COMET following the content planner share a common description of what is to be communicated. Just as modules accept input in the same formalism, they can also annotate the description as they carry out its directives. This design has the following ramifications:

- It lets text and graphics influence each other.
- Communicative goals are separated from the resources used to carry them out.
- It provides a mechanism for text and graphics generators to communicate.

4.1. Mutual Influence

Since both the text generator and graphics generator receive the same annotated content description as input, each knows which goals are to be expressed in text, in graphics, or both. Even when a media-specific generator does not communicate a piece of information, it knows that the information is to be conveyed to the user; thus, it can use this information to influence its presentation. Consider a portion of the explanation that COMET generates to instruct the user in how to install the holding battery. The second step of the explanation (Figure 2b) was generated from a complex LF that consists of one goal (to remove the holding battery cover plate) and two complex substeps that carry out that goal. As Figure 2b illustrates, the media coordinator determines that the goal is to be generated only in text ("Remove the holding battery cover plate:") and that the substeps are to be shown in both media.

Although IBIS depicts only the substeps of the LF, it receives the entire annotated LF as input. Since it receives the full LF, and not just the pieces assigned to graphics, IBIS knows that the actions to be depicted are steps that achieve a higher-level goal. Although this goal is not itself realized in graphics, IBIS uses this information to create a composite illustration [Seligmann and Feiner 1991]. This type of illustration consists of an integrated set of pictures that work together to achieve a common set of goals that cannot be accomplished in a single "simple" illustration. In this case, IBIS rules do not include any satisfactory way to show the radio with its cover plate and captive screws in different positions in one illustration.

If IBIS were to receive only the substeps, it would have no way of knowing that the substeps are being described in relation to a higher-level goal. It may end up producing two separate illustrations, just as it does for each simple LF, such as that shown in Figure 2a. Thus, information conveyed in the explanation as a whole, but not in graphics, influences how IBIS depicts other information.

4.2. Separation of Goals from Resources

Because we are using a common content-description language, content must be specified at a level that is appropriate for all generators. We have found that by expressing content as a combination of communicative goals and the information needed to achieve these goals, each generator can select the resources it has at hand for accomplishing its assigned goals. In text generation, this means the selection of specific syntactic or lexical resources (using passive voice to indicate focus, for example). In graphics generation, it means the selection of a conjunction of visual resources (modifying an object's material and the lights that illuminate it to highlight it, for example).

Consider again the explanation shown in Figure 1 and its associated annotated LF in Figure 4. The main goal of the first part of the LF is to describe an action (c-push) and its role (medium). Subgoals include referencing an object (for example, c-button-clr, the clear button) and conveying its location and size. IBIS and the text generator use different resources to achieve these goals. For example, the text generator selects a lexical item, the verb "press," to describe the action. "Press" can be used instead of other verbs because of the characteristics of the medium, c-button-clr. If the medium were a slider, a verb such as "push" or "move" would be required. In contrast, IBIS uses a *metaobject*, an object that does not itself represent any of the objects in the world being depicted [Feiner 1985]. In this case, the metaobject is an arrow that IBIS generates to depict the action of pushing the button. To refer to the clear button itself, the Sentence Generator uses a definite noun phrase, whereas IBIS highlights the object in the picture.

4.3.   A Mechanism for Communication

Since both generators understand the same formalism, they can provide more information to each other about the resources they have selected simply by annotating the content description. Thus, the content description serves as a blackboard to which all processes can write messages. We use this facility for coordinating the internal text structure with pictures.

5.   Bidirectional Interaction

Certain types of coordination between media can only be provided by incorporating interacting constraints between text and graphics. Two-way communication between the media-specific generators may be required as they carry out their individual realizations. Furthermore, coordination may only be possible once partial decisions have been made by the media-specific generators. For example, the text generator needs to know how the graphics generator has depicted an object before it can refer to the object's visual properties in the illustration. Here we discuss two types of coordination that require bidirectional interaction: coordination of sentence breaks with picture breaks, and cross-referencing text and graphics.

5.1. Coordinating Sentence Breaks with Picture Breaks

In addition to revealing several dimensions along which to assign information to media, our media coordination experiments also demonstrated a strong preference for tight structural coordination between text and graphics. Our subjects much preferred sentence breaks that coincided with picture breaks. While multiple sentences accompanying one picture were found satisfactory, subjects strongly objected to a single sentence that ran across several pictures.

Including this type of coordination in COMET requires two-way interaction between text and graphics. Both text and graphics have hard and fast constraints that must be taken into account to achieve sentence-picture coordination. IBIS uses a variety of constraints to determine picture size and composition, including how much information can easily fit into one picture, the size of the objects being represented, and the position of the objects and their relationship to each other. Some of these constraints cannot be overridden. For example, if too many objects are depicted in one picture, individual objects may be rendered too small for clarity.

This situation suggests that constraints from graphics be used to determine sentence size and thereby achieve coordination between picture and sentence breaks. However, some grammatical constraints on sentence size cannot be overridden without creating ungrammatical—or at least very awkward—text. Each verb takes a required set of inherent roles. For example, "put" takes a medium and to-location. Thus, "John put." and "John put the book." are both ungrammatical. Once a verb is selected for a sentence, this can in turn constrain minimal picture size; the LF portion containing information for all required verb roles should not be split across two pictures. Consequently, constraints from text must also be taken into account.

In COMET we incorporate this interaction by maintaining two separate tasks that run independently, each annotating its own copy of the LF when a decision is made, and querying the other when a choice about sentence or picture structure must be made. Once a verb is selected for a sentence, the text generator annotates its copy of the LF by noting the roles that must be included to make a complete sentence. At the same time, the graphics generator annotates its LF with the mapping from the pieces of information to be communicated by graphics to the identifiers of the illustrations in which it intends to communicate the information.

When different sentence structures are possible, the text generator uses the graphics generator's annotations to make a choice by unifying the graphics generator's LF with its own. Consider the example of clearing the display shown in Figure 1. IBIS generates one picture showing the action and its effect; the text generator produces one sentence incorporating the effect as a purpose role of the action (". . . to clear the display"). IBIS could depict this action in many ways, depending on the situation. For example, a pair of "before" and "after" pictures can be used, the first showing the action "push" about to occur and the second showing the cleared display. This picture structure can be especially useful in locating the objects participating in the action by showing their appearance prior to this event. Figure 5 shows what happens when IBIS's style rule base is modified so that a composite "before" and "after" pair is preferred. After consulting the annotated logical form, the text generator produces two separate sentences.

5.2.   Cross References

One important goal of media coordination is to allow material in one medium to cross-reference material in another. COMET provides for two kinds of cross-referencing: structural and content. The former refers to the coarse structure of the material being referenced. For example, a sentence could refer to an action by mentioning that it is depicted in one of the two pictures on the display. In contrast, a content cross-reference refers to the material's content, such as an object's position in a picture or the way in which the object is highlighted. Structural cross-references require only high-level knowledge of how the material being referenced is structured, whereas content cross-references require low-level knowledge of how the material's communicative goals are realized.

COMET's text generator can make both structural and content cross-references to IBIS illustrations [McKeown et al. 1992]. IBIS constructs a representation of each illustration it generates that is indexed by the LF. This representation contains information about the illustration's hierarchical structure, the identity and position of the objects that it depicts, and the kinds of illustrative effects used in constructing the illustration (like highlighting or cut-away views) [Feiner and Seligmann 1992]. The text generator queries this representation to generate cross-references. For example, it can refer to information that is communicated "... in the left picture" (structural cross-reference) or mention "... the old holding battery shown in the cutaway view" (content cross-reference).

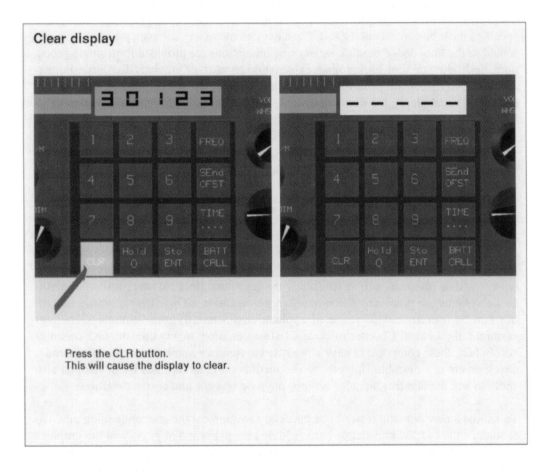

Figure 5. An alternative explanation for clearing the radio display. A composite illustration containing two pictures is generated with coordinated text. (Compare with Figure 1.)

6. Current Status and Limitations

COMET can provide instructions for maintenance and repair procedures in two different contexts. A user can directly request instructions for a specific procedure through a menu interface (essentially, asking "How do I do *x*?"). Alternatively, during symptom diagnosis, the user can request an explanation for any diagnostic procedure the system specifies must be carried out. COMET can explain over forty complex procedures represented in the knowledge base. A variety of explanations are provided for a single procedure, depending on user background, explanation context, or previous discourse. For example, COMET can vary the vocabulary (like not using the word "polarity" if it isn't in the user's vocabulary), the illustration design (like attempting to reuse the preceding illustration's viewing specification for the next illustration to avoid confusing camera motion), or the information communicated (like omitting an explanation for a procedural step if it was explained recently). COMET also has preliminary facilities for answering follow-up questions of the form: "What is an *x*?", "Where is the *x*?" or "Why should I do *x*?" [McKeown et al. 1992].

COMET was designed to be as domain-independent as possible. It can be adapted with minimum effort to a new task-based domain when tasks and actions are encoded using a standard plan-based representation [Sacerdoti 1977] and objects are represented using frames. The content planner can produce the content for explanations of tasks or actions represented as plans, as well as for follow-up questions. Because many artificial intelligence systems use plans and frame-based representations, COMET's explanation facilities can be used in a wide range of applications. Similarly, the Sentence Generator grammar, the Lexical Chooser rules, and IBIS rules apply to any domain, task-based or not. In fact, these components have already been used in a number of applications under development at Columbia University. The media coordination rules we developed also apply to any domain that includes actions, physical objects, and abstract relations.

To handle a new domain, it would be necessary to augment the lexicon (adding new vocabulary), the LOOM knowledge base (adding new plans and objects), and the graphics knowledge base (adding the new objects' detailed geometry and physical properties). These are currently substantial tasks, but so is the effort required to create conventionally authored explanations for a new domain. Also, note that some domain-dependent information, such as the graphics knowledge base, would ideally be available in CAD/CAM databases created when the objects to be documented were designed. COMET's rule bases were designed for domains involving physical objects. Therefore, handling domains that stress abstract relations among abstract concepts (like statistical analyses of numeric variables), would require major changes. These changes include different content-planning strategies, a different media coordinator grammar, and new graphics generation approaches (for example, adding a method for designing quantitative data displays [Mackinlay 1986b; Roth et al. 1991]).

7. Conclusions and Future Work

The COMET testbed has allowed us to explore many ways to coordinate the generation of text and graphics. Our present and future work on COMET and its components includes the development of additional generators that support the temporal media of speech and animation, as described in the following chapter [Feiner et al., this volume]. (IBIS already allows for direct, dynamic user control of the viewing specification [Seligmann and Feiner 1991].) Our work also includes the design of a browsing/navigation facility for COMET's explanations. We are developing a media layout component that will rely on the media generators' annotations to determine the relationships among pieces of text and graphics. This will allow COMET to group related items spatially.

We plan to allow feedback from the media generators to affect assignments made by the media coordinator and the selection of communicative goals made by the content planner. Our use of unification has the potential to make such feedback possible. Currently, we use an overall control structure for efficiency, calling the unifier separately for each grammar. Instead, we could call the unifier once for the combined series of grammars, thus allowing complete interaction through unification among thetypes of constraints. In this scenario, a decision made at a later stage of processing can propagate back to undo an earlier one. For example, information about the syntactic form selected can propagate back to the Lexical Chooser to influence verb choice.

While COMET is currently a research prototype, we believe that far more powerful systems will someday generate high-quality multimedia explanations for users in a variety of domains. Potential applications include education (explaining scientific phenomena), or even basic home repairs (coaching the user through troubleshooting a broken appliance). Although the hardware needed to run our current system is beyond the reach of most users, rapid improvements in the price-performance ratio will soon make high-performance real-time three-dimensional graphics a fundamental capability of any computer system. In our work on COMET, we have attempted to lay some of the groundwork for the kinds of knowledge-based user interfaces that technological advances will soon make feasible.

8. Acknowledgments

Research on COMET is supported in part by Defense Advanced Research Projects Agency Contract N00039-84-C-0165, an equipment grant from the Hewlett-Packard Company, National Science Foundation Grant IRT-84-51438, New York State Center for Advanced Technology Contract NYSSTF-CAT(88)-5, and Office of Naval Research Contracts N00014-82-K-0256, N00014-89-J-1782, and N00014-91-J-1872. COMET's development is an ongoing group effort and has benefited from the contributions of Michael Elhadad (FUF), Dorée Seligmann (IBIS), Andrea Danyluk (diagnostic rule base), Yumiko Fukumoto (media coordinator), Jong Lim (static knowledge base and content planner), Christine Lombardi (media coordinator), Jacques Robin (lexical chooser), Michael Tanenblatt (knowledge base), Michelle Baker, Cliff Beshers, David Fox, Laura Gabbe, Frank Smadja, and Tony Weida.

Supplement: Unification in COMET

COMET uses FUF, an efficient extended version of Functional Unification Grammar [Kay 1979], for media coordination. FUF also performs two text-generation tasks (selecting words and generating syntactic structure) and part of graphics generation (mapping the LFs to a communicative goal language supported by the graphics generator). Each component has its own "grammar" that is unified nondeterministically with the LF to annotate it with directives or further specifications. The result is a cascaded series of FUF grammars, each handling a separate task.

In FUF, both the input LF and the task grammar are represented using the same formalism, a set of attribute-value pairs. A value can be an atomic symbol or, recursively, a set of attribute-value pairs. For example, consider the following fragment of an input LF:

```
(substeps
[((process-type action)
(process-concept c-push)
(roles ( . . . )) . . .])
```

This fragment contains a single attribute, `substeps`, whose value is a set of attribute-value pairs. It contains three subattributes. The first, `process-type`, specifies the type of substep process as an `action`, the second, `process-concept`, indicates that the specific action is a knowledge-base concept called `c-push` that represents the action of pushing. The third, `roles`, specifies the actors and objects that participate in the action. The value of the `roles` attribute is a set (not shown here). Additional attribute-value pairs occur in a full LF.

Annotation is accomplished by *unifying* the task grammar with the input and is controlled by the grammar. For each attribute in the grammar that has an atomic value, any corresponding input attribute must have the same value. (Technically, it must have a compatible [Kay 1979] value. As one example, when the grammar attribute has the value ANY, the input attribute can have any value.) When the values are different, unification fails. When the attributes match and both values are sets, unification is applied recursively to the values, and the result replaces the input value. When the input LF does not contain the grammar attribute, the attribute and its value are added to the input. Any attributes that occur in the input but not in the grammar remain in the input after unification. Thus, unification matches only the relevant subsections of the input. Note that unification is similar to set union, since enriched attribute-value pairs from both input and grammar are merged.

A fragment of the media coordinator's grammar states that an action should be realized in both graphics and text:

```
(((process-type action)      ;; If process is an action
        (media-graphics yes)      ;; Use graphics
        (media-text yes)    ;; Use text
        ...))
```

On unifying this fragment of the grammar with the value of the `substeps` fragment of the input LF, FUF first checks whether the attribute `process-type` occurs in the input. Since it does and the value following it is `action`, FUF now checks whether the attribute `media-graphics` occurs in the input. Since it does not, FUF adds to the input the attribute-value pair `(media-graphics yes)`, a directive indicating that the action is to be realized in graphics. Similarly, it adds the directive `(media-text yes)`, specifying that the action is also to be realized in text. Thus, the first attribute-value pair is used as a test for this grammar portion. When it matches the input (the input LF describes an action), the input is annotated with the remaining attribute-value pairs. If the input LF had contained a different `process-type` (like `abstract`), unification with this portion of the grammar would have failed and FUF would have attempted unification with a new portion.

In most uses of the media coordinator grammar, a fragment is recursively applied to small nested segments of the input LF at least once. For example, the input LF can contain a causal relation, with two roles, both of which are actions. In this case, the grammar fragment as shown matches each role. A different fragment matches the causal relation (one that annotates it to be realized in text only). The roles of the actions are annotated recursively, as are their modifiers.

Chapter 6

Towards Coordinated Temporal Multimedia Presentations

Steven K. Feiner, Diane J. Litman, Kathleen R. McKeown, and Rebecca J. Passonneau

Abstract

In this chapter, we discuss some of the issues that must be addressed to generate multimedia presentations of temporal information automatically, especially when temporal media are to be used. By *temporal information*, we mean entities and relations that are defined at least partly in terms of time, such as events, points in time, durations, ordering relations, and overlapping intervals. We are especially interested in how temporal information can be expressed by *temporal media*, such as animation and speech, whose information content is presented over time in a way that is controlled by the presentation designer. In temporal media, a presentation designer must decide not only the temporal order in which information is presented, but also the point in time at which each communicative act occurs and its duration. In contrast, although material presented in *static media*, such as written text and static graphics, is examined by the viewer over time, the author does not have control over the material as it is being viewed.

1. Introduction

Over the past few years, researchers have begun to explore how to plan and coordinate multimedia presentations in which all material is generated by the system [Arens et al. 1991; Neal and Shapiro 1991; Roth et al. 1991; Badler et al. 1991; Feiner and McKeown, this volume; André et al., this volume; Maybury, this volume]. The majority of these projects have concentrated on static media: written text, and a variety of graphics including two-dimensional graphs and charts, maps, and illustrations of three-dimensional environments. Badler et al. [1991] generate animation from natural language instructions as a first step toward the production of narrated animation. Their emphasis thus far, however, has been on motion control.

In the work described here, we build on our experience in representing temporal plans [Devanbu and Litman 1991], in natural language processing [McKeown et al. 1990; Passonneau 1988], in knowledge-based graphics and animation [Karp and Feiner 1990; Seligmann and Feiner 1991; Feiner and McKeown, this volume], and in coordinating static multimedia [Feiner and McKeown, this volume; McKeown et al. 1992]. We will be extending COMET (COordinated Multimedia Explanation Testbed) [Feiner and McKeown, this volume; McKeown et al. 1992], a system that can generate explanations of field maintenance and repair procedures for a military radio. COMET includes knowledge bases that describe domain objects and plans, a diagnostic component, a content planner that determines what information should be presented, a media coordinator that determines which information should be realized in graphics and which in text, and separate text and graphics generators. It is described in the preceding article by Feiner and McKeown in this volume.

2. Example

A number of extensions to COMET will be required to make it possible to present complex temporal relationships using temporal media. We present an example to illustrate some of the representation and coordination issues. The text shown in Figure 1 is taken from a manual on preventive maintenance for the military radio that serves as COMET's current domain, and is the third step in a set of instructions for checking the rt (receiver-transmitter) remote I/O module.

Five actions are presented in linear order, all but the last of which must overlap in execution: (1) press and (2) hold CALL button, (3) key rt, (4) check display, and (5) show CALL (executed by the radio, not the user). Without prior knowledge about the causal dependencies between these steps, the text in Figure 1 is confusing. The important information about the potential delay in the displayed characters that indicate a successful test is presented late and is de-emphasized. Note also that in a well-integrated multimedia presentation, the italicized descriptors in Figure 1 would be redundant; here, however, they make it possible to read the text without having to see the pictures.

The underlying temporal relations can be clarified by the use of more explicit linguistic devices, such as well-chosen temporal adverbs, and judicious use of visual devices, such as zooming and highlighting. Figure 2 describes a proposed alternative explanation that illustrates how such devices could be coordinated to provide a more effective explanation. Each segment consists of an animation sequence (A) with a voice-over (V).

Press and hold *keyboard* BATT/CALL button and key rt, *using handset or intercom push-to-talk switch*. Check display; it must show CALL. (It might take up to 12 seconds before CALL is displayed.)

[The text is followed by a row of three figures showing (1) the keyboard and display (with an enlarged inset of the BATT/CALL button), (2) a hand holding the handset and pressing the switch, and (3) the desired final display.]

Figure 1. Original Documentation for a Maintenance and Repair Step
(italics added)

V:	Press and hold the BATT/CALL button.
A:	*Closeup of keyboard and display, with inset of BATT/CALL button.*
V:	While holding it, key the rt.
A:	*Zoom out to include handset, keyboard, and display.*
V:	Simultaneously, check the display.
A:	*Highlight display.*
V:	It must show call within 12 seconds.
A:	*Show "CALL" in the display with an inset iconic clock indicating elapsed time*

Figure 2. Proposed Documentation using Temporal Media

The explanation that uses temporal media is clearer because it conveys more explicitly how the separate actions overlap one another, and because it organizes the information in a way that controls what the user should attend to as the explanation progresses. Designing systems that could generate such explanations raises diverse issues pertaining to representation and control for each medium, and how to coordinate the media.

3. Representing Complex Temporal Plans

To represent both temporal domain and multimedia presentation plans, a plan language is needed that can capture complex temporal relationships between actions. Currently, COMET represents only sequential relationships. In the general case, plans may be composed from actions by relationships such as sequencing, choice, iteration, recursion, and concurrency [Georgeoff 1987]. Here we consider the use of Allen's interval-based temporal logic [Allen 1983a] to construct temporal plans. The goal of our current work on plan representation [Devanbu and Litman 1991] is in fact to make it possible to represent such temporal relationships in the framework of a terminological knowledge representation system (the type of system currently used in COMET). Here we discuss only the implications for generation of having such a temporal representation.

Allen's representation allows for the specification of thirteen temporal relationships between two intervals: *before*, *meets*, *overlaps*, *during*, *starts*, *finishes*, *equal*, and inverses of the first six relationships. These temporal relationships are shown pictorially in Figure 3.

The representation also permits the expression of a disjunction of these relationships between two intervals. By restricting the representation in this manner, computationally efficient algorithms for computing implicit temporal relationships between intervals are provided, based on constraint propagation techniques.

Allen's temporal logic can be applied to plans by associating temporal intervals with every action that makes up the plan, and using the logic to express explicitly the temporal relationships between the intervals. Consider the example introduced in the previous section. If we name the interval associated with each action after the type of the action (e.g., **press**, **hold**, **key**, **check**, and **show**), then the set of temporal constraints in Figure 4 describes the temporal relationships in the domain plan. (Note that the potential duration of 12 seconds between **key** and **show** cannot be represented using only Allen's relative relationships.)

X *before* Y	XXX YYY
X *equal* Y	XXX YYY
X *meets* Y	XXXYYY
X *overlaps* Y	XXX YYY
X *during* Y	YYYYY XXX
X *starts* Y	XXX YYYYY
X *finishes* Y	YYYY XXX

Figure 3. Temporal Relationships from [Allen 1983a]

Allen's representation could similarly be used to represent the presentation plan. In particular, the interval corresponding to each speech action should be related by *equal*, *starts*, *finishes*, *during* (or inverses) to the corresponding animation interval. Each pair of such speech and animation actions should also be related by *meets* to an interval representing a pause, which itself should *meet* the next speech and animation pair. Control over pause durations and speech rate are issues that need to be investigated.

4. Using Temporal Knowledge for Natural Language Generation

In determining the content of the multimedia explanation, we make use of a presentation strategy also represented in our plan representation formalism. By separating explanation presentation order from the order of task execution, a generation system can make use of a variety of constraints on presentation order including, but not restricted to, temporal sequence. For this example, most of the actions are not related by strict temporal sequentiality, so the presentation strategy must rely on other information. In the domain plan depicted in Figure 4, note that only the **press** action completely precedes any other actions. Of the four remaining actions, all are represented as having the same endpoint, and potentially the same onset as one or more other actions. Thus, the temporal order of the actions does not determine a linear order that could be used for language, where simultaneous presentation of actions is not possible. Other constraints on presentation order must play a role in determining how to describe the task. In this example, presentation order can be based in part on precondition-action sequences. Note that **press** is a precondition for **hold**, and the conjunction of **hold** and **key** is a precondition for **show**.

When presentation order does not follow the underlying task, speech can indicate the domain relation using a temporal adverbial such as "before," "after," or "while." Because temporal information in natural language is always partial, and is expressed both explicitly and implicitly, the generator must make decisions about what to express explicitly, and how to reason about what inferences the user might draw. There are many ways to express simultaneity in natural language, but none of them conveys exactly the relational information represented in the domain plan shown here.

---

meets(**press, hold**)
OR [*equal*(**key, hold**), *finishes*(**key, hold**)]
OR [*equal*(**check, key**), *finishes*(**check, key**)]
OR [*equal*(**show, check**), *finishes*(**show, check**)]

Figure 4. Temporal Relationships in Example Domain Plan of Figure 2.

In our sample utterances, the adverbial words and phrases ("while," "simultaneously," and "within 12 seconds") contribute explicit information about temporal overlap and duration. Implicit temporal information is also conveyed by the linear order of verb phrases or clausal constituents within utterances (e.g., "press and hold" versus "hold and press," or "while holding it, key rt" versus "key rt while holding it"). For example, the conjoined verb phrase "press and hold" does not necessarily lead to the inference that the two actions are in a *meets* relation, although in this case, *meets*(**press**, **hold**) is part of the underlying domain plan.

In our work, we use a Functional Unification Formalism (FUF) [Elhadad 1990] to represent lexical items, constraints on their usage, and inferences that they allow. It will allow us to handle interactions between different word choices (e.g., between the use of conjunction and the use of temporal adverbs) to select the set of devices in a text that best conveys the underlying temporal relations. Our work will draw on previous work in generating text containing temporal markers [Matthiessen 1985; Maybury 1990] and work on temporal focus [Webber 1988]. We are looking at the interaction that will be needed between the content planner and FUF. For example, the content planner can select a presentation order that does not follow the underlying temporal order when FUF can select linguistic markers that unambiguously convey the correct temporal relations.

5. Using Temporal Knowledge for Graphics Generation

Animation can be an especially effective medium for presenting information that involves complex temporal relationships. Dynamically controlled camera specification and editing effects are powerful resources for communicating such information [Karp and Feiner 1990]. For example, the context within which an action takes place can be established by starting with a wide shot and cutting or zooming in to a closeup. Then, within the closeup, the action itself can be depicted in detail. Spatial editing effects, such as multiple viewports, can be used to create a "split screen" that shows different concurrent actions or the same action from different viewpoints. Temporal editing effects, such as cuts, wipes, and fades, can be used to express the relationship between the actions depicted in the shots joined by the effect. For example, a dissolve (in which one shot is faded down as the other shot is faded up) is an effect that is used conventionally, although not exclusively, to indicate that time has elapsed between the two shots that it joins.

In Figure 2, we begin with a closeup of the keyboard and the display that shows the button being pressed, and then widen the shot to include the handset being keyed, emphasizing the simultaneity of the actions. Alternatively, the keyboard and handset could have been been shown side-by-side using a split-screen effect. (This would be especially effective if the two loci of action could not have been shown legibly in the same view.) Next, although the display is already visible, it is emphasized by highlighting it. If the text "CALL" is not legible in the selected view, an inset could be used to show a closeup. In this case, the alternative of zooming in on the display is less preferable, since it would fail to show the simultaneity of all four actions: holding the button, keying the rt, checking the display, and the appearance of "CALL".

Waiting up to 12 seconds may be shown using a combination of effects. For example, an iconic clock showing the amount of time to wait is a standard illustrative device that can be made available as one of a set of predesigned techniques for use in static graphics or animation. Although animation can portray events in the same time they take to occur, this is not an effective choice when the particular event (e.g., waiting) would not be explained better by doing so. A variety of effects are possible in this case that can indicate the wait. For example, time could be sped up by showing a quickly moving clock, or a cross fade might be used between the start of the wait, and the appearance of the word "CALL", emphasized by showing the change in the clock time.

In previous work on animation generation, we used a temporal representation that specified the precise times at which each action started and stopped; the same representation was used to encode both the input domain actions as well as the generated presentation actions [Karp and Feiner 1990]. Our animation presentation planning, however, was restricted to a single medium alone, and followed the strict temporal course of action: actions were shown as they took place, with no attempt to change their presentation order to emphasize important ones or linearize parallel actions for clarity. If temporal relationships among the domain actions are instead classified and represented explicitly, this makes it easier to invoke presentation strategies that correspond to some subset of these relationships.

5.1. Coordination Issues

We are particularly interested in the problems of coordinating multiple temporal media. By coordination we mean deciding what information to communicate in each of a set of media, how to communicate it, and when and for how long to communicate it. Since temporal media allow the presentation designer to specify the starting point and duration of each communicative act, communicative acts in different media can be synchronized at an extremely fine granularity. As discussed, not only could a spoken sentence be planned to start at the same time as an animated action, but a specific word in the sentence could be made to coincide with a particular point in the action. In contrast, although the viewer is aware of and affected by the overall appearance of a presentation that uses only static media, the viewer does not read text and view graphics simultaneously. Nevertheless, presentations that intersperse static graphics and text (e.g., comic strips) may approach this level of simultaneity. (In fact, this is why temporal presentations such as movies are often planned using storyboards that are similar to comics in appearance.)

Much of our early effort on COMET was spent on determining the assignment of information to media, and on the separate generation of material in text and graphics based on these assignments. More recently, we have addressed cross-referencing material in one medium from material in another, and other coordination issues that require one media generator to know *how* information is being generated by another generator, rather than *what* information is being generated [McKeown et al. 1992].

The need for temporal information is motivated by coordination tasks in multimedia generation, since certain temporal relations can be presented more effectively in one or another medium. For example, language imposes a sequential order on the presentation of events, even if the actual events occur simultaneously. Simultaneity thus must be conveyed by additional linguistic devices, such as the use of "while" to link two clauses representing the events. In contrast, graphics can depict several events simultaneously and thus might be a better medium for expressing such a temporal relationship. If simultaneous actions are linearized in an animation, perhaps because they are too complex to present together, the text generator may be called upon to make the temporal relationship clear. One global issue that must be addressed is that of duration—a presentation must fit within the time allocated it, and the length of its component parts must be constrained to make possible desired temporal relationships both within and across media boundaries.

6. Acknowledgments

This work was supported in part by the Defense Advanced Research Projects Agency under Contract N00039-84-C-0165, the Office of Naval Research under Contracts N00014-89-J-1782 and N00014-91-J-1872, the National Science Foundation under Grant IRT-84-51438, and an equipment grant from the Hewlett-Packard Company.

Chapter 7

Multimedia Explanations for Intelligent Training Systems

Bradley A. Goodman

Abstract

As intelligent training systems are emerging from the laboratories, the need for individualized multimedia explanations has surfaced. Multimedia explanations go beyond text, incorporating one or a combination of graphics, video, speech, and sound to convey information. Explanations in the past have typically been canned - unanticipated or tailored explanations were not possible. To make intelligent training systems more effective, we are performing research in techniques in multimedia explanation generation. Multiple media can concisely and accurately convey required information and promote better learning. As an initial test, we have prototyped our ideas in the form of a multimedia generation component for an intelligent help system that could be employed as part of an intelligent diagnosis training system for Apple Macintosh[1] repair. The prototype automatically coordinates generated spoken narration with appropriate video segments showing repair actions to reflect a repair plan devised by a student on the fly. The principal advantage of our technique is that it is not necessary to predict and film ahead of time all possible repair plans that a student might invoke. Instead the help component automatically sequences video segments of different repair actions to reflect the student's plan.

1. Introduction

Recently, there has been a major surge in the use of advanced instructional technology by industry and government. Multimedia explanations can play a central role in this ad-

---

[1] Apple and Macintosh are trademarks of Apple Computer Inc.

vancement by increasing the fidelity and bandwidth of the communication to the student. In the government sector, the Air Force, Army, Navy, and NASA are beginning deployment of intelligent training systems (ITS) to replace or supplement standard computer-based training systems (CBT) and instructor-based training. No longer are ITS simply in research laboratories, many are coming into direct use in training. For example, the HAWK Mach-III is an intelligent training system for teaching the diagnosis and correction of faults in the RAM/HIPIR of the HAWK air defense system [Massey 1986]. Until recently it was in use in the program for the HAWK Firing Section Mechanics conducted at the U.S. Army Air Defense Artillery School, Fort Bliss, Texas. As another example, The MITRE Corporation is helping the Air Force Human Systems Division prepare specifications for an intelligent training system for the instruction of advanced diagnosis techniques for F15 and F16 aircraft maintenance personnel to transition the basic jobs skill technology developed by the Air Force Human Resources Directorate [Gott 1987; Means 1988; Gott 1989; Lajoie and Lesgold 1989]. Another prototype intelligent training system, STEAMER [Stevens and Roberts 1983; Hollan et al. 1984], was developed for the Navy to help train the operators of large ships by employing an interactive, inspectable simulator of a ship's steam propulsion system. STEAMER was used for actual training at the Great Lakes Naval Training Center [Wenger 1987]. Each of these systems concentrated on providing students with a more robust learning environment through the use of such devices as simulators and coaching. Simulators are employed to provide a context for and to add realism to the learning process; coaching is used to provide guided learning to the student. Despite their novelty, all of these systems provide coaching through canned or template-filled explanations to students about the process being taught, requested help, and advice – no unanticipated explanations are possible and the explanations may become inconsistent with underlying system behavior if any system code changes.

Some of the ITS prototypes in the labs are beginning to go further, employing artificial intelligence natural language generation and user modeling techniques [McKeown 1985, Paris 1987a, Moore 1989] to provide on-the-fly, individualized explanations for students. Here we outline explanations from a few of the intelligent training systems developed the past 15 years and mention the underlying technique used to generate them. For example, explanations generated by one of the earlier intelligent training systems, SOPHIE II [Brown et al. 1982], can respond directly to a student's query about his or her hypothesis of a fault in an electrical circuit or can disclose how an expert would approach the fault. "...The current source is working then. The modules now left are CL, VL, OPF and DARL. I think I will make my next measurement on the Darlington amplifier. I want to know whether the BASE CURRENT of Q4 is OK..." [pg. 63, Wenger 1987]. SOPHIE II incorporated "pre-canned and handcrafted schemata" [pg. 116, Psotka et al. 1988] attached to nodes in a decision tree to provide explanations. The explanations are simply instantiated with appropriate values and put together to form a dialogue.

In contrast to SOPHIE II, explanations in STEAMER are generated directly from abstractions of the devices and processes that underlie the steam propulsion system as modeled in the simulation [Forbus and Stevens 1981; Wenger 1987]. A typical response to a student using the STEAMER system might be: "According to the principle which requires that whenever you admit steam into a closed chamber you should first align the drains, before opening valve 13 you should align the drain valves FWD-E254 and FWD-E239." [pg. 131, Gott 1989].

The SHERLOCK I system [Gott 1989] can convey one of five different levels of instruction in its explanations depending on the explicitness necessary for a particular trainee. It uses an estimate of a trainee's ability and a trainee's past queries to determine which level of explanation to furnish. A trainee in the highest level would receive a brief functional description, the next level down might get an explicit enumeration of the required steps to perform, and lower levels would leave out descriptions of required steps sizing up precisely instead the current state of component by listing expected measurements. Each explanation is encoded and prestored ahead of time based on an analysis of an expert's advice on proper approaches to solving a particular problem and the level of expertise of the intended student.

Multimedia goes beyond textual explanations as outlined above, incorporating one or a combination of graphics, video, speech, and sound to convey information. Typical combinations include text with graphics and speech with video. Computer-based training systems are taking the lead in multimedia for training by utilizing interactive videodisc. At the same time research in individualized, natural language explanation generation for ITS is moving forward using the research in artificial intelligence explanation generation (e.g., for expert systems, [Moore and Swartout 1990; Paris 1990]), intelligent training systems are making the jump to multimedia to provide explanations and help in the form of multimedia presentations. Explanations incorporating video, for example, are hardwired, i.e., each video segment to be played must be selected and indexed ahead of time and then called up when needed. They, thus, exhibit the same problem as canned natural language explanations - unanticipated (video tailored to user, task, and discourse) explanations are not possible. Multimedia intelligent training systems must address the complexity of multimedia explanations if they are to promote a better learning environment.

The remainder of this paper addresses the complexities of multimedia explanations for training. A discussion on different ways to employ multimedia for training is presented. The need for coordination of media is then addressed. Next, details on how to employ multimedia in intelligent training systems is provided. A description of a prototype multimedia explanation component for helping instruct a student on the repair of Apple Macintosh computers is then presented. Lastly, some proposed solutions to address problems with multimedia explanations for training systems are given.

2. Multimedia for Training

Interactive courseware (ICW) draws heavily on the use of multimedia, particularly through video. The video is often narrated and textual information is overlaid on top of it. Typical ICW follow an instructional design that provides demonstration, followed by guided practice, and then ending with exercises. Demonstration mode provides a tutorial (usually through narrated video) on an aspect of the topic to be trained. Guided practice is then presented by going through a typical problem scenario and solving it. The student's interactions with the system in guided practice mode are restricted. The student is presented a problem, shown how to solve it (using a combination of video, graphics, narration, and text), forced to look at help messages, and requested occasionally to take a specific action (e.g., point to a particular object on the screen). If the student does not follow the specified action exactly, the system immediately interrupts and shows the proper action. Lastly, the student is given exercises to carry out. Exercises include both multiple choice questions, and carrying out tasks by selecting objects on the screen and actions from menus. The student can ask for help at any time. The help is the same as presented in guided practice. It is usually in the form of canned, narrated video with text overlays. All explanations or advice in an ICW are prespecified by the courseware author.

Multimedia, especially through video, is making its way into intelligent training systems as well. SHERLOCK II [Gott 1989], for example, incorporates still video shots of equipment components (e.g., card pins) and test equipment. By overlaying graphics depicting such entities as knobs, test probes, and dial readings, SHERLOCK II allows students to simulate interaction with the actual equipment in the field. Students can place graphical "test probes" over the video-simulated "pins" to invoke the taking of a measurement. The realism afforded by such an interface provides easier transfer of the learned knowledge into the field. The procedure is also more concrete, making it easier for a student to comprehend than through some abstract way of specifying the same action. In a more traditional interface, for example, the student might have to use some esoteric notation like "Multimeter.TestProbe.+ = Pin[12].Card[3]" to specify the same measurement task. Thus, SHERLOCK II concentrates on using video on the input side but does not use video as part of explanations. It instead uses either text or graphics.

The Piano Tutor project [Joseph 1991] takes a broader approach to explanations for ITS. It provides multimedia presentations followed by student exercises on a MIDI keyboard to help teach beginning piano. The multimedia explanations incorporate digitized recorded voice, videodisc, computer graphics, and MIDI synthesized music. The presentations are specified using a multimedia editing system, the Presentation Builder, that allows the specification and storage of both sequential and parallel media along an event line for animated presentations. The Piano Tutor can incorporate complex multimedia presentations as part of a lesson. However, the presentations are strictly limited to ones previously specified by a courseware author. A little flexibility is provided to the presentations by allowing arbitrary LISP functions to be placed on an event line. The LISP functions can, for example, pause the presentation or solicit interaction from the student.

The two ITS projects cited highlight the principle current uses of multimedia in intelligent training systems. One makes for more realistic input while the other provides sophisticated, canned output. Since SHERLOCK II already incorporates the necessary video hardware, there is no reason not to also use it as part of its explanations. The Piano Tutor, on the other hand, can provide diverse multimedia explanations but, without encoding a massive database ahead of time, cannot respond to the needs of specific students in a particular learning context. Its explanations, instead, can only be targeted for a stereotypical student. Thus, the best features of an ITS, its tailored coaching, gets lost in the midst of the sophisticated media.

Figure 1 attempts to summarize the state of video-based courseware. As the involvement of the multimedia interaction between the student and the courseware technology rises (i.e., top to bottom in the table in Figure 1), the practice and coaching increases in quantity, complexity, realism, and fit. Other than for full multimedia ITS, the video and all its uses must be anticipated and authored ahead of time. The video can only be targeted at a stereotypical student; it is not adapted on the fly for a particular student in a

Courseware Technology	Unique Feature	Example	Ease of Use	Relevance to Student	Expected Overall Effectiveness
Videotape	Visual descriptions of tasks as an overview	Home repair video	Easy - play VCR	Moderate - should contain material that touches on some current student needs	Low - no practice and no help when performing the learned task; best at providing an overview
Videotape + Textbook	Complementary textual explanations to fill in details and summarize the video segments	Sun Microsystem intro to operating system fundamentals	Moderate - pause/play VCR, read textbook, perform exercises	Moderate - should contain material that touches on some current student needs	Moderate - some practice to reinforce viewed skills
Interactive Courseware	Student answerable queries as exercises on newly taught skills	Hill AFB F16 jet engine theory and repair [Walker 91]	Moderate - view PC display and videodisc, respond to queries and exercises	Moderate - should directly address some student needs since video integrated with course material	Moderate - some practice through multiple choice questions and problem exercises
Overlaid Graphics ITS	Realistic, simulated student actions "executed" on a simulated model as responses to exercises	SHERLOCK II [Gott 89] avionics test station diagnosis	Moderate - view PC display and videodisc, respond to exercises, perform simulated tasks	High - high level of integration with learning materials	High - good practice and review
Canned Multimedia ITS	Canned, coached visual explanations to provide help explanations and advice	Piano Tutor [Josephs 91]	Moderate - view/hear PC and videodisc, respond to exercises, perform tasks	High - high level of integration with learning materials	High - good practice with general coaching
Full Multimedia ITS	Tailored, coached visual explanations to supply help explanations and advice	Visual Repair [under development by author]	Moderate - view/hear PC and videodisc, respond to exercises, perform simulated tasks	High (expected) - high level of integration with learning materials	Very high (expected) - good practice with student and context adapted coaching

Figure 1. Video-Based Courseware

distinct context. Such video is most effective in an introductory overview of a domain where the objects involved in a task are described; it is less effective for teaching how to perform a task. For example, after describing and highlighting domain objects, viewing video segments of tasks that use the objects serve to improve recall. In demonstrating the execution of a task, however, the video segments are less effective since a student's involvement is only as a passive observer and no reinforcement occurs. Coordinated and integrated multimedia explanations composed on the fly in response to a student's actions have the potential for getting around these limitations.

The categories listed in the columns of the table in Figure 1 are self-explanatory except for the last two. "Relevance to Student" is an attempt to consider how well the video shown and its delivery mechanism fits the current training needs of the student with respect to the knowledge desired. A moderate relevance indicates that the student can expect to be shown video on aspects of the domain being trained. High relevance indicates the fidelity of the information conveyed through the video is deep and the information directly addresses current training requirements. While each courseware technology can be at times very relevant to a student, the column entries are meant to indicate the likelihood of course material presented using a specific courseware technology directly addressing a particular student's needs. The column on "Expected Overall Effectiveness" is intended to summarize the likely effectiveness of the courseware technology employed [Stafford 1990]. Low indicates the technology is not effective at teaching many domains to students. Moderate signifies that the student can expect to learn a great deal about the domain but that some important training aspects will be overlooked or given cursory treatment. Lastly, high designates that the courseware technology provides for maximal learning by the student in the domain being taught. The table shows "Expected Overall Effectiveness" being stronger as the bandwidth and fidelity increase through the use of tailored student interaction and multimedia.

3. Coordinated Media

Combining multiple media, such as speech and video or text and graphics, can provide for more effective explanations than afforded by a single medium. Many training domains cover complex concepts and devices. The operation and maintenance of equipment are two principle areas encountered [Hollan et al. 1984; Massey 1986; Gott 1989]. Mixed media communication can more concisely and accurately convey the required information. It will be less ambiguous, reducing any possible miscommunication between tutor and student. For example, text and graphics can be used one after the other as part of an explanation about computer maintenance. A textual description of how to remove the top lid of a computer can be followed by a picture of the computer with its top lid removed (Figure 2).

Integrated media is even more successful if the information conveyed in one medium is woven with that provided in the other medium(s) and not simply presented in succession (as occurs in Figure 2). It is easier to remember such material by associating a lot of details (given verbally or in written form) with a spatial visualization than on its own [Miller 1986]. It is also perceptually and cognitively less taxing for the student during the learning process since details are spread across more than one medium and trigger more than one sense. As an example of integrated media shown in Figure 3, a textual description of how to remove the top lid of a computer can refer to parts of a picture showing the top lid being removed.

1. Remove the Phillips screw at the top rear
    of the case

2. Push up on the tabs on the back of the lid
    and lift up the lid from the back to the
    front until the lid comes off the front
    end.

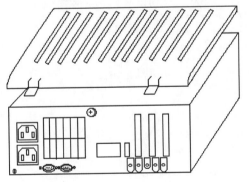

Figure 2. Removing the Top Lid without Coordinated Media

Research in coordinated and integrated media has begun in earnest. Recent research in coupling natural language explanations, and graphics for training that is most closely related and motivational to our effort has been performed by Feiner and McKeown [1990a, 1991]. Their research employs a content planner that plans media-independent explanations, and a media coordinator that determines the best way to realize them using mixed text and graphics. All graphics and text are generated on the fly. The decision on whether to present a particular piece of information as text or graphics is determined using a set of heuristics developed through experiments using hand-coded displays of text/graphics explanations [Lombardi 1989]. The study proposed presenting physical attributes and location information as graphics, abstract actions as text, and simple and compound actions as text and graphics. Feiner and McKeown [1990a] employ graphical "metaobjects" to emphasize the performance of an action. For example, an arrow can be drawn to show which direction to turn a knob. As an extension to their research, temporal information about the sequencing of information in an explanation is expressible using temporal media such as animation and speech [Feiner et al., this volume].

1. Remove the Phillips screw at the top rear of
   the case (Figure 1, #1).

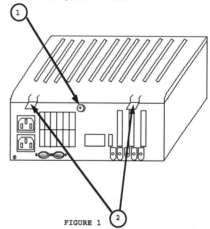

FIGURE 1

2. Push up on the tabs on the back of the lid
   (Figure 1, #2) and lift up the lid from the
   back to the front until the lid comes off th
   front end.

Figure 3. Removing the Top Lid Using Coordinated Media (adapted from page 2.3, Apple Technical Procedures Macintosh IIcx, 1989)

Other researchers are addressing issues in classifying, planning, and coordinating multimedia explanations (e.g., Arens et al., this volume; Maybury, this volume; André and Rist, this volume; Wahlster et al. 1991a]. Arens, Hovy, and Vossers [this volume] have attempted to capture factors that are important in multimedia communication. They categorize factors by the intentions, desires, and characteristics of the producer, the capabilities of the perceiver, the nature of the information to be conveyed, and the characteristic of the media used [Arens et al., this volume]. Maybury [this volume] extends the communicative acts used to generate textual explanations to include visual acts so integrated text and graphics can be planned for dynamic animation of routes. The research of André and Rist [this volume] considers the influence of graphical constraints on text generation, and text generation decisions on graphics generation to tailor the presentation of information to suit a specific context. André and Rist [this volume] describe a plan-based approach to generate illustrated documents based on such constraints. Maybury [this volume] and André et al. [this volume] view the issue of content selection and media allocation as co-constraining in contrast to the separation of the two processes in Feiner and McKeown [1990a, this volume].

A major thrust of this research that is different from the other multimedia explanation research is the concern with re-use of material (especially video) in many different situations. Re-use is a problem closer to the needs of current training systems than generating multimedia explanations from scratch. Coordinated and integrated media material can allow such re-use through devices such as automatic editing to patch previous video or graphics, or supplementing the explanation with more appropriate information through additional media. The next sections expand on this notion.

4. Effective Multimedia for ITS

The research described in this paper attempts to layout a better approach to using multimedia in ICW and ITS. It presents coordinated media and response planning techniques for providing effective multimedia in an intelligent training system. The previous section of the paper defined coordinated media and provided exemplars on how to provide multimedia explanations. Response planning will be elaborated here to explain how the coordinated media is derived.

The synthesis of coordinated media can be achieved through planning of a response. A response planner [Sidner et al. 1984; Burger 1989] can contemplate important factors about the training situation and the information to be conveyed. It can consider the student, his or her progress, the skills learned so far, and any difficulties he or she encountered; the material to be presented, e.g., whether it includes material that is spatial in nature, involves a difficult (to describe) action, or requires a lot of detail to convey; and the current contextual situation, e.g., the student has been bombarded with lots of details and needs the information summarized to reinforce the learning. A response planner must use its deliberation to determine the temporal order of presenting information and the points in time to start and stop each underlying communicative act [Maybury, this volume; Feiner et al., this volume] in the explanation. The construction ahead of time of canned multimedia explanations to cover most contingencies would be too burdensome a task if adequate coverage of a domain is to be achieved.

Once the ITS determines what information it wants to convey to the student, the response planner must contemplate the different ways to present it.[2] Considerations on how to communicate the information through particular media include higher-level factors like determining what piece of the information gets put into "focus" and how to ensure that the explanation is unambiguous. The response planner consults the student model to determine how to express the information in a unifying context that is easiest for the given student to understand. For example, if a referential phrase [Goodman 1986] would be verbally, very complex, possibly confusing the student, a decision could be made to present the information as an image. If the information to be conveyed is visual and the visual scene is especially busy, the planner might determine that the use of speech or animation (e.g., motion on the screen) [Feiner and McKeown 1990a; Vilain 1990] is crucial to "point" the student to the appropriate viewing position. Once it is determined how to best provide the information to avoid ambiguity, the planner can then determine how to present the information concisely.

At the same time multimedia explanations can provide a more effective learning environment, they can help reduce the cost of developing new lessons in an ITS. For example, the shooting of video is an expensive and time-consuming process. Re-use of the same materials is important. We propose to plan such re-use on the fly with a response planning component so the ITS can select and augment a video segment with superim-

---

[2]Actually, this process is a little more involved than is described here. The information to convey and the ways to present it could be co-constraining.

posed graphics and generated spoken or textual explanations. This way not only can the same piece of video be re-used in another lesson but even in the current lesson it could be refined to help more appropriately target and communicate information to a particular student.

Research in the area of text generation has led to a set of communicative acts (e.g., [Appelt 1985; Maybury 1991a]) appropriate for describing the actions followed by a speaker to communicate information to a hearer using language. In particular, speech acts [Searle 1969; Cohen 1981; Appelt 1985] convey underlying language purposes. Rhetorical acts (e.g., [Maybury 1991a]) are higher-level actions that provide structure to other communicative acts so that they may achieve specific goals (e.g., comparing two entities). Extensions to these text-based communicative acts are under development to provide for the assembling of multimedia presentations (e.g., [Wahlster et. al. 1991a, Maybury 1991a]). Additional categories of communicative acts include graphics and video acts [Feiner and McKeown, this volume; Maybury 1991a] and discourse acts [Litman and Allen 1987]. Figure 4 provides some sample communicative acts for multimedia presentations. A response planner must select from these communicative acts to develop a multimedia presentation to satisfy the communication needs.[3] Actions can occur sequentially, in parallel, or any combination. Feiner et al. [this volume] propose to use Allen's interval-based temporal logic [Allen 1983a] to represent the complexities of multimedia presentation plans. Figure 5 shows an example multimedia explanation plan on a time line that indicates the different communicative actions that take place sequentially and in parallel to demonstrate the removal of a fan module from a power supply module that contains it. The plan plays a video segment showing the fan being removed. As it plays, the fan module is circled to highlight it, a narration explains what is occurring, and a caption further states what is being shown.

5. Visual Repair

The research performed here has led to a demonstration multimedia explanation component - Visual Repair - that could be used in an intelligent training system for tutoring

---

[3]While the approach as described in this chapter is a bottom-up approach to explanation generation, top-down or mixed approaches are also possible (e.g., McDonald and Pustejovsky 1985; McKeown 1985; Moore and Swartout 1990).

technicians to repair Apple Macintosh IIcx computers.[4] It uses interactive video, speech, text, and graphics as part of an intelligent diagnosis and repair planning tool and a help tool. The help tool gives access to information about parts of the computer and particular actions that can be applied to them. The diagnosis and repair tool provides a realistic way to teach a student about complex systems, that is, learning about the complexities of a system through diagnosing and repairing problems with it. This approach purposely parallels those taken in current successful intelligent training systems, such as SHER-LOCK [Gott 1989] and HAWK Mach-III [Massey 1986]. It departs from the current approaches, though, through the increased fidelity of explanations given to the student.

Speech (Language) Acts	Rhetorical Acts	Graphics and Video Acts
Request	Explain	Highlight
Confirm	Identify	Circle
Inform	Compare	Fade
Warn	Describe-Object	Pan
.	Argue	Display-Object
.	.	Display-Action
.	.	.
	.	.
	.	.

Figure 4. Communicative Acts for Multimedia Presentations

With the diagnosis and repair planning tool, the student builds a diagnosis and repair plan that he or she intends to follow given a particular fault that arises. The student can specify the steps they would take in the repair process one step at a time or all at once (e.g., unscrew the top case cover, remove the top cover, and slide out the video board

---

[4]The Visual Repair multimedia explanation component is implemented in Silicon Beach's SuperCard on an Apple Macintosh IIci computer. A Sony LDP-1450 videodisc player is used to retrieve and playback the video. A Mass Microsystems Colorspace II genlock video board is used to mix the computer and videodisc signals.

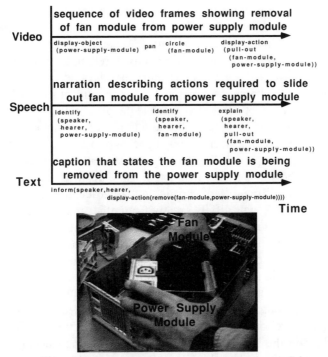

Figure 5. An Example Multimedia Explanation Plan on Fan Removal

from the NuBus slot). The plan steps can be input through multiple interface modalities: the student can enter the plan one step at a time either interactively by selecting actions from menus and parts to apply the actions from graphical or video stills of the computer, or textually by typing in a set of actions and part names in an English command language. The interface is illustrated in the upper part of Figure 6. The planning tool tracks the student's proposed actions against generalizations of known repair plans found in a procedures library (based on those suggested by an Apple Technical Procedures manual [1989] for the IIcx) in an attempt to determine which plan the student is proposing. The Apple procedures are currently stored in an augmented finite state machine network. States are nodes in the network; actions are outgoing links from a node. Actions that occur in parallel are grouped using a parallel operator construct; actions that can occur in any order are grouped by an any-order operator. Procedures with the same initial steps share nodes and outgoing links, to preserve space and to decrease search time, until steps in each procedure diverge. Tracking a student's actions entails matching each action to links and nodes in the procedures library. When no match is possible, that is, the student's action does not match any of the actions stored on the current node's outgoing links, then the diagnosis and repair tool assumes that the student has gone astray. It can recommend reasonable alternative steps and asks the student to choose from amongst them. Or, at the student's option, it can complete the plan by finding all reasonable ways to end the plan, asking the student to choose one if more than one option is available. The tool uses a speech synthesizer software package to narrate its explanations to the student (e.g., saying the particular plan step the student has requested or stating the complete plan that the student has constructed. More detailed explanatory information, such as warning about difficulties of carrying out a particular action, could be provided as well). Where Visual Repair differs greatly from other intelligent training system research is that a student at any point in the plan development can ask for an explanation in the form of a visualization of his or her plan when executed. The student can request to view how a single action under consideration is performed (e.g., to help decide the best "next" action to add to the plan), can ask to see how the current plan steps would look when executed (i.e., it plays back in sequence video clips of each action in the plan, retrieving and assembling them automatically from the videodisc to give the student a feel for the steps' appropriateness), and lastly can play back the completed plan (such as the one illustrated in the lower half of Figure 6) to give the student the perception of how it would work in the real world. Visual Repair assembles the (indexed) video segments from a videodisc composed of video of a service technician taking apart and putting back together the IIcx.[5] Narration is generated on the fly and added over the as-

---

[5]Notice that the video segments do not involve the technician performing a particular repair task. The goal was to film the most utilized actions of a service technician but outside of any particular repair context. In doing so, the hope was that the filmed segments were neutral in character so that they could apply in a number of very different repair contexts. While there will always be an art to determining the appropriate neutral clips to film, a standard procedure can be followed. Sample problem scenarios and (partial) solutions can be gathered. These scenarios and solutions can be abstracted. One can then film only once an action that is carried out often though instantiated in slightly different ways each time. Such video clips can be modified to fit a particular situation. For example, testing different pins on a connector with a voltmeter could be

sembled video segments to explain what is being seen so the same video segments can be re-used in other contextual situations by simply adding new narration.

The other piece of Visual Repair is a multimedia help tool that generates (for now canned) speech and text explanations but, more importantly, can retrieve pertinent video clips that can aid the user. There are two types of help video clips available, object and action. Object clips provide close-ups of each of the Macintosh IIcx's components (e.g., the power supply fan); action clips show the performance of a particular action (e.g., unscrewing the top cover screw from the case). The student selects graphically the part that he or she wants help on (e.g., buttoning the fan module in a graphic of the IIcx) and then selects from a menu the kind of help they want (e.g., "where is the part located?"). The help tool plays back video clips that respond to the student's question. Speech is synthesized to inform the student what clip is being shown (e.g., "this clip shows how to remove the video board"). More involved multimedia explanation generation is under development that can more precisely describe the video from the point of view of the underlying task being demonstrated. For example, when displaying a video on how to perform a particular task, the system can graphically highlight the part(s) that are the primary objects of focus in the task. While the system can not always show the students exact results of every action (e.g., if the service technician that was filmed for the video clip library removed the floppy drive before the power supply but the student specifies it in the reverse order in a plan), it does demonstrate to the students how to perform the action and the typical results of that action. The next phase of the research will incorporate a planning component that computes the actual results of the action so that spoken narration could be generated to fill in the missing detail in the video.

As the student creates a repair plan, a parallel multimedia presentation plan, that will be able to show and describe the student's plan is automatically created. That presentation plan takes each repair action in the student's repair plan and converts it into a plan step that directs the playing of a particular segment of video and the description of what is being shown in the video (Figure 7). First, the student's plan step is mapped to an appropriate video segment, by considering the action denoted by the plan step. Second, using information associated with each video segment about what is shown and what objects are present in the scene, Visual Repair constructs a sentence in English that de

---

shot in a neutral form once and then the particular pins under test could be indicated (cf. SHERLOCK II).

scribes the action. More details about the objects on which the action is being applied can be added to this presentation step if desired by other components in an intelligent training system. For example, if the student has never encountered the current objects in an earlier part of the current session with Visual Repair, then a description of those objects could be added. It is here that issues of coordination between the different media

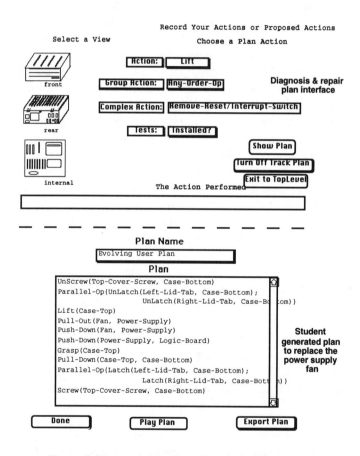

Figure 6. Diagnosis Plan Interface and Authored Plan

arise. Visual Repair currently narrates[6] in parallel with individual video segments and does not attempt to narrate across segments. While this works out well for Visual Repair's domain of procedural instructions, it would not necessarily work as well in a more complex domain where one would want to narrate across multiple video segments to make less complicated explanations. For example, if a student's repair plan had several consecutive steps that called for the removal of some components, Visual Repair would not generate one utterance that said each component was being removed (e.g., "The video board and power supply are pulled out from the logic board..."), but would instead generate individual utterances for each removal (e.g., "The video board is pulled out from the logic board. The power supply is pulled out from the logic board..."). The robust temporal representation for multimedia presentation employed by Feiner et al. [this volume] would allow for the planning of such an all encompassing utterance.

Coordination across video segments is provided by our focus mechanism by graphically highlighting relevant parts of the video as it is being shown. The beginning frame of each video segment has associated with it information about what is in that video frame (e.g., as shown in Figure 8, the name of important elements and the size and location of each element). That information can be used to automatically generate focus overlays that point out the recipient objects of important actions during the execution of the presentation plan. The focus overlays are superimposed on top of the video.[7] Figure 9 illustrates how a graphic overlay can focus a viewer's attention. A transparent, grayed overlay with a clear hole in it is placed so the clear hole is over the object of interest. By letting the student know what parts of the scene are in focus and which are not, it becomes clear what parts are relevant for the explanation. Focusing serves to lessen the

---

[6]It employs the software package MacInTalk to convert the English text into spoken form. This package was developed by Nigel Perry and is widely used on the Macintosh to perform basic text-to-speech conversion. Currently the speech is spoken over the selected video segment in Visual Repair. If that segment ends before the speech has completed, the video freezes on the last frame of the video segment. Given the step-by step nature of the procedural task underlying Visual Repair, the choice of freezing on the last video frame is not unreasonable.

[7]This is achieved using a genlock video board that mixes the video signal from the videodisc player with the graphics signal from the computer.

load on the student by limiting what has to be attended to, which can increase successful learning.

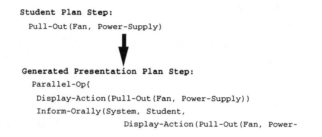

Figure 7. A Presentation Plan on Fan Removal

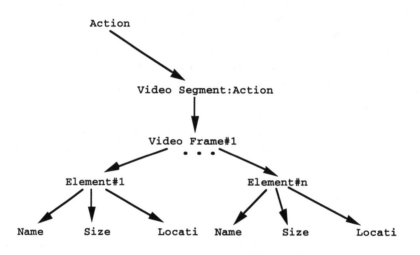

Figure 8. Describing a Video Frame

The Visual Repair multimedia help component was a first step towards effective multimedia explanations. Since the primary research goal behind Visual Repair was not the generation of natural language utterances (which could be better achieved through the work of current natural language generation researchers), a relatively canned object-oriented technique was employed that constructs explanations from phrases and templates. Visual Repair's emphasis was instead on taking the generated text and coordinating it with each video segment. The structure of the multimedia explanation is governed by the student's underlying repair plan and the action visually demonstrated in an indexed video segment. Visual Repair provides a testbed for experimentation with the automatic generation and coordination of multimedia explanations. More descriptive explanations than currently available in training systems can be generated and studied to determine if they promote better learning for students.

Figure 9. Highlighting the Focus of Attention

The Visual Repair system, however, is constrained by the availability of appropriate video clips in the video library and by the richness of the indexing provided. The level of detail of the representation of the video clip's content directly influences the ability of the response planner to select, sequence, and merge appropriate clips with other media into a suitable explanation. This problem is in contrast to the Feiner and McKeown [1990a, this volume] research where all necessary graphics is generated on the fly to fit the underlying representation. The Visual Repair research is following a different tack, modifying existing video and graphics to fit current needs since the approach is expected to be less computationally-intensive than generating the graphics on the fly. The Visual

Repair approach, thus, trades off completeness for efficiency. Once graphics generation becomes faster and cheaper, this tradeoff will become unnecessary. The next section provides a description on the techniques that will be employed in a future version of the Visual Repair system to improve the quality of multimedia explanations.

6. Future Directions

Visual Repair's multimedia explanations are currently limited to drawing from the indexed prerecorded video clips of repair actions and closeups of Macintosh components stored in the procedures library. Only a limited amount of video can be filmed and made available for multimedia explanations. Therefore, appropriate video to show the results of a student's actions might not be accessible. The particular representation of each video segment directly effects how successfully it can be drawn upon as part of a generated multimedia explanation. Even with a rich library of video clips, putting them together to form a clear, comprehensive explanation to address a student's needs requires much planning. Visual Repair is in the process of being extended to address issues of video clip selection, editing, and integration. Figure 10 shows the multimedia explanation generation component currently under development. The Realization Editor will modify multimedia explanations to make the explanation convey the planned explanation. For example, if the video clip library does not contain a clip that perfectly fits the explanation, steps are taken to modify one. Graphics can be superimposed on top of the video to provide a more appropriate scene; narration can be added to convey verbally the correct setting. Figure 11 shows how one can overlay graphics on top of video (or another graphic) so it properly reflects the current situation. The "diagonal lines" drawn on top of the components (the fan and the two memory SIMMs) denote that the components have been previously removed and are to be ignored. Narration can also be added, such as "Ignore the first and sixth RAM SIMM that have been crossed out to indicate prior removal...," to explain the example in Figure 11.

While the Realization Editor can modify video and graphics to make them more appropriate for a particular multimedia explanation, the Discourse Attenuator / Amplifier can guide the student to focus his or her attention to the most relevant pieces of the explanation to minimize ambiguity and to maximize information transfer. Text discourse techniques (e.g., [Reichman 1981, Litman and Allen 1987; Grosz and Sidner 1990]) can be extended to fit the multimedia environment. Pronominalization in text is often employed to focus a reader to a newly introduced object or concept (e.g., "...the left tab on the case top. <u>The tab</u>"). Similar highlighting can be achieved in multimedia explanations by employing techniques such as parallel spoken narration (e.g., "you see the tab on the left side of the case top...") or a graphic overlay. Cross-media references with static pictures has been done in the WIP system [Wahlster et al. 1991a; André and Rist, this volume].

Beyond the limitations of the multimedia explanation component of Visual Repair that were described, the plan tracker is impaired by the representation of the plans in the procedures library. The augmented finite state machine network representation of plans is

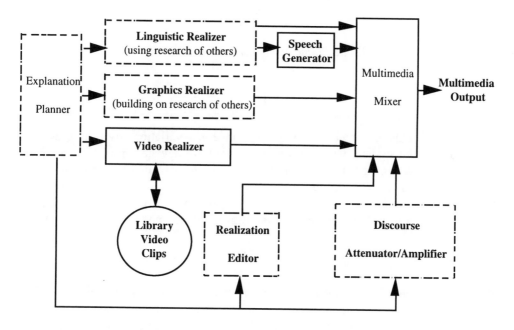

r ⁻ ⁻ ⌐
L _ _ ⌐ = Under development. Initial version used in current implementation.

Figure 10. Visual Repair Multimedia Explanation Generation Component

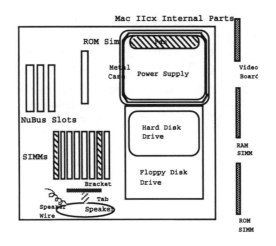

Figure 11. Indicating Removed Elements

too restrictive.[8] Students' creativity is stifled since any variation from the prestored plans results in the student being notified that they have deviated from known Apple recommended repair procedures. Any novel approach to solving a particular problem developed by a student would, thus, be challenged. An extension to plan tracking that tolerates novel actions is crucial to encourage originality. The concept of novel plan tracking is elaborated further in Goodman and Litman [1992] and Cohen et al. [1991].

---

[8]While we knew this before we implemented Visual Repair, we went ahead anyway since our research goal was to investigate the generation and coordination of multimedia explanations. However, if one is to implement our component for use directly in a fielded training system, a more robust plan representation technique, such as Kautz's graph-based approach [Kautz 1987; Goodman and Litman 1992] could be employed. In a graph-based approach, a library of plan schemas would be used to represent the knowledge of typical student plans for repair. Knowledge of plan schemas is represented as a plan hierarchy composed of two interrelated hierarchies: an abstraction hierarchy and a decomposition hierarchy.

7. Conclusions

Multimedia explanations can reinforce learning experience provided through intelligent training systems since they are more efficient and more effective than standard explanations. Visual Repair demonstrates the potential increased clarity afforded students through such explanations. They go beyond the standard canned text or prerecorded video explanations typically found in intelligent training systems. Multimedia explanations generated on the fly have the ability to provide much more relevant information to students than could have been anticipated during courseware authoring. They engage students, involving them directly in the learning experience, while addressing each student's particular needs by tailoring the content to both the student and the context.

8. Acknowledgments

I wish to acknowledge Kimberly Warren, Mark Maybury, and the anonymous reviewers for their helpful comments on drafts of this paper.

Intelligent Multimedia Interfaces

The chapters in this section focus on intelligent multimedia interfaces–interactive systems that exploit dialogue context to make presentation decisions or to interpret multi-channel input. In the first chapter of this section, John Burger and Ralph Marshall describe investigations into providing multimedia dialogue with expert systems, driven in part by their experience with typed natural language interfaces that failed to take into consideration all interactions between systems and users (e.g., deictic references to windows or items on the screen). Further, they found that different users would prefer different types of input mechanisms (e.g., menus versus types of natural language) and so generation of displays to facilitate alternative forms of input was important. The chapter describes AIMI (An Intelligent Multimedia Interface), a generalization of the KING-KONG portable natural language interface and exemplifies AIMI in action, interpreting multimedia input and automatically-tailoring multimedia output. The chapter describes influences on presentation design (e.g., content and size of the message, its purpose, the available means of communication). An interesting aspect of AIMI is that unlike previous systems in which deictic references were built into the grammar (e.g., [Neal et al. 1989]), one canonical form is used to represent both multimedia input and output (e.g., typed input, menu selection, and mouse clicks are translated into a common KL-ONE representation). Further, an explicit model of user attention and intention is acquired, represented, and exploited as the interaction proceeds.

In the second chapter, Oliviero Stock describes the ALFRESCO interactive system which investigates combining natural language processing and hypermedia in a domain of 14th Century Italian frescoes. This synergistic combination both helps avoid well-known disorientation and cognitive overload associated with large hypermedia networks, and also helps overcome the difficulty of using language to access unstructured, heterogeneous information. In ALFRESCO, users can ask questions in Italian, including making deictic reference in natural language and pointing to images on the screen (e.g., "Who is this person?"). Upon output, the system displays images and generated text with buttons that allow further interaction. A user model represents the interests of a user over the course of an interaction using an activation/inhibition network whose nodes one associates with ordered sets of individuals concepts.

The third chapter by Suhayya Abu-Hakima, Mike Halasz, and Sieu Phan also addresses hypermedia, however, in support of providing context-sensitive explanations for diagnostic expert systems. Their prototype, the Jet Engine Troubleshooting Assistant (JETA), tightly couples underlying troubleshooting knowledge to various help strategies. Users pose questions and requests for clarification via menus and buttons which the associated actions are instantiated with the current context established by the state of the diagnosis. Explanations can be generated from traces of the systems diagnostic reasoning, which include associations with text, images, and graphics (e.g., diagrams, schematics). Thus, while media allocation is fixed in advance by the programmer, hypermedia explanations can be dynamically generated based on the current state of the diagnosis.

In the final chapter of this section, David Koons, Carlton Sparrell, and Kristinn Thorisson focus on the integration of speech, gesture, and gaze. In their prototypes, interpretation of input occurs after initial processing, taking advantage of information from other modes and context. For example, in one prototype if the user says "that blue square below the red triangle" and looks in the upper right quadrant of the screen and points in that direction, these individual streams co-constrain the interpretation. When the system realizes that there are multiple blue squares in that region of the map, it resolves the linguistic reference by using information from the gesture and gaze channels. The system represents individual channels at multiple levels of abstraction to facilitate integration. For example, data from the physical input device is first characterized using features of posture, orientation, and motion, similar segments of which are then grouped by rules to form more abstract structures termed "gestlets". The eye tracker categorizes input into fixations, saccades, and blinks. This information has future utility beyond input disambiguation, such as indicating interest, suggesting turn-taking in dialogue, and indicating fatigue.

Chapter 8

The Application of Natural Language Models to Intelligent Multimedia

John D. Burger and Ralph J. Marshall

Abstract

One of the features that distinguishes intelligent multimedia interfaces from more static approaches such as preconfigured hypertext, is the ability to reason about how to present information to the user and how to interpret user input in the context of the ongoing dialog between human and computer. In this chapter, we describe an intelligent multimedia interface tool, and the internal mechanisms used to support this intelligent behavior. The central idea behind this work is the extension of existing work in natural language understanding to handle multimedia conversations. By incorporating context tracking and a knowledge representation, we are able to automate many of the interface decisions without seriously limiting the scope of the interactions.

1. Why Develop an Integrated Multimedia Interface?

An earlier project at The MITRE Corporation involved augmenting the MACPLAN[1] mission planning expert system with the KING KONG[2] natural language shell. It was during that work we reached the conclusion that it was not practical to have an intelligent interface that only accounted for part of the users' interaction with the underlying

---

[1] MACPLAN is an acronym for "Military Airlift Command Planner".

[2] KING KONG is not an acronym.

system. Since KING KONG was intended solely as a natural language interface tool, we decided to adapt and extend its communication models to attack the more encompassing problem of a complete interface. This project was known as AIMI,[3] and forms the basis of the ideas we present in this chapter.

1.1.   A Brief Description of MACPLAN

MACPLAN was an expert system designed to assist human planners in the task of devising cargo transportation schedules and routes (see [Kissmeyer and Tallant 1989] for details). It included a series of graphic displays that showed the selected routes and resource flows in the current plan, and both menus and a simple ATN-based natural language interface for issuing commands. The system focused around a small set of graphic displays that supported most of the planning and data entry work.

The goal of the KING KONG integration effort, was to replace the ATN-based parser with a full-fledged dialog system which would provide a much wider range of features to the users. The most important of the capabilities provided by KING KONG were the ability to issue commands and ask questions not anticipated by the menu designers, perform anaphoric reference resolution, and handle deictic introduction of items for later reference. However, we deliberately intended the port of KING KONG to be an extension to the existing MACPLAN interface rather than a complete replacement, since many of the graphic displays were popular with the users.

Users were initially disappointed by the rather low success rate of the natural language interface, but once they understood its limitations they found the ability to use anaphoric reference and deictic reference to be a decided improvement over the previous parser. However, when the users learned to take advantage of the context mechanism, they ran into the problem that it was only tracking user actions involving the language interface. Since the graphic interface was more natural for many types of interactions, users continued to rely on it to a large extent. They were confused by the fact that selecting an item on the screen only introduced it into the dialog context in certain circumstances, and we were never able to satisfactorily explain the distinction to them.

---

[3]AIMI is an acronym for "An Intelligent Multimedia Interface". Part of this work was funded through Rome Laboratories under Air Force Contract number F19628-89-C-0001.

1.2.   Lessons Learned

The MACPLAN experience convinced us that many of the advanced context-tracking mechanisms in KING KONG are of limited practical advantage if the system does not track the entire set of interactions between the system and users. Since there didn't appear to be a good way (short of extensive modification to the existing MACPLAN interface code) to improve the communication between the two systems, we concluded that the proper solution was to build an interface tool that could accommodate *all* of the necessary communication channels. By extending the internal dialog support tools of KING KONG to a complete multimedia interface system we were able to develop a seamless interface that was cognizant of all the activities performed by the user and could respond appropriately in a much wider range of situations.

Another important conclusion we reached during the MACPLAN work is that most casual computer users (especially those who do not touch-type) would much rather select from a limited set of menu options than have to enter a long command in text, even if the natural language system does an excellent job of interpreting their sentences. This reinforced the need for an interface tool that is not restricted to producing static displays, but rather one that is able to generate responses that can form the basis for follow-up queries or commands.

1.3.   A Brief Description of AIMI

Rooted in the work discussed above, AIMI'S project goals were to develop a portable intelligent multimedia/multimodal interface. By *portable*, we mean that much of the processing done by the system is independent of any particular back end system. The intent was to be able to connect AIMI to a new back end with minimum effort. (We use the phrases *front end* and *back end* to distinguish the interface from the underlying system with which the user wishes to interact.) AIMI reasons in detail about the meaning of user input, using a number of AI approaches discussed below. Similarly, when presenting information to the user, the system is able to intelligently choose among the presentation alternatives available to it and then design the most appropriate presentation. Currently, AIMI'S repertoire of modalities includes natural language, maps, mouse gestures, business charts, specialized interactive inspectors, still images, and non-speech audio.

Despite the existence of multiple communication modalities, AIMI deals with the meaning of input and output without respect to any particular modality. This is because many of the mechanisms developed for the KING KONG system have been generalized to allow for the intelligent processing of communication in general, regardless of the medium of the communication. Some of these mechanisms include a meaning representation component, an intentional context model that tracks the user's goals, and an attentional context model that tracks the entities introduced into the mutual focus of attention of the user and the interface. As we shall see, these mechanisms, as well as the presentation planning components of the system, do most of their reasoning at a level that is removed from the domain of the back end and the mode of input or output. This allows new input and output capabilities to be more easily added to the system. In addition, the interface front end can be more easily ported among different back end systems.

2. What We Mean by Knowledge Representation

As discussed above, many of the mechanisms of an intelligent interface can benefit from a rich and explicit representation of knowledge, including a system's representation of input and output. For example, in AIMI, at the heart of the representation machinery, there is a terminological reasoner that stores predicate subsumption hierarchies, as in KL-ONE (see Brachman and Schmolze [1985]). The information in these hierarchies can be used in virtually every processing step that is performed on input and output, from understanding the input, to discourse processing, evaluation and the selection of how to present the response.

The meanings of input and output events can be encoded as expressions in a sorted first-order language (with generalized quantifiers) whose predicates are drawn from the terms in the subsumption hierarchy. For example, the English sentence "London is reachable with what all-weather aircraft from airports in Scotland?" is represented in AIMI by the following expression:

```
(WH x (LAMBDA y
          (AND  (AIRCRAFT y)
                (AC-TYPE y All-Weather)))
       (EXISTS z (LAMBDA w
                    (AND  (AIRPORT w)
                          (AIRPORT-IN-COUNTRY w Scotland)))
          (REACHABLE London x z)))
```

In this example, the LAMBDA-terms are sorts, *à la* λ-abstraction, and WH is a generalized quantifier that is used to encode the meanings of Wh-terms such as "what" and "where" (see Bayer and Vilain [1991]). Again, the predicates in this expression, for instance AIRCRAFT and REACHABLE, correspond to terms in the knowledge representation's subsumption hierarchies. Examples of related approaches include such systems as KRYPTON, BACK, and KL-TWO [Brachman et al. 1985; van Luck et al. 1987; Vilain 1985]. Many kinds of knowledge are represented in AIMI using this logical language, including the system's model of the user's goals. Most of the system's reasoning is done at the level of expressions in this language, and is thus independent of the medium of the original input.

Given a meaning language such as that just described, a system can make use of a planner to determine how to accomplish goals expressed in the meaning language. This combination allows for a strong distinction between what to do and how to accomplish it. This enables a system to be more sensitive to factors external to a user's actual commands, and accomplish a given command in different ways, depending on such things as the user's implicit goals, the status of the display, the system's display capabilities, and other external information. Similarly, a system may satisfy its own goals in different ways. For example, when an anomalous situation occurs, a system may choose between a warning dialog box and an audio indication such as a siren.

Another useful feature of an explicit knowledge representation and a meaning language, is that it allows for an appropriate level of communication between sub-modules in an interface. This is especially useful when incorporating an existing interface component into a larger interface, for example, a self-contained map display system. The connection between the existing component and the rest of the interface can be in the high-level terms of the knowledge representation.

Finally, a rich and explicit meaning representation language allows more easily for "self referentiality", that is, for the user and the interface itself to refer to the artifacts of their interactions, such as graphical presentations. Such a capability is described in more detail in section 6.

3.   Knowledge Representation and Intelligent Interfaces

In order to effectively separate the user interface from the application, there must be methods for interpreting input and generating output that are not specific to the domain of the application. One convenient way to achieve this separation is to develop general purpose reasoning mechanisms for communication that extract the necessary domain-specific information from an instantiated knowledge representation. We feel that the style of knowledge representation outlined in Section 2 is suitable for organizing the information needed to generate both text and graphics. Using a single data source in this fashion helps to ensure that communication is consistent across modes and also enables the interface to select the most appropriate mode with fewer constraints on what can be said or understood.

3.1. Knowledge-Based Presentation Planning

A reasonable amount of research has been done on the problem of automating the design of information graphics, which is one requirement of a system like AIMI. Most of these approaches (see [Roth and Mattis 1990a] for one example) require a taxonomy of data types used by the system so that the design module can make decisions about appropriate ways to display a given set of data. While one can always build such a taxonomy into the system, using an existing knowledge representation that supports inheritance computations and automatic classification of data points eliminates the need for a separate component.

While a complete description of the methods for generating automatic displays is beyond the scope of this chapter, a brief description of one popular approach will serve to demonstrate the benefit of having a knowledge representation (and optionally an associated natural language component).

The basic notion behind automatic design of charts is that there is a generally accepted syntax and semantics of graphical displays that people rely on in order to decode a given presentation. For example, the syntactic restrictions on bar charts require that all of the bars have the same scale and baseline, and that the height (or length) of the bar is used to represent differing values for corresponding items. Finding a valid interpretation of these charts requires that we agree on the semantics of the bars as well. The height should correspond in a direct fashion to the value represented, and the value should be some measurement of amount. For example, a bar chart that attempts to represent the starting dates of events is semantically invalid because dates are points in time, not amounts. On the other hand, lengths of events are amounts and thus can be represented with bars. See Roth and Hefley [this volume] for a more comprehensive introduction to the issues of automatic graphic design.

While the specific requirements of a given automated designer will vary, most will need to ask questions about the data such as:

- Is this field quantitative or qualitative?
- Is there any natural ordering among the data points?
- Are any data points missing or unknown?
- How are data points from this set to be labeled?

Questions like these can be supported by the knowledge representation mechanisms used by AIMI, making it easy to include such a design component in the system without extensive modifications.

Another important use of a type taxonomy is the ability to store domain-specific information about preferred display methods. For example, if a system processes information about various countries, it may be desirable to attach an icon representing the flag of a given nation to the corresponding node in the taxonomy. When a presentation that includes a list of countries is being planned, the design can make use of the icons as appropriate. While the specific icon, color, or pattern to be associated with a data type is not something the presentation module should have built into it, the general knowledge that some data sets will be able to provide such information can be used to generate more effective graphics.

It should be noted that the requirements of presentation design at this level do not require the services of a full-blown knowledge representation. A more restricted taxonomy that simply classifies the data sets and provides a place to attach additional type-specific information is sufficient. Thus, the advantages of automatic presentation design can still be had even if the system has no other need for the sort of knowledge representation advocated here.

3.2. The Added Value of a Natural Language Generator

While we have just seen that an integrated knowledge representation can be used to support the generation of multimedia displays at run time, the quality of those displays can be further enhanced by the presence of an associated natural language generation facility. Labels need to be generated for the data points, chart axes, legends, and so on, and the resulting displays will be vastly improved by the use of natural language rather than computer-generated code words.

There are two broad types of text generation that will benefit the user: simple label generation, and full-text description. Generating reasonable names and labels for various chart elements can be done by associating a name generator with various concepts in the knowledge representation hierarchy. This will allow the chart to contain labels such as **Imogen Cunningham** rather than **Person-32**—an obvious improvement that does not require a large investment in additional code.

A more complete natural language generator can provide several additional levels of functionality. Presenting answers in text is often the most appropriate mode of communication. Such answers can also be communicated in speech if the system decides that it is the best channel under the circumstances. If the text generation is supported by the core system (rather than produced by a black-box approach) the interface can perform appropriate reasoning and control over the output as required for a system that is a well-meshed set of communication channels and not just a collection of display modules. For a more comprehensive exposition of the use of natural language generation in multimedia interfaces, see Maybury [this volume].

4. Context Models

Many natural language systems utilize various *context models* while processing. Although such models were initially formulated for linguistic interactions, they often prove to be of sufficient generality to accommodate non-linguistic interactions as well [Neal and Shapiro 1991; Wahlster 1991; Burger and Marshall 1991]. The notion of a *discourse* is central to such systems, and underlies much of the intelligent assistance that they are able to provide to their users. Discourse is broadly construed as the sequence of interactions, be they linguistic, graphic, or gestural, between a system and its user. By contextualizing the user's input and the system's output in the light of earlier interactions, a wide range of cooperative behavior can be provided that is focused on the task the user is trying to accomplish.

Many approaches to modeling this sort of discourse are based on the work of Grosz and Sidner [1986]. For purposes of this discussion, their model attempts to capture the interrelations between the discourse's *intention* structure, which models the respective goals of the discourse participants, and the *attentional* structure, which reflects the foci of the participants' attention.

Each of the interactions between the user and the back end system is associated with an intention (roughly, a goal) that the user and the back end system share. Each intention is represented as a logical expression in the sort of meaning representation language described in section 2. The relationships among intentions are also represented, for example, subgoal/supergoal. In addition, a context model must represent the attentional state of a discourse. Such a representation can be composed of a number of focus spaces (as described in Grosz and Sidner [1986]), each containing representations of the entities introduced explicitly during a particular segment of a discourse, or that become salient while interactions in that segment are produced or interpreted. Each focus space is associated with a particular intention; since it consists of the entities introduced by the utterances associated with that intention, a focus space contains only entities that are salient in the context of a particular goal.

An interface's intentional model can be used to disambiguate user input, and to understand *why* a user is doing something. An intention model as described here relies on the assumption that each interaction in a discourse is to be understood as contributing, directly or indirectly, to the satisfaction of a particular intention. Thus, an important part of discourse processing is the *recognition* of the intention motivating a particular utterance. We will not describe methods for accomplishing such recognition, but a number of algorithms exist.[4] Using this recognition of the goals underlying a user's input, an interface can engage in a number of cooperative behaviors, including disambiguating the input, providing information other than that directly requested (see [Schaffer Sider and Burger 1992]), and warning the user if her underlying assumptions are incorrect (see Schaffer Sider [1990]).

Maintaining the interface's attentional model involves identifying those entities that have been introduced into the discourse by each interaction, and adding them to the internal focus spaces appropriately. Simple models may merely keep a global focus space ordered by recency [Neal and Shapiro 1991], while others may segment the focus space, often in terms of the intentional state of the discourse (for example, [Schaffer Sider and Burger 1992]). Information from the attentional model is often used in natural language systems to resolve referring expressions, and this translates quite straightforwardly to the incorporation of deictic gestures. For example, in a mixed modality interface, a user

---

[4]See, for example, Carberry [1988], Kautz [1987], or Schaffer Sider and Burger [1992].

may point to items with a mouse, such as a city on a map, and then refer to them with natural language: "Send the plane there." This is a more general approach than those that incorporate the pointing gesture into the natural language grammar [Neal and Shapiro 1991], as it allows pointing gestures to be used in conjunction with other modalities, such as menu selections. Thus the user could point to the city, and then select the **Destination** command from a menu.[5]

Natural language systems often also use the attentional model when generating output to decide when to use referring expressions. Again, this notion translates to multimodal output quite straightforwardly. If an interface knows that a particular city has previously been displayed on a map, and later output refers to that city again, the system may merely be able to highlight the city, rather than generate new output. This often leads to smoother and less disjointed interactions between the user and the system.

Later, we shall describe other instances of the usefulness of context models such as these in interfaces without natural language.

5. Reasoning About the Dialog

One of the things necessary for an *intelligent* multimedia interface is the ability to determine how to communicate with the user at any given point in time. A number of factors should influence that decision:

- What is to be communicated?
- How much is to be said?
- Is this a question or a response, and should it be available for follow-up?
- What do we expect the user to do as a result of receiving this message?
- What communications channels are available?
- Which channels does the user prefer?

---

[5]For greater detail on the use of deictic gestures in both input and output, see Wahlster [1991].

• What modes of communication have we been using so far?

While taking full account of each of the above points is well beyond the scope of existing artificial intelligence technology, there are limited ways for the answers to each of the above questions to influence the choice we make. We will expand on the reasoning applied to each of these questions in the following sections.

5.1.   Content of the Message

The range of interesting communication that can occur between the user and a system is primarily determined by the area of expertise of the underlying application. We make the strong assumption that computing the answer, including any attendant data reduction or amplification, is the responsibility of the back end system. While the interface should provide facilities that make it easy for the user to ask follow-up questions or to request a modified version of the answer, we have made no attempt to do any such data analysis in the front end. This philosophy can be contrasted with the tighter integration between presentation and domain knowledge found in systems such as TEXPLAN (see Maybury [this volume]).

In many systems, the format of the response that is generated is either completely determined by the question or the user is required to specify it as part of the initial query. Since one main purpose of an intelligent interface is to support relatively unstructured dialog while assuming much of the burden of selecting appropriate methods of presentation, having the ability to generate responses based on the *answer* as well as the *question* is essential.

5.2.   Purpose of the Message

While the general guidelines for determining how the purpose should influence the form are easy to derive, applying them appropriately in different conversational contexts is important. Consider the following cases:

Yes/no response: This answer is probably going to be transitory, and most communication channels will be able to convey it effectively. Thus, printing "Yes" in response to a typed question or having the system generate a euphonious sound in response to mouse input are typically the best choices. Note that even here the input mode is important for determining how to respond.

Detailed listing of facts: As the size and level of complexity of the message increase, certain communications channels will be more or less able to convey a response effectively. Selecting the appropriate channel (audio for rapidly changing non-quantitative information, graphics for more static information) can best be done by weighing what the user is currently doing against the absolute best mode of conveying this particular answer.

Request for data entry: This may range from asking the user to select a file name to filling in a large set of values in a form. Here the method of eliciting the answer may consist of presenting a list of possible choices (if only a few responses are valid), providing a graphical presentation that allows the user to browse a directory structure, or presenting a blank input window for typing in a name. However, since the user must eventually provide a response, the format of the question should assist the user in specifying the answer. This means that linear, computer-driven methods (such as telephone menus) should be avoided if possible.

Alarm: Here the system needs to weigh the importance of the alarm, any other alarms that may also be active at the moment, and the probable focus of attention of the user. A well-known example concerns the problem of alerting airplane pilots to dangerous situations—if too many alarms are sounding simultaneously no real communication is possible. Also, if the user of a multi-screen display has been recently providing input to a particular screen the visual alarms should obviously appear on that device, and possibly move when the system detects that the user is focusing on another display. This ability can be greatly aided by the attentional context tracking mechanisms described in section 4.

5.3. Available Means of Communication

Clearly, the way a given message will be conveyed to the user depends heavily on the physical means at the system's disposal. While this is an obvious point, it means that the system must make its decisions in a manner that does not rely on knowing the choices in advance. The available hardware may change from user to user, session to session, or even within a session if equipment is subject to faults and subsequent repairs. Also, the system should make an effort to check the suitability of each available channel for the current audience. By marking some channels as inappropriate or less effective the system can accommodate handicapped users to a limited extent without a radical modification.

5.4.　Tailoring the Message to the Intended Recipient

While accommodating physical limitations of a particular user is important, in general, we want to try to adapt to the preferences of the user in more subtle ways as well. For example, if a given user is a slow typist, we would want to downgrade input choices that require extensive typing and thus tend to prefer more mouse- or voice-based methods. However, since these are merely preferences and not simple on/off switches, the system will still decide to prompt the user for typed input if the amount of information expected is large or if it is otherwise impractical to elicit it through other means. While it is possible to consider deriving these preference settings automatically by monitoring the user, there is no need for a complicated user preference learning subsystem in order to offer this level of customization.

5.5.　Maintaining the Flow of the Conversation

One of the problems with using the preceding criteria as the sole means of choosing how to express each new utterance is that a conversation composed of apparently randomly selected types of communication is quite disorienting. If the user is currently selecting items from a menu, any response or request for further input should weigh the fact that the user is currently looking at a given screen and holding the mouse, thus hopefully avoiding generating text on a distant window. Also, since the user is not simply engaging in isolated acts of communication, we want each response to contain as many possible ways for the user to select part of it for further detail, amplification, or otherwise use it to continue the discourse. Having a discourse model that tells us what goals the user is currently pursuing allows us to compare the advantage of these sorts of active responses with the potential benefits of more passive but also more appropriate methods of response.

6.　The Interface as a Domain

An important goal of intelligent interface design ought to be to create a unified presentation to the user of the information known to the system. This includes the information relevant to the interface itself, as well as the domain of the underlying system. When using an interface, users should usually not see two entities, the interface and the back end. They should see one unified entity. Accordingly, it should be as easy for the user to ask Which graphs display aircraft speeds?" as it is to ask "What is the speed of each aircraft?" A properly designed user interface should be well-integrated with the underlying domain, and thus can be the target of questions and operations in much the same way as the back end system. This follows from the philosophy that user interfaces are not ends in themselves; rather they exist to facilitate the work of the user on the tasks that he *really* needs to accomplish. Since that work usually involves significant operations on the interface objects, those manipulations should benefit from the strengths of the interface.

Accordingly, interface objects should be first-class citizens in the knowledge representation described in section 2. Windows, graphs, images; all of these should be available for discussion by the user. In particular, when information is presented to the user, the means of presentation can be introduced into the discourse model. Thus, if the user asks "How much does each employee earn?" and the answer is presented in a bar chart, the user can then say "Print that chart".

A recent trend in interface design is to decouple the interface from the back end system (for example, Foley et al. [1988] and Weicha and Boies [1990]). This is done for purposes of modularity, so that large changes in the back end do not necessitate large changes to the interface. This is quite appropriate, but, unfortunately, often results in the artificial distinction between the front and back end discussed above. We feel that the use of a declarative knowledge representation to model the back end *and* the interface gives the system the necessary modularity and also results in a more integrated product.

7. Examples

7.1. A Multimedia Dialog

The following example dialog is taken from a user's interaction with a back end mission planning system via the AIMI interface. It is a real example of AIMI's capabilities, and illustrates many of the issues of interface design we have discussed above..

At this point in the dialog, the user has already indicated that she wants to plan a mission from Alconbury to Oceana. AIMI has responded by presenting two views of the mission. One is a detailed, form-based "inspector" that we will not deal with here. The other representation of the unfolding mission is displayed on a simple cartographic system, as shown in Figure 1, and comprises the two endpoints of the mission, labeled, with an arrow drawn between them. In this example, bracketed text describes an action by the user or system, while unbracketed text is natural language input and output.

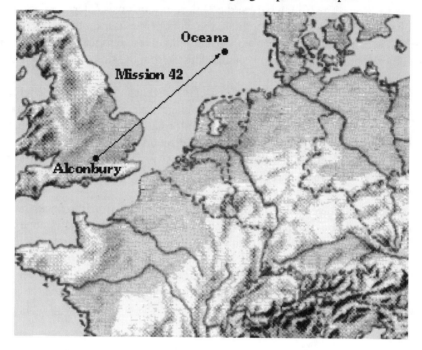

Figure 1. AIMI's Cartographic Representation of the Mission

What AC Are Appro... Text Print Kill		
F4C	F4D	F4E
F4G	F111E	F111F
F-15	F-15E	F-16

Figure 2. A "Flat List"

User: What AC are appropriate for the mission?

System: [A "flat list", or menu-like window, appears, displaying the names of several aircraft—see Figure 2]

User: [Clicks on F-4C in the flat list] What is its speed?

System: An F-4C has a speed of 260 meters-per-second

No F-4Cs are stationed at Alconbury

User: What are the speeds of the planes?

System: [Displays a bar chart—See Figure 3]

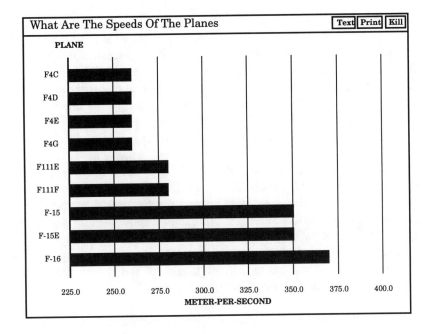

Figure 3. A Bar Chart

User: [Clicks on **Text** button of bar chart]

System: An F-4C has a speed of 260 meters-per-second, an F-4D has a speed of 260 meters-per-second, an F-4G has a speed of 260 meters-per-second, an F-4E has a speed of 260 meters-per-second, an F-111E has a speed of 280 meters-per-second, an F-111F has a speed of 280 meters-per-second, an F-15 has a speed of 350 meters-per-second, an F-15E has a speed of 350 meters-per-second and an F-16 has a speed of 370 meters-per-second

User: Print the chart

System:	[Prints a hardcopy of the bar chart]
User:	What bases have F-16s?
System:	[Adds and highlights three bases on the map—See Figure 4][6]
User:	[Drags the mission endpoint to one of the three highlighted airbases]
System:	Düsseldorf is the source of Mission 42

7.2. Commentary

A number of features are demonstrated by the previous example. One thing that should be made clear is that, although the "flat list" of Figure 2 appears to be a menu, clicking on one of the items does not do anything but introduce the corresponding entity into the discourse. All of the textual items in the charts generated by AIMI are similarly mouse-able, including the labels on the bar chart (Figure 3). After the user introduces an entity into context, the system resolves later references to it using the attentional context mechanisms described in section 4. This ability allows the user to more naturally integrate gestural and textual input, as in the question "What is its speed?" The system resolves references such as "the mission" and "the planes" in the same way.

After the system answers that question, it gives the user some additional information: "No F-4Cs are stationed at Alconbury". This unsolicited output is called a *cooperative response*. The system uses the intentional context mechanisms described in section 4 (and in further detail by Schaffer Sider [1990]) to reason about the user's goals in asking the question. This allows the system to infer that the user is considering using F-4Cs in the mission being planned. However, a necessary condition of this goal is violated, namely that the chosen airbase has the aircraft available. The system decides to inform the user of this problem using a natural language utterance.[7]

Note that the direct answer to the question "What is its speed?" could have been presented as a bar chart, just as were the nine aircraft speeds in the following exchange. Of

---

[6]When AIMI highlights graphic objects such as the three airbases, the system blinks them briefly.

[7]In point of fact, AIMI always uses natural language when giving the user unsolicited information (except for alarms). Presenting a graphical representation of such information was deemed to be too likely to be disorienting.

Figure 4. Highlighting Airbases, and Changing the Source of the Mission

course, AIMI's knowledge about graphical design tells it that a bar chart with only one bar is a very poor chart indeed. However, without the ability to generate natural language output, the system would have been forced to generate just such a chart.

Correspondingly, the set of nine aircraft speeds could have been realized as natural language. AIMI examined this presentation alternative when answering the original question, and determined that the bar chart was a more perspicuous realization than text (the reader will presumably agree). However, when the user clicks on the **Text** button of the bar chart, the system is forced to re-realize the underlying information as text. As well as being able to force the system to generate text output, the user ought to be able to choose various other graphic alternatives as well (a table, for example).

Just as the **Text** button forces the system to re-realize the information as text, rather than a bar chart, so the command to "Print that chart" causes the system to re-realize the information on a printer.[8] In this case, the type of graphic remains the same, a bar chart, but the device changes, from a color monitor to a black-and-white printer. The system actually re-designs the bar chart in this case, as the display capabilities of these two devices may be different, and re-renders it as POSTSCRIPT code. Also note that the user is able to refer to artifacts of the discourse with natural language, in this case "that chart". As discussed in Section 6, graphic presentations are introduced into the discourse just as are domain entities such as "the planes".

The system's use of the map to answer the question about airbases (Figure 4) is a good example of how a knowledge representation can aid response generation. Here, the system had at least three alternatives to choose from: text, a flat list, as in Figure 2, and the map. The latter was not an alternative for the information in Figure 2, because AIMI's knowledge representation informed it that the aircraft were not cartographic entities. The airbases are, of course, and the system's design knowledge was used to determine that a cartographic representation was to be preferred to a flat list, while text is usually used only as a last resort.

When the user drags the mission endpoint in Figure 4, she is able to take advantage of the fact that most of AIMI's presentations are designed to be interactive. When possible, changes in the graphical realization of information made by the user are translated into changes to the underlying information. Of course, when taken to its extreme, this would allow the user to stretch the bars in Figure 3, thus altering the speeds of the aircraft stored in the underlying database. Currently, such interactions are not allowed.

7.3.   Tailoring the Response to the Situation

As noted above, there are a number of factors that must be considered by the system when deciding how to convey a given piece of information. This section shows two examples of how the format of the response can differ depending on the anticipated use.

---

[8]Clicking on the **Print** button has exactly the same meaning.

These examples are taken from a travel reservation information system. While this domain has not actually been modeled by AIMI, the decisions and resulting graphs are representative of the processing actually performed by the system. We assume that the intentional model for this domain includes (at least) two distinct high-level goals: selecting a particular train for travel between New York and Washington, D.C., and maintaining the database of travel schedules.

When Do Trains ... Text Print Kill	
New York	Washington
8:00 am	**10:59 am**
8:20 am	11:41 am
9:00 am	**11:59 am**
9:40 am	12:35 pm
10:00 am	**12:55 pm**
11:00 am	**1:55 pm**
11:20 am	2:49 pm
Noon	**2:55 pm**
Bold MetroLiner Service Roman Normal Service	

Figure 5. The Answer as a Table

Figure 5 shows one possible response to the question "When do trains leave from New York for Washington?" Since the node corresponding to "database maintenance" in the intention model has been marked as favoring exact information over the ability to perceive trends or make comparisons, the system has decided to present the response in a table. This makes it easy to check the times for correctness, something that would be difficult or impossible with a more graphical response.

Note that if this response were being generated on a screen, most of the items in the table could be mouse-sensitive, allowing the user to continue the dialog from this point. For example, since the user is understood to be maintaining the database rather than using it to make a reservation, mousing on one of the times would most likely indicate that it should be changed. Thus, in this context the system's response to the mouse click would be to post the goal of allowing the user to modify the value. Similarly, clicking on one of the city names could allow the user to enter a new city, effectively asking the same question about a different pair of cities. It is because the system knows what it is presenting, and what question it is answering, that it can support follow-up interactions of this sort.

However, the system is also capable of generating a noticeably different type of response to the same question asked in a different context. If the intentional mechanism has concluded that the user is trying to select a particular train for making reservations, AIMI could present an interval bar chart (Figure 6) indicating when each train leaves and arrives. This would allow the user to base the selection on preferred time of travel, length of trip, or price (since MetroLiner service is more expensive than standard coach seating).

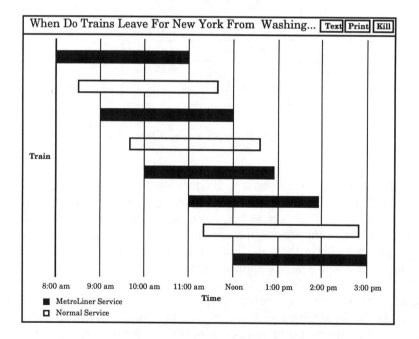

Figure 6. The Answer as a Bar Chart

The important point here is that the system does not have a single response that it generates for a given type of question, and it does not necessarily use the same format even if the same question is asked in two different settings. The extra levels of reasoning that are performed by the system independent of the particular domain allow us to provide this flexibility without having to tailor the machinery to each new domain. We believe that this capability is a strong indication of the need for knowledge-based infrastructure in multimedia interfaces.

8. Conclusion

In this chapter we have presented our vision of a system that can support an integrated multimedia dialog between computer and human. We feel that these interactions are similar in many respects to the text dialogs that have been the focus of linguistic study over a long period of time, and that we should thus adapt results from that field to this more general problem.

Building the reasoning machinery of the interface around a knowledge representation and the associated planning and context tracking mechanisms allows us to achieve many of the same results in multimedia that are already common in natural language systems. We are able to convert input in various surface forms (typed text, menu selections, and mouse clicks) into a canonical form that can be processed without becoming bogged down in the specifics of the original communication. This facility also allows us to generate responses and goals in the same abstract form, and then present them via any of the available and appropriate output methods.

Not only does this distinction between surface form and internal semantics allow us to multiplex the various communications channels, but it provides a modular system that can incorporate new methods of interaction simply by adding the appropriate tools to transform between their raw, mode-specific data and the actual information content. Since each such module is responsible for this transformation, there is no need to devise a monolithic interpretation and response planning scheme; each module is free to use whatever approaches are best suited.

Tracking the complete conversation is important, not only to provide a more consistent view to the user, but also because it allows us to use intentional context models to derive some insight into what the user appears to be doing at a given moment. This information, even at a coarse level of refinement, can be used to help select appropriate means of response without requiring that the user explicitly indicate what "mode" they are in.

Finally, we feel that the ability to model the interface itself is an important contribution of our method. By removing the distinction between the underlying application and the interface at this level we can greatly improve the user's ability to accomplish the job at hand.

While we would like to have had more opportunity to refine the specifics of this system, we were able to accomplish enough to convince ourselves that this is a viable approach to managing the complexity of an intelligent multimedia interface. It is clear that it would be unwise to ignore the long history of investigation into what constitutes effective communication merely because color graphics have been added to an interface.

Chapter 9

ALFRESCO:
Enjoying the Combination of Natural Language Processing and Hypermedia for Information Exploration

Oliviero Stock and the ALFRESCO Project Team[1]

Abstract

This chapter describes an investigation into the integration of natural language and hypermedia interfaces. This approach overcomes many of the limitations of these two types of interfaces when used in isolation (e.g., lack of coverage in natural language systems or the danger of disorientation in hypermedia interfaces) by providing complementary functionality (e.g., the ability to specify queries in natural language while at the same time utilizing hypertext to organize highly-heterogeneous and unstructured information.) This chapter describes the ALFRESCO interactive system [Stock 1991], a prototype built for accessing images and information about Fourteenth-Century Italian frescoes.

1. Introduction

Integration of natural language with other communicative modalities has a number of different motivations. One is that there are things that in absolute terms, "in nature," humans best communicate and understand if transmitted non linguistically. This is the

---

[1]The current and previous members of the ALFRESCO Project Team include: G. Carenini, F. Cecconi, E. Franconi, A. Lavelli, B. Magnini, F. Pianesi, M. Ponzi, V. Samek-Lodovici, C. Strapparava.

case for the analogical information we give when we transmit spatial information through maps, or through the act of pointing for indicating a direction. It would be nice to reproduce automatically our capacity for exploiting and choosing among different modalities, including providing graphics (maps, diagrams, etc.).

Another motivation is that the research community has recognized that unsolved problems in natural language processing (NLP), hinder delivering a sufficiently sophisticated system that can be realistically offered as the basis for complex real-world interfaces with computers. We should therefore, integrate NLP with other well developed techniques, so that problems for the language processing component can be circumscribed and solved in practical terms, while other technology helps the rest. In a way this happens with various kinds of menu driven systems integrated with NLP.

Yet another motivation is that computers embody a potential that goes beyond communication as we know it in human-human interaction, but that still seems to be cognitively realisable; this potential relies on the technological possibility of navigating a rich information space with rapid interleaving of different information and different media, and on the high-level integration of the different communication modalities. The role of language seems to be central even here but in a novel way (see also [Stock 1992]).

All these different motivations share the view that the so-called teletype approach is too narrow for NLP applications and envision a larger bandwidth of communication.

In recent years, there have been various projects sharing all or part of the above motivations and the chapters in this book give an excellent overview of the problems in designing an integrated multimedia system and of the proposed solutions. A central problem concerns the integration, in the system output, of text generation with forms of graphics. For instance, the combination of analogical images and text has been developed in several systems, notably in COMET [Feiner and McKeown, this volume], where the role of a coordinator that has to negotiate with the different mode specialists is emphasized. Particularly interesting is the case in which instructions are given so that temporal relations among actions are specified in a multimedia format [Feiner et al., this volume].

In the WIP system [André et al., this volume], concerned with the presentation of information for the use of a technical device, the multimodal system starts from a formal representation of the system's goal (for instance the mutual belief between system and audience that the system has the goal of a certain action being performed by the audience) as defined by the back-end application. This is common to other generation systems, then here the main question is how best to decompose this goal into subgoals to be realized by the mode-specific generators [André and Rist, this volume] so that they can complement each other. The interesting consequence is that semantic and pragmatic concepts such as coherence, focus, communicative act, implicature, discourse model, reference etc. acquire an extended meaning. An analogical representation of the technical device is also produced from an internal format. Another relevant aspect of the project concerns the capacity for incremental generation, i.e., of starting to realize output even when only part of the information to be conveyed is available.

One of the main problems shared by different researchers is how to represent the actions that the system may perform in a coherent and flexible way so that the overall behaviour of the system can be built to realize the goals. [Maybury, this volume] offers a very interesting proposal for starting the process of presentation from a communicative act perspective. What is proposed is an extension of the classical, linguistic-oriented representation to include visual acts, and the integration of rhetorical acts. This is then used by a planning system that organizes the overall multimedia presentation. The potential of the perspective described above is very high for applications to the design of training systems [Goodman, this volume]. In particular, the coherent integration of visual dynamics (videoclips, animation) becomes crucial.

Joint planning of text and diagrams has also been addressed by using presentation rules that hold for several media at once [Arens and Hovy 1990a]. Rules are generalized to take into account the system's communicative goals, a model of the reader, features characterizing the information to be displayed, and features characterizing the media available to the system. In [Arens et al., this volume], the parameters that influence what media to use and how to combine them are analyzed in detail.

All of these aspects are of central importance for the planning of multimedia presentations. Other work emphasizes the potential bidirectionality of interaction: for instance, pointing to images on a screen may individuate the objects involved in some direct action. Systems of this type have been developed for interfacing a user with a dynamic process such as the simulation of the operations inside a factory [Cohen et al. 1989], a simulated battlefield [MacLaughlin and Shaked 1989], or the activities of U.S. Navy ships [Arens et al. 1988]. Still other research has been carried out, with the aim of putting intelligence and dynamicity into a "static" multimedia interaction pardigm (see, for instance, [Cornell et al., this volume]), sometimes specifically inspired by research developed so far in the NLP area [Burger and Marshall, this volume].

The present work has a slightly different emphasis. It is about combining NLP with "hypermedia." Hypermedia is the generalization of the idea of hypertext to multimedia or as Halasz put it, "a style of building systems for information representation and management around a network of multimedia nodes connected together by typed links" [Halasz 1988]. Hypermedia has opened interesting perspectives on the problem of accessing loosely-structured information. Hypermedia systems promote a navigational, explorative access to multimodal information: the user, browsing around the network, is simultaneously exploring the network and searching for useful information. We believe that often the user wants exactly this double capability from the system, of dealing with goal-oriented behaviour, typical of language and exploration-oriented behaviour. The most ambitious motivation of this work is of the third type specified at the beginning (amplifying natural communication potential). In addition we propose a view that makes these concepts of practical use.

In particular, this chapter describes the ALFRESCO interactive system [Stock 1991], a prototype built for accessing images and information about Italian Fourteenth Century frescoes. We believe that the approach taken here is of particular interest for access to cultural information; an area where the shift from a mass-oriented to an individual-oriented creative offering, in which the user can "find his way", is really needed.

2. Hypermedia and NLP Combined

The main reason for trying to integrate two approaches that have up to now represented independent lines of research, is that there are a number of advantages that accrue to both:

(a) From the NL perspective: a means for organizing heterogeneous and unstructured information, for favouring the direct manipulation of all objects, integrated with language, and for facilitating explorative behaviour;

(b) From the hypermedia perspective: a solution to the problems of disorientation and of the cognitive overhead of having too many links;

(c) From an unbiased point of view that looks at all of this as an independent approach: the offer of a high level of interactivity and system habitability in which each modality overcomes the constraints of the other, resulting in the whole being more than the sum of the parts.

We shall briefly discuss these points.

Many of the problems that prevent NL systems from providing useful interfaces stem from the current inability to handle the difficulties, lack of knowledge and misunderstandings that arise during dialogs. Hypermedia has the virtue of offering a powerful means for organizing highly-heterogeneous and unstructured information, a kind of knowledge not easily handled by natural language systems (and artificial intelligence (AI) systems in general). For example, in situations in which an AI application has a formal representation of only a subpart of the relevant domain knowledge, it is not possible to generate natural language text about information not explicitly represented in the system. A possible solution is the dynamic generation of hypertext (possibly hypermedia) nodes pointing to a canned hypermedia network about those areas of the domain that have not been formally represented. Direct manipulation of images, buttoned text etc., integrated with the natural language channel is a powerful concept. On the *interaction strategy* side the crucial point is to integrate an exploration modality. With this, a user finds it easy to move around, see what is available here and there, possibly follow some exploration path, without being necessarily constrained by any definite goal.

Looking at interaction from the hypermedia point of view, one of the major problems is *disorientation*, as pointed out in Conklin [1987]. Hypermedia offers more freedom, more dimensions in which to move, and hence a greater potential for the user to become lost or disoriented; the user's problem is having to know where she is and how to get to some other place that she knows (or thinks) exists in the network. A solution is the integration of a query facility within the system, providing a way of jumping inside the network without having to follow predefined paths through it. Halasz [1988] identifies two kinds of queries:

1) *Content queries* allow retrieval of all objects (nodes or links) that satisfy some requirements; and

2) *Structure queries* allow retrieval of a subnetwork matching a given pattern

NL can be the best way for handling such queries, if we assume that the system has some information about the knowledge presented by the different nodes and about the semantics of the structure of the network. But there is more to it than just adding queries to an hypertext system.

The hypertext research community has begun to acknowledge the importance of user modeling. Conklin [1987] points out that a common difficulty arising in interacting with a hypermedia system is the *cognitive overhead* caused by the number of links that may be followed from each node. It would be very useful to be able to tell which links the specific user is less likely to follow, so as to display them all (or to display them with a lower degree of relevance). User modeling has a longer history and great power in NLP, basically representing the communicative context in which a sentence is uttered [Kass and Finin 1988; Kobsa 1988]. So, for instance in generation, a text can be naturally tailored (at all levels, from the rhetorical to the lexical choices) for the intended reader, yielding an effective communicative act [Hovy 1987; Paris 1987b].

The handling of initiative shifts and of different attitudes on the side of the user is of basic importance for the improvement of human-computer interaction. When a user encounters a system that she has never used before, she is very unlikely to have a clear idea of how to formulate a problem so that the system understands it. It is also possible that the user does not have enough information about the domain to be able to produce *any* clear problem formulation. We believe that at least in typically "explorative" and "individually creative" domains, a substantial global environment habitability is of the utmost importance, and does greatly benefit from a global, even if approximate user model arising through dialog.

The combination of the relative freedom provided by a natural language interface (with the power of making complex and precise requests and answers) and a visual presentation (with direct manipulation possibility) of some organized subdomains has immense potential impact. And of course the user can interleave precise requests with concrete exploration of "the surroundings."

This last aspect requires original studies on the cognitive side (one step in this direction is [Slack and Conati 1991]), while as far as work on the evaluation of the effectiveness of different modalities is concerned, the two fields are starting to address some of the related cognitive and methodological problems (see for instance [Nielsen 1990a] on the hypermedia side and [Oviatt and Cohen 1989] and [Whittaker and Stenton 1989] on the NLP side).

It may be useful to add here some notes on discovering art and the role of computer-based systems. Hypertext systems for museums are presently quite common, but they provide a very limited possibility. The main weakness lies in what we have emphasized before: the difficulty of expressing a precise, complex request, the lack of possibility of pursuing a particular goal through conversation, etc. It is well known that even without entering in the complex and subtle world of art *understanding*, art *curiosity* develops as a function of two factors: a) the cumulative effect of information (especially information answering free requests by the person or giving some limited further hints, relevant to her inclination); b) fruition of an art work when the experiencer is prepared and antici-pates it. Art *curiosity* grows slowly and autonomously, and imposing more data or ex-periences than the person is prepared to cope with has no positive effect at all. Only by combining information and perception with a sensation of driving the game and enjoy-ing circumscribed moments of mere exploration, can a user experience the possible de-velopment of an interest in art. A typical consequence might be that one takes a trip just to go and see a painting that they saw before among others and didn't even notice. Or else, in Italy, one learns of a minor fresco in a church in a remote village and goes there because they know they will find pleasure in seeing it and, indeed, in "discovering" it.

Now, in the design of an artificial system that provides an environment for a user inter-ested in art, the same concepts must be exploited. An interesting fact is that, as far as the modality of language communication is concerned, *written* language is acceptable even if not the most desirable solution. A user interested in this domain (as opposed to a generic user of an automatic counter at a station), is likely to know how to use a key-board.

3. ALFRESCO

ALFRESCO is an interactive system for a user interested in frescoes. It is implemented in Common Lisp and Interlisp and runs on a SUN 4 connected to a videodisc unit and a touchscreen. The particular videodisc in use includes images about Fourteenth Century

Italian frescoes and monuments.[2] Natural language and hypermedia are integrated both in input and output. In input, our efforts have been focused on combining the interpretation of NL deictic references with pointing to images displayed on a touch screen. For instance, the user can ask a question such as: *"Who is this person?"* while touching the image of a person appearing in the currently displayed fresco. Both the linguistic and the graphical deixes may be ambiguous, but usually the correct integration of the information provided by the two channels allows the identification of the intended reference.

In output, the actions performed by ALFRESCO are realized exploiting the media the system is based upon: a) the system can show images, b) give some punctual answer to a question by replying with instances such as the title and location of a painting, or dates etc., or, finally, c) give a more complex description of a fresco or some other entities, through natural language (see [Carenini et al., to appear]). All three different media allow the user to interact with them by direct manipulation. A higher-level, *ad hoc*, pragmatic component decides how to react in the given discourse situation, considering the type of request, the context, the model of user's interest, the things already shown or said to the user, and so on. The system's linguistic output includes buttons that allow the user to enter a hypertext mode. The dialog may cause zooming into details or changing the focus of attention onto other frescoes. The overall aim is not only to provide information, but also to promote other masterpieces that may attract the user. ALFRESCO will eventually provide, though not presently part of it, a proposal for a cultural tour appropriate for the particular user, through further negotiation with her.

A dialog fragment (taken from a real session with ALFRESCO) oriented to requests of information follows:

> U: Vorrei sapere se Ambrogio Lorenzetti ha dipinto un'opera che raffigura una scena sacra con un angelo.
>
> *I would like to know if Ambrogio Lorenzetti ever painted a work that represents a sacred scene with an angel.*

---

[2]The videodisc "Italian Art History" was provided by Rizzoli; we take this occasion to thank them.

S: Sì. Per esempio: A. Lorenzetti, l'Annunciazione. L'angelo é l'Arcangelo Gabriele.

Yes, for example, A Lorenzetti, the annunciation. The angel is the Arcangel Gabriel.

U: Chi è questa persona? [pointing at Mary on the touch screen]

Who is this person?

S: La Madonna.

Mary.

U: Puoi mostrarmi un ingrandimento che la contiene?

Can you show me an enlargement containing her?

S: [The system shows an enlargement]

U: C'è un pittore che ha influenzato l'autore?

Was the author influenced by some other painter?

S: Sì. Per esempio da Giotto.

Yes. For example by Giotto

U: Dove vide la luce questo maestro?

Where did this master see the light? [meaning "where was he born"]

S: Colle di Vespignano.

U: C'è un'opera di Ambrogio Lorenzetti a Trento?

Is there a work by Ambrogio Lorenzetti in Trento?

S: No.

U: Un affresco di Giotto a Assisi?

A fresco by Giotto in Assisi?

S   Sì. Per esempio la Predica agli uccelli.
    Yes. For example the sermon to the birds

U: Mostrami un dettaglio con questa scena. [pointing to some place about the centre of the scene]
    Show me a detail with this scene.

S: [The system shows the detail]

U: In quale città è nato Ambrogio Lorenzetti?
    In what town was Ambrogio Lorenzetti born?

S: Siena.

U: Mostramela.
    Show it to me.

S: [the system shows a small film segment about Siena]

U: Vorrei vedere un affresco del maestro in un monumento della città.
    I would like to see a fresco of the master in a monument of the town.

S: [the system shows a video segment about a large fresco, "the Effects of Good Governement," and outputs the name with a "description" button.]

At this point the user presses that button and a generated text is issued. Clicking on buttons the user can move inside a hypertext with comments written by art critics, or see related images, or explore the network. At any point it is possible to resume the dialog.

A sketch of the ALFRESCO system architecture is shown in Figure 1 and in the following we shall give an outline of some components of the system.

3.1. Knowledge Representation in ALFRESCO

The underlying knowledge base in ALFRESCO is expressed in YAK [Franconi 1990], a descendant of Kl-One [Brachman and Schmolze 1985]. YAK is a hybrid system, whose terminological component (T-box) consists of a tangled hierarchy in which generic concepts and attributes (roles) are defined. The assertional component (A-box) consists of instances that are represented as frames connected to the terminological box by a realizer that builds in the terminological hierarchy the most specific generic concept to which the particular instance belongs. The KB is used for defining everything the system can reason about: frescoes, monuments, painters, contents of frescoes, towns, etc., and provides the base for ALFRESCO's deductive inference capabilities.

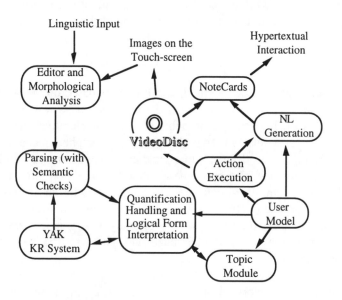

Figure 1. ALFRESCO System Architecture

In Figure 2 a view of a fragment of the ALFRESCO knowledge base is sketched.

A NoteCards hypermedia network is included in the system, containing unformalized knowledge such as art critics' opinions on the paintings and their authors. Monodirectional pointers link instances or features in the knowledge base to images and film fragments stored in the videodisc. Bidirectional pointers connect knowledge base entities to regions of images.

At this point, an explanation is due. Fourteenth Century frescoes have a content that almost always is centered on a sacred scene. The scene includes an event that can be reasonably well described (for instance the event "annunciation" performed by the angel Gabriel to Mary, where the contents of the message is another event, namely the forthcoming birth of Jesus) and includes a number of well-identified recurring characters–humans, animals, saints, angels, etc. The contents that we represent are the contents of the foreground of the paintings, while nothing is said about the background where the artist could have expressed any real world scene. In this particular context, the indexabilty of the objects and the related concept of the granularity of internal representation are quite easily made clear to the user at the beginning of the interaction.

3.2. Parser

As far as sentence analysis is concerned, ALFRESCO is based on the WEDNESDAY 2 parser (described in Stock [1989]). It is a chart-based parser [Kay 1980] that can cope with a large number of linguistic phenomena, including declarative, imperative and interrogative sentences, complex relative clauses (and other phenomena connected with so-called long-distance dependencies), idiomatic expressions, various kinds of ellipses, constituent coordination, etc. The parser bases its work largely on information stored in the lexicon. The only centralized data used by the parser – in the form of a (non-augmented) recursive transition network – deals with the distribution of constituents. One relevant capability of the parser is its ability to analyze idiomatic forms, with all the flexibility they may display in natural language. This characteristic is strictly integrated in the chart-based approach.

A morphological analyzer works on-line while the user types the sentence on the keyboard, thereby providing an immediate building of inactive lexical edges for the chart parser. If a word is mispelled, the error is signalled and either it is removed or the user enters a modality in which she can specify a new lexical entry. The editor, through which the sentence is input, provides a transparent behaviour. For instance, words can be deleted guaranteeing that the edges are reorganized accordingly. An important feature is that the user can point to the currently displayed fresco while they type the sentence, in correspondence to demonstratives.

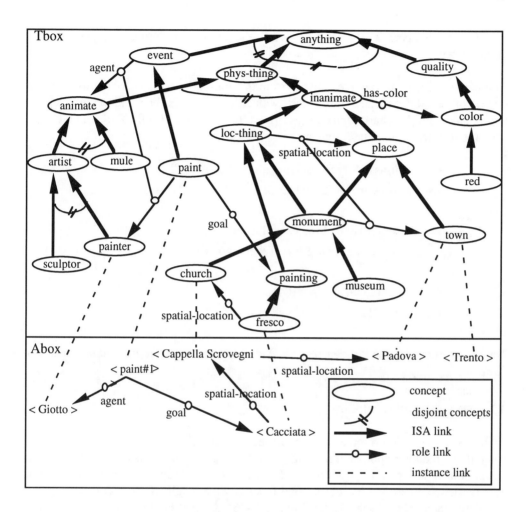

Figure 2. ALFRESCO Knowledge Base Fragment

In general, the parser *per se* would output a large number of alternative interpretations of a sentence (this is particularly unfortunate for Italian, which is a freer word-order language than English and in which even simple sentences can be ambiguous from a syntactic point-of-view). Through continuous interactions with the conceptual knowledge component via a lexical semantic analysis component, the possible functional relations are filtered. This permits a great reduction in the number of alternative representations of the sentence.

Another vital aspect for an interactive system that must allow good habitability and integration of modalities is the ability to deal with elliptical forms. The solution to this problem is built into the chart approach (see [Lavelli and Stock 1990]). For example, consider the following dialogue fragment:

> U: Giotto ritrasse S.Francesco in un'opera di Assisi?
> *Did Giotto portray St.Francis in a work located in Assisi?*

> S: Sì, ad esempio nella Predica agli uccelli.
> *Yes, for example in the Sermon to the birds.*

> U: Gioacchino in un affresco di Padova?
> *Gioacchino in a fresco located in Padova?*

The parser interprets the last sentence as *Does Giotto portray Gioacchino in a fresco in Padova?*

3.3.   Semantic Interpretation

As far as semantic interpretation is concerned, multimedia made it necessary to have a layered and modular approach. In some recently developed systems a multilevel semantics approach has been proposed in which various levels of representation, each with its own particular functionality, correspond to successive levels of abstraction of logical-linguistic phenomena [Scha 1983; Stallard 1986]. A level bound to lexical semantics (usually denoted as EFL, English formal language) can be individuated from a level of meaning representation (usually denoted as WML, world model language; see Figure 3). Meaning representation is therefore as much as possible independent from the application domain. In ALFRESCO, the interpretation modules' task is to present a meaning representation of the sentence that can be used by the various modules of the system.

The interpretative phase has several functions. In the first place it computes quantifier scopings. The algorithm is based on the concept of Cooper storage as in Hobbs and

Shieber [1987] and on: a) lexical classification of quantifiers; b) syntactic and surface order charcteristics; c) presence of disambiguating expressions. It solves definite expressions such as determinate NP's, demonstratives (for example deriving from pointing actions), and pronouns by interacting with the topic module. It interprets the sentence dynamically, exploiting the semantics of operators, quantifiers, verbal modifiers, various levels of coordination, and so on [Westerstahl 1986]. The resulting representation is intensional, i.e., it is possible to abstract it in relation to time and context. The integration with temporal and contextual interpretation modules is currently under investigation.

```
(indef x   (indef y   (and  (monument y)
                            (has-place nil y
                            (definite (town z))))
                     (and (fresco x)
                          (has-place nil x y)
                          (made-by nil x (definite (painter w)))))
          (want nil speaker (see nil nil x)))
```

Figure 3. A WML Form for
"Vorrei vedere un affresco del maestro in un monumento della città."
*(*I would like to see a fresco in a monument of the town..*)*

In our case, without passing to a DBL form (Data Base Language in Scha [1983]), WML expressions are dynamically mapped into YAK's assertional language. In the process, the topic module (see below) is called in. Translation is started, for example, when interpretation requires the extension of a certain concept or the truth value of a certain fact. For a description of the whole semantic interpretation process within the ALFRESCO system see [Strapparava 1991] and [Lavelli et al. 1992].

3.4. The Topic Module and Pointing

In a multimedia dialog system, the topic module must integrate global focus strategies [Grosz and Sidner 1986; Grosz 1977], local focus approaches [Hajicovà 1987] and deictic reference techniques [Wahlster 1991]. The main points of ALFRESCO's topic module are the following (see [Samek-Lodovici and Strapparava 1990]).

ALFRESCO basically structures discourse in turns, with confirmations of referents from previous turns into the current one. The user normally refers to entities bound to particular frescoes. So the basic idea is to combine: a) Grosz's idea of factoring the search for referents into topic-spaces [Grosz 1977]: our topic-spaces are typically built around frescoes; and b) Hajicovà's approach of allowing the entities that have been mentioned slowly fade away unless they are mentioned again with a certain functional role [Hajicovà 1987].

The system relies on two stacks: 1) a stack of turns, where each turn contains the referents inserted or confirmed by the user or by ALFRESCO, and 2) a stack of Topic Units, where each Topic Unit contains all the referents inserted by the user or by the system while discussing a particular fresco.

As far as the deictic context is concerned, in our case it changes whenever a new fresco is displayed on the screen. Similarly to XTRA [Wahlster 1991; Kobsa et al. 1986], we associate the accessible entities with the regions they occupy on the screen. Regions overlap significantly (e.g., the region of the "announcement" and the region of the angel Gabriel in Giotto's Announcement, or the region of the mule and the region of Mary in "The Flight to Egypt"), in contrast to the one-to-one mapping of previous systems between the pointed region and the intended one (e.g., [Brown et al. 1979]). As in CUBRI-CON [Neal 1990; Neal and Shapiro 1991], the ALFRESCO topic module permits both the use of linguistic input to solve ambiguous gestures and the use of gestures to solve ambiguous linguistic input. More specific, both a gesture and a linguistic expression may be ambiguous and yet yield a unique referent through mutual constraint.

3.5. The User's Interest Model

Presently, the most original part of the user model is the interest model. In ALFRESCO, in particular, interest for a given topic is assumed to be either a consequence of the activation of that topic in context (e.g., a specific request by the user) or of the anticipated exposition of the user to an art work (remember that the system includes a videodisc from where images of frescoes are retrieved). The interest model develops and becomes more focused in the course of the interaction between the user and the system.

The model consists of an activation/inhibition network whose nodes are associated with ordered sets of individual concepts. The grouping of the individuals is performed according to a measure of domain dependent pragmatic closeness; whenever a set is activated, all the entities composing it are considered to be somehow relevant. Each set represents an *interest area* and is identified by a particular individual or concept represented in YAK.

The top-level organization of the model is a set of *dimensions*. Each dimension is defined by a set of (assertional or terminological) concepts from the Knowledge base (KB). Such concepts are the heads of the interest areas associated to the dimension. An area is defined by an ordered set of A-Box individuals that are considered to be "connected" to the head of the area in the particular domain. The individuals are listed in order of decreasing relevance as interest indicators for the head concept. A dimension will typically represent a class that is particularly relevant for the current domain and its areas will be identified by (a subset of) its subclasses or individual instances. The sets associated to areas belonging to the same dimension are disjoint.

The A-Box shown in Figure 4 is structured along two dimensions: A (consisting of areas a-1, a-2, a-3, and a-4) and B (consisting of b-1, b-2 and b-3).

The areas of a particular model are all nodes of a single activation/inhibition network that connect them independently from the dimension they belong to. The links between the areas may be used to represent any kind of semantic/pragmatic proximity relevant for the domain. In the ALFRESCO system, the dimensions of the model correspond to painting schools, periods of time, and towns. We have drawn activation links between areas corresponding to towns that are geographically close, time periods that are temporally close, but also for instance between a painting school and the town in which the members of the school painted most of their works.

Each time a certain individual is designated by the user or is selected as a possible answer to a query, the areas to which that individual is associated receive an activation impulse proportional to the explicitness of the reference. Such impulses are then propagated through the network, decreasing in intensity according to the weights of the links traversed.

The current implementation supports both activation and inhibition links. In traversing an inhibition link, an activation (i.e. positive) impulse is transformed into an inhibition (negative) one. Such links should be used to connect interest areas that are mutually incompatible: they represent the fact that interest in certain topics generally implies a lack of interest for other aspects of the domain. Inhibition impulses are not propagated through inhibition links: a negative impulse at a certain node also inhibits those areas that are reachable from it through activation links; but such an impulse does not cause the activation of those areas that are reachable from that node through inhibition links.

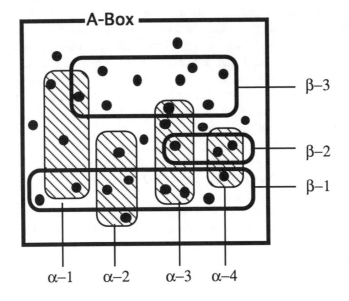

Figure 4. A-Box

For instance, if the a-3 area in the network in Figure 5 receives a positive impulse, it will propagate to a-2 and a-3; b-1 and b-3 will receive an inhibition signal that will propagate to b-2 from b-3, but not to a-1 from b-1.

In the networks we currently use, the individuals associated with a particular head, as well as their static ordering, are computed on the basis of the content of the A-Box. In general, each individual I is assigned to an area for each dimension. The area is that for which I scores the highest relevance level. Such level is computed on the basis of the number and the length of the minimal paths that connect I to the head of the area in the graph whose nodes are the individuals and whose edges are the roles of the Knowledge base. Individuals that are judged to be equally relevant for two or more areas of a dimension are not assigned to any area.

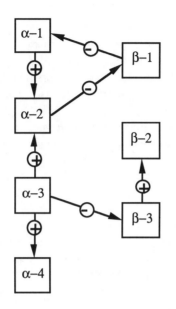

Figure 5. A-Box Network

The selection of the concepts to be used as heads of the interest areas and the links which constitute the network are not automatically computed and have to be explicitly defined. This cannot be avoided since the information embodied in the structure of the activation network implicitly contains a set of hypotheses about the relevance of the different entities of the domain and some relations between them that are not necessarily represented in the KB.

The status of the interest model provides a criterion for the computation of the relevance of the A-Box individuals with respect to the current interaction context: the interest areas are dynamically sorted in order of decreasing activation level. The selection between individuals associated to the same area depends on the static ordering specified when the areas are built. Such relevance criterion is exploited in choosing among different possible individuals to be introduced by the natural language generator and has a consequence in the hypertext access.

3.6. Generation in ALFRESCO

The generator has the purpose of expressing linguistically statements that are in an internal alinguistic format. The strategic task is actually to select the appropriate contents and to plan the structure of the resulting text . In pursuing these goals the generator must take into account the situation (see Figure 6): the user model, the discourse context, the characteristics of the particular user's request, and finally the configuration of the underlying hypertext. The strategic component then defines the input for the tactical component, which has the task of expressing the planned text in the best possible linguistic manner.

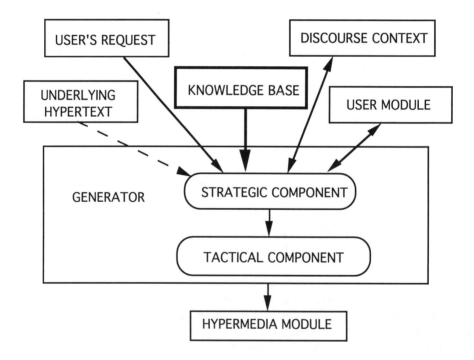

Figure 6. Generator Architecture and its Knowledge Sources

The communicative goal of the generation component, providing information about instances of the domain (i.e. frescoes), is achieved by execution of rhetorical schemata
(Figure 7) [McKeown 1985]. Briefly, a rhetorical schema is an abstract description of a
portion of coherent text coupled with processes that select and order the relevant knowledge.

The purpose of a schemata is to select and order appropriate attributes, generic-classes,
values, and instances (Figure 5) from a set of possible alternatives. The process of selection is driven by both an *a priori*, strongly domain-dependent ordering between the
knowledge base items and a sequence of queries to the knowledge base. For instance,
the selection of the comparative-attribute (Figure 7) for a fresco starts by asking the
knowledge base for other instances with a *similar* value for the *content* attribute (the
first in an *a priori* ordering) and values for the other attributes subsumed by concepts
stemming from the user modeling module. If the knowledge base returns one instance,
this is used as a comparative-instance and the selection process ends. If it returns more
than one instance another *a priori* ordering (this time between the instances) is exploited. In both cases the *content* would be the comparative-attribute. In the case that no
instance is returned, the selection process tries the steps described above for *content*
with the second attribute in the ordering i.e., *date-of-realization* and goes on in this way
until either it finds a comparative-instance (and so a comparative-attribute) or finishes
the possible comparative attributes.

```
SCHEMA S1
(1) [(instance1 (generic-description (attribute value M)*))
(2)  ((comparative-attribute not already used in (1) valueM)
          (S1 instance)*)
(3)  ((generic-description
          (recovered-attribute already used in (1) value)*)
          (S1 instance)*)]
```

*(2) introduces a new attribute of instance1 and makes a comparison with
other instances*
*(3) uses again some of the attributes already mentioned in (1), possibly
with a generalized value in order to introduce new istances*
 * = 0 or more iterations*
M *= possibility to add further information about the value*

Figure 7. Example Rhetorical Schema

As mentioned before, the dynamic knowledge source most involved in the construction of the queries to the knowledge base is the user modeling component. It provides a relevance criterion for making selections between the individual concepts described in the assertional box of the knowledge representation system. After this phase of determination of the rethorical schemata and of the particular contents, the syntactic realization component is called in. The algorithm works on a unification-based formalism in a bottom-up, head-driven fashion [Pianesi 1992] and yields complex natural language sentences.

4. Integrating Natural Language Generation and Hypertext

The system's output is a hypermedia node containing a generated text with links to the hypermedia network and possibly to images (retrieved from the videodisc in the case of ALFRESCO). In particular, the output of the tactical generator is passed to the hypermedia module which transforms the plain text into a hypertext entry point to the underlying hypermedia network. Buttons pointing to hypermedia information are associated with individual contents selected by the strategic generator.

The hypermedia module is based on the NoteCards system, a general hypermedia environment developed at Xerox PARC. We chose NoteCards for its powerful programmer's interface to a Lisp environment and general tailorability [Trigg et al. 1987]. Independence from the target task domain allows NoteCards to be successfully used in a generation system. The system provides an extremely flexible environment in which it is possible to integrate many of the different kinds of interaction that can take place in the exploration of a complex set of knowledge. The primitive constructs of the system are cards and links:

- Cards are usually displayed on the screen as standard Xerox Lisp windows containing a piece of text. NoteCards allows for the creation of new card types.
- Links are used to interconnect individual cards into networks; they are displayed as icons inside the substance of a card. Clicking the mouse in such an icon retrieves the destination card and executes the associated actions (usually the card is displayed on the screen).

The tailorability of NoteCards has been exploited in ALFRESCO in the implementation of virtual (dynamically-constructed) links that connect text cards to images and fragments of films stored in the videodisc. The generated text appears as a card providing the user with a dynamic entry-point both to images from the videodisc and to a static base of hypertext information. Figure 8 shows the card obtained applying the Similarity Schema Instantiator after the request: "Can you show and describe to me a fresco by Ambrogio Lorenzetti in Siena?"

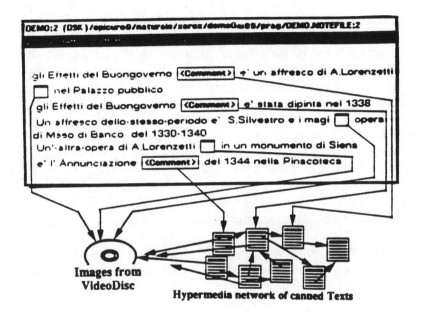

Figure 8. "The Effects of the Good Government *is a fresco by A. L. in the Public Palace. The Effects of the Good Government was painted in 1338. A fresco from the same period is S. Silvestro and the Holy Kings by Maso di Banco, painted in 1330-1340. Another work by A.L. in a monument of Siena is the Announcement, of 1344 in the Pinacoteca"*

The canned texts accessible through buttons deal with particularly complex topics (such as comparisons between styles as they are elaborated by art critics) definitely outside the expressive scope of current KR systems.

Presenting the user with a mix of generated and canned text in general can be misleading; in fact the unaware user might: a) make reference to canned text (the system is unable to understand), and b) over estimate the system's capabilities. The use of graphic containers overcomes this problem by making clear the difference between the two kinds of text: canned text has to be presented in an *evocative* graphical format, such as a simulated open book.

Another important aspect is the *Browser* construct. Browsers contain a structural diagram of a network of cards with different types of links visualized in different dashing styles. Browser cards can be automatically computed by the system and, when generated, have an active behavior (i.e., it is possible to click on a node of the displayed network in order to access the corresponding card.) The user can refer to this overall structure in her exploration.

The integration of NL generation with the NoteCards network is complete, since we have both links pointing to the cards containing the generated text and links pointing from such cards to "static" items of the network. NL generation provides a promising approach to the solution of some of the classical problems of hypertext interaction, such as the lack of sensitivity to the overall context of the interaction and the lack of adaptation to the characteristics of the particular user.

Dynamically-generated cards (being generated on the basis of specific queries and taking into account the status of the user model) result in often providing links between cards corresponding to individuals that are not connected in the knowledge base. Such a selective and structured access to a specific partition of the network could also help to avoid user disorientation.

In order to support the user in the exploration of the information stored in NoteCards, our system also makes use of the NoteCards "Browser" cards. The graphs (and the underlying hierarchy) are dynamically updated in order to take into account the cards generated during the interaction. For instance, after the generation of the card displayed in Figure 8, the graph in Figure 9a is modified as shown in Figure 9b.

The rationale for the different links correspond to user interests. Different graphical outlooks are used for lines that denote different interest dimensions. This helps make browsing less confusing: the cognitive overload of the user (see [Conklin 1987]) is reduced.

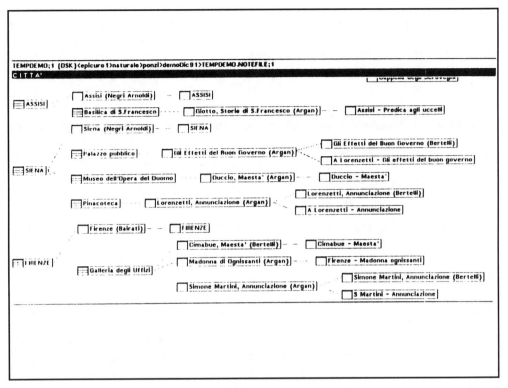

Figure 9a. NoteCards "Browser" Cards

Two general problems are worth discussing:

1) User modeling connected to linguistic communication may suggest the possibility of applying the same model to the control of hypertextual communication. "Coloured" links are provided so that exploration can be carried on preferentially along different dimensions. A more personalized view of the options may be studied and indeed there is work to bring user modeling into hypertext (see for instance [Stein et al. 1991]).

In any case, it is not clear whether a simple user model (such as that of ALFRESCO) could really improve the efficiency of hypertext interaction: it might be the case that only very sophisticated (and yet not understood) modeling techniques can help hypertext exploration, when another powerful means for focusing a request (e.g., natural language) is available in the same environment.

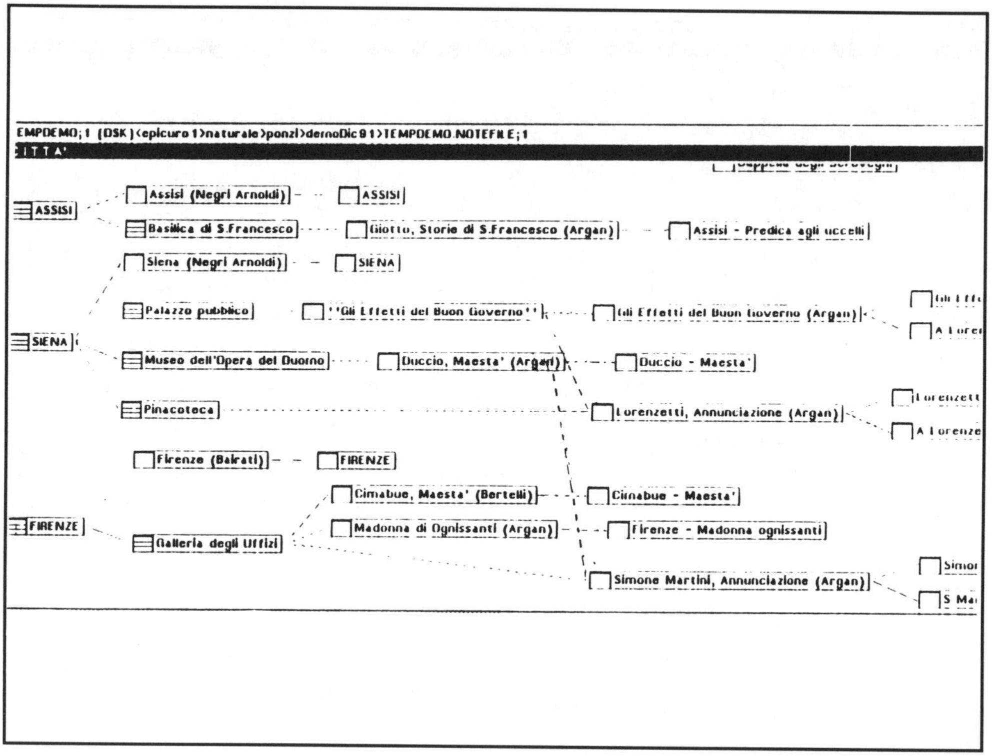

Figure 9b. Updated "Browser" Card

2) Would it be advantageous that the model of interest (to be used in the language-centered modality) be changed as the user browses through the network? We believe it may be wrong to constrain the behavior of the whole system in this way given a) the limited accuracy of current user models and b) the fact that hypertext on its own would only be used in a very limited way to explore the surroundings or have a general bird's eye view of the domain. It seems better to us not to build a user model through the hypertext modality thereby minimizing any consequences for the natural language-centered inter-action. In practice, the only real consequence is at the discourse level, where it is taken into account that the user has been provided with a hypertext access card that she has used.

With respect to the user interface, one possibility is to use an analogical device, e.g., a gauge, that can be set by the user to determine the degree of desired "intrusion" of the interest model in the explorative interaction, in both ways.[3] But let us reiterate that for the moment we believe that the interest model, at least with current understanding, should only determine the way in which one can begin exploration through hypertext, yielding two complementary yet integrated modalities.

Among various further research themes, we are investigating the possible extension of the interest model to include T-Box (as well as A-Box) concepts as members of interest areas. Such an extension would provide a criterion to operate selections among classes of individuals and for subparts of generic descriptions. In order to also make use of T-Box items during the activation phase, it will be necessary to take into account the concepts that appear in the logical-form representing the input request sentence. Of course, also the automatic generation of the contents of the areas will have to be modified. For instance, the generator will take into account a criterion for choosing dynamically a certain description of an individual (among various possibilities), and therefore relate it to other individuals on the basis of that particular conceptual framework. Also, the selection of attributes and the focusing on certain subspecifications of a structure of an individual would be dynamically performed for the particular interest of the user. This feature will provide both a text better tailored for the circumstance, focusing on what the user may be really looking for, and a better focus on the access to the underlying hypertext. A more limited number of relevant links will appear in the generated text, but more importantly, these links can be semantically qualified in a sense that the user is supposed to understand.

Recently there has been other work [Reiter et al. 1992] aimed at combining text generation and hypertext. Their work and ours are different. Reiter and colleagues address the problem of new hypertext being dynamically generated as the user performs further requests by clicking the available buttons in the current text. The fact that, as the user moves further, new specific text is generated presupposes that all the relevant knowledge is coded in an internal format and can be expressed linguistically on request. The typical browsing modality is not really the goal for Reiter and colleagues. For instance the user is not supposed to move around the network with a bird's eye view just to have an idea

---

[3]Phil Cohen suggested this possibility.

about what information is available for certain areas. Instead, hypertext buttons are a way for guiding and limiting the local follow-up requests that the user may wish to express (see also [Moore and Swartout 1990]). Our view is different. We maintain that natural language and hypertexts can be combined, yielding their specific contribution, both in input and in output. In the first place, hypertexts exist exactly for the kind of information that it is difficult to express in an internal format (for instance art critics' views). So they constitute *per se* a level of representation with a very limited number of entry points. In the second place, we believe that the role of hypertext in a natural language centered interactive system is to consent to the user to explore the area surrounding the focus of her attention and to provide a noncommitted modality of interaction, characterized by a fast turnaround. Of course, the generator starts from an internal representation also in our case but the result is a text linked to other preexisting text in a personalized way.

5. Conclusions

We have discussed the combination of natural language dialog and hypermedia within an artificial intelligence view of information exploration. We claim that the habitability of a system that provides an active integration of these two paradigms is greatly enhanced. The exploratory dialog system ALFRESCO has been presented: a natural language and hypermedia system connected to a videodisc that gives information about Italian frescoes of the Fourteenth Century.

Many points remain to be explored. Apart from more particular aspects, we intend to pursue the idea that the system can eventually provide, through further negotiation, a suggestion for a personal cultural-touristic itinerary. We believe that this area has great potential because cultural tourism is of increasing material relevance, especially in Italy, but also because it is an area that requires a shift from a mass-oriented, impersonal perspective toward an individual-oriented, creative opportunity for all. On the other hand, we believe that as we understand more about how exploration (as in hypermedia interaction) and goal-oriented behaviour (as in natural language) can be coherently modeled and integrated, a new perspective may be opened for intelligent interfaces that goes beyond what we are used to and amplifies our cognitive capabilities.

We would like to thank J. Slack for many helpful discussions.

Chapter 10

An Approach to Hypermedia in Diagnostic Systems[1]

Suhayya Abu-Hakima, Mike Halasz, and Sieu Phan

Abstract

User interfaces in knowledge-based applications have become more sophisticated in their use of multi-media. In this position paper we will describe a means of achieving hypermedia-based interfaces for diagnostic systems, in particular for the Jet Engine Troubleshooting Assistant (JETA). We will also describe how such an approach to hypermedia can be extended for explanation in diagnostic systems.

1. Introduction

For a diagnostic application to properly support hypermedia, one requires a structured manner by which to represent the knowledge, reason about it interactively, display it dynamically and explain it to the user. This is why it is essential to first describe the knowledge representation, reasoning algorithm, user interface and explanation strategies.

Figure 1 illustrates the typical architecture for a knowledge-based system. Its hypermedia user interface includes template-based text, graphics, images and icons which represent linked objects that in some implementations can communicate by messaging as in a typical object-oriented system (as was described for RATIONALE's

---

[1] Canadian National Research Council Document number 35031.

hypermedia interface in [Abu-Hakima 1989] and as is the case for the Jet Engine Troubleshooting Assistant - JETA). The interface shields users from application details of the reasoning algorithm and allows them to request explanations when needed. Both the reasoning algorithm and the explanation facility access the diagnostic frames that are organized in a hierarchical structure in the knowledge base. Other supporting knowledge such as descriptions of diagnostic parameters and glossary definitions are also accessible. Assuming that graphs and schematics are also required implies that the knowledge base must have links or pointers to the files or database where such information is stored.

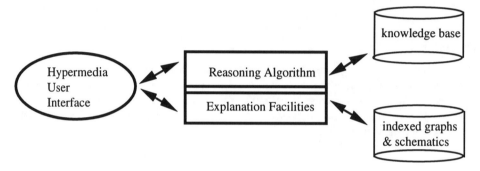

Figure 1. Hypermedia Architecture for Knowledge-based Systems

How the knowledge can be represented and reasoned about while accessing graphs and schematics is described under the knowledge representation and reasoning strategies in Sections 2 and 3 respectively. How the hypermedia user interface supports the user is described in Section 4. A user scenario is given in Section 5.

Explanation is tightly coupled to the explicit knowledge representation and reasoning in a system [Neches et al. 1985; Abu-Hakima 1988]. It is also strongly linked to the user interface, a hypermedia interface in the case of JETA [Halasz et al. 1992]. Thus, to discuss explanation strategies for diagnostic systems such as JETA, it is necessary to first describe their knowledge representation, reasoning strategies and hypermedia interfaces. Subsequent to this a means of achieving hypermedia explanations for JETA and other diagnostic systems is described in Sections 6 and 7.

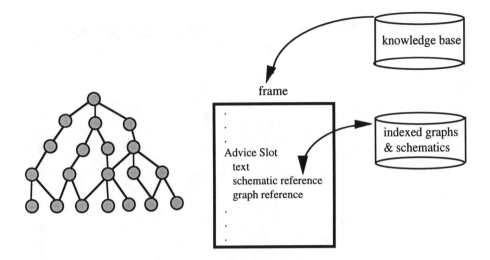

Figure 2. The Path of Information to Index and Retrieve Graphs and Schematics for Reasoning and Explanation

2. Diagnostic Knowledge Representation

A scenario for how hypermedia information can be represented and accessed is illustrated in Figure 2. In current diagnostic systems, advice generating slots are included in the frame and their contents are output to the user as diagnoses or procedures to follow to find a fault. The advice is likely to be supported with a schematic or a graph. It is proposed that an indexed database of schematics and graphs be kept. Thus, rather than storing an entire schematic in a frame, only its pointer to the database is kept. Once advice text and any indexed schematic are to be output to the user, the reasoning algorithm makes a request to the database for the schematic. A display function belonging to the user interface is then sent the schematic and the advice text for output. The current implementation of JETA links text, graphs and schematics in this manner.

Such an approach can be enhanced further by indexing electronic manuals so that the advice slots for text can simply access pointers to paragraphs that are to be output to the technician. Note that in the current implementation of JETA there are pointers that reference paragraphs and schematics that the technician can access in the hardcopy

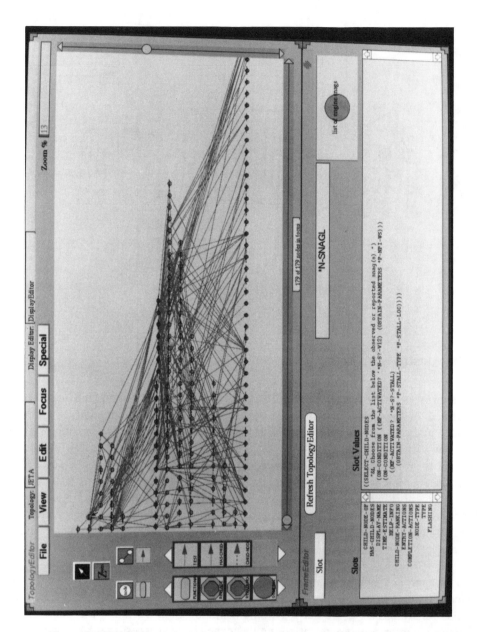

Figure 3. JETA's Diagnostic Network for the J85 Engine Shown in the Browser

manual. There are plans underway to transfer the full text of hardcopy manuals to an electronic format using scanners and optical character recognition. When such an electronic manual exists, JETA can easily have pointers to specific paragraphs and scanned in schematics and images so that the technician may access them directly.

JETA's troubleshooting knowledge is represented as a diagnostic network that is hierarchical in nature. Figure 3 shows JETA's J85 knowledge base in the browser. The browser includes a display and a frame editor for the knowledge base. Each node in the network corresponds to a decision point in the troubleshooting process and the links represent relations directing the flow of control between nodes. The overall network is much broader than it is deep since there are many components and associated symptoms. The number of nodes along a network path varies from four to twelve. Possible next moves in the network are represented as children of a node. Any node can have multiple parents since a component malfunction may be due to many causes. The troubleshooting knowledge is encoded at each node or decision point in a frame using a custom command language.

2.1. Frames

Frames offer a great deal of flexibility in constructing and reasoning about knowledge. Each node of the diagnostic network is represented by a frame. JETA also supports two other types of frames, diagnostic parameter frames and glossary frames. The interaction between these frames is illustrated in Figure 4. Diagnostic network frames have activation rules that fire based on the values of diagnostic parameters. Glossary frames hold the definitions of terms output to the user in interactions involving the diagnostic network frames or the parameter frames.

2.2. Diagnostic Network Frames

The frame for a diagnostic node holds a substantial amount of local information relevant to a particular node that is used dynamically in a diagnostic session. The diagnostic frame template is shown in Figure 5. It has fourteen slots. The *display-name* holds a domain-specific node name the user is familiar with. The *time-estimate* specifies the estimated time to carry out a procedure described in the node. The *line-of-maintenance* indicates whether a maintenance action is carried out at first (engine tested on aircraft), second (engine removed off aircraft) or third (engine assembled or disassembled) line of maintenance. The *help-info* slot provides backup contextual help to the user about the node. The information in this slot is accessed dynamically by the hypertext handler during a diagnostic session upon request by the user.

The *node-type* specifies one of the different types of diagnostic nodes which can exist. The *child-node-of* indicates the preceding nodes (parents) to the current node. Note that more than one parent can exist for any one node. The *activating-observation* holds a rule that triggers the node based on activated diagnostic parameters. The *child-node-ranking* prioritizes the children of a node. This priority is dynamically altered during a session based on collected evidence (see [Halasz et al. 1992]).The *blocking-if-user-selected* slot is used by the developer to block entry to a node or to warn the user about outstanding issues before entering the node.

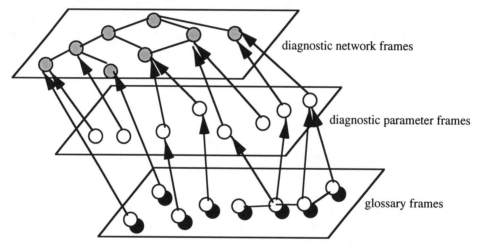

Figure 4. Interaction Between JETA's Three Types of Frames

The *entry-actions* are a sequence of commands which are carried out on entering a node. The *after-fixup-actions* are pertinent command sequences to be carried out after the *entry-actions*. The *completion-actions* are a sequence of actions to be carried out upon leaving the node. The *functional-tests-required* directs the user to carry out tests that are required to ensure the correct operation of a component after it has been repaired, adjusted or replaced. The *component-affected* slot allows the system to update a specific record in a parts database once a component has been replaced on the engine.

Note that the slots contain command sequences that often require the reasoning algorithm to dynamically interact with the user interface to organize what information is displayed where to the user. This is done by sending messages to the user interface objects in keeping with standard communication in object-oriented systems. This is discussed further in the user interface section, Section 4.

defnode:	node name
display-name:	displayed node name for user
time-estimate:	time estimate for recommended actions (displayed on node entry)
line-of-maintenance:	severity of repair (1st, 2nd or 3rd line)
help-info:	help information on node including hypertext markers
node-type:	type of diagnostic network frame
	- general (default),
	- all-ok,
	- snag,
	- functional test,
	- incorrect test setup,
	- adjust,
	- replace,
	- adjust/replace,
	- check/replace
child-node-of:	kinship to parent nodes
activating-observation:	rule expression which could be used to activate node
child-node-ranking:	relative child-node priority list (default = equally likely)
blocking-if-user-selected:	check to see if other conditions which
	may block entry to node
	(if user opts for direct selection to move in network).
entry-actions:	sequence of operations carried out upon node entry.
	examples
	- general advice,
	- advice which depends upon path through network, status of other
	nodes or parameter values,
	- asking for intermediate parameter values,
	- intermediate servicing of another node,
	- setting states of other nodes,
	- ask user to make selections from the list of sub-nodes.
after-fixup-actions:	sequence of operations to execute after executing **entry-actions**
completion-actions:	sequence of operations to execute before returning to the
	invoking node (see those for "**entry-actions**")
functional-tests-required:	validation tests to check that repair was carried out correctly
component-affected:	component in engine parts database with serial numbers, etc.

Figure 5. Diagnostic Network Frame Template

2.3.   Parameter Frame

Parameters are variables which represent the user's observations about the current state of the engine and the environment it operates in. They are used by the rule expressions in the *activating-observation* slot of a diagnostic network frame. The rule characterizes the symptoms of a particular node. For example, the actual temperature (a particular parameter) is compared to a value, and from this, the symptom *high operating temperature* or *low operating temperature* is determined and reasoned about. The parameter frame has slots pertaining to the type of value, a user displayed textual or graphical prompt generated based on the parameter type and contextual help information used to describe the parameter in more detail if the user asks for it. The parameter frame template is shown in Figure 6.

---

defparam: parameter name

display-name: displayed parameter name for user
help-info: help information for parameter including hypertext markers
parameter-spec: type of value for parameter
                                   examples
                                   - numeric (with associated interval(s) of acceptance),
                                   - alphanumeric,
                                   - one-of (a list of selections),
                                   - function (calculated parameter: function or simulation).

Figure 6. Parameter Frame Template

2.4.   Glossary Frame

The glossary frames are used to link the hypertext information. For example, if a term in a paragraph of text requires clarification or definition, one would simply select it (with the mouse) and the information linked to it would be displayed. In the case of JETA, if there are any common abbreviations required by: the *help-info* slot of the diagnostic network or parameter frames; another definition slot of a glossary frame; any displayed advice or system prompts; they are linked through the use of glossary frames. The glossary frame template is shown in Figure 7. Glossary information is displayed to the user in the context it is asked for as illustrated in the user scenario of Section 5.

defglossary:	glossary name
display-name:	displayed name for user
definition:	definition of glossary term including hypertext markers.

Figure 7. Glossary Frame Template

3. Reasoning Strategy

JETA's reasoning strategies are quite versatile. The path of information between the encoded knowledge in the diagnostic frame and the user display is illustrated in Figure 8. The reasoner interprets commands encoded locally in the diagnostic nodes of the network and outputs requests for information to the user in the user interaction area. Any advice or procedural information the technician is given is presented in the advice area. From the advice the technician can access other linked information such as supporting schematics, images or text.

The reasoning strategy, while interpreting JETA's frame command language, addresses those strategies inherent in engine diagnosis. It blocks entry to a particular node if certain pre-conditions have not been cleared. Logical 'jumps' in the network are permitted in order to abort the current line of reasoning should new observations lead to other nodes becoming more probable. Nodes are activated by rules that depend on network status and relevant parameters. Postponement of certain procedures at various nodes is allowed by a technician who may have a 'hunch' that a certain path is incorrect, or who may be limited by time or a parts shortage. Dynamic help, graphics and hypertext that describe nodes or terminology is provided. Advice is customized at the node level before it is displayed to the user. Allowances for instrument mis-readings or failures are made. Nodes can be re-visited if it seems that a faulty component has been used. Parameters are updated as the diagnosis extends over time. For example, temperature will change during the day making initial values invalid for later tests requiring the same information. Looping is controlled in the network by setting and monitoring node states. The reasoner lets the user select from a list of prioritized tests and failure modes. The list order is based on the difficulty of a test and the likelihood of the failure and can be dynamically re-ordered depending upon observed snag combinations.

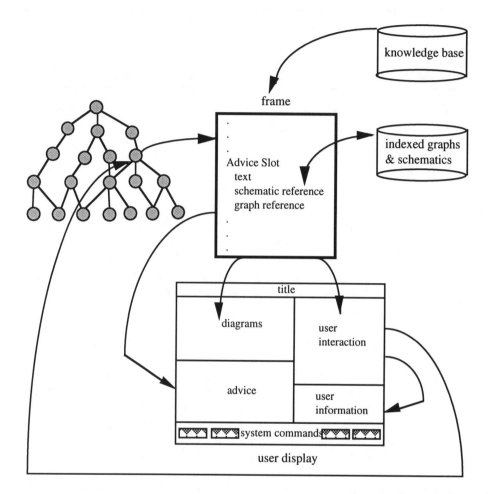

Figure 8. Information Path Between Reasoning Algorithm and User Environment

Troubleshooting tasks cannot be fully planned since they are essentially investigative [Fikes and Kehler 1985]. JETA has a mixed initiative approach that allows a user to either directly select a path for reasoning or to let the system deduce a diagnosis since the technician can respond *unknown* at any point during reasoning. If the user controls the path of reasoning in the network JETA provides some guidance but acts mainly as a bookkeeper and keeps a trace of the user's actions. Any pending and ruled-out diagnoses are always displayed to the user in the user information area of the display.

The diagnostic nodes in the network assume states that are monitored by the reasoner. This controls the search by pruning the network and provides trace information to track sessions for explanation generation. Node states can be set locally by the knowledge-base designer once certain conditions are met. When starting a session all diagnostic nodes have open status. If the user provides feedback to the system that a component replacement, adjustment or repair has been carried out successfully, the node state is 'done'. If a node is activated by its associated preconditions evaluating to true or through user selection, the state is set to 'activated'. If a node is removed from further consideration it is set to 'ruled-out'. The system assigns 'eliminated' status when all offspring of a node have been set to either done, ruled-out or eliminated. The reasoning module also maintains a status to track node traversal. The system assigns the state 'being-visited' when the node is currently being visited or 'has-been-visited' when a node was visited. The system or the user can postpone a decision, thus setting a node status to 'postponed'.

4. Hypermedia User Interface

The user interface module accepts input from the user and passes it to the reasoning module for processing. It also receives output from the reasoning module and displays it for the user. The interface is designed for three types of users: the maintenance technician, the system manager and developers of JETA. This distinction is necessary since technicians require an interface tailored to their maintenance tasks whereas developers require special access to the knowledge-base and reasoning module. A system manager has access and authority to update lists of user names and passwords as well as engine serial numbers.

Three main objectives exist for the user interface. The first is to accommodate different levels of troubleshooting expertise and computer proficiency. A seasoned technician may need to be reminded of specific details, whereas a novice may need more detailed guidance. A second objective is to provide context-sensitive information and automated cross-referencing. A third objective is to provide links between text and graphics. This is important since future technical manuals will likely be in electronic format due to the advantages of enhanced information access and more efficient means of distributing revisions [Bonissone and Johnson 1983].

JETA's user interface addresses its objectives by having a reasoning process that intervenes only when the user requests assistance. It provides glossary and context-sensitive help throughout a diagnostic session that a novice technician may use continually whereas a seasoned technician may access infrequently. User input is made by menu and iconic button selection with a mouse. Keyboard input is minimized. System commands are always visible on the bottom of the display. The use of multiple function buttons has a tendency to impede user acceptance, since the user must focus on both the options displayed on the screen and on the mouse. For this reason, a single button is used so that users that are not computer proficient do not have to struggle to use JETA. The glossary and definition functions which are cross-referenced meet the objective of providing context-sensitive information and automated cross-referencing. The interface uses hypermedia links between graphics and text to provide the user with hypermedia-based advice.

The four tools used in the development are: Common LISP, PostScript, NeWS and HyperNeWS 1.4. Figure 9 shows the development environment. The reasoning strategies and knowledge-base representation are implemented in LISP. The multiple stack interface runs under HyperNeWS, which itself runs under the Sun Micro Systems Network Windowing System (NeWS). NeWS runs under the Unix operating system.

4.1.   HyperNeWS

HyperNeWS is an object-oriented interface design tool developed at the Turing Institute in Glasgow, Scotland [van Hoff 1991]. It is similar to HyperCard™ but can also be interfaced to client programs such as LISP, Quintus Prolog and C. It is written in PostScript and makes use of NeWS graphics primitives. It provides a complete windowing environment, colour graphics, drawing tools and use of captured images. A HyperNeWS window is referred to as a stack. HyperNeWS objects placed on the cards include: text/menu objects (static and dynamic), check boxes, push and arrow buttons, sliders, and iconic buttons (created using the built-in drawing tool). Objects communicate with each other and client programs by sending messages.

The primary advantage of using HyperNeWS is its ease and flexibility for user interface development. The look and feel of a HyperNeWS user interface can be developed interactively on the screen and more importantly, any subsequent modification can be viewed immediately without having to re-code or re-compile as is the case with other graphical user interface development tools (such as DevGuide™ from Sun Micro Systems for example).

4.2. JETA's User Interface Stacks

JETA's user interface initially presents an introduction to the system and a login before bringing the user to the main environment. The technician is first given a choice of engine type to diagnose as displayed for the JETA user scenario in Figure 12. Once selected, a login is required. The user selects their name from a menu, enters a password and the engine serial number. The serial number is required to enable reasoning based on the past history of the specific engine and the fleet once a significant number of cases are tracked by the system.

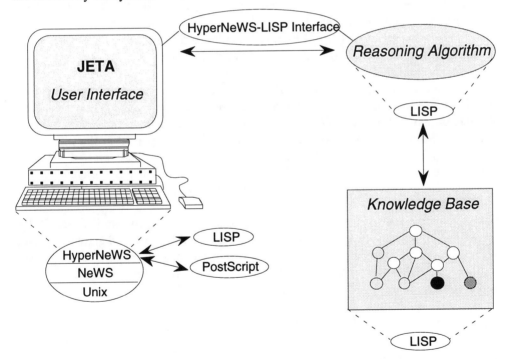

Figure 9. Development Environment

After login the user is brought to the main user environment. JETA takes advantage of a multi-window layout which subdivides the main user screen into six areas that distinguish different types of information. On each screen area, stacks (windows) may be overlaid according to system reasoning or user interaction. This layout creates an ordered and stable look while offering depth in certain areas of system functionality. It also ensures that all system functions are accessible and eliminates the need for the user to memorize different screen configurations.

A flowchart of JETA's stacks is shown in Figure 10. The user is first presented with a Title stack (shown below in Figure 12 under JETA's user scenario) from which they can access a Help or a Background stack. Once the user selects the engine to troubleshoot from the Title stack, a Login stack is presented. After the user logs in, the main user environment is displayed on the screen (shown in Figures 12 to 17). This environment includes the Default User Interaction, the User Information, the JETA Advice, the Default Diagrams, the System Commands and the Titlebar stacks. Several of these stacks have secondary stacks which are displayed based on user actions or the selection of certain commands. A JETA Busy stack is displayed to the user when the reasoning module is busy processing information for extended periods.

When a node in the diagnostic network is reached, the user may be prompted for a selection of sub-nodes. Direct selection may be made according to user knowledge, or a *continue* button may be selected to imply *unknown* which allows the system to offer guidance. Definitions and kinship relations of the nodes displayed in the menus are available by button selection. This allows the user to choose the degree of detail or assistance required on a node-by-node basis. A Snag window provides a reference to the state of the snags (a snag is the reason an engine is removed or snagged off the aircraft).

Maintenance manuals emphasize diagrams that illustrate instructions to the user. JETA provides an equally efficient, if not improved, synergy between text and graphics. Raster images have been scanned from the manuals with a digital scanner. At relevant nodes, pertinent diagrams are accessible by means of hypermedia links. Diagrams can be displayed in a default or enlarged mode.

5. JETA User Scenario

Assume the engine has just returned from a maintenance action and is undergoing acceptance testing in the test cell. The technicians note that while performing an acceleration test, the main engine experiences a loss of flame and is shut down. The technicians are experienced with the engine but none of them has seen a flameout for a quite some time so they turn to advice from JETA.

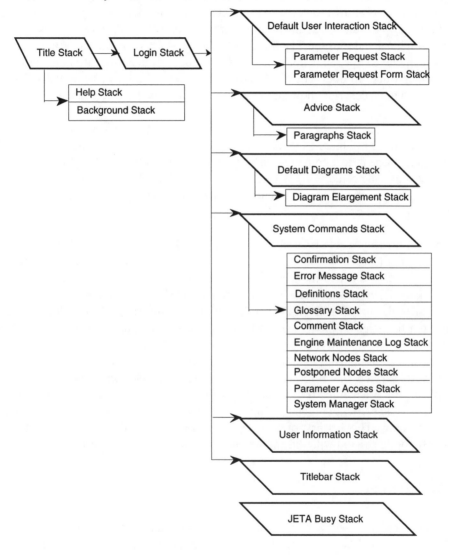

Figure 10. Flowchart of User Interface Stacks

The engine flameout subtree shown in the browser illustrates the path of reasoning for this scenario (Figure 11). Upon starting JETA, the technician is asked to select an engine to troubleshoot as shown in Figure 12. Note that an image of the engine the user selects to troubleshoot is shown to confirm user selection. Once Joe has logged in he is asked for pre-start up conditions as shown in Figure 13. The NPI reading request provides him with a graphical slider to set. The ram position request asks him for numeric input which the system checks for range consistency. If he inputs an inconsistent value, he is asked for another value. In both requests the user could select buttons (A8 or VEN RAM for example) to get a description of the parameter and its contextual relevance.

The technician has elected to troubleshoot the engine on the basis of a snag as shown in User Interactions in Figure 14. From the list of snags, Joe selects engine flameout. JETA refines this problem to a combination of general problems (loss of fuel flow, decrease in fuel flow and undetected stall) as well as specific replace (P&D valve) and repair (P3 to MFC line, combustion liner and main fuel nozzles) nodes. Joe then selects decrease in fuel flow.

JETA then presents a set of possible causes for the decrease in fuel flow. The technician is given repair (fuel forwarding system, water contamination of fuel and fuel filter - 120 micron or 200 mesh) and replace (MFC - main fuel control) options. Before making a decision, he decides to look at a hypertext definition of the MFC as shown in Figure 15. He then decides to select it. JETA warns and blocks him from selecting the MFC since he has not investigated the less costly options (it takes 16 hours to replace an expensive MFC which may not be faulty at all). Joe then decides to repair the 120 micron fuel filter as shown in the user interaction in Figure 16 (a). JETA provides him with advice on how to service the filter as shown in Figure 16 (b). Once the technician has completed the procedure, JETA asks for feedback on whether the filter was repaired according to specification. The technician confirms that it was and clears the engine flameout snag. The history of the engine is then updated internally for the next troubleshooting session with the engine known by its 8581 engine serial number.

6. Explanation

For a knowledge-based system to explain its reasoning, it should be built with four objectives in mind [Abu-Hakima 1988, 1990]. First, it must tell the user what the system

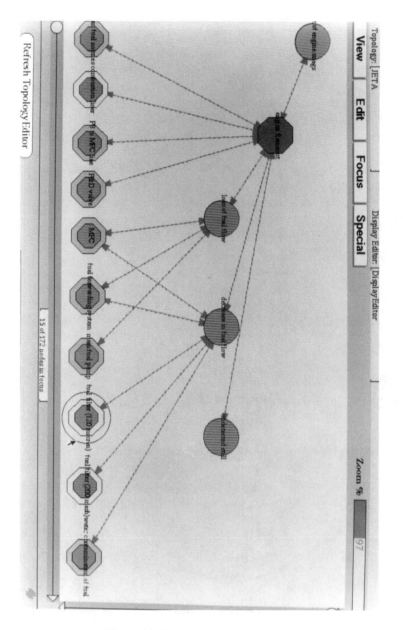

Figure 11. Engine Flameout Subtree

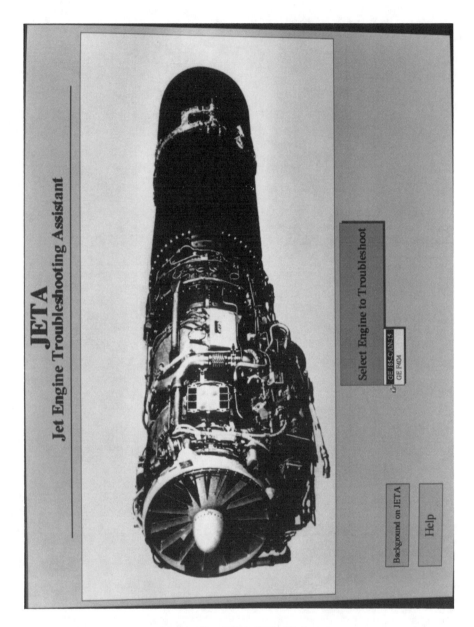

Figure 12. JETA's Title Stack

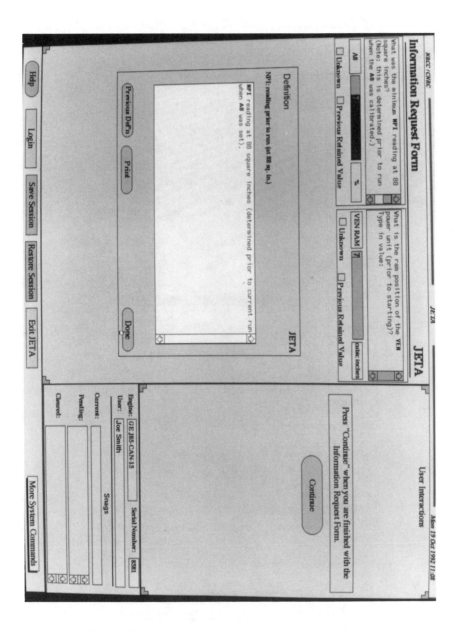

Figure 13. Information Request Form on Start of Session

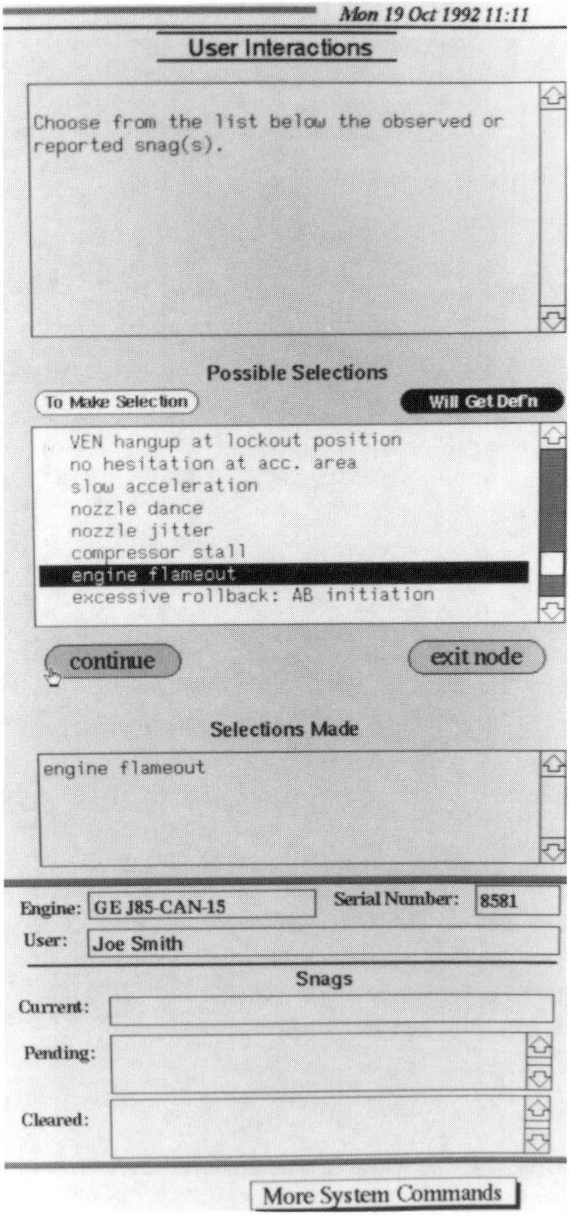

Figure 14. User Selecting Engine Flameout

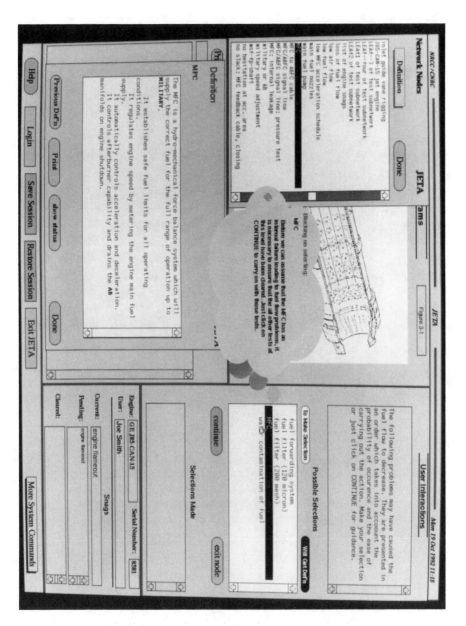

Figure 15. User Exploring Troubleshooting the MFC

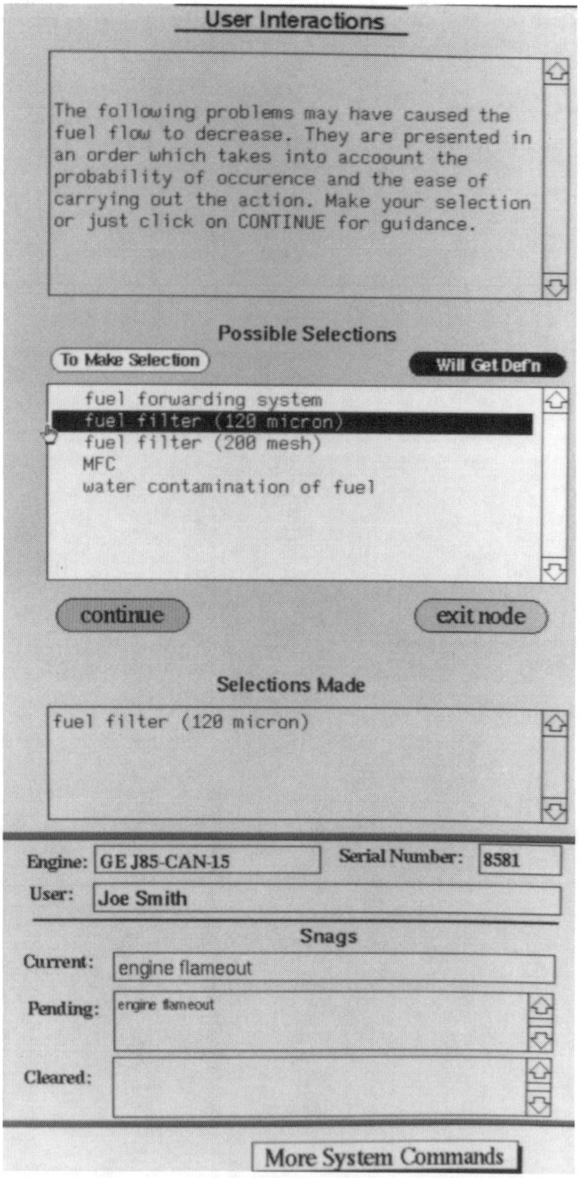

Figure 16 Checking the 120 Micron Fuel Filter.

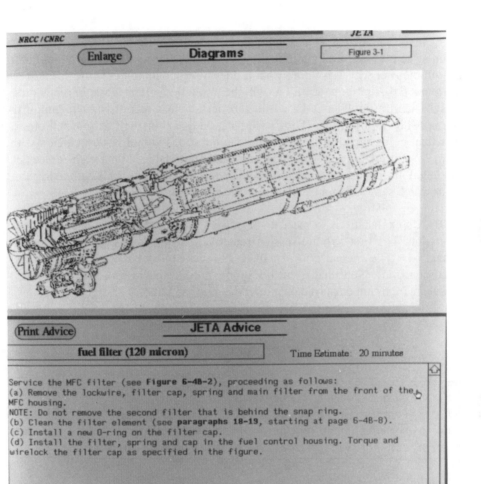

Enlarge   **Diagrams**   Figure 3-1

Print Advice   **JETA Advice**

fuel filter (120 micron)   Time Estimate: 20 minutes

```
Service the MFC filter (see Figure 6-48-2), proceeding as follows:
(a) Remove the lockwire, filter cap, spring and main filter from the front of the
MFC housing.
NOTE: Do not remove the second filter that is behind the snap ring.
(b) Clean the filter element (see paragraphs 18-19, starting at page 6-48-8).
(c) Install a new O-ring on the filter cap.
(d) Install the filter, spring and cap in the fuel control housing. Torque and
wirelock the filter cap as specified in the figure.
```

Help   Login   Save Session   Restore Session   Exit JETA

Figure 17 Advice on Troubleshooting the Fuel Filter

can or cannot do. Second, it must tell the user what the system has done. Third, it must explain system objectives by telling the user what the system is trying to do. Fourth, it must tell the user why it is doing what it does by responding to the user's clarification questions. Explanations in JETA will be modelled after those implemented for RATIONALE, a knowledge-based diagnostic tool that reasons by explaining [Abu-Hakima 1988, 1990]. Thus, JETA's explanation questions will be selected off menus rather than being typed in by the user. The questions would be instantiated with the current context established with node states and node status in the reasoner (see Section 3). In addition, supporting diagrams would be indexed using JETA's current hypermedia facility which shows diagrams relevant to the current line of reasoning.

For JETA's explanations to meet its objectives, it should give the user four types of explanation. The first two are session sensitive, and they are event and hypothetical explanations. The second two explain system capabilities, and they are ability and factual questions. Note that event questions, unlike system capability questions, are dynamic and thus are displayed only after the user has started a session.

For my current problem, why do you need these symptoms?
For my current problem, why do you NOT need these symptoms?
For my current problem, why did you conclude this problem?
For my current problem, why did you NOT conclude this problem?

example:
For my engine flameout, why did you NOT conclude an MFC problem?

JETA has established that your engine flameout problem was refined to a decrease in fuel flow problem. A decrease in fuel flow problem could be refined to a fuel forwarding system problem, a fuel filter (120 micron), a fuel filter (200 mesh), a water contamination problem or an MFC problem. It is attempting to eliminate the other problems before the MFC problem can be deduced.

Figure 18. Event Questions and Explanations

6.1. Session Sensitive Explanations

System event explanations are directly related to the reasoning in the current system session. Event questions that a user is able to ask are directly related to the parameters and diagnostic nodes the knowledge-based system is working with. JETA activates a node on the basis of user selection, an activating condition or as a descendent of a currently activated node. Thus for event questions, a technician should be allowed to ask *why*, *how* and *what-if* questions from the JETA explanation menu.

6.1.1. Event Questions

Why questions would address JETA's immediate actions. *How* questions require explanations of reasoning strategies related to the symptoms and diagnostic nodes within the current context. The emphasis in these questions is how the system achieves its objectives. Such explanations would be supported by subtrees that represent the current line of reasoning as shown in Figure 11. Event questions in JETA could also include *why-not* questions. These give the technician an idea of why the system failed to use particular symptoms or deduce particular problems. Figure 18 presents the types of event questions the user selects from the menu and an example explanation that would be displayed in a pop-up explanation window. The example is based on the engine flameout user scenario described previously.

6.1.2. Hypothetical Questions

Hypothetical explanations are often referred to as what-if explanations. They could explain to the technician the result of adding new symptoms to an established problem or of replacing an established problem with a new one with a modified set of symptoms. Hypothetical explanations can be both event dependent and independent. In the event dependent case, new symptoms are associated with an already established problem. In the event independent case, a new problem with new symptoms could replace the established problem. They can be generated using a parallel trace of the session in which the technician defines hypothetical symptoms and hypotheses as was implemented for RATIONALE. Such explanations are valuable for users testing the knowledge of the system. Hypothetical explanations, unlike Event explanations, are not readily available in most knowledge-based systems. This is mainly due to the overhead associated with tracking a user's current and hypothetical sessions. The types of hypothetical questions the JETA user would select from the explanation menu and respective responses to be shown in the pop-up window for the engine flameout example are shown in Figure 19.

What-if these symptoms were also true for my current problem? What-if this problem replaced my current problem with these symptoms?

example:
What-if the symptom fuel pressure at inlet to engine is less than 5 psi is also true for my decrease in fuel flow problem?

If the symptom fuel pressure at inlet to engine is less than 5 psi is also true for your decrease in fuel flow problem, then a problem with the fuel forwarding system may be deduced.

Figure 19. Hypothetical Questions and Explanations

6.2.   System Capability Explanations

Questions about system capabilities would allow the technician to get explanations about reasoning strategies and the use of symptoms and problems, independently of any particular context.

6.2.1.   Ability Explanations

Ability questions are independent of user sessions and can be asked at any time, thus giving the technician an insight into what the system is capable of. Ability explanations would be useful in helping the user test as well as learn the reasoning strategies of JETA. Ability questions allow one to ask questions about what the system can do with particular symptoms to arrive at particular problems. The types of ability questions selectable from the explanation menu and respective responses are illustrated in Figure 20.

6.2.2. Factual Explanations

Factual questions allow the technician to query JETA's static knowledge by asking for definitions and information about parameters and diagnostic nodes. This is illustrated in the engine flameout example and more specifically in Figure 15 where the technician is accessing definitions and contextual help to explore troubleshooting the main fuel control (MFC).

How do you deduce this problem?
How do you refine this problem?

example:
How do you deduce a fuel forwarding system problem?

JETA deduces a fuel forwarding system problem if the symptom fuel pressure at inlet to engine is less than 5 psi and either a loss of fuel flow or a decrease in fuel flow problem is activated.

example:
How do you refine an engine flameout problem?

JETA refines an engine flameout problem by trying to deduce a loss of fuel flow, a decrease in fuel flow, a P3 to MFC line problem, a P&D valve problem, a combustion liner problem, an undetected stall problem or a main fuel nozzles problem. These problems are subsequently refined based on user selection, descendent problems or activating conditions.

Figure 20. Ability Questions and Explanations

7. Generated Explanations

Generated explanations in current knowledge-based systems are frequently clumsy and hide the reasoning strategies. Ideally, generated explanations should be considered as important as providing the explanation capability itself. There are five important considerations for generated explanations that facilities would benefit from adhering to. These considerations were adhered to in the implementation of explanations for RATIONALE and will be carried over to JETA. JETA's explanations will be template-based. This form of explanation connects pieces of text to variables that are instantiated from the knowledge in the system. This allows explanation templates to be independent of the domain to which JETA is applied. It also simplifies the task of generating dynamic explanations according to the current context.

7.1.   Contextually Dependent References

Once a context is introduced in a user question, the generated explanation should reference it much as a human explaining within a particular context would. This has been implemented for RATIONALE [Abu-Hakima 1990]. An example of the explanation template that could be used for JETA for a session dependent question follows. An example of its use based on the engine flameout user scenario is given (Note that '/' separates the template phrase choices - the choices are made based on the current context of the session.)

User Question:	Why did you not deduce problem B?
Explanation:	Problem B could not be deduced since / the related problem's activating symptoms Sa, of current subproblem A could not be concluded / its parent problem A could not be concluded / none of the selected problems could lead to it.
example:	
User Question:	Why did you not deduce a loss of fuel flow?
Explanation:	A loss of fuel flow could not be deduced since the activating symptom sharp drop in fuel flow could not be concluded.

7.2. Anaphoric References

These are references to an already introduced entity. RATIONALE's explanations make use of anaphoric references by establishing and maintaining a contextual view (see [Abu-Hakima 1990] for examples). Thus, JETA users could ask questions with anaphoric references and the explanation facility would be expected to understand the reference and hence deduce the entity referred to.

example:	
User Question:	How did you use the selected symptoms?
Explanation:	A moderate drop in fuel flow was used to establish a decrease in fuel flow problem.

7.3. Elliptic References

Such references involve indirect references to introduced entities. Again such interpretation of user questions attempts to follow the human model of explanation.

User Question 1:	Why did you not deduce problem A?
User Question 2:	What were its symptoms?
Explanation:	Problem A's activating symptoms are Sa.

7.4. Echo User's Question

This is the ability to include several messages in one generated explanation. Such an explanation could echo the user's question subtly to assure the user that their intentions were understood as illustrated in the examples above.

7.5. Clarification Questions

Questions about the user's intent should be specific and well directed and understandable by the facility itself. Clarification is mostly applicable to a dialogue-based interface versus a menu-based interface such as JETA's. The system's request for clarification may be open ended which may leave the user confused as to the system's expectations of a response. It is imperative for the facility that requires explanation clarification questions to be able to question the user in a meaningful manner. An example of a clarification interaction would be:

User Question:	What is the basis of problem A?
Clarification:	Do you mean, what are the activating symptoms for problem A?
	versus
	Clarify 'basis' please?

Note that elliptic references, echoing the user's question and clarification questions would all be required for a natural language question and answer interface versus a menu-based interface. Since both RATIONALE and JETA have menu-based interfaces and are designed to allow the user to select contextual explanation questions from menus, the problems of question and answer responses are avoided altogether.

7.6. Implementation

Explanations are generated from traces of diagnostic reasoning. As described for RATIONALE in [Abu-Hakima 1990] they allow the user to ask questions about dynamic and static knowledge. They also allow the user to ask about deductive and abductive methods of the system and how conclusions are drawn from both the static and dynamic knowledge. Although explanations in RATIONALE have been generated in a hypermedia interface environment, their content has been textual thus far. We are currently in the process of defining how we can integrate graphical and schematic information in the content of the explanations.

As in the case of adding pointers to the advice slot in a frame so that relevant schematics and graphs are shown, explanations on the system's capabilities and methods would access pointers to graphs and schematics that would enhance the content of the explanation. We have found this approach to be quite practical and flexible in meeting user requirements. A use for hypermedia links between template-based text and graphics is in explaining to the user why it is necessary to follow certain steps in dismantling a subsystem. With a schematic of the subsystem, the user could have arrows with numbers attached to them to show what steps are taken in what order. In this manner it may be easier for the user to understand why steps are followed in a certain order since they have a visual aid to the procedure. This approach communicates causal information quite easily. At this point temporal information is not required but it could be integrated in a similar manner. The approach is related to the concepts discussed in [Feiner and McKeown 1990b].

Another graphical enhancement to the content of an explanation would be the use of two to three level subtrees of the diagnostic hierarchy to illustrate the relations between nodes. If, for example, the user asks why a certain conclusion was made. If the conclusion was due to a refinement of the original hypothesis, the root of the subtree would be the original hypothesis and the subsequent refinements of that node would be illustrated using children of the root. In the case of a trace which required the traversal of several levels of nodes to reach a conclusion, a mechanism such as that used in RATIONALE's textual explanations [Abu-Hakima 1988] could rank the nodes for explanation content in terms of relevance and complexity. In the cases where explaining the node is overly complex compared to its relevance to the current line of reasoning, it is omitted from the explanation. In the cases where it is relevant and not overly complex it is included.

8. Conclusions

Causality in JETA is not as explicit as it is in RATIONALE since JETA does not distinguish between enabling, invalidating or alternate symptoms that are used for problem refinement. However, JETA has a more complex node activation algorithm which combines symptoms, node status and descendent nodes. The tradeoff between representational complexity and clarity is a key problem in generating explanations in knowledge-based systems. In more complex representations, the explanation facility must compensate to clarify the reasoning strategies for the user. Such will be the case for JETA. Building an explanation facility requires interaction with technicians who are the end users. JETA's explanation facility will have to be evaluated by the technicians to provide feedback for its enhancement.

This paper illustrates that hypermedia is the approach to follow in the implementation of diagnostic systems, especially the implementation of the user interface and explanation facility. The overhead associated with the integration of text, graphics and images has to be addressed further so that hypermedia explanations are achievable. Some of these issues will be resolved when JETA's hypermedia explanation facility is completed.

9. Acknowledgements

The authors would like to thank Dave Peloso of GasTops Ltd. and Tim Taylor of Phalanx Research who were contracted to implement the user interface and the generalized knowledge browser respectively.

Chapter 11

Integrating Simultaneous Input from Speech, Gaze, and Hand Gestures

David B. Koons, Carlton J. Sparrell, and Kristinn R. Thorisson

Abstract

The focus of this chapter is the integration of information from speech, gestures, and gaze at the computer interface. We describe two prototype systems that accept simultaneous speech, gestural and eye movement input from a user. The three modes are processed to a common frame-based encoding and interpreted together to resolve references to objects in the map. In the first proto-type, a user can interact with a simple two-dimensional map. The computer responds in synthe-sized speech and by manipulating the map display. The second system uses a three-dimensional blocks world and demonstrates a more flexible interpretation strategy for handling full-hand ges-tures. Speech-related hand movements are processed to an intermediate level of representation without automatically assigning a deictic or symbolic meaning. Interpretation occurs later and takes advantage of information from the other modes and from the context.

1. Introduction

With increasing computer and robot intelligence, it is becoming more desirable to *com-municate* with machines rather than *operating* them. We have at our disposal a wealth of techniques to communicate our thoughts and intentions. To get ideas across quickly, our communication system relies on a very efficient mix of spatial and semantic knowledge. We can switch instantly between various modes for communicating the same ideas: speech, hand gestures, facial gestures, intonation, etc. Together, these features signifi-cantly increase the "bandwidth" between two communicating parties.

One of the problems encountered when interpreting simultaneous input from multiple modes is the timing of events. With a free mix of input modes, actions are not coordinated according to a script or a set sequence. This puts a higher burden on the interpretation methods used. A second problem is the level of abstraction. If the signals from the disjoint modes are separate pieces of a particular message, the question becomes how far we should process the given "evidence" in each mode before trying to integrate it with the information from the other modes. A related problem is *how* to combine the information once it has been extracted. In this paper, we focus on integrating information from speech, gestures, and gaze at the computer interface. We have built two prototype systems that accept speech, gestural and eye movement input from a user. The first one allows interaction with a simple two-dimensional map (for an overview and hardware description, see [Thorisson et al. 1992]). Through a free mixture of speech, deictic gestures and glances the user can request information or give commands to modify the contents of the map database. The second system extends the repertoire of free gestures to include iconic and pantomimic gestures and replaces the two-dimensional graphics with a three-dimensional blocks world.

2. Related Research

2.1. Multi-Modal Interfaces

The most widespread example of a computer interface that offers multiple input channels is the combination of keyboard and mouse found on most modern workstations. These systems offer the user a choice of modes for many tasks: entering text is best accomplished with the keyboard; moving the cursor or other objects around on the screen is easily carried out with the mouse or other pointing device. Interface designers must constrain the possible actions that a user may carry out and develop an unambiguous mapping between the context of an action and its interpretation. In addition to a highly-constrained interaction, these interfaces do not allow the use of the multiple input channels in parallel (except for a few cases such as the click-drag).

"Put That There" [Bolt 1980] used speech-recognition and a three-dimensional sensing device to simultaneously gather input from a user's speech and the location of a cursor on a wall-sized display. CUBRICON, a more recent multi-modal interface prototype, provides for simultaneous speech, keyboard and mouse input [Neal and Shapiro 1991]. Although these are important contributions to the development of multi-modal interfaces, both systems reduce gestures to the location of a simple two-dimensional cursor. Hauptman [1989] conducted a "Wizard of Oz" study (a person monitors the user's actions and translates them into computer commands) and found that, when given the task of manipulating objects displayed on a computer display, there is an advantage in allowing a person to communicate using a free mixture of speech and gestures. However, the study also showed that two-dimensional input devices severely restricted the types of gestures that could be made by the person.

2.2. Gestures

Human hands are powerful tools for directly interacting with the environment and exerting influence on it. This may be one of the reasons why research on hand gestures (both in three-dimensional interactive graphics and computer generated environments as well as telerobotics) has focused on *tool-level* manipulation (e.g., [Butterworth et al. 1992; Sheridan 1992; Sturman 1992; Weimer and Ganapathy 1989; Fisher et al. 1986]). In these interfaces, gestures either imitate real-world actions (like grasping and throwing) or are purely symbolic, with a single and complete meaning attached to a pre-defined motion, posture, or combination of the two. While tool-level interfaces can be very efficient and sometimes intuitive, they often become unwieldy when functionality is hidden under layers of hierarchical modes and menus.

Another characteristic of these interfaces is their limitation to a small set of gestures [Tyler et al. 1991b; Wahlster 1991] that the user sometimes has to learn, and even train for, to be able to apply. Wahlster [1991] has a good example of such a system using deictic gestures. In his interface the user selects the desired type of gesture from a menu of icons; the interpretation of the subsequent deictic gesture (a mouse click in a chosen region of the screen) is based on the type of icon selected. While the interpretation is context dependent, the interface still forces the user to learn specific rules for operating the computer.

In addition to tool-level manipulation our hands play a large role in communication because of their natural link to the spatio-temporal world in which we live [Rimé and Sachiaratura 1991]. People use their hands to show three-dimensional relationships between objects and temporal sequences of events: a hand can in one instance take the role of an object and in the next, serve as a pointer to fictional constructs created in the gesture space. These types of gestures at the interface have received very little attention.

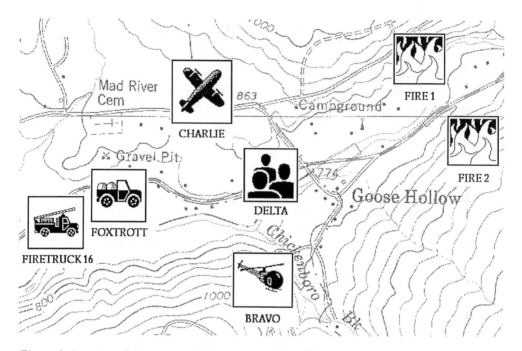

Figure 1. A section of the screen with icons representing helicopters, airplanes, trucks, fire crews and fire locations. The user can move, create and change these objects by referring to them in a free mixture of speech, gaze, and gestures.

2.3. Eyes

If an object of discussion is in someone's vicinity there is a natural tendency to glance in its direction, make gestures toward it, and to look directly at it, in coherence with the flow of the conversation [Kahneman 1973]. This feature of gaze can augment the interpretation of deictic references when the input from other modes is partial or segmented. Starker and Bolt [1990] describe an interface that bases its output on the data from a user's looking behavior. Whereas their system used only eyes as input, they made an effort to interpret the deictic behavior of the eye on more than one level, making the interface potentially more responsive to the user's looking. Jacob [1990] devised an eye tracking interface that allows a person to use gaze, or gaze and keyboard input in combination, to make selections on a computer screen. However, in this system, eye tracking plays a role similar to a mouse or other pointing device. In our system, the user is not required to use eyes as a pointer. We are specifically looking to incorporate eyes into the interaction process in a non-intrusive manner.

3. Prototype for Three Modes

To explore the issues related to multi-modal interpretation, we designed a prototype system that can gather input from speech, gestures and eye movements. The primary goal was to design a computer interface that could collect, process and interpret the different channels into a single integrated meaning.

A simple two-dimensional map is used as the subject of the interaction with the computer (Figure 1). Through a free mixture of speech, gestures and glances the user can request information or give commands to modify the contents of the map database. The prototype is composed of three major components: the input system, the map database, and the interpretation module (Figure 2).

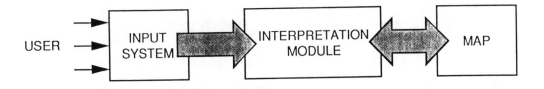

Figure 2. The interpretation module receives information from both the user's actions and the map database, which allows it to interpret the actions in the context of the map.

3.1. Input System

The user's speech is recognized using a PC-based discrete word recognition system. Hand and arm movements are sampled using full hand sensing hardware, and data on eye movements is collected using a corneal-reflection eye tracker. All three streams of data, the words from the speech recognizer, the position and posture of the hand and the point of gaze, are collected on a central workstation (Figure 3). Each incoming data record is assigned a time stamp as it arrives on the host computer. This timing information is later used to realign data from the different sources.

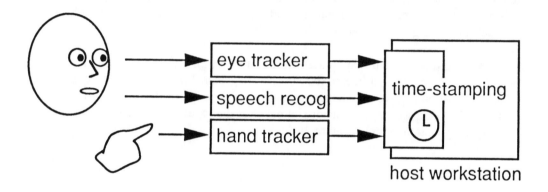

Figure 3. The data from speech, eye and hands are collected and sent to a real- time interface where they are time stamped. The time stamping allows for a later reconstruction of the input based on the exact time of occurrence.

3.2.   Map Database

The map, displayed on the workstation display, serves as the shared subject for the human-computer interaction. The graphic presented is a simple two-dimensional color map and a number of colored icons representing objects. An object-oriented database manages the attributes and locations of the map objects. A command-language interface allows the interpretation module (and external simulation modules) to make queries to the database contents or to modify selected objects. When the system is initiated, the map database reads a stored configuration and displays the map for the user.

3.3. Interpretation Module

Based on the observation that a message is often composed of at least two very different kinds of information, the interpretation module includes two different representational systems that are interconnected: the first system is used to encode categorical information; the other is used to encode geometrical or spatial information. Information from the map database is used to build and maintain a knowledge base that spans the two representational systems. Map objects are represented both as nodes in a semantic network within the categorical system and as models in the spatial system. The interpretation module's task is to gather information from the input system and match the message to elements within the knowledge base.

The user input is processed in two major steps. First, the three input streams are parsed to produce a frame-like description of the structure of the incoming data. Second, the frames are interconnected and evaluated. Some frames can be encoded and evaluated in the categorical system where others find values in the spatial system. Together the expression guides the evaluation of the user's utterance. Once the expression is completely evaluated and all references have been resolved, the computer can then respond to the user's request. An example of this process is given in Section 3.6.

3.4. Parsing

Each mode has its own parser that takes advantage of the structure or syntax inherent in the corresponding data stream. The output of the three parsers is an expression in a common intermediate frame-based representation.

A parse tree is produced from the incoming words in the speech channel (Figure 4). As syntactic tokens are created and added to the parse tree, frames associated with those tokens are created and arranged into nested expressions. The timing information of individual words is carried up through the syntactic tokens and into the frames.

For this prototype, gestures and eye movements are treated in a simplified way and have only deictic interpretations. Posture and movement data from the hand-sensing hardware are processed to recognize postures and movements directed at the workstation display.

When such a movement is detected, a frame is created with the glove and time data. Data from the eye tracker is analyzed to detect characteristic features in the motion of the eyes: fixations, saccades and blinks. A frame is created for each fixation containing the associated tracking data and time stamp.

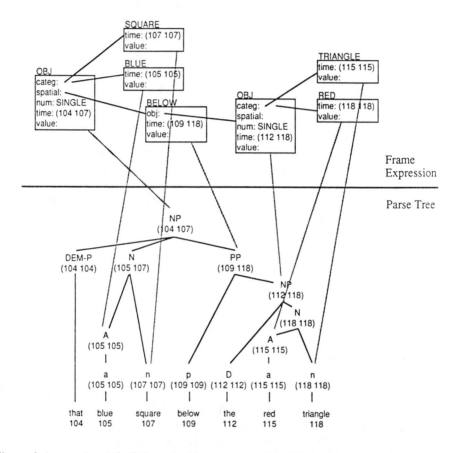

Figure 4. A parse tree is built from the incoming speech and then connected to the frame-based system. Here the parsed utterance is "... that blue square below the red triangle." Figure 5 shows frames produced from the other two modes.

3.5.   Evaluation

Each frame produced during parsing has a corresponding "evaluation method" that controls the search for that frame's value within the knowledge base. Depending on the type of frame, values can range from *nodes* in the propositional system (representing attributes or individual objects) to *points* or *regions* in the spatial system. When an evaluation method is successful, the resulting value for the corresponding frame is now available to other evaluation methods. (Frames can serve as slot values in other frames, creating nested expressions similar to LISP functions.) If a problem arises in the evaluation of a frame, a "problem method" is started. A new subgoal is then created that attempts to find the missing information in other modes or by asking the user for additional information.

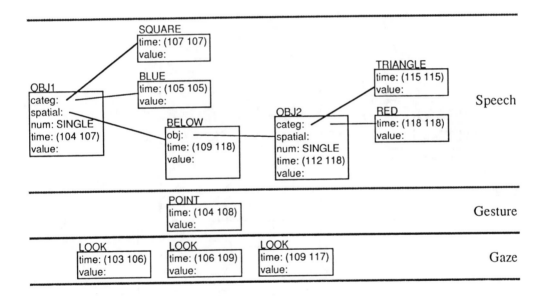

Figure 5. An idealized example of the frames produced from all three input modes during utterance "...that blue square below the red triangle"

3.6.   Example Evaluation

Suppose the user is sitting in front of the display. He now says, "That blue square below the red triangle" while looking at the upper right quadrant of the screen and pointing in a similar direction. After this speech input is parsed, a nested expression of frames will be produced (Figure 5). Parsing the hand data and eye tracking data will produce additional, but at this time, disjoint frames. The evaluation methods attached to each of the frames begin to search for values for their frames in the representational systems. Because all gestures in this prototype are treated as deictic, an evaluation method attached to a gesture frame will produce a *point* in the spatial system; this *point* is the frame's value. The fixation frames are treated in a similar manner.

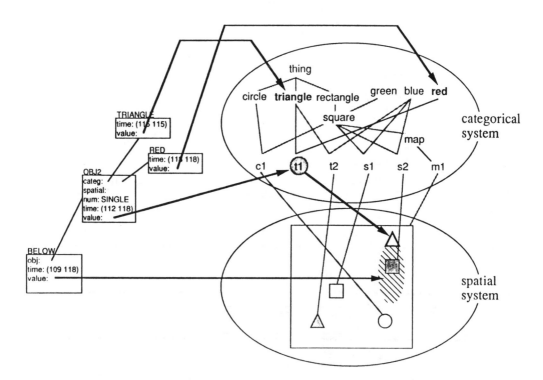

Figure 6. The expression associated with "below the red triangle" is evaluated by finding values for each frame. Frame values include object models and regions in the spatial system as well as nodes in the categorical system.

The evaluation method attached to the speech frame labeled OBJ2 (and associated with the speech input "the red triangle") in Figure 6 first attempts to use the propositional system to find an object that is both *red* and a *triangle*. This object, represented as a node in the propositional system (with links into its representation in the spatial system), is now available to the evaluation method attached to the BELOW frame. This method accepts the *red* triangle *t1* as an argument and shifts to the spatial system to produce a region that is in the proper spatial relation to the red triangle (below it). Meanwhile, the evaluation method attached to the OBJ1 frame (associated with the speech input "that blue square") attempts to find a single object in the propositional system but finds that there are multiple blue squares within the current map. A problem method now searches the other information sources and finds the frames in the gesture and eye modes that have an acceptable temporal relation to its frame (determined by temporal proximity). With the additional information from these deictic frames, and the BELOW frame from speech, the evaluation method for the OBJ1 frame can now use the spatial system to find the only blue square that is in the correct location on the map (Figure 7). Once the utterance has been successfully evaluated (all references have been resolved), the computer will react to the user's input. For this example, the result of evaluation is the square *s2* (for example, as the user's answer to an incomplete command). In the case of a query or a command, the interpretation module will send the appropriate commands to the map database and generate a simple statement that is sent to a speech synthesizer.

3.7. Discussion

This prototype system highlights many important points in attempting to interpret simultaneous multi-modal inputs. First and most obviously, this interface is a departure from current computer interface design. Unlike the interaction on a modern workstation, the user is able to use any combination of modes to communicate the request. For example, the user can choose to use speech alone with a request like "Delete all the blue squares." Or, speech can be reduced to "Move that to here" with gestures or glances filling in the necessary information. This opens up a highly flexible communication style for the user (and the interface designer).

A related point demonstrated in the prototype is that the interpretation of multi-modal input must be handled in a way that takes advantage of the interdependencies between the information supplied by each mode. While one mode may carry a significant portion of the information (usually speech), most messages cannot be interpreted without using the information from the other modes. These interdependencies require an interpretation process that is able to build up a single meaning by using all the modes simultaneously in a process similar to constraint satisfaction.

A shortcoming of this first prototype is its oversimplification of gestures and eye movements. Contrary to the idea that interpretation should not be carried out in any one mode, gestures and fixations in the prototype were automatically assigned a deictic interpretation. This treatment ignores the rich and subtle communicative abilities of both gestures and eye movements in natural discourse.

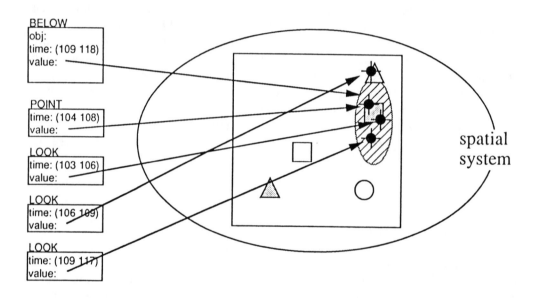

Figure 7. Spatial values for frames originating in the speech, gesture and eye tracking channels are compared in the spatial representation system.

4. Beyond Pointing

Gestures are most often integrated with our speech and other channels of communication. We fluidly switch context in the process of communicating a message, such that two identical hand movements might represent different actions, objects or ideas even when performed in the space of one verbal phrase. What are the different ways that a speech-related movement might be interpreted? Several taxonomies have been proposed for categorizing gestures that occur with speech. The taxonomy proposed by Rimé and Schiaratura [1991], which is a revision of the Efron classification system, proposes the following gesture types:

Symbolic gestures can be translated directly to some verbal meaning (such as the "OK" *posture* made by touching the forefinger to the thumb and extending the other fingers). Gestures such as these are normally part of a culture and have come to represent a single unambiguous meaning within that culture.

Deictic gestures include pointing or motioning to direct the listener's attention to objects or events in the surrounding environment.

Iconic gestures are used by a speaker to display information about the shape of objects, spatial relations, and actions.

Pantomimic gestures usually involve the manipulation of some invisible object or tool in contact with the speaker's hand.

Of these possible interpretations of speech-related hand movements, only the symbolic gestures can be interpreted immediately (within a given cultural context). Deictic, iconic and pantomimic gestures usually cannot stand alone and must be interpreted with additional information from the other channels and/or the surrounding context.

4.1. Representational Level

In order to extract meaning from the streams of gestural data, an appropriate level of abstraction must be chosen. At the lowest level, we have the constant flow of raw data from the full-hand input device hardware. At the highest level of abstraction would be a pure symbolic language (such as American Sign Language) in which complete gestures are specifically categorized to have an exact meaning.

It has been previously stated that using the highest level of abstraction, as in a symbolic language, limits the flexibility of the hands. This method changes the hands into "tools" and restricts their communicative power, creating problems such as the "Midas Touch." We have tried to find an intermediate level of abstraction that refines and reduces the information from the raw data and faciltates interpretation in the broader context of information available from other sources.

4.2.   Gesture Features

Two layers of abstraction are built before the final interpretation of the gestures (Figures 8 and 9). First, the hand data is classified into features of *posture, orientation*, and *motion* at each discrete sample point. Currently, the posture features for each finger are *straight, relaxed*, or *closed*. For orientation of the hand, we look at the direction of two vectors coming out of the hand. The first is a normal vector out of the palm (vector A in Figure 10). The second is a longitudinal vector indicating where the hand is pointing (vector B in Figure 10). The general direction of both vectors is quantized into the values *up, down, left, right, forward*, or *back* (relative to the person's trunk). Hand motion is currently only specified as *moving* or *stopped*. While relatively crude, these descriptive tags are useful in detecting important changes in the hand data.

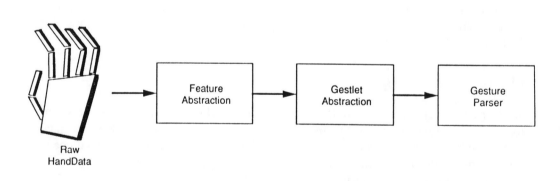

Figure 8. Raw hand data are processed successively on three separate representational levels.

The features are first used for data reduction: when a record is received with one or more of the values differing from the preceding record, it is extracted for further processing. These extracted records are passed to the next abstraction layer. Subsequent identical records are saved but not processed. (The unprocessed records are preserved for cases where the exact path is important, such as in the case of a person drawing out a detailed shape with their hand.)

4.3.   Gestlets

A second layer of abstraction is created by collapsing the stream of features into structures similar to speech phrases (Figure 9). We refer to these structures as *gestlets*. The gestlets are pieces of gestures that have been formed by grouping portions of the feature stream together using certain rules. The most useful rule for this purpose has been to group all contiguous data sets where the hand is moving together with the preceding and following records when the hand is stopped.

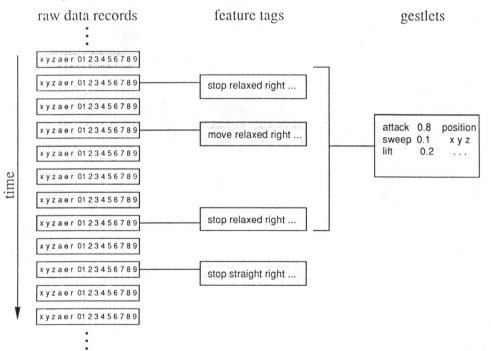

Figure 9. Parsing the raw hand data involves extracting features (feature tags) and combining these into meaningful units to produce gestlets.

The resulting stream of gestlets is buffered. If evidence in the speech channel suggests that important informaion may be found in gestures, the interpretation module searches the gestlet buffer for specific categories of gestures. The gesture parsing routines produce a broad description of the hand motion that occurred, using various weighted parameters. A pointing gesture, for example, would include *attack* (motion towards the gesture space), *sweep* (motion from side to side), and *end reference space* (position of hand at the end of the motion). By adding up the parameter weights, and looking for various logical combinations of gestlets, the parameters provide a way to estimate the likelihood that a certain categry of gesture happened. For this specific example, if a deictic gesture is gound, the hand orientation would be used to find a vector in three-space that intersects the screen.

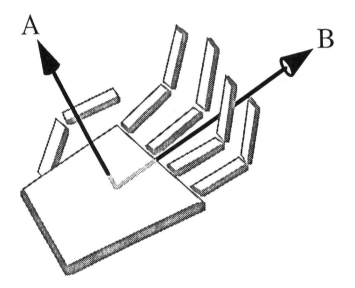

Figure 10. Normal and Longitudinal Vectors from Palm

4.4.   Example Evaluation

A second prototype system, based on these modifications, enables a user to manipulate objects in a simple "blocks world" by using not only deictic but iconic and pantomimic gestures as well. A typical interaction is shown in Figure 11. The user in this example wishes to move and rotate a cylinder so that it ends up in a particular orientation next to a cube. It is important to note that gesture types are fluidly mixed in situations such as this. The raw data must be processed in a way that these motions can be separated and interpreted in the context of the accompanying speech.

While the hand data is being processed into gestlets, the speech recognizer is converting the voice input into words. The eye tracking module is also working in parallel determining fixations, saccades and blinks. Each channel of information is brought to a similar level of abstraction allowing for close examination of the interdependencies of the modalities.

Figure 11. Typical Interaction

Processing the speech produces a structure as shown in Figure 12. The first part of the command to be resolved is the reference with the phrase "that cylinder." The use of "that" in the utterance *"Place that cylinder"* strongly suggests a deictic gesture. The speech and gesture phrases are tied together and interpreted in the spatial representational system to determine a referent in the environment. The remainder of the directive, "next to the red cube," indicates the possibility of either a deictic or an iconic gesture.

The phrase "next to the red cube" allows for several interpretations. The first might be that the user doesn't care about the exact location and orientation of the cylinder, only that it is in close proximity to the cube. In that case, no gesture information would have been given, and the exact placement of the cylinder could be arbitrary. Alternatively, the person might use a deictic gesture and point to a location near the cube where the cylinder should be placed.

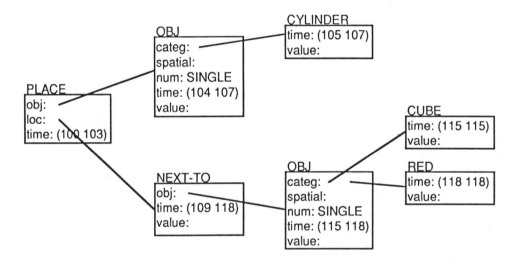

Figure 12. Structure After Speech Processing

A third possibility is the one shown in Figure 11. The person has used a two-handed iconic gesture to indicate not only the relative position of the cylinder with respect to the cube but also the orientation. The movement of both hands is important. First, the left hand is brought up to represent the cube. Then the right hand is moved in next to it to show the relative positioning of the two objects. Orientation information is provided by the right hand: it is placed in a curled posture suggesting that an invisible cylinder is being held.[1] With one command the user has accomplished a selection, a three-dimensional translation, and a rotation around all three axes.

5. Beyond Looking as Deixis

Most uses of gaze at the computer interface have been interpreted as deictic gestures indicating the user's interest [Thorisson et al. 1992; Starker and Bolt 1990; Jacob 1990]. However, like gestures, eye movements can be interpreted in many different ways, depending on the context in which they are performed. For example, gaze is a good indicator of a person's attention over time [Kahneman 1973] and could be useful in predicting the user's behavior in the context of a broader task. The eyes also play a very special role in social interaction; they are important in the regulation of turn-taking between participants in a dialog (who has control of the "floor") [Argyle and Cook 1976]. Turn taking is crucially important in both clarification and negotiation [Whittaker and Walker 1991]. Additionally, eye movements have been found to play a significant role in conveying personality, emotional states, and interpersonal attitudes [Argyle et al. 1974; Kleinke 1986].

Future work should include the ability to incorporate this eye behavior information in an integrated interpretation process. Someday, significant looks, tired stares, winks and rapid searches can all be useful in our interaction with machines.

6. Summary

We have shown a frame-based method of interpreting multi-modal input. The system takes into account various types of gestures, fairly complex speech and deictic gaze. By

---

[1]The point might also be argued that the user is representing the cylinder by the shape of his hand. According to Rimé and Schiaratura's modified Efron classification, this would be an iconic gesture. In many cases this distinction will not make a difference for interpretation.

bringing gestures to an intermediate representational level, interpretation of hand data is made more flexible. The gesture parsing method described can currently handle deictic references, pantomimic and iconic gestures, but should be easily extended to accommodate other categories as well.

Future work should include extensions such as full-arm and full-body descriptions. We are currently working on methods to accommodate more complex interpretations of looking and are exploring other gesture categories in a variety of contexts.

Acknowledgments

We would like to thank our director, Dr. Richard Bolt, and acknolwedge the contributions of graduate students Brent Britton and Edward Herranz, and assistants David Berger, Brian Brown, Michael Johnson, Mathew Kaminski, Brian Lawrence, Christopher Wren, and research affiliate Masaru Sugai, NEC, Japan.

This research was supported by the Defense Advanced Research Projects Agency (DARPA) under Rome Laboratories, contract F30602-89-C-0022.

Architectural and Theoretical Issues

The papers in this final section address architectural and theoretical issues that underlie intelligent multimedia interfaces. The first chapter by Yigal Arens, Eduard Hovy, and Mira Vossers addresses the media allocation problem, that is how and on what basis should information be apportioned to different kinds of media (e.g., text, charts, maps, tables, menus). They first ague that information (e.g., ships locations) should not be directly allocated to particular media (e.g., text or maps) rather characteristics of information (e.g., data with spatial denotations) should be assigned to characteristics of media (e.g., graphs, tables, and maps are planar media). They identify four classes of knowledge that are required to allocate information to media – the characteristics of the information, the characteristics of the media, the goals and nature of the speaker, and the nature of the perceiver and the communicative situation. For example, information characteristics include dimensionality, transience, urgency, quantity; media characteristics include dimensionality, temporal endurance, visual/aural nature. They formalize a range of these features in a systemic network and indicate interdependencies among features as rules or constraints between producer goals, information content, and surface features of presentations. They conclude by illustrating how these knowledge sources could be used to produce and interpret multimedia displays, in particular to indicate the location of Paris and to analyze an illustrated instruction explaining how to adjust a Honda car seat.

Andrea Bonarini also discusses the kinds of models required to support multimedia communication, however, in the context of the communication between a driver and an artificial co-pilot. Bonarini discusses the need to model the features of interaction tools, including general features such as the sensory channel used (e.g., auditory, visual) as well as particular characteristics (e.g., the type of action and attention required to manipulate a tool, the fidelity of the tool). A model of the driver is derived from his behavior (e.g., using a history of the velocity and acceleration of the vehicle, braking and steering patterns, horn use) which includes knowledge about his psychological state such as the level of attention devoted to performance of his current task, degree of agitation, and degree of fatigue. Each of these features are associated with interface functions (e.g., if the driver's attention is overwhelmed, communicating additional information is not advised). Other components of the driver model include a model of his goals and knowledge along with a probabilistic, rule-based model of his preferences or biases to react to situations in stereotypical ways. Use of the driver model is exemplified in an example interactive route guidance in which the system infers (using uncertainty management techniques) and reasons about driver properties such as the level of awareness and agitation to decide what, when, and how to communicate information (e.g., display information on a map using arrows versus using synthetic speech). This chapter highlights the value of user models for tailoring multimedia communication.

In contrast to the view of automating mode allocation, Matthew Cornell, Beverly Woolf, and Daniel Suthers describe a multimedia framework in which users choose how to view information in various ways (e.g., as animation, text, graphics, sound). Because all of the displays in their prototypes are generated from underlying knowledge structures, users can ask questions like "What is that" and receive context dependent responses which they can then view from multiple perspectives. Because the underlying knowledge base relates the presentations on the fly, there is no need to author explicitly connections between presentations as in traditional hypermedia systems. The authors describe IKIT, an application which supports creation, organization, access, and communication of information. IKIT includes media displayers, display hierarchies, and the ability to interactively or programmatically bind gestures to underlying actions. The authors illustrate their notion of "live information" with several examples, including an explanation dialogue from an electronics tutor. Users are able to reuse parts of or entire previous presentations or queries by simply selecting them. When users linguistically reference or physically point to these, this modifies the attentional model as in Burger and Marshall's [this volume] AIMI. They discuss how their framework also has utility for hypermedia authoring and distributed multimedia collaboration.

In addition to the development of prototypes such as those described above, there is an important and largely unfulfilled role for empirical testing and experimentation with intelligent multimedia interfaces. Jurgen Krause provides an empirical perspective to these issues based on a set of human computer interface (HCI) experiments and prototypes. He does not restrict the kind and scope of the combination of different modalities to that found in human-human communication, rather he argues that we ought to preserve their advantages but avoid their disadvantages. This leads to a need for a range of empirical studies from formally testing existing prototypes and systems to simulating potential systems via wizard-of-oz experiments. For example, studies of menus in commercial systems which convey possible actions (menu choices in text), application states (check marks next to menu items), and disabled actions (greyed out menu items) indicate that even this simplest integration of text and graphics encourages high error rates in users. This, in part, is a consequence of individual differences in the naming of actions and functions but also a result of the lack of consistency in action grouping (within and across applications) and the failure to adequately encode semantic distinctions in presentations. The mixed-media menu case questions the conventional wisdom that multiple media will improve communications. Other evidence implies that, at least with the current state of the art, users adapt their communication to a kind of "computer talk" when interacting with machines (i.e., they restrict sentence complexity, become more direct, avoid elliptical constructions). Rather than assuming users will interact as in human-human communication, Krause argues for further empirical studies to discover the actual and most effective modes of communication so that these can be supported.

Chapter 12

On the Knowledge Underlying Multimedia Presentations

Yigal Arens, Eduard Hovy, and Mira Vossers[1]

Abstract

We address one of the problems at the heart of automated multimedia presentation production and interpretation. The media allocation problem can be stated as follows: how does the producer of a presentation determine which information to allocate to which medium, and how does a perceiver recognize the function of each part as displayed in the presentation and integrate them into a coherent whole? What knowledge is used, and what processes? We describe the four major types of knowledge that play a role in the allocation problem as well as interdependencies that hold among them. We discuss two formalisms that can be used to represent this knowledge and, using examples, describe the kinds of processing required for the media allocation problem.

1. The General Problem of Presentations Using Multiple Media

When communicating, people almost always employ multiple media. Even natural language, which is after all the most powerful representational medium developed by hu-

---

[1] The first author was supported in part by Rome Laboratory of the Air Force Systems Command and the Defense Advanced Research Projects Agency under contract no. F30602-91-C-0081. The second author was supported in part by Rome Laboratory of the Air Force Systems Command under RL contract no. FQ7619-89-03326-0001. The third author, a graduate student at the University of Nijmegen, Nijmegen, The Netherlands, spent six months at USC/ISI and has since graduated. Views and conclusions contained in this report are the authors' and should not be interpreted as representing the official opinion or policy of DARPA, RL, the U.S. Government, or any person or agency connected with them.

mankind, is usually augmented by pictures, diagrams, etc., when written, or by gestures, hand and eye movements, intonational variations, etc., when spoken. And this preference for multimedia carries over to communication with computational systems, as evidenced by the explosive growth of the field of Human-Computer Interfaces. Since the early dream of Artificial Intelligence – of creating fully autonomous intelligent agents that would interact with people as equals – has proved impossible to achieve in the near term, the thrust of much AI work is on the construction of semi-intelligent machines operating in close symbiosis with humans, forming units. For maximum ease of communication within such units, natural language and other human-oriented media are the prime candidates (after all, computers are easier to program than humans are).

How then can computers construct and analyze such multimedia presentations? A survey of the literature on the design of presentations (book design, graphic illustration, etc., see [Tufte 1990; Bertin 1983; Tufte 1983]) underscores how this area of communication remains an art and shows how hard it is to describe the rules that govern presentations. But people clearly do follow rules when they use several media to construct communications; textbooks, for example, are definitely not illustrated randomly. Psychologists have been studying multimedia issues such as the effects of pictures in text, design principles for multimedia presentation, etc. for many years [Hartley 1985; Twyman 1985; Dwyer 1978; Fleming and Levie 1978], although most of their results are too general to be directly applicable in work that is to be computationalized. On the other hand, cognitive science studies of the past few years have provided results which can be incorporated into theories about good multimedia design [Petre and Green 1990; Roth and Mattis 1990a; Mayer 1989; Larkin and Simon 1987]. They address questions such as whether graphical notations are really superior to text, what makes a picture worth (sometimes) a thousand words, how illustration affects thinking, the characterization of data, etc.

Artificial Intelligence (AI) researchers and other computer scientists have been addressing aspects of the problem of automatically constructing multimedia presentations as well. Mackinlay [1986a] describes the automatic generation of a variety of tables and charts; the WIP system [Wahlster et al. 1991b; André et al., this volume; André and Rist, this volume] plans a text/graphics description of the use of an espresso machine, starting with a database of facts about the machine and appropriate communicative goals, and using text and presentation plans. The COMET system [Feiner 1991; Feiner and McKeown 1990b] plans text/graphic presentations of a military radio using text schemas and pictorial perspective presentation rules. The TEXPLAN [Maybury 1991a, this volume] and AIMI [Burger and Marhsall 1991, this volume] systems plan text/map/table presentations of military information, also using presentation plans. Similarly, the INTEGRATED INTERFACES system [Arens et al. 1988] and the CUBRICON system [Neal 1990] plan and produce presentations involving maps, text, and menus. Other work is reported in the collections [Sullivan and Tyler 1991; Ortony et al. 1992].

One lesson that is clear from all this work is the need for a detailed study of the major types of knowledge required for multimedia presentations, encoded in a formalism that supports both their analysis and generation. For the past few years, we have been involved in various studies of one aspect or another of this problem. In particular, we ask: why and how do people apportion the information to be presented to various media? And how do they reassemble the portions into a single message again? This paper contains an overview of some of our results. Section 2 describes our methodology and formalisms. Section 3 provides details about the features and their interdependencies that we have managed to collect, and Section 4 provides some examples of the use of this knowledge.

2.   Our Approach and Methodology

2.1.   The Problem of Media Allocation

In order to focus our efforts, we have concentrated on the media allocation problem: given arbitrary information and any number of media, how, and on what basis, is a particular medium selected for the display of each portion of the information? This question, a particularization of the question why people use different media and other gestures and movements when they communicate, in our opinion lies at the heart of the general multimedia issue.

Rather than start with a literature study, we here describe the problem from the computational side. In most systems, the media allocation problem is addressed simply by the use of fixed rules that specify exactly what medium is to be used for each particular data type. This is clearly not a satisfactory solution, given the inflexibility and non-portability of such systems. Our approach is a *two-stage generalization* of this straightforward approach. We take an example from a hypothetical data base about ships in a Navy to illustrate. Under the straightforward approach, a typical rule may be:

1.   Ships' locations are presented on maps.

Our first generalization is to assign a medium not to each data type, but instead to each feature that characterizes data types. Thus instead of rule 1, we write the rule:

1. Data duples (of which ships' locations are an example) are presented on maps, graphs, or tables.

Of course, when considering subsets of features, one invariably gets under-specific rules. To provide more specificity we formulate such additional rules as:

2. Data with spatial denotations (such as locations) are presented on media with spatial denotations (such as maps).

However, note that this rule deals not with the medium of maps but instead with a characteristic of this medium. It suggests the second step of the generalization.

The second generalization is to assign characteristics of data not to media, but instead to characteristics of media. The two example rules now become:

1'. Data duples (of which locations are an example) are presented on planar media (such as graphs, tables, and maps).

2'. Data with spatial denotations (such as locations) are presented on media with spatial denotations (such as maps).

In this example, the two rules together suffice to specify maps uniquely as the appropriate medium for location coordinates. Of course, though, one can present the same information using natural language, as in *"the ship is at 15N 79E"*. Thus one is led to rephrase rule 2' to arrive at a more general but very powerful formulation:

2" Data with specific denotations are presented on media which can convey the same denotations.

Since language, pictures, and maps can carry spatial denotations (while, say, graphs or histograms usually do not), we once again require additional rules in order to specify a unique medium. However, since each of the three mentioned media can be perfectly suitable in the right context, the rules we formulate might not absolutely prohibit a medium; rather, the rules should be context-dependent in ways which enable the selection of the most appropriate medium. Thus we are led to rules such as:

3. If more than one medium can be used, and there is an existing presentation, prefer the medium/a that is/are already present as exhibits in the presentation.

4. If more than one media can be used, and there is additional information to be presented as well, prefer medium/a that can accommodate the other information too.

Rule 4 has important consequences. If one is to present not only the location of a ship, but also its heading, then both language and a map would do, since both media have facilities for indicating direction (in the case of language, an appositive phrase with the value *"heading SSW"* and in the case of a map, an icon with an elongation or an arrow). If in addition to this now one adds the requirement to present the nationality of the ship, natural language has such a capability (the adjective *"Swiss"*, say) but due to limitations of the map medium, one of the icon's independent characteristics (say, its color) must be allocated to convey nationality. Of course, this requires the addition of a description of the meaning of the different values the icon's independent characteristic can have (for example, a table of color for nationality). Such additional presentational overhead makes a map a less attractive medium than natural language for presenting a single ship's location/heading/nationality (though possibly not that of several ships together).

We formalize and discuss this point later in more detail. Here it is enough to note that the two-stage generalizations provide collections of rules that relate characteristics of information and characteristics of media in service of good multimedia presentations. In general terms, the medium allocation algorithm required can be described as a constraint satisfaction system, where the constraints arise from rules requiring the features of the information to be presented (i.e., the data) to be matched up optimally with the features of the media at hand.

2.2.   The Four Types of Knowledge Required

We illustrated the use of knowledge about media and information type. But what additional factors play a role in multimedia communication?

In our previous work in multimedia human-computer interactions [Arens et al. 1993; Vossers 1991; Hovy and Arens 1991; Hovy 1990a; Arens and Hovy 1990a,b], we addressed this question from several angles, trying to build up a library of terms that capture all the factors that play a role in multimedia human-human and human-computer communication. Drawing from an extensive survey of literature from Psychology, Human-Computer Interfaces, Natural Language Processing, Linguistics, Human Factors, and Cognitive Science, (see [Vossers 1991] as well as from several small analyses of pages from newspapers such as the *USA Today* and instruction manuals for appliances such as user manuals for a motor car, a sewing machine, a VCR, and a cookbook, we collected well over a hundred distinct features that play a role in the higher-level aspects of the production and interpretation processes, as well as over fifty rules that express the interdependencies among these features. Where appropriate, we applied the two-step generalization method to come up with features of the right type and at the right level of detail.

These features classify naturally into four major groups:

- the characteristics of the media used,
- the nature of the information to be conveyed,
- the goals and characteristics of the producer, and
- the characteristics of the perceiver and the communicative situation.

Section 3 provides more details about each type of knowledge resource and the rules interlinking them. Before getting to this seyction, however, we describe our attempts to find an adequately flexible and powerful representation formalism for the knowledge.

2.3. An Adequate Representation Formalism

Though we did not study all four aspects iny equal detail, we needed a representation formalism that could capture the requisite individual distinctions as well as their underlying interdependencies, that was extensible, and that did not hamper our research methodology.

As illustrated in Section 2.1, the two-step generalization process provides features and rules simultaneously. Features and their values we tried to tabulate straightforwardly, until we discovered that the underlying intyerdependencies between features – for example, the subclassification of some but not all values for a feature into finer classes, or the combination of values from several features to give rise to a new feature – and the interdependencies between rules made the simple tabular format cumbersome. In the spirit of our work on various media, we decided to codify our results in a more visual way, following the paradigm of AND-OR networks of features and values used in Systemic Functional Linguistics to analyze language and write grammars [Halliday 1985]. This is the notation used in the network fragments that appear in this chapter. The tables in this chapter can be drawn as networks as well, but more clearly illustrate the points being made here.

Processing of the networks is to be understood as similar to discrimination net traversal; one enters the network, makes the appropriate selection(s) at the first choice point(s), records the feature(s) so chosen, and moves along the connecting path(s) to the next choice point(s). In the network, curly brackets mean AND (that is, when entering one, all paths should be followed in parallel) and square brackets EXCLUSIVE OR (that is, at most one path must be selected and followed). Square brackets with slanted serifs are INCLUSIVE OR (that is, zero or more paths may be selected and followed). Whenever a feature is encountered during traversal, it is recorded; the final collection of features uniquely specifies the eventual result.

Using this notation, we follow a three-step research methodology: First, we identify the phenomena in some aspect of a presentation (e.g., the fact that the producer usually wants to affect the perceiver's future goals, or the fact that different media utilize different numbers of presentation 'dimensions'); second, we characterize the variability involved in each phenomenon (e.g., a producer may want to affect the perceiver's goals through warnings, suggestions, hints, requests, etc., or language is expressed 'linearly' while diagrams are two-dimensional); and third, we map out the interdependencies among the values of all the phenomena (e.g., the goal to warn selects a feature value 'urgent', and this value is interdependent with values such as 'high noticeability' which are tied to appropriate media such as sound or flashing icons). In the resulting AND-OR networks of interdependencies, each node represents a single phenomenon and each arc a possible value for it together with its interdependencies with other values.

One advantage of the network notation is its independence of process; one can implement the knowledge contained directly in network form, in a traditional rule-based system, or a connectionist one. We maintain the network form because several other presentation-related software at USC/ISI use the same formalism. The Penman sentence generator [Mann and Matthiessen 1983; Penman 1988] and associated text planning system [Hovy et al. 1992] contain a grammar of English and various factors influencing text structure all represented as AND-OR networks; sentence generation proceeds by traversing the grammar network from 'more semantic' toward 'more syntactic' nodes, collecting at each node features that instruct the system how to build the eventual sentence (see [Matthiessen 1984]). Parsing proceeds by traversing the same network 'backwards', eventually arriving at the 'more semantic' nodes and their associated features, the set of which constitutes the parse and determines the parse tree (see [Kasper 1989; Kasper and Hovy 1990]). This bi-directionality of processing is an additional advantage of the network formalism.

With respect to multimedia presentation planning and analysis, our overall conceptual organization of the knowledge resources is shown in Figure 1. Each knowledge resource appears as a separate network; the central network houses the interlinkages between the other ones. When producing a communication, the communicative goals and situational features cause appropriate features of the upper three networks to be selected, and information then propagates through the interlinkage network (the system's 'rules') to the appropriate medium networks at the bottom, causing appropriate values to be set, which in turn are used to control the low-level generation modules (the language generator, the diagram constructor, etc.). For multimedia input, a communication is analyzed by identifying its features in the relevant bottom networks for each portion of the communication, and propagating the information upward along the internetwork linkage to select appropriate 'high-level' features that describe the producer's goals, the nature of the information mentioned in that portion, etc. Examples appear in Section 4.

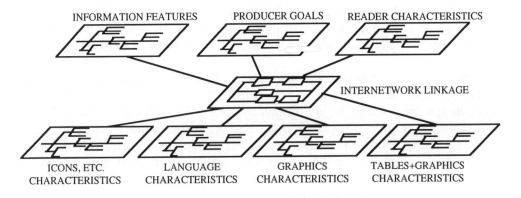

Figure 1. Knowledge Resources that Support Multimedia Communication.

3. The Knowledge Resources

In this section we describe the four major classes of features that influence multimedia presentation planning. In the fifth section we discuss the rules expressing interdependencies among the features in the four classes.

3.1.   Characterization of Media

3.1.1.   Definition of Terms

The following terms are used to describe presentation-related concepts. We take the point of view of the communicator (indicating where the consumer's subjective experience may differ).

Consumer: A person interpreting a communication.

Medium: A single mechanism by which to express information. Examples: spoken and written natural language, diagrams, sketches, graphs, tables, pictures.

Exhibit: A complex exhibit is a collection, or composition, of several simple exhibits. A simple exhibit is what is produced by one invocation of one medium. Examples of simple exhibits are a paragraph of text, a diagram, a computer beep. Simple exhibits involve the placement of one or more Information Carriers on a background Substrate.

Substrate: The background to a simple exhibit. That which establishes, to the consumer, physical or temporal location, and often the semantic context, within which new information is presented to the information consumer. The new information will often derive its meaning, at least in part, from its relation to the substrate. Examples: a piece of paper or screen (on which information may be drawn or presented); a grid (on which a marker might indicate the position of an entity); a page of text (on which certain words may be emphasized in red); a noun phrase (to which a prepositional phrase may be appended). An empty substrate is possible.

Information Carrier: That part of the simple exhibit which, to the consumer, communicates the principal piece of information requested or relevant in the current communicative context. Examples: a marker on a map substrate; a prepositional phrase within a sentence predicate substrate. A degenerate carrier is one which cannot be distinguished from its background (in the discussion below the degenerate carrier is a special case, but we do not bother explicitly to except it where necessary. Please assume it excepted).

Carried Item: That piece of information represented by the carrier; the 'denotation' of the carrier.

For purposes of rigor, it is important to note that a substrate is simply one or more information carrier(s) superimposed. This is because the substrate carries information as well.[2] In addition, in many cases the substrate provides an internal system of semantics which may be utilized by the carrier to convey information. Thus, despite its name, not all information is transmitted by the carrier itself alone; its positioning (temporal or spatial) in relation to the substrate may encode information as well. This is discussed further below.

Channel: An independent dimension of variation of a particular information carrier in a particular substrate. The total number of channels gives the total number of independent pieces of information the carrier can convey. For example, a single mark or icon can convey information by its shape, color, and position and orientation in relation to a background map. The number and nature of the channels depend on the type of the carrier and on the exhibit's substrate.

3.1.2.   Internal Semantic Systems

Some information carriers exhibit an internal structure that can be assigned a 'real-world' denotation, enabling them subsequently to be used as substrates against which other carriers can acquire information by virtue of being interpreted within the substrate. For example, a map used to describe a region of the world possesses an internal structure – points on it correspond to points in the region it charts. When used as a background for a ship icon, one may indicate the location of the ship in the world by placing

---

[2]Note that from the information consumer's point of view, Carrier and Substrate are subjective terms; two people looking at the same exhibit can interpret its components as carrier and substrate in different ways, depending on what they already know. For example, different people may interpret a graph tracking the daily value of some index differently as follows: someone who is familiar with the history of the index may call only the last point of the graph, that is, its most recent addition, the information carrier, and call all the rest of the graph the substrate. Someone who is unfamiliar with the history of the index may interpret the whole line plotted out as the information carrier, and the graph's axes and title, etc., as substrate. Someone who is completely unfamiliar with the index may interpret the whole graph, including its title and axis titles, as information carrier, and interpret the screen on which it is displayed as substrate.

its icon in the corresponding location on the map substrate. Examples of such carriers and their internal semantic systems are shown in Table 1.

Other information carriers exhibit no internal structure. Examples: icon, computer beep, and unordered list. An internal semantic system of the type described is always intrinsic to the item carried.

Carrier	Internal Semantic System
Picture	'real-world' spatial location based on picture denotation
NL Sentence	'real-world' sentence denotation
Table	categorization according to row and column
Graph	coordinate values on graph axes
Map	'real-world' spatial location based on map denotation
Ordered list	ordinal sequentiality

Table 1. Internal Semantic Systems

3.1.3.   Characteristics of Media

In addition to the internal semantics listed above, media differ in a number of other ways which can be exploited by a presenter to communicate effectively and efficiently. The values of these characteristics for various media are shown in Table 2.

Carrier Dimension: Values: *0D, 1D, 2D*. A measure of the number of dimensions usually required to exhibit the information presented by the medium.

Internal Semantic Dimension: Values: *0D, 1D, 2D, >2D, 3D, #D, ∞D*. The number of dimensions present in the internal semantic system of the carrier or substrate.

Temporal Endurance: Values: *permanent, transient*. An indication whether the created exhibit varies during the lifetime of the presentation.

Granularity: Values: *continuous, discrete*. An indication of whether arbitrarily small variations along any dimension of presentation have meaning in the denotation or not.

Medium Type: Values: *aural, visual*. What type of medium is necessary for presenting the created exhibit.

Default Detectability: Values: *low, medlow, medhigh, high*. A default measure of how intrusive to the consumer the exhibit created by the medium will be.

Baggage: Values: *low, high*. A gross measure of the amount of extra information a consumer must process in order to become familiar enough with the substrate to correctly interpret a carrier on it.

Generic Medium	Carrier Dimension	Internal Semantic Dimension	Temporal Endurance	Granularity	Medium Type	Default Detectability	Baggage
Beep	0D		transient	N/A	aural	high	
Icon	0D		permanent	N/A	visual	low	
Map	2D	>2D	permanent	continuous	visual	low	high
Picture	2D	∞D	permanent	continuous	visual	low	high
Table	2D	2D	permanent	discrete	visual	low	high
Form	2D	>2D	permanent	discrete	visual	low	high
Graph	2D	1D	permanent	continuous	visual	low	high
Ordered List	1D	#D	permanent	discrete	visual	low	low
Unordered List	0D	#D	permanent	N/A	visual	low	low
Written Sentence	1D	∞D	permanent	discrete	visual	low	low
Spoken Sentence	1D	∞D	transient	discrete	aural	medhigh	low
Animated Material	2D	∞D	transient	continuous	visual	high	high
Music	1D	∞D	transient	continuous	aural	medhigh	low

Table 2. Media characteristics

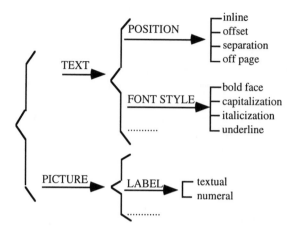

Figure 2. Portion of the Media Network: Values for some Text Channels

3.1.4.   How Carriers Convey Information

As part of an exhibit, a carrier can convey information along one or more *channels*. For example, with an icon carrier, one may convey information by the icon's shape, color, and possibly through its position in relation to a background map. The number and nature of the channels depends on the type of carrier and the substrate. The semantics of a channel may be *derived* from the carrier's spatial or temporal relation to a substrate which possesses an internal semantic structure; e.g., placement on a map of a carrier representing an object which exists in the charted area. Otherwise we say the channel is *free*.

Among *free* channels we distinguish between those whose interpretation is *independent* of the carried item (e.g., color, if the carrier does not represent an object for which color is relevant); and those whose interpretation is *dependent* on the carried item (e.g., shape, if the carrier represents an object which has some shape).

Most of the carrier channels can be made to vary their presented value in time. Time variation can be seen as an additional channel which provides yet another degree of freedom of presentation to most of the other channels. The most basic variation is the alternation between two states, in other words, a flip-flop, because this guarantees the continued (though intermittent) presentation of the original basic channel value.

The fonts and positions of letters and words in a text are also free channels for the words as carriers. Figure 2 contains a fragment of the network describing some possible values for these channels.

3.2. Characterization of Information

In this section we develop a vocabulary of presentation-related characteristics of information.

Broadly speaking, as shown in Table 3, three subcases must be considered when choosing a presentation for an item of information: intrinsic properties of the specific item; properties associated with the class to which the item belongs; and properties of the collection of items that will eventually be presented, and of which the current item is a member. These characteristics are explained in the remainder of this section.

Type	Characteristic	Values
Intrinsic	Dimensionality	0D, 1D, 2D, >2D, ∞D
Property	Transience	live, dead
	Urgency	urgent, routine
Class	Order	ordered, nominal, quantitative
Property	Density	dense, discrete, N/A
	Naming	identification, introduction
Set Property	Volume	singular, little, much

Table 3. Information characteristics by type.

Dimensionality: Some single items of information, such as a database record, can be decomposed as a vector of simple components; others, such as a photograph, have a complex internal structure which is not decomposable. We define the *dimensionality* of the latter as *complex*, and of the former as the dimension of the vector.

Since all the information must be represented in some fashion, the following rule must hold (where *simple* dimensionality has a value of 0, *single* the value 1, and so on, and *complex* the value ∞):

The Basic Dimensionality Rule of Presentations

Dim (Info) ≤ Dim (Carrier) + Free Channels (Carrier)
+ Internal Semantic Dim (Substrate)

In addition, we have found that different rules apply to information of differing dimensions. With respect to dimensionality, we divide information into several classes as follows:

- *Simple:* Simple atomic items of information, such as an indication of the presence or absence of email.
- *Single:* The value of some meter, such as the amount of gasoline left.
- *Double:* Pairs of information components, such as coordinates (graphs, map locations), or domain-range pairs in relations (automobile × satisfaction rating, etc.).
- *Multiple:* More complex information structures of higher dimension, such as home addresses. It is assumed that information of this type requires more time to consume.
- *Complex:* Information with internal structure that is not decomposable this way, such as photographs.

Transience: Transience refers to whether the information to be presented expresses some current (and presumably changing) state or not. Presentations may be:

- *Live:* The information presented consists of a single conceptual item of information (that is, one carried item) that varies with time (or in general, along some linear, ordered, dimension), and for which the history of values is not important. Examples are the amount of money owed while pumping gasoline or the load average on a computer. Most appropriate for *live* information is a single exhibit.
- *Dead:* The other case, in which information does not reflect some current state, or in which it does but the history of values is important. An example is the history of some stock on

the stock market; though only the current price may be important to a trader, the history of the stock is of import to the buyer.

Urgency: Some information may be designated *urgent*, requiring presentation in such a way that the consumer's attention is drawn. This characteristic takes the values *urgent* and *routine*:

- *Urgent:* This information relates to the user's persistent goals (involving actions which could cause personal injury or property damage, whether an imminent meltdown or a warning to a person crossing the road in front of a car) and must therefore be reinforced by textual devices such as 'boldface', 'capitalization', etc. For more details see [Hovy and Arens 1991].
- *Routine:* The normal, non-distinguished case.

Order: Order is a property of a collection of items all displayed together as a group of some kind. Values here are:

- *Quantitative:* This characterizes items belonging to a conceptually and/or syntactically regular but not presentationally ordered set, such as temperature readings for various parts of the country.
- *Ordinal:* This characterizes items of a set ordered according to their semantic denotations (e.g., steps in a recipe).
- *Nominal:* The items are not ordered.

Density: The difference between information that is presented equally well on a graph and a histogram and information that is not well presented on a histogram is a matter of the density of the class to which the information belongs. The former case is *discrete* information; an example is the various types of car made in Japan. The latter is *dense* information; an example is the prices of cars made in Japan.

- *Dense:* A class in which arbitrary small variations along a dimension of interest carry meaning. Information in such a class is best presented by a medium that supports continuous change.
- *Discrete:* A class in which there exists a lower limit to variations on the dimension of interest.

Naming (function): The role information plays may be defined relative to other information present. A good example is the information that names and introduces, such as that in headings of text sections, titles of diagrams, and labels in pictures. We identify just two of the many types here:

- *Identification:* This information identifies a portion of the presentation, based on an appropriate underlying semantic relation such as between a text label and a picture part; see [Hovy et al. 1992].

- *Introduction:* This information identifies and introduces other information by appearing first and standing out positionally.

Volume: A batch of information may contain various amounts of information to be presented. If it is a single fact, we call it *singular*: if more than one fact but still little relative to some task- and user-specific threshold, we call it *little*; and if not, we call it *much*. This distinction is useful because not all media are suited to present *much* information.

- *Much*: The relatively permanent media such as written text or graphics leave a trace to which the consumer can refer if he or she gets lost doing the task or forgets, while transient media such as spoken sentences and beeps do not. Thus the former should be preferred in this case.

- *Little*: There is no need to avoid the more transient media when the amount of information to present is *little*.

- *Singular*: A single atomic item of information. A transient medium can be used. However, one should not overwhelm the consumer with irrelevant information. For example, to display information about a single ship, one need not draw a map.

The features listed here are only the tip of a large iceberg. They can be subclassified in several ways. One way is by whether the feature is apparent by virtue of the information itself or by its juxtaposition with others, as in Table 3; another way is by its teleological status, as partially shown in Figure 3.

3.3.   The Producer's Intentions

Particularly in the field of natural language research, there has been much work identifying and classifying the possible goals of a producer of an utterance – work which can quite easily be applied to multimedia presentations in general.

Automated text generators, when possessing a rich grammar and lexicon, typically require several producer-related aspects to specify their parameters fully. For example, the PAULINE generator [Hovy 1988b] produced numerous variations from the same underlying representation depending on its input parameters, which included the following presenter-oriented features:

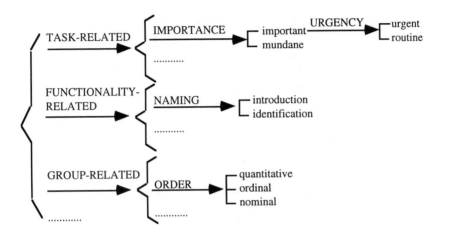

Figure 3. Fragment of the Information Features Network.

Producer's goals with respect to perceiver: These goals all address some aspect of the perceiver's mental knowledge or state, such as:

Affect perceiver's knowledge. This feature takes such values as teach, inform, and confuse.

Affect perceiver's opinions of topic: Values include switch, reinforce.

Involve perceiver in the conversation: Involve, repel.

Affect perceiver's emotional state: Of the hundreds of possibilities we list simply anger, cheer up, calm.

Affect perceiver's goals: Values include activate and deactivate. These goals cover warnings, orders, etc.

Producer's goals with respect to the producer-perceiver relationship: These address both producer and perceiver, for example:

Affect perceiver's emotion toward producer: Values include respect, like, dislike.

Affect relative status: Values here determine formality of address forms in certain languages, etc.: dominant, equal, subordinate.

Affect interpersonal distance: Values such as intimate, close, distant.

For our purposes, we have chosen to borrow and adapt a partial classification of a producer's communicative goals from existing work on Speech Acts. Figure 4 provides a small portion of the network containing aspects of a producer's communicative intentions that may affect the appearance of a presentation (see [Vossers 1991] for more details). In this network fragment *warn* is distinguished from *inform* because, unlike inform speech acts, the semantics of warnings involve capturing the attention of the reader in order to affect his/her goals or actions. To achieve this, a warning must be realized using presentation features that distinguish it from the background presentation.

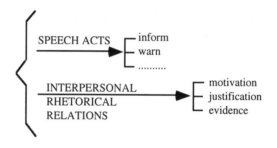

Figure 4. Portion of the Producer Goals Network.

3.4.   The Perceiver's Nature and Situation

Our work has only begun to address this issue. Existing research provides considerable material with a bearing on the topic, including especially the work in Cognitive Psychology on issues of human perception which influence the appropriateness of media choices for presentation of certain types of data. A survey and discussion of these results is presented in [Vossers 1991]. On the computational side, the abovementioned text generation system [Hovy 1988b] contains several categories of characteristics of the perceiver, including (with example values):

• *Knowledge of the topic:* Expert, student, novice.

- *Interest in the topic:* High, low.
- *Opinions of the topic:* Good, neutral, bad.
- *Language ability:* High, low.
- *Emotional state:* Calm, angry, agitated.

3.5. Interdependencies and Rules

The factors that affect multimedia presentations are not independent. Their interdependencies can be thought of as rules which establish associations between the goals of the producer, the content of the information, and surface features of presentations to constrain the options for presenting information (during generation) and disambiguate alternative readings (during interpretation). A small portion of these rules, also represented in network form, appears in Figure 5. Moving from left to right through the network (that is, in the direction of presentation interpretation), one first finds the presentation forms which express the information, then features of the information which are linked to various presentation forms, and finally the producer goals. That formalism is essentially equivalent to standard "Rule" writing, as below. We use one formalism or the other, depending on what we feel is most suitable to the task being addressed.

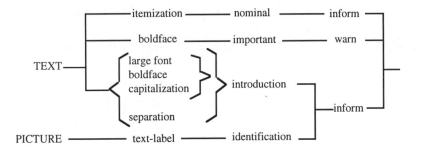

Figure 5. Portion of the Internetwork Linkage.

Below, in traditional form, is a more comprehensive list of rules, organized by characteristics of data being considered for presentation. The terminology is defined in Section 3.2.

Dimensionality

- Simple:
  - ◊ Rule: As carrier, use a medium with a dimension value of 0D.
  - ◊ Rule: No special restrictions on substrate.

- Single:
  - ◊ Rule: No special restrictions on substrate.

- Double:
  - ◊ Rule: As substrate, use media with internal semantic dimension of 2D.
  - ◊ Rule:As substrate, use media with discrete granularity (e.g., forms and tables) if information-class of both components is discrete.
  - ◊ Rule: As substrate, use media with continuous granularity (e.g., graphs and maps) if information-class of either component is dense.
  - ◊ Rule: As carrier, use a medium with a dimension value of 0D.

- Multiple:
  - ◊ Rule: As substrate, use media with discrete granularity if information-class of all components is discrete.
  - ◊ Rule: As substrate, use media with continuous granularity if the information-class of some component is dense.
  - ◊ Rule: As carrier, use a medium with a dimension value of at least 1D.
  - ◊ Rule: As substrate and carrier, do not use media with the temporal endurance value transient.

- Complex:
  - ◊ Rule: Check for the existence of specialized media for this class of information.

Transience

- Live:
  - ◊ Rule: As carrier, use a medium with the temporal endurance characteristic transient if the update rate is comparable to the lifetime of the carrier signal.

◊ Rule: As carrier, use a medium with the temporal endurance characteristic permanent if update rate is much longer.

◊ Rule: As substrate, unless the information is already part of an existing exhibit, use the neutral substrate.

- Dead:
  ◊ Rule: As carrier, use ones that are marked with the value permanent temporal endurance.

Urgency

- Urgent:
  ◊ Rule: If the information is not yet part of a presentation instance, use a medium whose default detectability has the value high (such as an aural medium) either for the substrate or the carrier.

  ◊ Rule: If the information is already displayed as part of a presentation instance, use the present medium but switch one or more of its channels from fixed to the corresponding temporally varying state (such as flashing, pulsating, or hopping).

- Routine
  ◊ Rule: Choose a medium with low default detectability and a channel with no temporal variance.

Density

- Dense:
  ◊ Rule: As substrate, use a medium with granularity characteristic continuous (e.g., graphs, maps, animations).

- Discrete:
  ◊ Rule: As substrate, use a medium with granularity characteristic discrete (e.g., tables, histograms, lists).

Volume

- Much:

◊ Rule: As carrier, do not use a medium with the temporal endurance value transient.

◊ As substrate, do not use a medium with the temporal endurance value transient.

- Little:

  ◊ Rule: No need to avoid transient media.

- Singular:

  ◊ Rule: As substrate, if possible use a medium whose internal semantic system has low baggage.

4. Some Examples

In this section we present a few simple examples of how the knowledge and rules outlined earlier can be applied to produce and interpret sample displays. Each example utilizes only a portion of the knowledge resources we have collected.

4.1. Example 1: Identification of Appropriate Media

We present three simple tasks in parallel. Given the following:

- **Task:** the task of presenting Paris (as the destination of a flight, say).
- **Available information** (three separate examples): the coordinates of the city, the name *Paris*, and a photograph of the Eiffel Tower.
- **Available media:** maps, spoken and written language, pictures, tables, graphs, ordered lists.

The characteristics of the media available appear in Table 2, and the characteristics of the information to be presented appear in Table 4.

The allocation algorithm classifies information characteristics with respect to characteristics of media, according to the rules outlined in Section 3.2. The medium with the most desired characteristics is then chosen to form the exhibit.

	Coordinates	Name	Photograph
Information	48N 2E	Paris	Eiffel Tower
Dimensionality	double	single	single
Volume	little	singular	singular
Density	dense	discrete	discrete
Transience	dead	dead	dead
Urgency	routine	routine	routine

Table 4. Example information characteristics.

4.1.1.   Handling the coordinates

As given by the rules mentioned in Section 3.2, information with a *dimensionality* value of *double* is best presented in a substrate with a *dimension* value of *2D*. This means that candidate substrates for the exhibit are maps, pictures, tables, and graphs. Since the *volume* is *little*, *transient* media are not ruled out. The value *dense* for the characteristic *density* rules out tables. The values for *transience* and *urgency* have no further effect. This leaves tables, maps, and graphs as possible media. Next, taking into account the rules dealing with the internal semantics of media, immediately everything but maps are ruled out (maps' internal semantics denote spatial locations, which matches up with the denotation of the coordinates). If no other information is present, a map medium is selected to display the location of Paris.

4.1.2.   Handling the name

The name Paris, being an atomic entity, has the value *single* for the *dimensionality* characteristic. By the appropriate rule (see Section 3.2), the substrate should be the neutral substrate or natural language and the carrier one with *dimension* of *0D*. Since the *volume* is *singular*, a *transient* medium is not ruled out. None of the other characteristics have any effect, leaving the possibility of communicating the single word Paris or of speaking or writing a sentence such as *"The destination is Paris"*.

4.1.3. Handling the photograph

The photograph has a *dimensionality* value *complex*, for which appropriate rules specify media with *internal semantic dimension* of ∞D, and with *density* of *dense* (see Section

3.2) – animation or pictures. Since no other characteristic plays a role, the photograph can simply be presented.

This example illustrated how data characteristics can help limit the selection of media appropriate for displaying a particular item. The features we discussed can be used to establish a number of possible display media (or media combinations). Further knowledge can then be applied to make the final media determination.

4.2. Example 2: Rule Simplification and Generalization

This example involves the analysis of a figure taken from the 1990 Honda Accord Owner's Manual page explaining how to adjust the front seat [Honda 1990].

On first inspection, the section heading **Front Seat** and the label **Pull up** in Figure 6 look very different; indeed, the heading is analyzed as including the features *text-in-text*, *boldface*, *large-font*, *separation*, and *short*, while the label includes the features *text-in-picture* and *short*. But upon following the internetwork linkage rules in Figure 5, both items are seen to serve almost-identical producer goals: *introduce* and *identify*, respectively. Thus they are both instances of the *naming* function (see Figure 3); the features that differ are simply those required to differentiate each item from its background. Thus the operative rule can concisely be expressed as:

◊ Rule: To indicate the *naming* function, use *short* text which is *distinct* from the background presentation object.

How to achieve distinction is a matter for the individual presentation media, and has nothing to do with the communicative function of *naming* per se. Within a picture, *distinction* is achieved by the mere use of text, while within text, *distinction* must be achieved by varying the features of the surrounding rendering of the language, for example by changing the font type and size or the position of the item in relation to the general text body.

The notion of *distinction*, having crystallized out of the above two presentations, somewhat unexpectedly turns out to be quite generally applicable. Consider the text bullets at the bottom of the figure. Since their function is to *warn* (and not merely to *inform*, which is the purpose of the preceding paragraphs), the text has the feature *bold*. This serves to *distinguish* the warning text from the background, thereby signaling the special force required for a warning. Using the rule stated above, we can now predict that, within the context of a diagram or picture, one can effect a warning simply by placing text within the non-textual substrate.

Thus, though the notion of *distinction* was not explicitly developed for the individual networks influencing presentations, Figure 5 suggested its utility with an appropriate collection of specific features. Its importance was discerned in the course of investigating the internetwork linkage rules and their application to presentations such as this manual page.

The example illustrates the generality of the rules that can be used to generate and parse multimedia presentations, but, when described, it may seem obvious. However, it can only be explained by using such notions as *distinguished/separated* (both the positional/off-text distinctiveness and the realizational/text-vs-graphics distinctiveness) and *communicative function* (one part of the communication serves to name/introduce/identify another part). When one constructs a vocabulary of terms on this level of description, one finds unexpected overlaps in communicative functionality across media.

In the domain of presentations containing text and line drawings, we demonstrated that media selection rules can be written so that the same rule can be used to control the analysis and generation of some aspect of both a diagram and a piece of text. This is extremely significant, in that the resulting parsimony and expressive power of these rules simultaneously motivates the particular representational level we have used and also suggests how the complex task of multimedia communication is achieved with less overhead than at first seemed necessary. The assembly of a vocabulary of media-independent (or at least shared by multiple media) features of the kind we discuss is an important future research task.

5. Conclusion

The enormous numbers of possibilities that appear when one begins to deal with multiple media, as illustrated by the psychology, cognitive science, and automated text generation and formatting work mentioned above, is daunting. We believe that systematic analysis of the factors influencing presentations, such as the types described here, is required before powerful general-purpose multimedia human-computer interfaces can be built. Appropriate formalisms for representing the underlying knowledge may serve to uncover unexpected overlaps of functionality which serve to simplify the rules upon which such interface systems will depend. It appears that the dependency network formalism and feature-based analysis methodology described in this paper hold some promise for untangling the complex issues involved, and, perhaps, may one day help explain why multimedia communication is so pervasive in human interaction.

Chapter 13

Using "Live Information" in a Multimedia Framework[1]

Matthew Cornell, Beverly ParkWoolf, and Daniel Suthers

Abstract

We have developed an integrated multimedia information environment to support the creation, organization, and communication of information. The underlying theme is that information is interconnected, can be shared among people, and can be viewed in different ways. An object-oriented direct manipulation approach is taken towards all components of the architecture, including specification of underlying information, definition of user-invoked procedures, bindings of user gestures (like dragging and clicking to actions), and definition of display-related objects that show information in different ways. This approach has three major advantages. First, the user can choose how information will be displayed, changing for instance between animation, text, and graphics. This reduces the need for computer applications to perform extensive reasoning about media mode decisions. Second, users can share and reuse information because objects are defined in terms of a persistent object store and because all needed displayers and user procedures are, themselves, made available as objects in an object hierarchy. Third, hypermedia capabilities come naturally because references between objects are links whose semantics are specified by the underlying object. Ongoing work focuses on issues such as the tension between allowing full functionality in a *live information* environment and how to maintain informational integrity.

1. Extending Multimedia Environments

This chapter describes a principle of interface design to support the creation, organization, access, and communication of information. *Live information* is the name given to the central theme and supporting ideas behind this design principle. The interface prin-

---

[1]This work is supported in part by External Research, Apple Computer Inc., Cupertino, California.

ciple requires that information be fully connected and retains all links to the conceptual structures from which it was generated. Media or data in a *live information* interface does not terminate upon display. The motto is "No ink on the screen," or no presentation without an understanding by the system of the semantics behind that presentation. Implementation of this principle requires retention of the full functionality of each underlying data structure for displayed information on the screen. A central theme is the separation of form and concept, or maintenance of a distinction between the appearance (form) of information and its conceptual message or semantics while retaining the links between the two.

One goal behind the *live information* design principle is to give the computer "knowledge" of the displays on its screen and to provide a research environment to support rich information handling operations. For example, a user should be able to interrupt either a textual or video program, point to the screen and ask "What is actually happening here?" or "Tell me about that item." The system should respond based on dynamic evaluation of both the context of the human-machine interaction and knowledge of the data structures underlying the visible screen presentation. *Live information* supports users in directing their own learning by enabling them to choose how to distribute research responsibilities among applications (e.g., on-line encyclopedias, explainers, tutors, simulations, etc.), to compose and integrate the results, and to share the learning results with colleagues. Additionally, computer applications can effectively do less reasoning about selection of a multimedia element (e.g., text, graphics, animation, or sound) since alternative media can be selected by the user if the original choice by the application resource is not appropriate.

To provide a context for further discussions, consider the following hypothetical example shown in part in Figure 1. A user types "What is electricity?" and runs and intelligent tutor such as described in [Woolf and Cunningham 1987] or [Suthers 1993]. The system responds with text describing static electricity and refers to a diagram that shows a person's hand approaching a door knob and shows charges as plus and minus signs (see Figure 1). After reading the explanation, the user selects a minus and plus sign in the diagram and types "What is the difference?" The explanation program analyzes the difference in the diagram and follows-up with more text and a model simulating the charge transfer process (displayed as an animation). After reading the text and running the simulation (and enjoying the animation), the user creates a specialized process window that lists the processes in each step of the animation. Now, as the simulation runs, a marker in the process window cycles from step to step in synchronization with the first window's animation frames. The user opens yet another window, describes what she saw (referencing the two explanations), and sends the entire multimedia composition to her classmates. Upon receiving the composition, the classmates follow each of the encoded references by double clicking, reviewing the presentations (e.g., explanation, simulation, or animation) for themselves, and making comments back to the first user.

Figure 1 suggests how a *live information* interface presents this information to the user enhancing presentations available from an explanation or tutoring system by providing several interface features. *Live information* supports users in conversation with a computer application by enabling them to query the application about portions of its presentation, either graphic or text, which were not understood and to ask for new presentations that were not anticipated by the author nor originally provided by the application. In this example, the user was able to move from one graphic presentation that references the concept "charge," to another, which provided a textual explanation. A conventional hypermedia system would only allow moves between presentations expressly provided by the author and previously encoded in the application.

The perspective of learning as design, research, and composition requires an integrated multimedia research environment in which the following functionality is available: *creation of information*, such as text, drawings, digitized pictures, notes, and references to other information; *organization of information* by connecting items, grouping and ungrouping items, moving items around spatially, marking and classifying items, and looking at the same item differently; *access to information* by listing all items of a certain type, filtering lists of items, and searching for patterns; and *communication of information* by sharing work and ideas between people and programs regardless of its source. Existing systems are inadequate because they do not fully integrate resources, do not allow complete information sharing, do not support viewing information in different ways, and limit how users interconnect and use information. Traditional systems require that an author previously establish links and presentations before a user can select a new media type. Within such a system a user cannot change how something looks (whether it is animation or text), cannot follow all references to a textual or graphical entity, and cannot reuse information in follow-up questions or in her own notes.

2. Principle of Live Information

The principle of *live information* addresses several areas of the interface design issues suggested above, including multimedia presentation (display of information in alternative media) and multimedia composition (support of users in producing artifacts they can share and critique) [Pea 1990; Guzdial and Soloway 1991]. It instantiates both a perspective of learners as researchers and composers [Harel and Papert 1990] and of learning as a process of knowledge communication [Wenger 1987]. The principle is premised on the availability of fully interconnected information so that displayed information is as functional and reusable as its internal representation. A central theme of *live information* is the separation of form and concept and the retention of links between them.

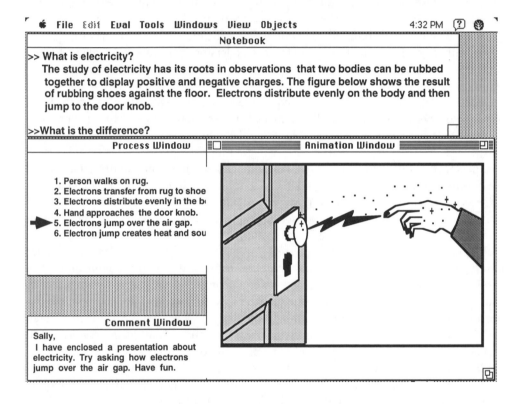

Figure 1. A Hypothetical Live Information Interface

"Concept" is the underlying data structure or topic being displayed, linked-to, edited, or referenced; "form" is a particular media-dependent representation of that concept (e.g., textual, graphic, animation, or sound). Thus, the same concept displayed in different forms will show different but related information; the actual presentation will depend upon the specific concept and the form chosen.[2] This separation allows alternate views on information so that a user or application program can choose a form that elucidates an important aspect, e.g., to describe a process by presenting a simulation or to describe a structure by presenting a graphic. As an example, Figure 2 shows a single concept -- personal schedule items -- displayed in three different forms: as an icon, as a text string, and as a list of its component items. (This figure was created using the Information Kit, described in Section 3.)

To do list: 4 items	
8:00a:	Call Bob
12:00a:	Lunch w/Mary
2:00p:	KCSG group meeting
8:00p:	Movie!

Figure 2. A List Shown Three Ways

Separation between form and concept exists in limited ways in current PC applications. For example, word processors allow a user to view documents in edit (or text entry) mode, in page preview (or shrunken page) mode, and in outline (or hierarchical) mode. Spreadsheets enable a user to view cells as formulae or as their computed values. Graphical file systems allow a user to view directory contents in an icon mode or in outline mode, and allow sorting by name, type, and date. In each example, alternative views activate a different subset of operations and emphasize different facets of the information, e.g., an icon view of a file system allows a kind of fast pattern recognition and enables icons to be arranged into meaningful spatial groupings. Existing applications,

---

[2]In our current design, the burden of managing the presentation falls upon computer applications using the framework, not on the framework itself.

however, do not modularize the separation between form and concept either internally or to other applications, as prescribed by *live information*.

One outstanding feature of the separation between form and concept is the reduced need for an application program to focus on media choice. This is because after a presentation is made by an application, a user can refine the information's appearance, since links to underlying data structures are maintained. This enables the application to "get it close and encourage fixing" or make "good" initial media mode choices and then dedicate more effort to tasks such as content selection. Application programs cannot always make optimal first-time media presentation choices, and thus the *live information* approach supports human-computer collaboration to satisfy user goals by effectively allowing the user to access underlying computer information.

The principle of separation of form and concept also provides all the features of hypermedia for free (see [Conklin 1987; Nielsen 1990b]). Because it treats *concept-to-concept* references as links, a user can connect related information and move between different presentations of the same information, effecting hypertext jumps. Separating form and concept also provides advantages over existing hypermedia systems, such as Hypercard, which have links between *presentations* (*form-to-form* links), since it allows users to move between all possible references and presentation of a single object, not just among those links pre-specified manually by the author. Conventional hypermedia systems constrain a user's motion to just those links pre-built and attached by the author or previous user; for example, to link additional explanations to prior ones new links must be made for each desired traversal.

Several supporting ideas and advantages follow directly from the primacy of the principle of separation of form and concept. For instance, information consistency results since each piece of information is a first class entity and no distinction is made between program data, system data, and personal data. This feature, combined with the fact that all actions and displayed types are available in all contexts, maximizes application usefulness.

3. A First Implementation of Live Information

This section describes Information Kit (IKit), a first implementation of the *live information* principle, and shows how key features have been implemented to provide the functionality described above, specifically support for the creation, organization, access, and communication of information. Section 4 describes how this functionality can be extended to three additional applications. Key elements of IKit are *objects*, *displayers*, *actions*, and *object references*. All information is represented either as objects or as references between objects, and both can be shared among applications independent of their source. Objects are viewed in different ways by placing them in different displayers.

3.1. The IKit Implementation

Information is managed using a direct manipulation interface which supports operations on viewed objects via specialized viewing regions in windows [Apple 1987]. A *displayer* is such a specialized area which is built to view a specific media type, and presents information to users in that type, determining the "form" in the separation of form and concept. The displayed object retains a link to the underlying semantic data structure, which is the "concept" in the separation of form and concept. Figure 2 showed a sequence object displayed, from left to right, in an icon displayer, a text displayer, and a sequence contents displayer. IKit includes textual, iconic, graphic, animation, and simulation media-type displayers. A user determines the media type of presentation by dragging and dropping a screen representation of an item into the preferred displayer.

Figure 3 shows a window from the IKit implementation. On the left side of the figure, a person object is displayed in three ways (from top to bottom): (1) textually as a generic "identifier" (used in our system as a persistent object store), (2) both textually as a name and graphically as an icon, and (3) textually as its component parts. On the right side of the figure a sequence object, **Sequence1**, which contains a list of objects, is displayed in three ways: (1) as an identifier, (2) as a number of elements and their type ("T" means the sequence can hold any type of object), and (3) as the sequence's textual elements. The boldface **Matthew** in (3) is a reference to the person object shown on the left in Figure 3. In the bottom right corner of the figure a person object is displayed graphically as a digitized picture. This graphic was realized by dragging the boldface **Matthew** from the textual displayer into the graphic displayer. Each class of displayer displays objects in one media mode using one kind of description in that mode. For example, the person object is displayed textually in two ways ("Matthew Cornell" on the left and just "Matthew" on the right) and graphically in two ways (as an icon on the left and as a digitized picture on the right). Some implementation-specific names of objects are listed to the right of the figure and further explained in Figure 4.

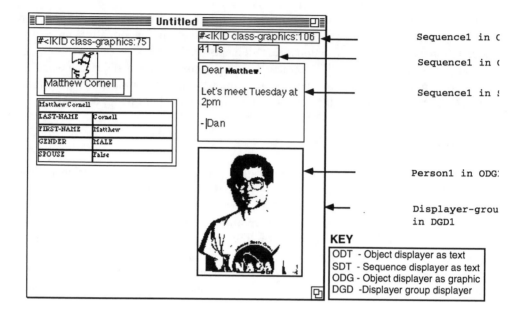

Figure 3. Multiple Representation in the Information Kit

3.2.   Objects

Users manipulate objects and each object represents a piece of information. The kinds of objects manipulated include class instances representing people, places and things, as well as instances representing multimedia information types such as text, graphics, and sound.[3] (Recall Figures 2 and 3 which showed concepts, including a sequence object and a person object, displayed in several ways.) Objects are representations of data structures (i.e., the "concept" in the separation of form and concept) with which users

---

[3]We use *objects* in the sense of instances whose structure is defined by classes and whose behavior is defined by class messages (or generic functions), such as specified by the Common LISP Object System [Bobrow et al. 1988].

work. Users create information by making new instances of objects and links between objects, and they share information by exchanging objects. Associated with each object are descriptions of the ways it can be represented in various media modes (e.g., as text, graphic, etc.) and procedures for returning the media elements corresponding to each mode (strings, pictures, etc.)[4] Objects are viewed in different ways by placing them in different displayers as shown in Figures 2 and 3. An object representing a person may be shown in a text displayer as a text string, e.g., "Dr. Smith" or "Jane Smith." The same person object, when moved into a graphics displayer is shown as a graphic, a drawing, or a photo (in Figure 3 above). The boldfaced name "Matthew Cornell" was shown as text in one window, as a graphic when dropped into the graphic displayer on the bottom right, or as the underlying textual information associated with that name when dropped into the bottom displayer on the left.

3.3. Displayers and the Display Hierarchy

Figure 4 shows the display hierarchy corresponding to the right side of Figure 3 and indicates the relationships between display elements and the underlying objects being presented. The hierarchy shows entries for two objects, **Person1** and **Sequence1**, which are labeled on the right side of Figure 3. Figure 4 shows the implementation-specific object names as boxes with arrows pointing to related boxes. We distinguish between the data structure of the main piece of information being shown (called the *directly displayed object*) and other objects being shown that are connected to it by a pointer from the main object's data structure (called *indirectly displayed objects*). For example, the three top displayers on the right in

Figure 3, ODT1, ODT2, and SDT1, display **Sequence1** directly, and only the sequence displayer above the digitized picture displays an object indirectly (specifically, reference to **Person1**, shown in bold as **Matthew**).

Arrows in the display hierarchy of Figure 4 indicate the kind of relationship: the *directly displayed* arrow means that the displayer at the foot of the arrow directly displays the el-

---

[4]Storing fixed forms for each type is an implementation choice. Another approach is to generate different forms from form-free representations, perhaps using text generation technology [Feiner and McKeown, this volume].

ement at the arrow's head, and the displayer at the foot of the *indirectly displayed* arrow indirectly displays the element at the arrow head. *Children* displayers are contained by the displayer enclosing it. For example, listed at the top of the hierarchy is *displayer-group-displayer1*, corresponding to the enclosing window in Figure 3. The directly displayed object, *displayer-group1*, has seven children displayers (four are shown in Figure 4). Three of these children directly display **Sequence1** and the fourth directly displays **Person1**. One of the children, *sequence-displayer-as-text1*, has both a directly displayed object (**Sequence1**) and an indirectly displayed one (**Person1**).

3.4. Actions

As described above, users interact by selecting displayed objects and performing gestures on them to run operations defined on a set of object types (called *actions*). For example, a "Mail" action might be defined for a multi-selection of a person and a sequence, and would send the sequence object to the person (via the person's stored electronic mail address). Thus, in Figure 3 a user might select the sequence object in the right displayer, select the mail recipient person in the bottom right displayer, the run the Mail action, perhaps by making a menu selection.[5] All actions and displayers are available in any context (due to the persistent object store), a functionality which supports composition and collaborative work. Each displayer follows its own policy of allowing selection of indirectly displayed objects within it. For example, the middle right displayer in Figure 3 lets users insert and delete object from the sequence, but all other displayers shown let users select only the directly displayed objects.[6] Information can be viewed in different ways by changing within-mode object representations in a displayer instance (such as changing to another text representation) or by displaying the object in an instance of a different displayer class.

Information can be organized by using *displayer-group* instances, which group collections of displayers to form nested presentation. This clustering ability allows an individ-

---

[5]Because the sequence and person objects have multiple representations the user can select the most convenient (or most appropriate) one when running an action.

[6]The composite displayer on the bottom left of figure 3 is actually a displayer group with child displayers for each component.

ual to group related items, to collapse them to reduce clutter, and later to re-expand them. Displayer-groups can maintain constraints on their members' spatial relationships, which enables enforcing relationships such as keeping all objects' left sides aligned with ten pixels of vertical space between each. As an example, the second displayer on the left of Figure 3 shows a person object displayed by a displayer-group in both graphic (iconic) and text displayers. In this one displayer group, both displays are centered horizontally. Constraints like this are important because spatial layout of cells greatly affects human interpretation: for example, objects that are aligned are understood to be on the same dimension.

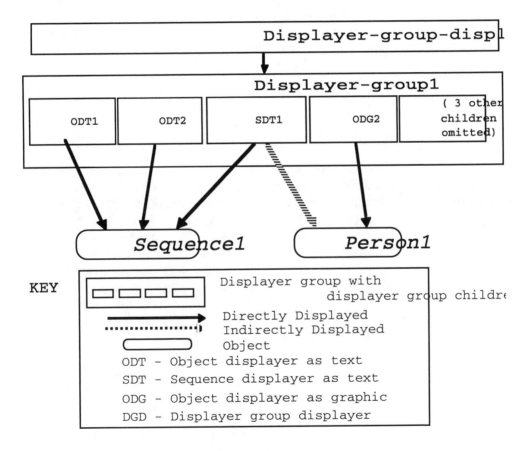

Figure 4. Display Hierarchy for Figure 3.

3.5.   Object References

Object references, or pointers between objects, are easily made by a user. Dragging and dropping an object into another object creates a reference, the equivalent of a hypertext link. The student described in the first hypothetical example made object references by selecting the plus and minus signs and asking a follow-up question. Hypertext-like jumps to other objects are made by displaying referenced objects in a local window (i.e., by "bringing them up"); referenced objects include those objects that point to an object as well as those objects an object points to. For example, suppose the student in the original hypothetical example mailed a colleague a summary object and the second person also wanted to see the animation of static charge build upon a person's hand. The colleague would select the reference to the animation in the text (which would appear in bold print), issue the 'animate' command, and see the original animation in its own dis-player.

3.6.   Defining New Functionality

A general mechanism enables users to define *actions* independent of the particular *gestures* used, much like the EMACS family of text editors allows independence between keystrokes and the text manipulation functions they invoke. For example, a user might assign the gesture of "dropping a textual object into a tutor displayer" to invoke a tutor on the dropped object, presumably a question. In such a case, the automated tutor would parse the question and construct an appropriate response (see description of the Explainer in Section 4 below). Currently, actions are defined for operations such as displaying, selecting, and changing an object, creating and saving instances, binding gestures and actions, getting help with gestures an actions, inserting objects into text sequences, and following (jumping to) references. All action/gesture bindings can be so customized programmatically or interactively.

For example, the help dialog box in Figure 5 shows documentation of each action/gesture. The "Describe" action on the left is selected and a description and bound gestures for this action listed on the right. The documentation says the chosen action will describe objects currently selected, and is invoked by two gestures: 1) selecting an object and choosing a menu item, or 2) double clicking on the object to be described.

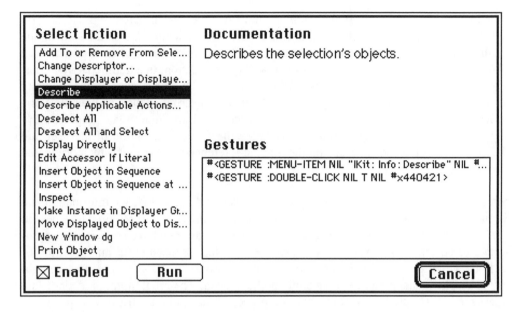

Figure 5. User Definition of Action and Gestures

3.7. Implications of the Interface

Application programs designed for this paradigm must generate media objects that maintain links to internal representations after presentation. For example, in the application described in Section 4, the first answer in Figure 6 contains the text "When the switch S1 is closed, the light bulbs light up." This piece of text is linked to a hierarchical knowledge base structure, allowing the user to select smaller textual pieces such as, "switch S1," "switch," "light bulbs light up," etc., and to use them in follow-up questions. The full implementation will support similar segmentation of images. The links to internal representations not only save an application from reparsing input, but provide specific knowledge base structures underlying the input. Since users can reference objects in their own media documents, it may be necessary to retain objects across sessions. We have implemented a persistent object store to address this need.

Since *live information* applications can associate conceptual structures with presentations, they can in some cases track the user's focus of attention using less processing.

For instance, consider an explanation session after the system has discussed several electrical devices using circuit diagrams. Suppose two capacitors are on the screen, one within a DC circuit in which the capacitor is used to store charge, and another within an AC circuit in which the capacitor performs a filtering function. In a traditional system, if the user types "What is the purpose of the capacitor?" the user's focus of attention and exact reference to a particular capacitor could only be determined through heuristics or a clarifying dialogue. However, from a mouse selection on the appropriate graphic, a *live information* application can immediately know the focus of attention of the user and begin planning a response based on the graphic referenced by the user which originated the query.

Programs can use this framework to provide ways to help users manage information and reduce the overload of too much information or too many activities required to access it. One way is to shrink previous presentations to icons after they have become less appropriate to current tasks. Another way involves developing meaningful interpretation of actions which otherwise would be considered inappropriate. For example, a user might try to display a static picture in an animation displayer. The program might deduce that the user is interested in related dynamic processes and might retrieve and present a simulation, avoiding the need to interrupt learning activities with clarifying dialogue.

Because users are free to edit information after its presentation, and because some programs depend on preserving the information's underlying structure, there is a tension between allowing the user to modify the *live information* interface and maintaining informational integrity. For example, a program might present a particular model of a process but the user might interactively change the order of the processes' steps, possibly invalidating the model. Further research is needed to determine when previous links to underlying structure are invalidated, and whether user editing actions should be restricted in such situations.

4. Applications of this Technology

This section outlines the use of *live information* within four program applications and demonstrates how its functionality can generate more effective and more intuitive human-computer interfaces. The first application is fully implemented and results produced by the system are shown. The last three applications are hypothetical.

4.1. An Explanation System

The principles of *live information* have been implemented and integrated with research on explanation planning [Suthers et al. 1992; Suthers 1993]. Figure 6 shows a human-computer dialogue which occurs within the *live information* direct-manipulation interface.[7] Within this interface, each conceptually-significant segment of displayed information retains the full functionality of the underlying data structure from which it was generated; it is not just "ink on the screen". Each display serves as a representational medium through which the activities of the machine and human are coupled. This kind of coupling, in which both the human and machine can interpret and reuse information, is a step towards shared "representations" in which information in the interface is available for perception and manipulation by both human and computer dialogue participants.

The domain knowledge for the explanation system is basic electricity and electrical networks and the circuit at the top of Figure 6 is under discussion. In Q1, the student typed a query which was parsed by a natural language parser, using dialogue history to disambiguate the referent of "the switch." The machine response, A1, was planned using internal representations before translation into natural language. While composing the second question, Q2, the student mouse-selected and dragged two phrases from the explainer's first response (shown in boldface) in addition to typing the non-bold text.[8] Since displayed information remains attached to its internal representations, the machine accessed the referents of the boldface phrases directly. Mouse-selections are also used to update an internal focus of attention data structure by bringing the selected context into the foreground. This data structure is used to disambiguate ambiguous referents and to

---

[7]We present this example to show IKit integrated with an existing application, not to explain the architecture of the explanation system. Readers interested in more detail should see the articles referenced above.

[8]As mentioned in "Implications of the Interface" in the previous section, responses to queries are actually structured objects containing pointers to subobjects. These structured objects are presented in specialized displayers that allow users to select and drag portions of the response corresponding to parts of the uttered statement. Section 5 describes the process of developing new object types and displayers in more detail.

determine which concepts are currently under active consideration. The student constructed Q5 by selecting and double clicking on the entire machine response, A4. The explainer constructed a menu of questions applicable to its response and the student selected the question echoed as Q5. The explainer interpreted this next question as a request to elaborate on the previous explanation.

This dialogue illustrates how information displayed in IKit can be mouse-selected to obtain a menu of questions or to reference an object in follow-up explanations. Other relevant functionality is also available. For example, the user can incorporate display elements into her own documents (by mouse-dragging across windows) where they retain their underlying semantic representation. This enables a student to construct a "live" document including the models or discussions around a topic in a session with the system. Appearance of the model is determined by the kind of "displayer" in which the information object is presented, allowing the same information to be displayed under alternate views. For example, a user can mouse-drag a unit of text into a graphic displayer and obtain a picture of the underlying information (provided one is available). Also, once *simulation displayers* are added to IKit a student will be able to drag a model into a simulation displayer to obtain a working simulation. Thus, the users can refine the information's appearance after it has been presented, which is desirable because application programs cannot always make optimal media choices.

4.2.   Text Processing, Mail Applications, and Academic Collaboration

Now we consider three hypothetical applications of IKit. In text processing, one frequently cites remote parts of a document (sections, figures, charts, etc.), other documents, and other authors, by cutting and pasting text from the remote part of the text, other documents, etc. As document elements are moved, edited, and deleted, the document must be manually updated accordingly. A *live information* approach to text processing would present every text element, e.g., words, sections, figures, and charts, as objects. This suggests very powerful improvements to the resulting text processor. For example, a reference to an unknown section might be realized by selecting an element in a convenient displayer and dragging and dropping it into the desired position. Suppose a user is working on a document shown in two displayers: an outline displayer which presents sections and subsections hierarchically, and a text displayer which presents a single page view. The user might type into the text displayer "as shown in" and then refer to a section conveniently shown in the outline displayer by dragging the section object from the outline displayer to just after the word "in." The framework would insert a reference and select a default textual representation for it, so that the sentence appears as "...as shown in **Section 7, page 14**." Subsequently, as the referenced section's position in the document and order relative to other sections changes during editing, all reference appearances will be automatically updated, so the text might become "...as shown in **Section 6, page 11**." Similarly, a user could reference output objects of an explanation system (described above and shown in Figure 6) such as a picture or simulation. Documents could be shared with other users (collaborators, teachers, and peers) by mailing document objects to people who could then examine the documents and all referenced elements.

Currently, sophisticated text processors on microprocessors, such as LaTeX, handle renumbering references to section, figures, and tables as suggested above. However, this process requires two passes of the text processor and all place holder references must be written manually. Within such text processing systems, commands are often difficult to perform and references to other kinds of objects (people, other documents, etc.) are not supported. New PC operating systems are starting to incorporate a "dynamic linking" functionality which allows "publishing" objects from their source application to which other applications might "subscribe." However, no support is given for declaring different mode appearances (text, graphics, etc.), and switching to original applications to edit objects is required. (IKit switches applications implicitly via gestures.)

A *live information* implementation automatically supports academic collaboration by providing a multimedia research notebook via the functionality described above. To collaborate with peers, for instance, an individual would perform the operations discussed in the text processing example application. Quick referencing would be a powerful collaboration tool since much scientific and technical writing involves referencing objects, including publications, books, journals, people, research groups or projects, and other parts of the document (as in "see Section IV" or "see Figure 4"). Objects could represent personal events (such as appointments, meetings, demonstrations, and presentations), and times (including days, weeks, etc.). Calendar and "to do" displayers would provide a researcher with different ways to view her schedule, such as daily, weekly, and monthly views of personal events. Since events will reference people, places, and projects, one could search for information based on reference patterns, for example, "Display all events that reference **Project A** and **DAN**."

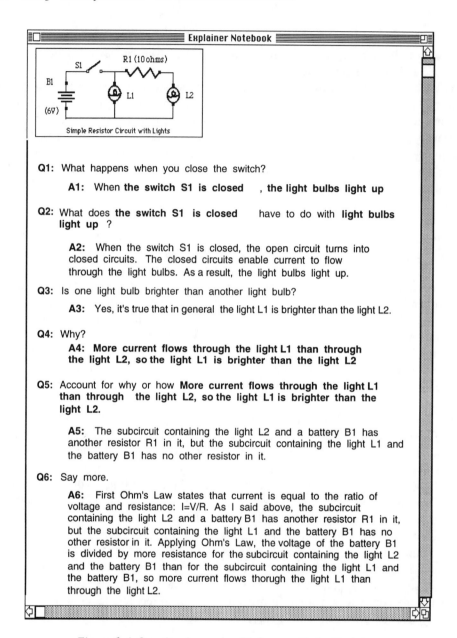

Q1: What happens when you close the switch?

    A1: When **the switch S1 is closed**   , **the light bulbs light up**

Q2: What does **the switch S1 is closed**   have to do with **light bulbs light up** ?

    A2: When the switch S1 is closed, the open circuit turns into closed circuits. The closed circuits enable current to flow through the light bulbs. As a result, the light bulbs light up.

Q3: Is one light bulb brighter than another light bulb?

    A3: Yes, it's true that in general the light L1 is brighter than the light L2.

Q4: Why?

    A4: More current flows through the light L1 than through the light L2, so the light L1 is brighter than the light L2

Q5: Account for why or how **More current flows through the light L1 than through the light L2, so the light L1 is brighter than the light L2.**

    A5: The subcircuit containing the light L2 and a battery B1 has another resistor R1 in it, but the subcircuit containing the light L1 and the battery B1 has no other resistor in it.

Q6: Say more.

    A6: First Ohm's Law states that current is equal to the ratio of voltage and resistance: I=V/R. As I said above, the subcircuit containing the light L2 and a battery B1 has another resistor R1 in it, but the subcircuit containing the light L1 and the battery B1 has no other resistor in it. Applying Ohm's Law, the voltage of the battery B1 is divided by more resistance for the subcircuit containing the light L2 and the battery B1 than for the subcircuit containing the light L1 and the battery B1, so more current flows thorugh the light L1 than through the light L2.

Figure 6. A Question Answering Dialogue with the Explainer

Research notes taken using a *live information* system could be annotated to aid review and processing. One method would be to have objects representing *ideas, to do items, questions*, and *issues*, displayed as icons in an easily-accessed window. When an item came up that fit into a category, one would drag it into the appropriate icon, which would mark the item accordingly. Later, one could perform queries like "Show me all **Ideas** referenced since last week" or "Display all **To Do** items."

5. Advantages over Existing Approaches

Existing multimedia systems use limited or restricted versions of the functionality discussed in this chapter and do not encode the functionality described here. For example, Hypercard [Michel 1989] and other conventional hypermedia systems do not separate form and concept. In such systems, information is typically presented in a single way and that form cannot be changed. Smalltalk [Goldberg and Robson 1985] supports separation of form and concept via the model-view-controller approach, but is oriented toward programmers, does not provide explicit handling of object references, and does not provide user-level methods of changing views on information or following references. Object Lens [Kum-yew et al. 1988] has separation of form and concept through objects and views, but does not generalize the separation to all object types, and does not allow the definition of additional types of views. As mentioned above, some operating systems have added dynamic links between application programs, but do not support alternate views, and require the user to switch between applications when working.

Live information treats each piece of information as a first-class entity, and all actions and displayer types are available in all contexts. This maximizes the usefulness of information and applications. Further, adding new functionality is relatively easy and seamless. A developer starts with a standard higher-level object hierarchy providing common data structures and displayers. Upon these she 1) defines object subclasses to represent her application's internal data structures, 2) defines new displayer subclasses to allow viewing and editing information, 3) defines new actions for the new classes, and then 4) binds those actions to desired gestures. From the end-user's perspective, these just-developed classes, displayers, and actions are "dropped into" the environment to become a fully integrated part of the *live information* functionality as described above.

More specifically, the developer will implement new functionality for two cases: 1) exiting information to be displayed in new ways, and 2) new information to be stored and displayed. Developing for the first case involves simply creating a new displayer subclass that shows the already-stored information. A hypothetical example might be to extend an IKit-style spreadsheet to include a scatter-chart given that a two-dimensional array object and a corresponding numeric table displayer are already defined. Adding a scatter-chart displayer involves creating a displayer subclass that plots table values on a scaled Cartesian coordinate system. In this case, the user could immediately utilize the new scatter-chart displayer class on all existing data of the appropriate type (e.g., upon two-dimensional array objects). Developing for the second case, to store and display new information, requires creating a subclass that stores the additional information and defining displayers that show it. An example using our spreadsheet example is defining a new three-dimensional array class and a corresponding three-dimensional bar chart displayer. In addition to displaying instances of the new data type in the new displayer, the user can display the new data in any applicable existing displayer. So one might drop the three-dimensional array object into a text displayer to see its name or (perhaps) its size and number of elements. (In IKit one can select an object and ask for a list of all applicable displayer types and all within-mode displays, so that users can select which text string or which picture is displayed if the default choices do not suit them.)

In sum, *live information* is a principle for merging multimedia objects with alternate media representations of information and hypertext using an interconnected set-of-objects architecture. A synergistic framework was described which supports personal computer users in actively creating, organizing, accessing, and communicating subject matter. Information Kit (IKit) is a first Lisp implementation of the principle of *live information* [Cornell 1991]. The prototype is currently integrated with the explanation planner described in Section 4. A full implementation of IKit is nearing completion, based on extensive design specifications. The full implementation is written in Common Lisp on the Macintosh and uses CLOS for the base object representation. Currently, classes represent text sequences (e.g., strings, pictures, sounds, research groups, and projects), in addition to classes which represent explanations. Displayer classes enable the user to present and edit objects as text and pictures, as characters in a sequence or as lists, and objects as their component parts. A persistent object store handles paging objects to and from memory as needed, and a general change propagation mechanism facilitates notifying referencing objects of changes in a referenced object (such as when its appearance changes).

6. Vision

Advances in information and communication technology will one day produce a global infrastructure enabling easy access to information in remote libraries, museums, databases, or institutional archives. We expect artificial intelligence technology to play a central role in bringing multimedia systems to new levels of realism and usefulness and to provide gateways to encyclopedia clearinghouses of knowledge and stores of widely available knowledge-bases. Intelligent agents will be needed to learn an individual's preferences and prior knowledge, to facilitate easy access remote information, and to move among databases and bring back specific information. *Live information* provides a design principle and basic technology for building such intelligent agents.

The principle of *live information* uses objects to represent models. In time, the models themselves might be developed and shared for the purpose of communicating knowledge directly. These models would represent things like "tectonic plate activity" (with an appropriate animated displayer) and "historical population movement." The models would be decomposable facilitating the presentation of multiple models, and would be of the "glass box" type, enabling student exploration and experimentation [Papert 1980]. Inexpensive stylus-based "table" computers (as suggested by [Mel et al. 1988] and [Kay and Goldberg 1977]) will be available and *live information* media will cultivate a "model culture" in which users build and share models. Perhaps one day research will enable development of models which configure themselves to the learner based on her current goals and knowledge.

"As the planet comes on line" the individual will become the center of a large electronic global communication network [CasaBianca 1988]. Ultimately, on-line libraries will provide global access to information (see [Nelson 1980]) and intelligent tutors will help users retrieve, construct, understand, and modify conceptual models. However, intelligent information resources, such as described here, will be needed to provide the focus for the new global wired society. Through mechanisms such as *live information*, the individual will gain more access to knowledge and to a variety of media forms. The multimedia framework described here provides foundation technology for establishing an intelligent and global multimedia infrastructure.

Chapter 14

A Multilayered Empirical Approach to Multimodality: Towards Mixed Solutions of Natural Language and Graphical Interfaces

Jürgen Krause

Abstract

An empirical approach for a merging of different modalities is suggested which is not restricted to the simulation of human-human communication. Empirical research for multimedia seems useful and necessary as an additional component after technological and architectural oriented research has created a promising start, based on the imitation of "natural" modality mixtures such as, e.g., deictic gestures in speech. The examples given come from the activities of the Linguistic Information Science Group at the University of Regensburg (LIR), dealing mainly with human-computer interaction (HCI) and the combining of graphics and natural language. They underline the usefulness of intensive empirical research at all levels of the system development cycle, from low level design decisions like using check marks correctly up to the question of how to build a theoretical model of multimodal HCI. In keeping with this, the main focus of the paper is on methodological questions of developing multimedia interfaces, exemplified by findings from a set of HCI experiments and prototype development projects.

1. Introduction

Currently, multimedia interfaces, which combine, e.g., motion sequences, pictures, graphics, sound and natural language, are one of the main areas of scientific research in data processing, artificial intelligence, cognitive science and information science. Simultaneously, commercial interest at the PC level also concentrates on this theme; multimedia products have become possible with respect to hardware as well as to standard software. This development follows the prosperity of graphical interfaces, which have become the dominating standard for everyday software usage on PC's. There are now technical solutions not only for graphic screen design but for the integration of video or

CD players, motion pictures or audio. As people are again intuitively fascinated by computers with these new capabilities - as in the eighties by the Rank Xerox-derivates - and software companies create products which also need powerful PCs, the user must continually buy anew. This situation raises the reoccurring question of whether the upcoming multimedia paradise has a plausible theoretical background; whether the new possibilities are desirable for the user and not just for industry; and whether the implemented details of existing design solutions are a reasonable realization of the general idea of multimedia. A technological driven approach does not only exist in the development of commercial products but also in science as well. The fascination for interactive devices like the data glove, seen as the key for opening the door to three dimensional virtual realities, is only one example [Zimmermann et al. 1987]. At the same time the architectural-driven approach is one of the most powerful development lines today. The integration of different media and modalities in one coherent model demands sophisticated solutions for system architecture, concerning, e.g., the representation of different sensations, the retrieval of information in different media, or the usage of communicative act analysis [Arens et al., this volume]. The discussion of multimedia communication as a goal-based activity can be a starting point for modeling this new form of human-computer-interaction [Maybury, this volume].

Summarizing the recent development lines, it can be said that:

a)   Technology has reached a point of development where the old hardware barriers for the integration of different media are gone. Initial multimedia applications for a broad PC usage are now feasible.

b)   Considerations concerning systems architecture are still at their infancy, but the initial proposals show that complex multimedia systems are possible; prototypes like the WIP system are promising [André et al., this volume; André and Rist, this volume; Dannenberg 1990].

So, what's the next step? We have to answer the question, which information should be given through which medium and how should these different parts be mixed? No one would design a town information system where the geographical information (maps) was given verbally, and the abstract information (e.g., on the historical development of the town) was presented visually. Each medium should be used where it is the best solution for the conveying and processing of information.

2. Beyond Simulating Human-Human Multimodal Communication

What and how different modalities are integrated is generally answered by the simulation approach, beginning with an observation of a multimodal presentation of information found in our natural environment, e.g., text-picture combinations in catalogues or deictic references in question answering dialogs [Schmauks 1991a]. In many situations deictic gestures or the presentation of sketches prove to be more efficient than verbalization [Schmauks and Reithinger 1988]. That human communication itself shows a merger of different modalities suggests a combination of the advantages of various natural communication modalities in human computer interaction (HCI) as well. Therefore, systems like WIP and XTRA of the University of Saarbrücken (Germany) use the human situation as an analogy for the interface (see also [Schmauks 1991b]). Here - like so often in the history of artificial intelligence - the simulation approach is important and leads to interesting results; but simulation is not the only possible approach. The computer allows new ways of combining different media and has other possibilities for handling them. These new forms can already be found in present graphical interfaces. They are not merely copies of our visual environment, as when using the mouse for pointing actions instead of the light pen or touch screens, or when integrating menu subsystems to present possible actions of the desktop objects. Graphical interfaces, in many cases, merely use the experience people have in their environment as a starting point for a self-reliant solution, only oriented to the aim of creating the best possible interface style and presentation of information.

The projects of the Linguistic Information Science Group at the University of Regensburg (LIR) concentrate on aspects of multimodality not necessarily using the simulation approach. Our work centers on a merger of natural language and graphics in HCI, for which we use the term multimodality. Most publications in artificial intelligence, however, do not differentiate between modality and media in general, thus addressing the LIR activities with the latter term as well (see also [Zoeppritz 1988]). The LIR-activities do not restrict the kind and scope of the combination of different modalities to an imitation of human communication. We try to preserve as many of the advantages of the different access modes as possible and at the same time avoid their disadvantages, independent of the biological patterns existing outside the technical context of HCI. If aiming at features not analogous to human-human communication, then progress in multimodal HCI is to be heavily dependent on empirical questions. Therefore, prototypes are developed, empirically tested in user studies, and profit is gained by using the evaluated data in designing the next prototype. The empirical approach is the next step necessarily following the technological and architectural considerations and the first realized prototypes that are oriented towards the simulation of the corresponding mixture of modes and media in the non-computer environment.

3. Different Levels of Empirical Research Activities

Following the empirical approach also means that multimodal HCI research can and must be carried out at different levels of system analysis. At the lowest level, details like icons, or the syntax and form of buttons are analyzed by testing existing systems or prototypes. The examples discussed here come from graphical systems of text processing like AMI, Word for Windows or COMFOTEX, which are broadly used today [Lotus 1991; Microsoft 1992; Siemens 1991].

At the highest theoretical level, the basic assumptions of multimodal HCI-models are founded on empirical results from simulated prototype tests (wizard of oz experiments). The examples forthcoming are taken from the computer talk experiments of the LIR and the metaphorical usage of language. The term "computer talk" addresses - roughly speaking - the language differences applied in the communication between humans and natural language oriented HCI (and the question of whether such differences exist at all).

At an intermediate level, a plausible agreement on a first multimodal prototype must be found: which parts of the dialog and the presentation of information should be coupled with which mode? Contrary to the simulation approach, the detailed merging of modalities and the consequences of switching between, e.g., textual and graphical information, cannot be explained by the experience of human-human communication. The situation is especially difficult for the development of the first prototype of a multimodal system where only indirect empirical results can render plausible design guidelines for the mixing of different modes. The LIR development of an intelligent multimodal interface for a material database is an example in this area.

The following discussion will be restricted to multimodal HCI and to two modalities: natural and graphics. Surely, multimodality encompasses more than HCI and more than the integration of these two basic "natural" modalities. Nevertheless, handling the question of how to combine both basic modalities in HCI can be seen as a prototypical problem space for the theoretical, methodological and practical questions connected with this field. Our multilayered empirical approach will also show that it is impossible to restrict methodology to one paradigm, e.g., to the preferred method of artificial intelligence, to program models which are afterwards tested by input examples, or to that of cognitive psychology's "hard" statistical hypothesis tests. The LIR activities in the area of multimodal HCI follow the methodological tradition of cognitive science research as formulated in Slack [1984:156f]:

> "The original ideas are transformed into hypotheses that have to be potentially falsifiable. The researcher then constructs controlled situations within which these hypotheses can be tested. The results of the research mould the theory into shape. As the body of empirical findings grows, the original theory is required to account for more and more behavioral data. To do this the original theory invariably needs to be extended or modified. Changes to the theory stimulate further empirical work that may lead to further changes in the theory. In this way the theory is 'bootstrapped up' from its original core propositions to produce a complex set of interrelated hypotheses. The range of analytical tools that are available ... is quite diverse ... Some of these tools require the ability to create rigorously controlled tasks, whereas others are dependent on the selection and analysis of some appropriate sequences of behavior ... Although experimentation has tended to be the dominant form of empirical research ..., cognitive scientists do not restrict the types of empirical evidence they are willing to incorporate into a project."

4. Low-Level Analysis of Details: Menu Subsystems in Graphical Interfaces

The following hints, addressing the low level of detailed design decisions in the software development cycle, come from the LIR project COMFOLIR. In cooperation with (and sponsored by) SIEMENS, the COMFOLIR team has been working at the development of a sophisticated text processor and further office communication software on the basis of direct manipulation and graphics since 1986 (ComfoWare). The software developed by SIEMENS (Germany) for the commercial market has been iteratively evaluated by the LIR team. One task (relevant in the context of this paper) is to make proposals on the basis of knowledge of software ergonomics, assessing beta versions (as well as earlier ones) of the software and testing new prototypes. The empirical findings of the LIR user tests help influence the successive stages of development. Until now, protocols of about 100 users have been analyzed. In the context of this software ergonomic analysis, other graphic based software packages which compete commercially with the COMFO products are also tested. Additionally, we work at the development of intelligent active help systems, intelligent tutorials, and analyze the possibilities to integrate higher level natural language features. A first prototype of an intelligent active help system, developed and tested at the LIR, will be integrated in the commercial product COMFOTEX.

Looking at desktop software such as COMFODESK [Siemens 1991] or at powerful text processing systems like Word for Windows or COMFOTEX one can argue that there already is a mixture of natural language and graphical elements in commercially available programs. Objects are visualized as icons. In some cases the user may manipulate objects directly, e.g., when deleting a document by grasping it with the mouse and dragging it over the paper basket icon (function object). But most of the functions available are presented by the menu subsystem, where possible actions are organized hierarchically in menu panels with natural language words as menu items. One might argue that the usage of verbal items in a graphical context appears at such a low level of natural language usage that it has nothing to do with the idea of multimodal systems. But looking at the problems from the cognitive perspective, one can find some of the same crucial points which have to be solved when integrating more complex natural language components as well.

- The problem of finding the most efficient terms of the menu hierarchy is also a linguistic one, outside the scope of traditional software ergonomic knowledge.
- There is no "natural" way of combining verbal menu subsystems with graphics. We can't look at human-human communication - as in the case of deictic expressions - to find out which kind of mixture is efficiently manageable for human information processing.
- Therefore an artificial switching problem exists for the user, who has to combine the verbal memory with the visual.
- There are general software ergonomic problems like consistency, transparency, or the resolution of ambiguities for combining syntax and semantics coming up in a new form, e.g., when combining verbal menu items with check marks (see below).

Additionally, the COMFOLIR findings include a warning: Menu systems, which seem to have been investigated so intensively, and which are so simple in structure, do not work satisfactorily. The LIR tests with different menu subsystems inside a graphical system and different versions of menus constructed in accordance with our proposals repeatedly led to the displeasing result that the menu system was the largest source of error. Before the empirical results we did not worry about the menu subsystem. It seemed to be well understood and without major problems. We also had to accept that most of the reasons for error in this area were directly or indirectly associated with principles of combining natural language terms with graphics. Justification for this conclusion is to be provided in the following sections.

4.1.   "Natural" Naming and Hierarchies

Following software ergonomic guidelines, the designer of a menu has to observe and question users, as to the name they connect with some function the software package provides and then use these names, as well as the observed "natural hierarchies" for constructing the menu. Unfortunately reality doesn't fit this proposal. Trying to follow the above rules we repeatedly tried to reformulate the COMFOTEX-menus, but the basic problem remained. Users did not find desired commands in the menu efficiently. They spent much of their time opening inappropriate pull down menus. This corresponds with an experiment by Furnas et al. [1984]. The authors concluded that the probability of two people generating the same name ranged from 8% for editing commands to 18% for recipes. Another observation, when looking at the menus of powerful graphic based text processors, is that the naming and grouping of the commands differs extensively between the software packages. Partially, these observations have to be charged to the lack of rigor with which commercial software designers follow software ergonomic rules. But the more important point of these observations is according to the linguistic fact that there are application areas where hierarchies can be constructed easily and others where no "natural" term hierarchies exist (see also [Bengler 1990]).

There are hints in the COMFOLIR tests that text processing commands partially belong to this latter class. The consequence of this hypothesis would be to leave the verbal command terms without superimposed reference concepts. Unfortunately building menu hierarchies is forced by the amount of available space on the screen. The number of possible commands in large systems is too high to give up hierarchical structuring. Therefore, designers refer to artificial terms the user has - in the best case - to learn.

4.2.   Beyond the Optimal Menu Breadth and Depth

The depth-breadth trade-off is one of the most intensively analyzed and tested areas of software ergonomics (see [Paap 1988] for a survey). Therefore, it is known rather exactly how wide a menu panel should be (maximum 10 terms/level) and how many levels in the hierarchy should exist (2-3). Transgressing these boundaries means that the cognitive processing of the menu subsystem becomes suboptimal. Designers try to avoid not optimal solutions, but as the functions of complex graphic systems grows steadily, the possibility of stopping at these boundaries becomes more and more illusionary. The designers have to ignore optimal usage boundaries, even if they know that an increase in the work load, difficulties of finding commands and other errors will occur.

4.3.   Check Marks, Changing Items and Disabled Commands

The hierarchical verbal term structure integrated in a menu system, with pull-down menus and dialog boxes, is an intrinsic mixture of the graphical and the verbal mode. But also inside the menu, at the item level, a combining with visual elements occurs.

- Commands that are equivalent with a state description get a check mark, when activated with the mouse (= toggle commands). The sign is an analogy to the physical world, where we also use check marks (e.g. for checking an item off on our shopping list).
- Commands that cannot be activated at an actual system state are grayed (disabled menu items).

Another technique necessary for the following explanations are the changing menu items. In COMFOTEX, an example would be 'Extended menu' versus 'Reduced menu' in the 'Options' pull down menu. Similar options, adaptable by the user, are to be found in almost all large text processors. If the user activates the short menu form he will only get the most important entries in the menu system. Most special functions he seldom needs are deleted. After the user has activated 'Reduced menu' the menu system will become smaller and at the same time the entry under 'Options' changes to 'Extended menu'. That's a hint to the rule that menu systems mainly contain action options. If the reduced menu is active, the only open option for the user to choose is 'Extended menu'.

The LIR tests showed very clearly that users are not able to build up a mental model of the check mark usage as it is realized in graphical text processors (and other systems). Even after three months, users' reactions were based on trial and error. To show why that effect is not surprising, the following example given in the Microsoft Windows Application Style Guide of the Software Development Kit [SDK 1990:18] will be analyzed, with the only alteration being the extension of 'Underline' to 'Single Underline' and 'Double Underline' which is in keeping with many systems.

Style	
√ Normal	
Bold	
Italic	
Single Underline	GROUP 1
Double Underline	
Outline	
Strikeout	
Left Aligned	
Centered	GROUP 2
√ Right Aligned	

Toggle commands are a good example of the danger of new techniques interfering with well-known software ergonomic rules, like the disambiguity or transparency claim.

a) Basically check marks are a difficult additional concept which superimposes the rule that the menu system is the place for showing the user his action options. Since options can be contrary to the state description, the potential for confusion is intrinsically large when both aims are merged.

b) There exist two main types of toggle commands: The second group of our SDK-example 'Left Aligned/Centered/Right Aligned' is mutually exclusive (type 1). The items cannot be check marked at the same time. A check mark can also not be deleted by activating a check marked item. But in the second main type, the user can check mark 'Bold/Italic/Single Underline/Outline/Strikeout' together. The setting of one check mark does not remove former settings. The user can also remove single check marks by activating the item. Both types are not differentiated in form, only semantically.

c) If the user turns on 'Normal' in the first group, a third kind of action takes place. All check marks of group one are deleted, as 'Normal' is a metacommand which defines inherent features of text style. Technically, it turns on a defined number of features and turns off all others that are deviations from the standard style. Therefore, the check mark of 'Normal' cannot be deleted simply by activating the entry anew.

d) In group two the user can notice the focus of the mutually exclusive toggle commands by the line separator, but 'Single Underline' and 'Double Underline' in group one are also mutually exclusive. They are a type 1 subgroup in a type 2 environment. Therefore, the line separator is not used.

e) Additional to the basic types 1 and 2 there are mutually exclusive toggle commands with two items such as 'Object fixed' versus 'Object movable' in COMFODESK, the desktop for COMFOTEX. There are also groups of one item (like 'Save automatically'), where the check mark indicates the activation of the command and the removing of it (by activating the marked item again). In both cases there are also formal alternatives: changing items or disabled items.

In none of the above cases a formal differentiation between all the types and subtypes discussed in a) - e) exists.

The LIR-tests showed empirically that users cannot handle such complicated and over-crowded interface structures, whatever their actual mixture of verbal and graphical modes may be:

- Disambiguity should not be totally dependent on semantics, as in many cases the user is not able to determine the exact semantic content of a command.

- Different types should be differentiated syntactically. There should also exist only one formal type for the same semantic command group.

- Different design styles for commands the user conceptualizes as being equivalent impede the building up of a mental model.

- The number of different formal types should be kept as small as possible; no additional differentiation should be made where it can be replaced by an already existing one.

These difficulties in Section 4.3, which led to severe user irritation in the LIR tests, are only indirectly connected with the combining of verbal items and the graphical mode. They are mainly the result of general user interface inconsistencies, thus indicating that these design details have to be crafted according to general and well-accepted software ergonomic rules like transparency or consistency as well. Software packages using a merger of graphical and verbal elements do not utilize this insight at the detail design level.

4.4. Summary

Menus can be seen as a low level example for merging graphical and verbal elements, which is already widely used in commercial applications. The methodological advantage of research on this multimodal system level is that there already exists broadly used software which can be tested in real life situations. Menus are also an example of artificial combinations of different modes, and the detailed design decisions at the deepest level of the design process connected with this combination. These decisions are not guided by the simulation of the human-human dialog but by gathering detailed advantages of the dialog in a computer environment containing other possibilities of optimizing interaction. The results obtained from commercial software tests are not promising, as they show how much work has still to be done at this level. The consequences of the LIR-findings - not discussed here - range from reconstructing the irritating design details to a partial reduction of the tasks of the menu subsystem with verbal items in favor of sophisticated toolboxes, to broadening the direct manipulation facilities, up to a reinterpretation of object orientation in user interface.

5. Metaphorical Use of Language in Multimodal Interfaces

Combining graphical and natural language elements does not only lead to problems at the level of designing details like check marks adequately, but also at a high theoretical level. Currently, theoretical models of both the "pure" modalities contain conflicting elements, which makes it hard to imagine a fruitful combination of both in one model of multimodal HCI. To discuss the problem of finding a common point of departure in constructing a multimodal HCI model, let us first have a closer look at the two modalities to be combined.

5.1. The Basic "Natural" Modes: Natural Language and Graphics

5.1.1. Natural Language

The "naturalness" of natural language interaction is established by the fact that users are already familiar with this (almost literally self-explanatory) mode of communication. The underlying thesis - widespread in computational linguistics and artificial intelligence - states: There is a 1:1 analogy between the user's behavior in HCI and human communication (see e.g., [Grishman 1986; Kanngießer 1989]). The need to learn new ways of interacting, prevalent in command-oriented systems (such as SQL) is eliminated by the user's already existing and well-trained skills in human communication.

Following this thesis two problematic aspects arise:

a) No natural language interface covers the whole range of human communication. Thus the question is whether the partial solution designed for an application area meets the requirements of the actual retrieval situation. In the worst case the advantages of taking over knowledge from human communication get lost, if the handling of the implemented subset of language requires learning and recalling efforts comparable with those of formal language alternatives.

b) It is not yet clear whether users in a special application domain use the same natural language utterances and show the same behavior in HCI as in human communication. If differences ("computer talk") exist, they have to be determined empirically and must be considered in the design of natural language input components.

Problem a) leads to the subset discussion, which shall not be discussed further here (see [Krause 1982]). The subset problem can be seen (although not necessarily) as a practical difficulty in technologically transferring natural language algorithms to software products, resulting from the fact that currently and in the near future this transfer has to be done before the linguistic knowledge and computer systems have been sufficiently advanced to enable the adequate simulation of human communication. But these arguments are not valid for problem b). It questions whether the model of 1:1 analogy between human communication and natural language HCI is theoretically adequate and practically useful. The thesis of an almost 1:1 analogy is a very simple design thesis; it is also very practical because the only thing the software developer has to do in order to construct a natural language interface - "pure" or merged - is to copy the existing knowledge of linguistics, the knowledge of human communication. But what will happen if the thesis of the 1:1 analogy is not correct, if users do not behave in HCI as they do in human communication, but use different syntactic constructions, different words or different dialog strategies?

In this case, natural language algorithms imitating human communication will be constructed which would only work in an interface where the user looks upon the machine as another kind of human being. But if the users of natural language interfaces do not think in this way, if differences exist, we have to explore them to come to feasible solutions.

5.1.2.   Graphical/Direct Manipulative Interaction

This second basic form of "natural" HCI can mainly be characterized - apart from the use of icons, pull-down menus, and windows - by two features:

a) Underlying metaphors.

A central but simple insight, provided by cognitive science, justifies the use of metaphors: new phenomena (new knowledge) are easier to learn and remember if tied to knowledge that already exists. For the word-processing domain and office communication the physical office environment represents such a relationship. Therefore, the screen is designed as a desktop and the functionality of word processors is realized in analogy to the familiar typewriter. For functions that go beyond the desktop or typewriter (e.g., the clipboard concept), the whole office is taken as a metaphor for electronic objects (icons representing bookcases, folders, paper baskets etc.). Thus the work of the user is simplified; he can draw conclusions in analogy to the familiar office environment.

b) Direct manipulation and mouse.

The term direct manipulation was coined by Shneiderman, who also gives the classic example of this principle of HCI in Shneiderman [1983]. He characterizes the difference between graphical interaction and conventional (command-oriented) systems by a comparison with car driving as a prototypical example of the application of direct manipulation. Instead of using function keys to determine the desired direction ("right", "left", specification of angles) or giving natural language input ("turn the steering wheel 30 degrees to the left"...) we turn the steering wheel itself. We get an instant feedback of the changes caused by the action and can perform appropriate corrections. Instead of verbalizing we act without intervention. In the same way the user operates by means of visual objects and the mouse as the pointing device on his electronic "desk" or in his "office". He is explicitly encouraged to think in physical (instead of electronical) terms and real actions.

It would be an illusion to think that these techniques and theories will lead by themselves to systems that can be used without mistakes and require no practice at all. The use of the mouse has to be practiced to perform the desired movements precisely. Neither is the technique of clicking (single-click, double-click, holding down the button in pull-down menus) self-explanatory nor can learning be dispensed with.

Beyond that the theory of metaphors implies - different to the postulated 1:1 analogy of natural language usage discussed above - that there will always be deviations, that is, violations of the metaphor. For instance, the electronic desk in office communication does not really correspond with the real desktop in every respect and the analogy with the typewriter is incomplete at best. The electronic world is equal to the physical office world only insofar as there are analogies with a lot of details that help the user in becoming familiar with the functions of the software.

5.1.3. Conclusion

The first observation is that the two primary modalities have both advantages and disadvantages that cannot be avoided, given the state of the art in system development as well as theoretical considerations. That seems, at a first glance, to be a good starting point for combining the advantages of both modes and thus reducing their disadvantages.

The second observation is less promising: The two primary modalities for the design of "natural" user interfaces are based on different theoretical assumptions, which are similar in the sense of being based on the simple but central insights provided by cognitive science: new phenomena are easier to learn and remember, if tied to existing knowledge. But there are important differences that can be expressed by the terms "1:1 analogy" versus "metaphorical use". It is hard to imagine (although not completely impossible) that a theoretical model of HCI can be constructed, where these cognitive differences coexist. That is, the user would have to switch from his "simulation" point of view when interpreting verbal expressions to the "metaphorical" one when processing visual elements.

With this difference in mind we tried to find a common point of departure for both modalities in two steps:

First Step:

Neither natural language HCI nor natural language components in a multimodal environment will work if there are differences between human communication and natural language HCI neglected by conforming to the thesis of 1:1 analogy. For this reason, the next question to be answered is, whether such differences between human communication and natural language HCI exist at all. The answer to this question is important for all kinds of pure or merged interfaces and the majority of computational linguists have put stock in this analogy until now and still build up their systems on the basis of neglecting possible differences. Therefore, we have tried to prove the existence of such differences, that is, the existence of something like computer talk, empirically. The theoretical background chosen to interpret the empirical data was that of a language register like foreigner talk or baby talk. What does that mean? Registers like foreigner talk, or baby talk, are mainly seen as a special kind of simplification of "normal talk". A set of different parameters of the language-in-use situation is correlated with a set of structural features (like missing morphological endings or articles). The basic idea is that not only do people talk differently in different situations, but that they do it predictably: specific types of situations have definable properties, which in turn, have determinate consequences on language. Register theory wants to make explicit the links between the situational features and the linguistic features [Ferguson 1985; Halliday 1967; Paris and Bateman 1990].

Second Step:

The common point of departure for a multimodal model of HCI, consisting of a merger of natural language and graphics, will be based on the interpretation of the computer talk results from step one. Beyond the initial concept of a language register computer talk, I argue that language in HCI is used metaphorically - not in 1:1 analogy to human communication - in a similar sense as the metaphorical use of the desktop metaphor in graphical HCI. Thus the concept of metaphorical use can form the basis for both modes. The initial differences between "simulation" and "metaphorical usage" no longer form an obstruction in the building up of a common model of multimodal HCI.

5.2.   The DICOS/ASL Experiments and Computer Talk

DICOS/ASL (financed by the German Ministry for Research and Technology from March 1988 to July 1992) conducts controlled experiments focusing on the special language-in-use situation of natural language HCI (computer talk) and on the metaphorical usage thesis of language in HCI. The DICOS/ASL team did experiments within two application domains: information seeking dialogs within a railway information system and within a library environment. Two hidden operator experiments were conducted, each simulating four information systems with different capabilities, representing the capabilities of present day and future information systems.

System 1:
> The user is told that he is communicating with a railway or library employee, who does the lookup in a database and answers his questions through a computer as a special input/output channel. The system has no restrictions in language utterances or cooperativity. The user gets an echo describing his information need.

System 2:
> System 2 behaves exactly like System 1, but the user is told that he is communicating with a computer understanding natural language without any restrictions. The user may ask whatever he wants. The only difference between System 1 and System 2 is the mental concept of the systems in the head of the user.

System 3:

The cooperativity of System 3 is restricted. The user has to formulate his information need according to given restrictions (no vague or modal expressions, literally interpretation of time phrases etc.). If the user neglects the restrictions, his utterances are rejected and he is told by the system which mistake has occurred.

System 4:

System 4 introduces additional restrictions. It behaves identically to System 3, except that it does not analyze errors.

The experimental design involved two experimental factors:

a)   the input mode (voice input or keyboard input), and

b)   the system variation (System 1, System 2, System 3, System 4) as described above.

This led to an experimental design with eight cells and five subjects each:

	System 1	System 2	System 3	System 4
voice	5	5	5	5
keyboard	5	5	5	5

For each experiment (railway and library) 40 subjects were given eight tasks, which took them approximately two hours. The chosen tasks represented different scenarios as shown in the example below:

"Your infirm grandmother wants to travel to Hamburg. Find a traveling possibility as convenient as possible for her."

Statistical experiments set up hypotheses so that comparisons concerning the factor levels can be carried out by so called hypothesis tests. Within these tests the null hypothesis, which says that there is no difference between the factor levels, is compared with another hypothesis. The null hypothesis can be rejected, if a significant difference has been shown within a specified probability of making a wrong decision. In DICOS statistical hypotheses were formulated to contrast human communication with HCI (S1 vs. S2, S3, S4), a cooperative human dialog partner with a cooperative computer system (S1 vs. S2), a restricted communication situation with a non-restricted situation (S1, S2 vs.

S3, S4) and voice input with keyboard input (S1, S2, S3, S4 voice vs. S1, S2, S3, S4 keyboard). More details about the DICOS/ASL tests can be found in Krause and Hitzenberger [1992]. Here we want to summarize only some examples of the results that are important for our reflections on mixed HCI. Significant results could be achieved for some of the features of computer talk. Further qualitative interpretation of the DICOS/ASL protocols led to additional differences in language use.

There were differences between S1 (human dialog) and S2-S4 (HCI) and also between S2 and S3/S4 (unrestricted vs. restricted HCI).

a) There is a linear tendency, from S1 to S4, in the restriction of sentence patterns variation. The complexity and number are highest in S1, the human dialog situation. They decrease in S2, i.e., unrestricted HCI, and lead partly to question form patterns, where only slots (mainly the specifications of place and time) are filled differently. The reduction from S1 to S4 mainly concerns subordinate clauses.

b) Indirect interrogation, including imperative, declarative and *optative* clauses, occurs mostly in S1 and least frequently in S4, in contrast to the direct interrogative clauses, which are rare in human communication, and become frequent in man-machine dialogs S2 - S4. This tendency is augmented by the restrictions in S3 and S4.

c) Features - especially in spoken language - which are interpreted as dialog disturbances or errors are reduced in S2 - S4 in contrast to the human communication in S1 (e.g., different kinds of ellipsis like abandoning a construction or subsequent correction, additions and appositions). The user seems to feel more obliged to express himself correctly when the addressee is a (stupid) computer than when speaking with a human. There are also indications of special features of restricted systems (S1 - S2 vs. S3 - S4).

d) The elliptical constructions are clearly more numerous in the unrestricted systems S1 and S2. This seems to be an effect of the tendency to surpass the restrictions of S3 and S4. When the user knows that the system is restricted, he is (also unintentionally) hesitant to leave the limitations of the language capabilities. He is also hesitant to refer to unusual topics. For example, in S1 and S2 asking for the valid conditions of certain reduced tariffs is such a topic, which does not appear in S3 and S4.

Summarizing the observations of DICOS/ASL we can say that the existence of differences between human communication and HCI has been proven. There is no 1:1 analogy; specific rules and regularities cannot be captured by looking at linguistic grammars or by observing human dialogs. Additional experiments with speech output [Kirch 1990] and more informal tests with a simulated natural language interface for a material database (chapter 6, therein) confirmed these results. Nevertheless, this conclusion would be too simple if it were not restricted to our present HCI world. The experiments were done with subjects who have current attitudes and beliefs about what machines can do. We cannot predict, however, whether the computer talk conclusion would generally hold true in the future where systems could be so widespread and actually understand languages as well as a person can, and in which people knew this and were accustomed to it. The statistically valid results of the DICOS/ASL experiments do not (and cannot experimentally) exclude the possibility that computer talk as shown above might be a phenomenon of people's belief on and familiarity with the limitations of current interfaces, despite what the S2 users have been told about the unrestricted capabilities of the experimental systems. In this sense, computer talk research is intrinsically psycho- and socio-historically bound.

5.3. Metaphorical Use of Language in HCI

Besides the indications discussed in Section 5.2 there were also some examples of HCI-discourse, leading to the thesis that computer talk means more than some aberrations describable within a linguistic model of language use. Here we can only give one example [Krause 1990a, 1992], first published in Krause [1982] (without further interpretation) as an isolated anomaly.

No.	Question
14	Wieviele Schüler haben welche Englischnote in Quarta?
	(How many students have which grade in English in seventh grade?)

Note (Grade)	Anzahl (Number)
1	22
2	77
3	144
4	112
5	42
6	2
.	.
.	.
.	.

29   Welche Deutschnote in Quarta hat wieviele Schüler ?
        (Which grade in German in seventh grade has how many students?)

        U32410W: SPALTENNAME: VON NICHT ENTHALTEN IN   TABELLE:
        SCHÜLER

        (U32410W COLUMN NAME: FROM NOT FOUND IN TABLE:
        STUDENT)

30   Wieviele Schüler haben welche Deutschnote in Quarta?
        (How many students have which grade in German in seventh grade?)

The question number 29 is not acceptable in German. This did not, however, bother the user. He chose this form because the answer to question number 14 showed Note ('grade') in the first column and Anzahl ('number of the students') in the second. The user wanted to make it easier for the computer to answer questions such as number 14. Therefore, in number 29, he adapted his query to the (correctly) assumed internal sequencing. It is important to note that this destruction of an acceptable language structure, which proved to be successful in HCI, took place without being requested. There was no error situation and no unusual result. To interpret this and similar examples adequately, we have to admit that the user leaves our language system. He does not vary it (or it cannot be explained as such) by taking something away, adding a small new rule or simplifying regularities of general language. He chooses a vantage point outside his own language competence and appeals to the idea that a computer cannot talk: 'it's only a trick of the designers.' From this external position, he uses language parts as movable scenery, primarily subject to the general logic of computer actions, and not to language competence, (slightly) adapting the needs of the language-in-use situations.

If one accepts this interpretation, an alternative or additional concept has to be found to cope with these situations: It seems that natural language is used here in the same metaphorical sense as the desktop concept. The user builds a mental model of his natural language HCI, which is based on the view of human communication in natural language, which however, has no one-to-one correlation. In the context of this section the most important property of the metaphorical concept is that metaphors can break down. Metaphors do not work in all cases, but very often nevertheless.

5.4.   Conclusion to Metaphorical Usage

Besides the proof of differences between human communication and natural language HCI in the sense of a language register computer talk, there are also strong indications for the metaphorical use of natural language in a similar way to that of the graphical mode when using the desktop metaphor. The user builds up a mental model of his natural language HCI which is based on the view of human communication in natural language but which is not in one-to-one correspondence. Accepting this interpretation we have obtained the common point-of-view we searched for to interpret natural language HCI and the graphical interaction techniques. Both can be based on the concept of metaphorical use.

6. Prototyping a Multimodal Interface for a Material Database

The last example for empirically driven research about multimodal HCI belongs to an intermediate level of the software development cycle. The construction of a multimodal system for a special application domain like material databases requires more than some high level theoretical insights of how to model multimodal HCI and ideas on how to merge different modes at a detailed level of design. What we need is to find plausible suggestions for an initial multimodal prototype, to be improved later on by iterated empirical testing (rapid prototyping). One possible solution to do empirical research at this level will be exemplified by the ongoing activities of the LIR project WING-IIR. The main idea here is: Start with "pure" prototypes ("pure" concerning the modalities) and test them empirically in a prephase. Resulting insights on advantages and disadvantages of the pure solutions with respect to a special application from the basis for the construction of a first merged prototype and then further tested. The first prototype of a multimodal interface can only be a very tentative one, as the conclusions drawn from the empirical data are still very indirect. At this starting level, we employ the heuristic (surely wrong in some cases) that advantages in the pure modes will remain advantageous in the multimodal interface and that difficulties particularly due to the merging itself will be detected in the tests of the following prototypes with integrated modes.

6.1. WING-IIR and Influences of "Intelligent" Components

The aim of this project (financed by the German Ministry for Economics from April 1989 to July 1994) is to develop an intelligent multimodal interface (graphics and natural language) for the material database of our industrial partner MTU (Munich). The methods used are rapid prototyping in combination with intensive user-participation and empirical evaluation.

In WING-IIR the decision of how to combine graphical and natural language elements into a multimodal interface is strongly influenced by the second claim, to build up an "intelligent" interface in the sense of "intelligent information retrieval" (IIR, for a survey see Krause [1992]). The question of search can - almost independently from the chosen modality - be modeled conceptually in completely different ways, e.g., as a mapping of cognitive structures of a specific task, or built on a computer centered data model (e.g., SQL). The possible search strategies also differ considerably, as in hierarchical access, or associative hypertext relations. This, however, doesn't imply an obligatory correspondence with one of the two basic modalities. Furthermore, general concepts of software ergonomics, e.g., adaptivity, adaptability, or user-modeling, have to be included in studies of multimodal interfaces, as well as considerations from the domain of IIR [Bauer 1990; Krause 1992; ACM SIGIR 1988]. On the one hand, IIR includes the two natural interaction modes graphics and especially natural language as an increase of "intelligent" system behavior in contrast to formal languages, on the other hand, IIR goes beyond these techniques. The terms IIR or expert systems for information retrieval [Hawkins 1988] articulate the intention to make accessible ideas, methods, and techniques developed in artificial intelligence research; they do not, however, outline a well-defined topic, despite the definitions given for IIR (see e.g., [Croft 1987]). Thus, one can say, IIR means to improve traditional information retrieval by adding artificial intelligence components like user modeling or active help systems. Such intelligent components will also affect design decisions concerning details of a multimodal interface. For example it is impossible to build up the same interface for a traditional descriptor search system using Boolean algebra as for an artificial intelligence system heavily dependent on user models and inferential processes. Therefore, we have to take into account all these additional dimensions. It is possible to focus on the multimodal aspect of interaction, but IIR components cannot be neglected. A direct consequence of these interdependencies concerning the empirical approach had been that eight different types of interaction were tested in WING-IIR instead of two basic modalities only.

6.2.   The Eight WING-IIR Basic Types of Interaction

It has been argued here that it doesn't seem to be reasonable to disregard additional dimensions of interaction like those articulated in IIR. Therefore, the test of pure interaction types is not meant to be pure with respect to the additional concepts discussed in Section 6.1. Such empirical tests would not correspond to the reality of commercial and experimental interface types existing today either. We separated the two basic modalities but embedded them in an environment of additional features which are considered promising. These considerations led to eight types, realized and tested in WING-IIR:

1) Hierarchically organized search paths.

2) Hypertext structures.

3) Pure formal language query SQL.

4) Graphical supported SQL formulation.

5) Cognitive oriented graphical/direct manipulative interaction.

6) Query by example.

7) User driven natural language query (realized at the University of

Munich by F. Guenthners team).

8) Descriptor search with Boolean algebra for document retrieval.

The eight types are described extensively in Krause et al. [1990] and Krause [1990b]. Most of them are well-known interaction techniques and have been adapted to the special needs of the WING-IIR domain. Here, only types 1 and 5 will be briefly discussed.

6.2.1. Hierarchically -Organized Search Paths

The presently implemented access to the MTU-database is built upon a hierarchical structure, that is, query of information is made up by a sequence of individual decisions. Both entry points into the network of relations between generic and specific verbal terms and the ordering of query stages are determined by the system. In this hierarchical access mode, the potentials of graphical and direct manipulation interaction have not been exploited yet: to avoid interaction problems, the hierarchical access mode to the MTU-database was modeled in a graphical direct manipulation environment in accordance to the rules of software ergonomics.

6.2.2. Subject-Domain Driven Query Support for Factual Databases in a Direct Manipulation Environment

The first prototype COGRA (COgnitive/GRAphical) in the WING-IIR environment is an example for this mode of access [Wolff 1991]. Within COGRA, the following query types, extracted from typical information needs of material experts, have been modeled: "information about specific materials", "search by specification profile", "display of general qualities of materials" and "comparison of materials". Especially the last mode underlines the fundamental idea of a graphical query aid designed according to the subject domain of the application: The user simply selects the materials and specifications to be compared from two lists into a search matrix. A direct conversion of this cognitive pattern into a strategy for building the correlating and very complex SQL-query is undoubtedly a highly difficult task which cannot be expected to be solved by non-expert users. During the initial design stages of the different COGRA access modes, potential problem types of materials database users were analyzed and problem solving strategies that match structurally with human problem solving patterns have been modeled. An essential point of this solution is that different types of access exist in parallel, that is, the different problem types of one application have each their own query window.

6.3.   State of the System Development and First Prototype

In 1992 all WING-IIR prototypes of the prephase ("pure" solutions) have been implemented under MS-WINDOWS V. 3.1 mainly using the Software Development Toolkit and the SQLBASE Application Program Interface for C. The hypertext prototype was built up with TOOLBOOK. The natural language parser provided by our project partners at Munich University (Guenthner et al.) exists as a small demonstration prototype and will be extended in 1993. It is implemented in Prolog II (later Prolog III) running in a UNIX environment on a SUN workstation.

Informal tests with material experts of MTU have been conducted for all types under consideration; extended empirical tests took place with prototypes based on the interaction types 1 (hierarchical), 2 (hypertext) 5 (cognitive oriented graphical interaction), 6 (query by example) and a simulation of an ideal natural language system (7). The empirical material of the prephase has been analyzed (all together 45 test hours of 45 user sessions) and the first merged prototype exists since December 1991. A description of the first multimodal prototype is contained in Marx et al. [1992]. As mentioned above, in WING-IIR merging apart from the modalities graphics and natural language mainly concerns research strategies, interaction style and the integration of intelligent components in the sense of IIR.

Concerning the combination of the two modalities graphics and natural language, several hypotheses were derived from the empirical observations of the prephase:

a)   The cognitively motivated graphical/direct manipulative interaction type (number 5 in Section 6.2) turned out to be the most promising general approach for a material database.

b) Difficulties at the first interaction step, i.e., choosing the appropriate query-type like "search by specification profile" or "comparison of materials," which mirror typical information needs of material experts, could be observed. This seems to be a naming as well as a psychological problem, not a conceptual one. The postulated COGRA query types matched with the users' problem solving patterns but users preferred to formulate the initial query in natural language. This entry option has been modeled, but the reaction of the system leads the user to the graphical/direct manipulative environment, where a refinement of the information needs is possible by means of clicking buttons, choosing items from lists, and similar techniques.

c) Instead of single names for items in the relational database structure connected by operators like AND, OR, and NOT, at all levels of graphics nominal phrases (which will be analyzed by the natural language processor as elliptical expressions) are accepted. An intermediary language then has to build a link between the semantic of graphical elements and the nominal phrases.

d) The WING-IIR tests, as well as that of DICOS/ASL, demonstrated that users tend to formulate natural language queries in situations where they have lost confidence completely. If there are serious problems, particularly when other means of communication have broken down, users automatically shift to the natural language mode. The same observation was made by an evaluation study with GOETHE, a natural language help system for the domain of text processing (see [Heyer and Kese 1991; Heyer 1992].

"... context help and task help are the only tasks where GOETHE has been judged superior to UNIX and the graphical user interface. From the point of view of language technology, it may be important, therefore, to distinguish between a command entry and help request mode, and to consider, where possible, a combination of GUI [=graphics] and natural language interface components where natural language is mainly used for formulating general help requests." [Heyer 1992:9f]

7. Conclusion

Intelligent multimedia is a research domain full of unresolved issues of considerable complexity at all levels of development. As all these issues are still in their formative stage, definitive solutions even of small isolated problems can scarcely be expected soon. To comprehend the technical aspects of combining different media does not imply comprehending either the architectural problems or the conceptual ones arising with software ergonomic design decisions, although all these aspects are crucial to the problem at hand. For a long time to come we will have to experiment in an interdisciplinary context with as many different ideas and methodologies as possible; thus, finding starting points for system development in intelligent multimedia that are theoretically well founded and practical in application. The multilayered empirical approach and the LIR prototypes discussed have to be seen in this context. The focus on empirical research is an additional component in the overall endeavor of the multimedia research community that the papers in this volume on intelligent multimedia interfaces reflect.

Chapter 15

Modeling Issues in Multimedia Car-Driver Interaction

Andrea Bonarini

Abstract

The management of the communication between a driver and his artificial co-pilot is a challenging application for multimedia interaction. In the near future, cars will be equipped with screens, keyboard, displays, speech synthesizers, and other interaction tools. The artificial co-pilot will support the driver in his activities, interacting without distracting him from his task. We make decisions about the best media to use, and coordinate the communication through inferential activities basing on models of: the interaction tools, the driver, the environment, the situation, and the communication. Whereas the first type of models is static, the others are updated in real-time by inferential analysis of the driver's actions, as they are perceived from sensors. We represent and consider uncertainty about the results of this inferential activity. Heuristics working on the models choose the best mix of media to issue messages. The system performance gracefully degrades when information becomes poor, and the available time becomes scarce. In this chapter, we present in detail the models and how they can be updated using information coming from sensors. We also discuss uncertainty representation and management, proposing a solution feasible with the scarce resources available on board. Finally, we present the architecture of a system able to produce multimedia messages in real-time, satisfying the requirements of such a hard task.

1. Introduction

The interaction between driver and co-pilot is becoming an important research issue. Many car firms, but also national and international research agencies, are interested in the development of the "car of the future," where an intelligent co-pilot supports the driver's activities, enhancing safety and making the use of the vehicle easier. We present a part (Multimedia Interaction Manager - *MIMa*) of the whole Man-Machine Interface

(MMI) being developed within the EUREKA project PROMETHEUS. *MIMa* is in charge of bringing on the exchange of information between driver and co-pilot using different types of media.

The typical scenario is a car equipped with many different interaction tools, where all the actions done by the driver are interpreted as (possibly indirect) messages to the co-pilot. The Interaction Manager shall interpret the driver's messages, shall maintain models of the driver, of the environment, of the situation, and of the communication, and shall decide when and how to issue messages. The system should do this activity on-line, while different sensors contribute to update both the environment and the situation models.

Among the most studied practical applications for driver co-pilot interaction we may find interactive planning of the way to the destination (e.g., [Adorni et al. 1989]) and interactive route guidance (e.g., [Streeter et al. 1985; Hallen et al. 1989]).

We defined a set of features describing the interaction tools. *MIMa* uses these features to decide which tool may bring a message to the driver in a specific situation, or from which tool it may expect a driver reaction to a stimulus. We discuss the interaction tools features in Section 2, with special concern to what is available on a car now, or in the near future. More fascinating tools can be imagined, but driver co-pilot interaction is a real application for vehicle designers who have strong constraints on the costs of everything on board. *MIMa* [Bonarini 1991a] uses the driver model features we discuss in Section 3. The approach to uncertainty representation in user modeling is presented in Section 4. Section 5 is devoted to architectural issues, and, in Section 6, we provide some examples of the application of the driver model for effective multimedia driver co-pilot interaction.

2. The Interaction Tools Models

In this section we propose features describing interaction tools. These features take values ranging on verbal scales (*linguistic variables*). This solves problems of numerical representation of knowledge coming from people and inferential activities (see [Clark 1990] for a discussion about numerical representation of uncertainty), and reduces the complexity of a free semantic representation [Lenat and Guha 1990] where the meaning of each term should be fully described. We explicitly reject the possibility of modeling these features using numbers, since this may introduce problems such as:

- The difficulty of interpreting the meaning of the numerical measure–a value of 0.7 for a feature has no immediate meaning and different users can interpret it differently;

- The inability to normalize the scale of values–values supplied by different sources cannot be compared;

- No statements about the precision of the measure can be issued–it is impossible to know whether a value of 0.7 has to be considered as 0.7±0.1 or as 0.7±0.001;

- A false perception of precision–people may feel that the number coming from number-based reasoning is an exact representation of the corresponding features; this is misleading, since the initial values are mostly approximate and subjective;

- A possible discontinuity in the combination of numerical values when they are close to critical values;

- No cognitive plausibility–people reason in terms of classes and can keep distinct only a small number of values.

2.1. General Features

We call "input tools" the tools used by the driver to *communicate* messages to the co-pilot. *MIMa* uses "output tools" to *issue* messages to the driver. Two features common to both input and output tools are the:

- **Complexity** of the message a tool can convey. It ranges on a verbal scale from *two states* messages to *natural language* messages. For instance, a light indicator (or a switch) can only be *on* or *off*, whereas a speech synthesizer may issue a full natural language message.

- **Sensory system** involved in the interaction. We consider only the *auditory* and the *visual* systems, since we cannot realistically see the involvement of other senses in driver co-pilot communication in the near future. Moreover, we do not require any special action from a driver entering a car (such as putting on a mask or a body sensor). We assume that data-like body temperature or blood pressure will not be available in the near future, although they could be useful for driver modeling.

More than one sensory system can be effectively stimulated at a time, if we carefully choose the information given on the different channels. For instance, some experimental results (in part obtained within PROMETHEUS [Hallen et al. 1989]) show that producing the same information both on auditory and visual media may result in a worse message comprehension than when the same information is presented using only speech. Considering that car-driving is a heavy resource-demanding task, we may interpret this result as an overload of the driver's attentional abilities.

2.2.   Input Tools

Here is a list of features describing only input tools.

- **Intentionality** of the driver to use a tool to exchange information (communicate) with the co-pilot. This feature takes a Boolean value. Most of the input tools now available are intended to produce a change in the car behavior (e.g., the light switch makes lamps enlighten). These actions bring useful information, but usually the driver does not do them with communicative intention. Probably, a driver switching the lamps on would not explicitly communicate to the co-pilot that there is scarce visibility, whereas, he is surely starting a communicative sequence when he asks whether he should turn right or left at the next corner.

- **Type of action** needed to use the tool. For instance, some tools shall be *touched by hands* (e.g., levers, buttons), others *touched by feet* (e.g., pedals), others *vocally activated*. This feature is important since the co-pilot should not ask to use a tool that the driver cannot use in a specific situation.

- **Attention** needed to use a tool. Speaking in a microphone only requires the attention to produce the correct message, but it should be preferred that the driver stops the car to operate on a keyboard. *MIMa* asks only for messages which the driver can issue using those tools requiring a quantity of attention compatible with his current activity.

- **Quality** of the message reception, intended as a measure of the possible degradation of the message resulting from the specific conditions under which the tool can be operated.

In Table 1 we summarize the features describing input tools, with their possible values.

Features	Possible Values			
intentionality	yes	no		
kind of action	hand_touch	feet_touch	vocal	
attention	auto-motion	speak	single_motion	motion_seq
quality	good	medium	low	

Table 1. The Input Tools Features and Their Possible Values

2.3.   Output Tools

Here are the features specific to output tools.

- **Mergeability** is the feature modeling the possibility to use two tools simultaneously to convey a multimedia message or two interrelated messages. This feature depends on both the involved media and ranges on a verbal scale from *low* to *high*.

- **Attention** needed to understand the message is related both to complexity and to the sensory apparatus. While a map showing the way to a destination needs some attention to be interpreted if presented on a screen, the same information is more easily understood, if told step by step, at each road crossing.

- The degree of **awareness** needed by the driver to be conscious of the message *MIMa* is producing is different from attention. This feature models the driver's possibility to get in contact with the co-pilot issuing a specific message, whereas attention models the possibility to understand the message content. If the driver has to consider a message immediately, *MIMa* will choose an output tool calling for a low degree of awareness, such as a loud sound.

- **Agitation** induced in the driver by the output tool is related to the last two features. Whereas the driver could consider a red lamp more exciting than a green one, a blinking red lamp is even more exciting, and a siren may bring the driver to panic. The most sophisticated output tools may vary their induced agitation level: a natural language speaker may tell information about weather with a calm, firm voice, whereas it may use a screaming voice to inform there is fire on board. Agitation takes a value in a linguistic range from *calm* to *panic* and the most sophisticated tools are also associated with a range of possible agitation values.

Features	*Possible Values*			
mergeability	high	medium	low	
attention	map_or_nl	sentences	word_or_icon	two_states
awareness	high	medium	low	
agitation	panic	alarm	uneasiness	calm

Table 2. The Output Tools Features and Their Values

3. The Driver Model

The driver model we are proposing contains five types of knowledge:

- Knowledge about *psychological states* of the driver, such as attention and agitation;
- Knowledge about *attitudes* (attitude to a particular type interaction, to get slept after a given driving time, and so on);
- Knowledge about *preferences*;
- Knowledge about *what the driver knows*;
- Knowledge about *what the driver would like to get*.

We discuss each one of them in this section.

3.1. Psychological States

We describe psychological states in our driver model by variables which take values on a verbal scale. *MIMa* uses these variables as descriptors of the state of the driver both to choose the most appropriate interaction tool to issue a message, and to better understand the driver's behavior. The choice also depends on the description of the interaction tools available on board. For instance, if the driver's attention is dedicated to a dangerous activity (say a left-turning maneuver), *MIMa* should use a tool with a low degree of *awareness* needed, if it wants the driver to dedicate some attention to the message.

As example of inference of driver's behavior, let us consider the same attention-consuming situation, happening just after *MIMa* issued a question to the driver. He may not react, since the left-turning maneuver may take all his attention. *MIMa*, knowing the driver's state, may not insist to get any immediate answer, possibly planning to repeat the question at a later, more suitable moment.

In this section we present the features describing the driver's psychological state. We assume all the values for these variables are inferred by data patterns coming from sensors. Particularly, we are testing the possibility to consider only data coming from the interaction with the car, typically done to control it. Therefore, we defined a network mapping how the driver uses pedals, steering wheel, and control switches into psychological states.

Data from the interaction tools are continuously collected. The system infers from their modification the support to the nodes of the network corresponding to pre-defined, characteristic *ways to* use the tools. Whenever a *way* is supported enough, it triggers propagating its confidence measure (filtered by a link force) to nodes corresponding to psychological states, contributing to their confidence values. This architecture enables smooth, and quickly computed updates of the opinions *MIMa* has about the driver. Notice that at a given moment we may have different values for the same variable, supported by different confidence measures.

When presenting the psychological states, we will provide some relationships with data patterns, used to support their values. We identified them by methodical observations of some drivers in Milan, Italy. Probably, they need to be adapted to different types of traffic and driver's local idiosyncrasies. For instance, in southern Italy the use of horn is more common than in Milan, and, there, we cannot consider it as a good indicator for driver nervousness. Moreover, there could also be differences from driver to driver. These problems are only partially solved by the approximation of the model: the limited number of values for each state limits the possibility of errors in state identification. However, there are enough values to differentiate the interaction behavior of *MIMa*, giving the different situations and the different driver's states. Anyway, dynamic adaptation of the interpretation mechanism on specific users and situations is beyond the scope of our present research activity.

Here is the list of the driver's psychological state variables, their possible values, and some hints about how they are deduced from the driver's behavior.

- **Attention** dedicated by the driver to its current activities. It varies on a scale related to the type of activity the driver is involved in:
  ◊ null: the driver is completely free, he is not driving (this value can be deduced trivially);
  ◊ *routine*: the driver is doing some standard activity, such as driving in a normal situation (smooth use of accelerator, brakes, and steering wheel, eventually preceded by arrows switching at a proper time);
  ◊ *low-effort*: the driver is doing some extraordinary activity needing some attention (few sudden brake hits, few missing arrows);
  ◊ *absorbed*: the driver dedicates all his attention to his activity (sudden brake hits, some use of the horn, missing arrows);
  ◊ *life-danger*: the driver is doing some special activity needing more than the maximum of his attention (hard brake hits, small steering activity).

MIMa uses this feature to deduce how much attention the driver could dedicate to communicate with his co-pilot.

- **Agitation**. This feature describes how much the driver worries about something happening. For instance, not being in time for a meeting, or the car producing black smoke may cause agitation. It ranges on the following scale:
  ◊ *calm*: low speed, smooth use of pedals, no horn;
  ◊ *uneasy*: quick and disordered steering activity;
  ◊ *alarm*: sudden horning sounds, lights flashing, sudden small brake hits, quick, and large steering actions;
  ◊ *panic*: sudden, long horning sounds, sudden hard brake hits, action on friction without changing speed gear, no acceleration.

  MIMa can use this feature, for instance, to avoid the choice of interaction tools rising agitation over a critical threshold (such a siren), or to decide to issue messages to lower it.

- **Irritation**. This feature describes how much the driver is irritated. For instance, a long queue may irritate the driver, but also a discussion with his wife sitting in the car. It ranges on the following scale:
  ◊ *calm*: low speed, smooth use of pedals, no horn;
  ◊ *uneasy*: quick and disordered steering activity, some quick acceleration, some flashing;
  ◊ *nervous*: occasional quick accelerations followed by hard braking, frequent short flashing and horning, sudden changes of lane;
  ◊ *angry*: frequent hard accelerations, hard braking, long horning.

MIMa can use this feature to interpret ambiguous situations/messages such as a sequence of short horn sounds–is the driver addressing some of his friends he saw in the street, or would he like to escape from an endless queue?

- **Tiredness**. *MIMa* may use this feature to decide whether to present messages in the most plain and easiest possible way. It ranges on this scale:
  ◊ *fresh*: everything is standard;
  ◊ *almost tired*: some discontinuity in the use of the acceleration, few speed changes, some missed arrows switching;
  ◊ *tired*: sudden brake hits, preceded by normal use of the accelerator, almost no speed change (also when starting at the green lamp), missing arrows;
  ◊ *sleepy*: smooth lane changes with smooth deceleration, possibly followed by braking, sudden starting at the green lamp, almost no speed change, missing arrows.

3.2.   Attitudes

Attitudes are driver's tendencies to react to some situation in some stereotypical way. We assume some attitudes as standard for most people. For instance, most of us become tired after a long trip, or nervous after a two hour queue. Attitudes simplify data acquisition for the driver model. Other attitudes are more driver-specific, and should be inferred from typical driver behaviors. Each attitude has the form:

if <description of the situation> *then* <reaction> *with force* <force>

where the <description of the situation> is the name of the interpretation of a sensorial data pattern, <reaction> is a relationship between a psychological state and one of its values, and <force> is the force of the rule. When a sensorial pattern matches the left hand side of an attitude, the combination of the confidence in it with the force of the rule becomes the confidence attributed to the reaction. Since the reaction is a relationship belonging to the psychological states part of the driver model, two cases are possible: either no knowledge was already present about this relationship (and the obtained value becomes the current one), or something had already been stated about it (and the obtained confidence value is aggregated to the present one).

We list here some derived attitudes.

> *if* long_queue *then* irritation ≥ nervous *with force* extremely-likely
> *if* long_trip *then* tiredness ≥ tired *with force* meaningful-chance
> *if* serious_message *then* agitation ≥ alarm *with force* it-may

We may use attitudes to add information to a poor driver model, or to check the consistency of a rich one.

3.3.   Preferences

Preferences describe typical biases shown by the driver for a specific choice. For this type of knowledge, the same considerations done for attitudes are valid. Since this is knowledge that a system should infer from historical data, it is not realistic to think that it will be available on a car in the next few years. Only if their relevance will be proved by experiments will we insert preferences in the next version of the system. For the tests we are doing now, we represent them in the form:

> <u>prefers</u> <preference> <u>among</u> <class of choice>

Here are some examples:

> <u>prefers</u> visual messages <u>among</u> messages
> <u>prefers</u> long messages <u>among</u> messages

MIMa may use references to tune the interaction on the driver, choosing appropriately (when possible) the interaction tools and their use.

3.4.   Driver's Knowledge

This is what the interaction system assumes the driver knows and believes. We represent it in a KL-ONE-type [Brachman and Schmolze 1985] knowledge representation language, and it is updated by modules of the MMI different from *MIMa.*

3.5.   Driver's Goals

This is what the interaction system assumes the driver would like to do. We represent it in the same language used for driver's knowledge, and it is updated by modules of the MMI different from *MIMa.* Both the last two types of knowledge are standard components of user models, and we will not discuss them in this paper, since we did not implement anything new about them in *MIMa.* Interested readers can refer to [Kobsa and Wahlster 1989] or to [Allen 1987] for a state of the art overview in the field.

3.6.   The Initial State for the Driver Model

We defined *a priori* some general knowledge giving a sort of "default" initial state to the driver model. This describes the driver when he enters in the car at the beginning of the trip. It is possible to define different initial states for the different drivers of a car.

MIMa could refine the given initial states interacting with the actual driver. The interaction system will do this only if it has enough resources, since it is computationally expensive and affected by uncertainty–it has to dedicate some of the scarce resources to infer standard driver's features from his behavior while the interaction activity is running.

As a simple example of initial state for the driver model we consider that *attention* is *routine*, *agitation* is *calm*, and so on. We assume some generic attitudes (like the ones cited in Section 3.2), although it is impossible to quantify exactly the terms for the specific driver. For instance, I can drive for three hours with little effort, but my wife (using my car) is usually tired after a one hour trip. We cannot define *a priori* any *preference* for a generic driver. Moreover, we consider that, at the beginning, the driver does not know anything special and that he intends to get somewhere by car. One of the first goals of the whole MMI will be to define where the driver would like to go.

3.7. A Classification of the Proposed Driver Model

We classify our driver model using the grid presented in [Brajnik et al. 1990], to compare it with other proposals. This grid is a classification tool for user modeling in expert man-machine interfaces, and we believe it can be successfully used to classify driver models.

Given this grid, our driver model is:
- *Explicit,* since it is explicitly defined within the MMI architecture;
- *Inferred*, since it contains information which is *a priori* unknown, such as the attentional state of the driver, or whether he knows the current traffic situation;
- *Dynamic*, since its content is time-variant;
- *Individual*, since it is useful only if it models the driver currently on board.

The information present in the driver model may come from:
- External acquisition, and more specifically from dialogue inspection;
- Internal activity, mainly based on inferences drawn from the information already present in the current user model.

4. Knowledge Qualification: Confidence

We qualify each knowledge element present in our models by a *degree of confidence*, since the driver modeler mostly gets knowledge through inferential activities from the interaction with the driver. The semantics of the *degree of confidence* is: "a measure of how much *MIMa* believes that it can consider a knowledge element as a part of a correct description of the real world." Let us point out that a large part of the knowledge used in *MIMa* comes from the interpretation of how the driver controls the car (steering, accelerating, braking, horning, and so on).

To represent this type of meta-knowledge (confidence about knowledge) we cannot use any numerical measure. Refer to [Clark 1990], and [Bonarini 1991b] for a discussion about this topic, which follows the lines motivating linguistic values for models features, as presented above. A semantic qualification (such as the one proposed by [Lenat and Guha 1990]) does not seem feasible, since the computational resources on a car are usually under dimensioned for the activities they should carry on.

Therefore, we decided to represent the different components of confidence about a piece of knowledge with a unique *measure*, the *degree of confidence,* represented by a *belief interval* [Driankov 1986], i.e., a pair of variables (*support* and *plausibility*) each one ranging on a set of *linguistic labels* [Bonissone and Decker 1986], namely: *impossible, very-low-chance, small-chance, it-may, meaningful-chance, extremely-likely, certain.* Therefore, we can represent at the same time a measure of the evidence for a proposition (*support*) and of its negation (inversely proportional to *plausibility*). For instance, if there is much evidence that the driver is tired (e.g., he is not changing speed appropriately, he is forgetting to switch on arrows when turning), the support associated to the statement "*tiredness high*" is *extremely-likely*. On the other side, if the driver is answering promptly to messages, there is some evidence that he is not tired, represented by associating a high plausibility (such as *extremely-likely*) to "*tiredness high*."

Using this approach, it becomes natural to explicitly represent *contradiction* (high support and low plausibility) and *ignorance* (low support, and high plausibility), using a small set of values (only seven for each of the two components of the measure) related to terms which have meaning both for the Driver Modeler and its designer.

You may find details about belief intervals and how they are combined in [Driankov 1986, 1991; Bonarini et al. 1992]. The *degree of confidence* is associated to feature values with a time stamp, stating when it has been lastly updated. The time stamp implements a sort of decay of the validity of the degree of confidence with time: the actual degree of confidence considered by the inferential activities is always weighted by the time passing from its last update. This is an efficient way to keep track of some values thatmight have been updated by situations that no longer hold. For instance, if the driver's *agitation* value *panic* has a high support because the driver suddenly stopped the car, this will become less and less relevant as time passes, if no other evidence supporting it becomes available.

5. Architectural Issues

In Figure 1, we show the architecture of *MIMa* and how it interfaces with the other parts of the MMI. In Figure 1, the parts belonging to *MIMa* are shaded. We represent passive knowledge bases by boxes, and active modules (either procedural or inferential) by ovals. The other parts of the MMI are grouped in the white box on the left. Since they are being implemented at the same time as *MIMa*, we assume they have the features planned to be achieved by the end of the project. Specifically, we assume that: the knowledge is represented in a KL-ONE-type language, communicative acts [Austin 1962; Searle 1969; Allen 1987] are used to represent knowledge related to forms and contents of messages, and beliefs and intentions of the user are represented by logical forms. Notice that, as other people in this field (e.g., [Maybury, this volume; Awada et al. 1991]), we consider that communicative acts can adequately represent knowledge also about messages not to be output in natural language.

Data from the actual input interaction tools are first translated by different *Translators*, some of which belong to *MIMa*. The system uses data coming from car controls to infer *Psychological States* (represented as shown above) and a description of the external *Environment* (represented by KL-ONE-type statements). From these last, the *Attitudes* module generates other contributions for the *Psychological States* model. The MMI manager decides the message to output and puts its description, expressed in a logical form, in the queue of the output messages to be assigned a tool, a part of the *Communication Model*. From the contents of this queue, the *PsychologicaStates* of the driver, his *Preferences*, and the *Interaction Tools Models*, the *Tools Chooser* chooses the best tool to issue the message. The *Tools Chooser* is an inferential module which evaluates these data and ranks the candidate tools. It picks the best one and communicates its decision to the MMI manager, which will shift the message to another part of the *Communication Model*–the queue of the messages ready to be output. Then, the MMI starts the proper translator to issue the message; if this activity is successfully done, the message goes in the list of issued messages.

In this cyclic behavior there are some problems of synchronization. Each active module is implemented on a conceptually-different computational unit, so that the translators can continue their activity while the interpreters infer environmental descriptions and psychological states. Therefore, all the models are updated asynchronously. We assume that changes are smooth during the time the *Tool Chooser* chooses. Therefore, although it works on changing knowledge, its choice is coherent enough with the actual situation.

Two other lists are in the *Communication Model*. The first is the list of expectations, where the MMI puts the expectations of communicative responses to the issued messages, as stated by the postulates of good communication [Levinson 1983; Bonarini 1987]. The second is the list of the communicative acts recognized from the driver's behavior. As discussed above, many driver's actions implicitly convey messages, whether the driver does these actions to communicate, or not.

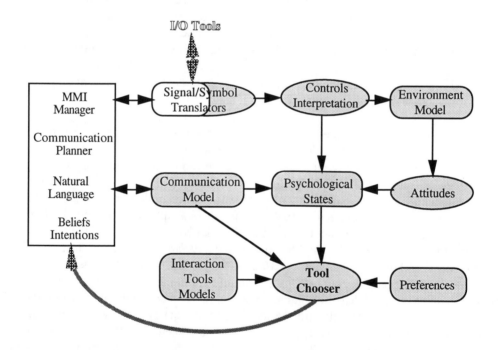

Figure 1. The Architecture of MIMa

6. An Example

As an example of the activity of *MIMa*, let us consider the case where the driver is *calm*, and its level of attention is *routine*. In Figure 2 you may see the situation. The driver's car is the gray one on the bottom. In the figure we also show: the track the driver will follow in the example, a queue, another car (black) he will meet, and the blocks delimiting streets.

Given the stated trip plan, he should turn right at the next crossing and, at the current speed, he will reach it in about 10 seconds. The MMI Manager queues a request of issuing this message to the list of messages to be assigned a tool in the *Communication Model*:

```
(inform Co-pilot Driver
     (should Driver (turn Driver right (next crossing)))) [1]
```

The fact that this queue has a new item triggers the *Tool Chooser*, which picks the best available tool for such a message, given the present *Psychological States*, the driver's *Preferences* and the available interaction tools. The chosen form for the message is a blinking arrow-shaped icon on the monitor, since this tool satisfies the requirements of the situation. The *Tool Chooser* communicates it to the MMI manager, which moves the message [1] to the queue of messages to be output in the *Communication Model*, associating to it the following description of the chosen tool:

```
media:          monitor,
message_form:   (icon),
contents:       (arrow left),
modalities:     (blinking)
```

On the monitor, there are pre-defined positions for icon messages, since this reduces the driver's recognition time. Then the MMI manager starts the proper *Symbol/Signal Translator*, which will issue the message. The last action done by the MMI manager is to set an expectation about a reaction of the driver to the issued message. Five seconds later, the driver did not operate on the right arrow switch, yet. Therefore, the MMI manager again puts the message request on the list of messages to be assigned a tool. From this, *MIMa* decides to decrease the *level of awareness* needed, and again starts the process of media assignment. Now, the chosen tool is the speech synthesizer, which needs a lower level of awareness. The MMI manager starts the translator which triggers the speech synthesizer. So, the loudspeaker says: "You should turn left at the next crossing." The driver reacts to this new stimulus, and turns right, using direction indicators properly.

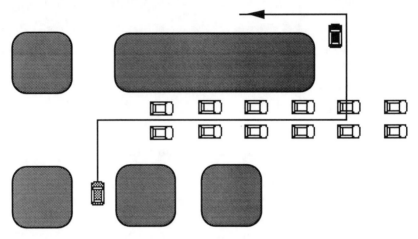

Figure 2. The Driving Situation Presented in the Example

Unfortunately, a queue begins just around the corner. The driver suddenly brakes. He is late, and he tries to find a way to gain positions on the queue. The controls interpreters add support to the fact that he is becoming *uneasy*, and that his *attention level* is becoming *absorbed*.

At the next crossing, he should turn left. Given the situation, *MIMa* decides to issue the message using the voice synthesizer, mainly because this media has a low level of *attention* needed. No blinking icons are now activated, because the quantity of attention the driver could dedicate to communication is low.

Fortunately, the street taken is a way out from the queue. The driver accelerates, but the car in front of him suddenly stops. He brakes, and pushes the horn button for some seconds. *MIMa* interpret this as *panic*. The next message should have been a suggestion to take the left way at the next traffic-light. None of the available tools are compatible with the current situation.

This is communicated to the MMI manager, which delays the message. The driver continues his way. We recall that *support* is a measure of the evidence for a fact. Here, from the behavior of the driver, the *support* to the value for the driver's *agitation* increases. As cited above, confidence values decay with time–this is what happens to the *support* for the value *panic* of the driver's *agitation. Plausibility* is inversely proportional to the measure of evidence against a fact. Since the value *panic* for the driver's *agitation* contrasts with the value *uneasy*, evidence against the first increases with evidence for the second. In other words, if there is evidence for the driver being uneasy, this is against the fact that his *agitation* takes the value *panic*. This decreases the plausibility of this value. This mechanism of uncertainty updating is implemented in a belief network [Bonarini et al. 1992] which does it automatically.

Given the new driver's state, the left-turning message can now be issued. Since there is only a short time before the next crossing, and the support for the level of *attention* value *absorbed* is becoming old, the message is issued by combining voice and visual natural language messages.

Moreover, since in the last minutes the co-pilot suggested three direction changes, the map showing the actual track is also presented on the screen to prevent driver's questions about the suggested route. This is triggered by the MMI reasoning on the current situation.

7. Conclusions

We have presented modeling issues to manage multimedia interaction between driver and co-pilot on a vehicle in the near future. The problem is quite different from the typical problems in the area of "intelligent multimedia man-machine interfaces." Most of the applications in this area are devoted to the interaction between a *user* and a *computer*, which can issue messages in different forms (mainly natural language and pictures). Here, the interaction is between a *user* and a *vehicle*: the computer is just a means to give the car the possibility to cooperate with the user. This sub-area (driver co-pilot interaction) is borning in these years, since the technology for such applications is becoming mature only now. One of the problems specific of this sub-area is that communication flows in parallel with a strong resource-consuming activity, which does not concern primarily exchange of information. This makes time-constraints critical. [Gerlinger et al. 1991] consider this problem, and propose an architecture where asynchronous tasks do short activities coordinated by strategic knowledge. This approach minimizes the risk of unexpected interrupts. We take another approach: all our modules produce some information which is not critical for the system performance. All the knowledge present in the modules is always consistent with some state of the world at a previous time, and the *Tools Chooser* may do its activity– any choice can be justified by the knowledge status at some time.

Most of the media used in our application are different from those used in traditional multimedia interfaces. Also, when the media are similar (such as a screen) the way they are used is different, since the situation is different. For instance, the problem of the screen layout, although important also for driver co-pilot interaction (see, for instance [Pleczon and Kessaci 1991]), is not a central issue for our research. We consider we have pre-defined places for icons, maps and messages on the small screen available on-board. Each message may only be output at his own place on the screen, according to the *Principle of the Least Astonishment* [Thimbleby 1990]. We are more interested in the choice of the most suitable message for the current situation, within a set of pre-defined types of messages on the different media.

The proposal of Arens, Hovy, and Vossers [this volume] is related to ours. They present a framework to classify knowledge, communication acts, and presentation features. Their classification, although very general, does not cover some features typical of our application domain, such as the *user model* features, and the *interaction tools* features. A future extension of our work will consider their proposal to enrich the present representation.

The proposal by Maybury [this volume] stimulated plans for future extensions of our work, too. He presents a model for planning communicative acts in a multimedia environment. We consider communicative acts as a means to represent knowledge corresponding to messages. We did not yet organize the communicative acts we work on in a clean framework as the one proposed by Maybury. This will help to design in a better way the inferential activities underlying tools selection.

We implemented *MIMa* in C on an MS-DOS machine, simulating the parallel activity of the different modules. We are now testing this prototype in a simulated environment.

The next step of our research activity will concern the collection of data from actual sensors in different driving situations. We will use these data to test the assumptions we made and to refine the elements of the models we defined.

8. Acknowledgments

The research here described has been supported by the CNR (the Italian National Research Council) within the Progetto Finalizzato Transporti, Obiettivo PRO-ART, and it is part of the EUREKA Project PROMETHEUS. We would like to thank Alfred Kobsa for encouragement about continuing our research activity about driver modeling, and Alessandro Taurino for the implementation of the system.

References[1]

[Abu-Hakima 1988] Abu-Hakima, S. 1988. RATIONALE: A Tool for Developing Knowledge-Based Systems that Explain by Reasoning Explicitly. Masters thesis, Carleton University, Ottawa, Canada, May, 1988.

[Abu-Hakima 1989] Abu-Hakima, S. and van Hoff A. A. 1989. An Intelligent Environment for Developing Knowledge-Based Applications. In [Arens et al. 1989], 1-11.

[Abu-Hakima 1990] Abu-Hakima S. and Oppacher F. 1990. Improving Explanations in Knowledge-Based Systems: RATIONALE. *Knowledge Acquisition* 2(4):301-343.

[Abu-Hakima et al., this volume] Abu-Hakima, S.; Halasz, M.; and Phan, S. 1993. An Approach to Hypermedia in Diagnostic Systems. In this volume.

[ACM SIGIR 1988] ACM SIGIR (ed.) 1988. *Proceedings of the 11th International Conference on Research and Development in Informatoin Retrieval.* Grenoble, France. June 1988.

[Adorni et al. 1989] Adorni, G.; Poggi, A.; and Ferrari, G. 1989. Natural Language Interaction in Navigation. In *Proceedings of the 2nd PROMETHEUS Workshop*, 110-116. Stockholm, Sweden.

Abbreviations:
International Joint Conference on Artificial Intelligence (IJCAI)
National Conference on Artificial Intelligence (NCAI)s
American Association for Artificial Intelligence (AAAI)
European Conference on Artificial Intelligence (ECAI)
Association for Computational Linguistics (ACL)
European Association for Computational Linguistics (EACL)
Object Oriented Programming Systems, Languages, and Applications (OOPSLA)
Human Computer Interaction (HCI)
Conference on Human Factors in Computing Systems (CHI)
Deutsches Forschungszentrum für Künstliche Intelligenz GmbH (DFKI)
 (German Research Center for Artificial Intelligence)
Association for Computing Machinery (ACM)
Institute for Electrical and Electronic Engineers (IEEE)

[Allen 1983a] Allen, J. F. 1983. Maintaining Knowledge About Temporal Intervals. *Communications of the ACM,* 26(11):832-843.

[Allen 1983b] Allen, J. F. 1983. Recognizing Intentions from Natural Language Utterances. In *Computational Models of Discourse,* eds. M. Brady and B. Berwick, 107-166. Cambridge: MIT Press.

[Allen 1987] Allen, J. F. 1987. *Natural Language Understanding.* Menlo Park: Benjamin Cummings.

[Allen et al. 1989] Allen, J. F.; Guez, S.; Hoebel, L.; Hinkelman, E.; Jackson, K.; and Kyburg, A.; and Traum, D. 1989. The Discourse System Project, Technical Report 317, Department of Computer Science, University of Rochester.

[Anand and Kahn 1992] Anand, T. and Kahn, G. 1992. SPOTLIGHT: A Data Explanation System. In *Proceedings of the Eight Conference on Artificial Intelligence Applications,* 2-8. Monteray, CA, March 2-6. Los Alamitos, CA: IEEE Computer Society Press.

[André and Rist 1990a] André, E. and Rist, T. 1990. Synthesizing Illustrated Documents: A Plan-Based Approach. In *Proceedings of InfoJapan 1990,* 2:163-170. Tokyo, Japan. Also DFKI Research Report RR-91-06.

[André and Rist 1990b] André, E. and Rist, T. 1990. Towards a Plan-Based Synthesis of Illustrated Documents. In *Proceedings of the Ninth ECAI,* 25-30. Stockholm, Sweden, July 1990. Also DFKI Research Report RR-90-11.

[André and Rist, this volume] André, E. and Rist, T. 1993. The Design of Illustrated Documents as a Planning Task. In this volume. Also DFKI Research Report RR-92-45.

[André et al., this volume] André, E.; Finkler, W.; Graf, W.; Rist, T.; Schauder, A.; and Wahlster, W. 1993. WIP: The Automatic Synthesis of Multimodal Presentations. In this volume. Also DFKI Research Report RR-92-46.

[Appelt 1981] Appelt, D. E. 1981. Planning Natural-Language Utterances to Satisfy Multiple Goals. Ph.D. diss., Stanford University.

[Appelt 1985] Appelt, D. 1985. *Planning English Sentences.* England: Cambridge University Press.

[Apple 1987] Human Interface Guidelines: The Apple Desktop Interface, 1987. Apple Computer: Cupertino, CA.

[Apple 1989] *Apple Technical Procedures Macintosh IIcx.* 1989. Cupertino: Apple Computer.

[Arens et al. 1988] Arens, Y.; Miller, L.; Shapiro, S. C.; and Sondheimer, N. K. 1988. Automatic Construction of User Interface Displays. In *Proceedings of the 7th NCAI (AAAI-88),* 808-813. St. Paul, MN: NCAI. Also available as USC/Information Sciences Institute Research Report RR-88-218.

[Arens et al. 1989] Arens, Y.; Feiner, S.; Hollan, J.; and Neches, B. (eds.) 1989. *Workshop Notes from the IJCAI-89 Workshop on A New Generation of Intelligent Interfaces*, Detroit, MI, 22 August.

[Arens and Hovy 1990a] Arens, Y. and Hovy, E. H. 1990. How to Describe What? Towards a Theory of Modality Utilization. In *Proceedings of the 12th Cognitive Science Conference*, 487-494. Cambridge, MA.

[Arens and Hovy 1990b] Arens, Y. and Hovy, E. H. 1990. Text Layout as a Problem of Modality Selection. In *Proceedings of the 5th Conference on Knowledge-Based Specification*, 87-94. Syracuse, NY: Rome Air Development Center Workshop.

[Arens and Hovy 1991] Arens, Y. and Hovy, E. 1991. Categorizing the Knowledge Used in Multimedia Presentations. In [Maybury 1991c], 70-77.

[Arens et al. 1991] Arens, Y.; Miller, L.; and Sondheimer, N. K. 1991. Presentation Design Using an Integrated Knowledge Base. In [Sullivan and Tyler 1991], 241-258.

[Arens et al. 1992] Arens, Y.; Dale, R.; Kerpedjiev, S.; McKeown, K.; Stock. O.; and Wahlster, W. 1992. Panel: Extending Language Generation to Multiple Media. In [Dale et al. 1992] 278-292.

[Arens et al. 1993] Arens, Y.; Hovy, E.; and Van Mulken, S. 1993. A Tree-Traversing Prototype that Allocates Presentation Media. In *Proceedings of the 13th IJCAI*, Chambéry, France, August, 1993.

[Arens et al., this volume] Arens, Y.; Hovy, E. H.; and Vossers, M. 1993. The Knowledge Underlying Multimedia Presentations. In this volume.

[Argyle et al. 1974] Argyle, M.; Lefebvre, L.; and Cook, M. 1974. The Meaning of Five Patterns of Gaze. *European Journal of Social Psychology* 4(2):125-136.

[Argyle and Cook 1976] Argyle, M. and Cook, M. 1976. *Gaze and Mutual Gaze*. England: Cambridge University Press.

[Austin 1962] Austin, J. 1962. *How to do Things with Words*, ed. J. O. Urmson. England: Oxford University Press.

[Awada et al. 1991] Awada, A.; Evrard, F.; and Jacoboni, E. 1991. Pilot Co-pilot Communication Acts. In *Proceedings of the PROMETHEUS Workshop on Intelligent Co-Pilot*, 83-92. Grenoble, France.

[Bandyopadhyay 1990] Bandyopadhyay, S. 1990. Towards an Understanding of Coherence in Multimodal Discourse, Technical Memo DFKI-TM-90-01, Deutsches Forschungszentrum für Künstliche Intelligenz, Saarbrücken.

[Bauer 1990] Bauer, G. 1990. Verfahren zur Unterstützung und Verbesserung des Rechercheprozesses. WING-IIR Arbeitsbericht 3. LIR Regensburg.

[Bayer and Vilain 1991] Bayer, S. and Vilain, M. 1991. The Relation-Based Knowledge Representation of KING KONG. *SIGART Bulletin* 2(3):15-21. Reprinted from *Working Notes of the AAAI Spring Symposium on Implemented Knowledge Representation Systems*, Stanford, CA, 1991.

[Badler et al. 1991] Badler, N. I.; Webber, B. L.; Kalita, J.; and Esakov, J. 1991. Animation from Instructions. In *Making Them Move: Mechanics, Control, and Animation of Articulated Figures,* eds. N. I. Badler, B. A. Barsky, and D. Zeltzer, 51-93. San Mateo: Morgan Kaufmann.

[Beach 1985] Beach, R. 1985. Setting Tables and Illustrations with Style. Ph.D. diss., Dept. of Computer Science, University of Waterloo, Ontario.

[Bengler 1990] Bengler, K. 1990. Experimentelle Untersuchung zur Representation Semantischer Strukturen. Diplomarbeit Regensburg.

[Bertin 1983] Bertin, J. 1983. *Semiology of Graphics*, trans. by J. Berg. Madison: University of Wisconsin Press.

[Bieger 1984] Bieger, G. R. and Glock, M. D. 1984. The Information Content of Picture-Text Instructions. *The Journal of Experimental Education* 53(2):68-76.

[Bieger 1986] Bieger, G. R. and Glock, M. D. 1986. Comprehending Spatial and Contextual Information in Picture-Text Instructions. *The Journal of Experimental Education* 54(4):181-188.

[Binot et al. 1990] Binot, J. L.; Falzon, P.; Perez, R.; Peroche, B.; Sheehy, N.; Rouault, J.; and Wilson, M. 1990. Architecture of a Multimodal Dialogue Interface for Knowledge-Based Systems. In *Proceedings ESPRIT 1990,* 412-433. Dordrecht, Germany: Kluwer.

[Blattner and Dannenberg 1992] Blattner, M. M. and Dannenberg, R. B. (eds). 1992. *Multimedia Interface Design,* Reading, MA: ACM Press/Addison-Wesley.

[Bobrow et al. 1988] Bobrow, D.; DeMichiel, L.; Gabriel, R.; Keene, S.; Kiczales, G.; Moon, D. 1988. Common Lisp Object System Specification, X3J13 Document 88-002R.

[Bolt 1980] Bolt, R. A. 1980. "Put-That-There": Voice and Gesture at the Graphics Interface. *Computer Graphics* 14(3):262-270.

[Bonarini 1987] Bonarini A. 1987. User Modeling in Person-Machine Communication: A Computational Approach, In *Proceedings MARI-87* , 377-382. Paris, France: CESTA.

[Bonarini 1991a] Bonarini, A. 1991a. User Modeling for Multimedia Car-Driver Interaction: Issues and Proposals. In *Proceedings of the PROMETHEUS Workshop on Intelligent Co-Pilot*, 61-70 Grenoble, France.

[Bonarini 1991b] Bonarini, A. 1991b. Uncertainty Components: Issues and a Proposal for their Integrated Management in Expert Systems. In *Proceedings of the World Congress on Expert Systems*, 1833-1842. New York: Pergamon Press.

[Bonarini et al. 1992] Bonarini, A.; Cappelletti, E.; and Corrao, A. 1992. Network-Based Management of Subjective Judgments: A Proposal Accepting Cyclic Dependencies. *IEEE Transactions on Systems, Man, and Cybernetics* 22(5):1-16.

[Bonarini, this volume] Bonarini, A. 1993. Modeling Issues in Multimedia Car-Driver Interaction. In this volume.

[Bonissone and Johnson 1983] Bonissone, P. P., and Johnson, Jr., H. E. 1983. DELTA: An Expert System for Diesel Locomotive Repair. In *Proceedings of the Joint Services Workshop, AI in Maintenance*, 391-405. Boulder, CO, October.

[Bonissone and Decker 1986] Bonissone, P. P. and Decker, K. S. 1986. Selecting Uncertainty Calculi and Granularity: An Experiment in Trading-off Precision and Complexity. In *Uncertainty in Artificial Intelligence,* eds. L. N. Kanal, and J. F. Lemmer, 214-247. Amsterdam: Elsevier Science Publishers.

[Borning 1987] Borning, A.; Duisberg, R.; Freeman-Benson, B.; Kramer, A.; and Woolf, M. 1987. Constraint Hierarchies. In *Proceedings of OOPSLA 1987*, 48-60. Orlando, FL, October 4-8.

[Bory 1990] Bory, B. 1990. Intelligent Support During Display Design for Dynamic Systems. In *Ergonomics of Hybrid Automated Systems II*, eds. W. Karwowski and M. Rahmimi, 545-552. Amsterdam: Elsevier Science Publishers.

[Bösser and Melchior 1992] Bösser, T. and Melchior, E. 1992. The SANE Toolkit for Cognitive Modeling and User-Centred Design. In *Methods and Tools in User-Centred Design for Information Technology*, eds. M. Galer, S. Harker, and J. Ziegler, J., 93-125. Amsterdam: Elsevier Science Publishers.

[Brachman et al. 1985] Brachman, R. J.; Gilbert, V. P.; and Levesque, H. J. 1985. An Essential Hybrid Reasoning System: Knowledge and Symbol Level Accounts of KRYPTON. In *Proceedings of the Ninth IJCAI*, 532–539. Los Angeles, CA.

[Brachman and Schmolze 1985] Brachman, R. J., and Schmolze J. G. 1985. An Overview of the KL-ONE Knowledge Representation System. *Cognitive Science*, 9(2):171–216.

[Brandt et al. 1983] Brandt, M.; Koch, W.; Motsch, W.; and Rosengren, I. 1983. Der Einfluß der kommunikativen Strategie auf die Textstruktur - dargestellt am Beispiel des Geschäftsbriefes. In: *I. Rosengren (Hrsg.), Sprache und Pragmatik, Lunder Symposium 1982*, 105-135. Almqvist and Wiksell: Stockholm, Sweden.

[Brajnik et al. 1990] Brajnik, G.; Guida, G.; and Tasso, C. 1990. User Modeling in Expert Man-Machine Interfaces: A Case Study in Intelligent Information Retrieval. *IEEE Transactions on Systems, Man, and Cybernetics*, 20(1):166-185.

[Brooke 1989] Brooke, N. M. 1989. Visual Speech Synthesis: Investigating Their Analysis, Synthesis and Perception. In *The Structure of Multimodal Dialogue*, eds. M. M. Taylor, F. Néel, and D. G. Bouwhuis, 249-258. Amsterdam: Elsevier Science Publishers.

[Brown et al. 1979] Brown, D. C.; Kwasny, S. C.; Chandrasekaran, B.; Sondheimer, N. K. 1979. An Experimental Graphics System with Natural Language Input. *Computer and Graphics*, 4:13-22.

[Brown et al. 1982] Brown, J. S.; Burton, R. R.; and de Kleer, J. 1982. Pedagogical, Natural Language and Knowledge Engineering Techniques in SOPHIE I, II, and II. In *Intelligent Tutoring Systems,* eds. D. Sleeman, and J. S. Brown, 227-282. London: Academic Press.

[Bruce 1975] Bruce, B. C. 1975. Generation as a Social Action. In *Proceedings of Theoretical Issues on Natural Language Processing-1*, 64-67. Urbana-Champaign: ACL.

[Burger 1989] Burger, J. D. 1989. User Models for Intelligent Interfaces. In [Arens et al. 1989], 17-20.

[Burger and Marshall 1991] Burger, J. D., and Marshall, R.J. 1991. AIMI: An Intelligent Multimedia Interface. In [Maybury 1991c], 23-28.

[Burger and Marshall, this volume] Burger, J., and Marshall, R. 1993. The Application of Natural Language Models to Intelligent Multimedia. In this volume.

[Butterworth et al. 1992] Butterworth, J.; Davidson, A.; Hench, S.; and Olano, T. M. 1992. 3DM: A Three Dimensional Modeler Using a Head-Mounted Display. In *SIGGRAPH '92, Symposium on Interactive 3D Graphics*, 135-138. New York, NY: ACM Press.

[Carberry 1988] Carberry, S. 1988. Modeling the User's Plans and Goals. *Computational Linguistics*, 14:23–37.

[Card 1983] Card, S. K.; Moran, T. P.; and Newell, A. 1983. *The Psychology of Human-Computer Interaction.* Hillsdale: Lawrence Erlbaum.

[Carenini et al., to appear] Carenini, G.; Pianesi, F.; Ponzi M.; and Stock, O. 1992. Natural Language Generation and Hypertext Access. To appear in *Applied Artificial Intelligence, An International Journal.*

[CasaBianca 1988] CasaBianca, L. 1988. "Publishers' Notes". In *Hypermedia: The Guide to Interactive Media Production, special publication of Mix--The Recording Industry Magazine.* Emeryville: Mix Publications.

[Casner and Larkin 1989] Casner, S. M., and Larkin, J. H. 1989. Cognitive Efficiency Considerations for Good Graphic Design. In *Proceedings of 11th Annual Conference of the Cognitive Science Society*, 275-282. Hillsdale, NJ: Lawrence Erlbaum.

[Casner 1990] Casner, S. M. 1990. A Task-Analytic Approach to the Automated Design of Information Graphics. Ph.D. thesis, University of Pittsburgh.

[Casner 1991] Casner, S. M. 1991. A Task-Analytic Approach to the Automated Design of Information Graphic Presentations. *ACM Transactions on Graphics* 10(2):111-151.

[Clark 1990] Clark D. A. 1990. Numerical and Symbolic Approaches to Uncertainty Management in AI. *Artificial Intelligence Review* 4(2):109-146.

[Cleveland and McGill 1984] Cleveland, W. S., and McGill, R. 1984. Graphical Perception: Theory, Experimentation, and Application to the Development of Graphical Methods. *Journal of the American Statistical Association* 79(387):531-554.

[Cohen 1978] Cohen, P. R. 1978. On Knowing What to Say: Planning Speech Acts, Technical Report TR-118, University of Toronto.

[Cohen 1981] Cohen, P. R. 1981. The Need for Referent Identification as a Planned Action. In *Proceedings of IJCAI-81,* 21-35. Vancouver, B. C., Canada.

[Cohen et al. 1989] Cohen, P. R.; Dalrymple, M.; Moran, D. B.; Pereira, F. C. N.; Sullivan, J. W.; Gargan Jr, R. A.; Schlossberg, J. L.; and Tyler, S. W. 1989. Synergetic Use of Direct Manipulation and Natural Language. In *Proceedings of CHI 89*, 227-233. Austin, Texas.

[Cohen et al. 1991] Cohen, R.; Song, F.; Spencer, B.; and. van Beek, P. 1991. Exploiting Temporal and Novel Information from the User in Plan Recognition. *User Modeling and User-Adapted Interaction*, 1(2):125-148.

[Coutaz 1992] Coutaz, J. 1992. Multimedia and Multimodal User Interfaces: A Taxonomy for Software Engineering Research Issues. In *Proceedings of the East-West International Conference on Human-Computer Interaction (EWHCI '92)*, 229-240. Moscow: International Centre for Scientific and Technical Information.

[Conklin 1987] Conklin, J., 1987, September. Hypertext: An Introduction and Survey, *IEEE Computer* 20(9):17-41.

[Cornell 1991] Cornell, M. 1991. IKit Design Specification. Part of an unpublished Masters Project, Computer Science, University of Massachusetts.

[Cornell et al., this volume] Cornell, M.; Woolf, B.; and Suthers, D. 1993. Using "Live Information" in a Multimedia Framework. In this volume.

[Croft 1987] Croft, W. B. 1987. Approaches to Intelligent Information Retrieval. *Information Processing and Management*, 23(4):249-254.

[Dale et al. 1992] Dale, R.; Hovy, E.; Rösner, D.; and Stock, O. (eds.) 1992. *Aspects of Automated Natural Language Generation.* Springer Verlag Lecture Notes in Artificial Intelligence No. 587: Proceedings of the 6th International Workshop on Natural Language Generation, Trento, Italy, April, 1992. New York: Springer Verlag.

[Dannenberg 1990] Dannenberg, R. B.; Sanchez, M.; Joseph, A.; Capell, P.; Joseph, R. L.; Saul, R. 1990. A Computer-Based Multi-Media Tutor for Beginning Piano Students. *Interface* 19(2-3):155-173.

[Dannenberg and Blattner 1992] Dannenberg, R. B., and Blattner, M. M. 1992. Introduction: The Trend Toward Multimedia Interfaces. In *Multimedia Interface Design*, eds. M. M. Blattner, and R. B. Dannenberg, xvii-xxv. New York: ACM Press.

[Dannenberg and Joseph 1992] Dannenberg, R. B., and Joseph, R. L. 1992. Human-Computer Interaction in the Piano Tutor. In *Multimedia Interface Design*, eds. M. M. Blattner, and R. B. Dannenberg, 65-78. New York: ACM Press.

[Davis 1991] Davis, M. E. 1991. Director's Workshop: Semantic Video Logging with Intelligent Icons. In [Maybury 1991c], 122-132.

[Devanbu and Litman 1991] Devanbu, P. T. and Litman, D. J. 1991. Plan-Based Terminological Reasoning. In *Proceedings of the Second International Conference on Principals of Knowledge Representation and Reasoning (KR '91)*, April 22-25, Cambridge, MA, 128-138.

[Diaper 1989] Diaper, D. 1989. *Task Analysis for Human-Computer Interaction*. Chichester: Ellis Horwood.

[Driankov 1986] Driankov D. 1986 Uncertainty Calculus with Verbally Defined Belief-Intervals. *International Journal of Intelligent Systems,* 1(3):219-246.

[Driankov 1991] Driankov, D. 1991. Towards a Many-Valued Logic of Quantified Belief: The Information Lattice. *International Journal of Intelligent Systems,* 6(2):135-166.

[Dwyer 1978] Dwyer, F. M. 1978. *Strategies for Improving Visual Learning*. State College: Learning Services.

[Edmonds 1992] Edmonds, E. (ed.). 1992. *The Separable User Interface*. London: Academic Press.

[Edwards and Mason 1989] Edwards, J. L. and Mason, J. A. 1989. The Structure of Intelligence in Dialogue. In *The Structure of Multimodal Dialogue*, eds. M. M. Taylor, F. Néel, and D. G. Bouwhuis, 85-105. Amsterdam: North-Holland.

[Elhadad et al. 1989] Elhadad, M.; Seligmann, D. D.; Feiner, S.; and McKeown, K. A. 1989. Common Intention Description Language for Interactive Multi-media Systems. In [Arens et al. 1989], 46-52.

[Elhadad 1990] Elhadad, M. 1990. Types in Functional Unification Grammars. In *Proceedings of the 28th Meeting of the ACL*, 157-164. Pittsburgh, PA: ACL.

[Elhadad 1993] Elhadad, M. 1993. Using Argumentation to Control Lexical Choice: A Unification-based Implementation. Ph.D. diss., Computer Science Department, Columbia University.

[Feiner 1985] Feiner, S. 1985. APEX: An Experiment in the Automated Creation of Pictorial Explanations. *IEEE Computer Graphics and Application* 5(11):29-37.

[Feiner 1988] Feiner, S. K. 1988. A Grid-Based Approach to Automating Display Layout. In *Proceedings of the Graphics Interface '88*, 192-197. Los Altos, CA: Morgan Kaufmann.

[Feiner 1990] Feiner, S. K. 1990. Authoring Large Hypermedia Documents with IGD. *Electronic Publishing: Origination, Dissemination and Design* 3(1):29-46.

[Feiner 1991] Feiner, S. 1991. An Architecture for Knowledge-Based Graphical Interfaces. In [Sullivan and Tyler 1991], 259-279.

[Feiner and McKeown 1990a] Feiner, S. K., and McKeown, K. R. 1990. Generating Coordinated Multimedia Explanations. In *Proceedings of the Sixth IEEE Conference on Artificial Intelligence Applications (CAIA90)*, 290-296. Santa Barbara, CA: IEEE Computer Society Press. March 5-9, 1990.

[Feiner and McKeown 1990b] Feiner, S. K., and McKeown, K. R. 1990. Coordinating Text and Graphics in Explanation Generation. In *Proceedings of the Eighth NCAI (AAAI-90)*, 442-449. Boston, MA: AAAI/MIT Press. July 29-August 3, 1990.

[Feiner and McKeown 1991] Feiner, S. K., and McKeown, K. R. 1991. Automating the Generation of Coordinated Multimedia Explanations. *IEEE Computer* 24(10):33-41.

[Feiner and McKeown, this volume] Feiner, S. K. and McKeown, K. R. 1993. Automating the Generation of Coordinated Multimedia Explanations. In this volume.

[Feiner and Seligmann 1991] Feiner, S., and Seligmann, D. 1991. Dynamic 3D Illustrations with Visibility Constraints. In Patrikalakis, N. (ed.), *Scientific Visualization of Physical Phenomena (Proceedings of Computer Graphics International '91, Cambridge, MA, June 26-28, 1991*, pp. 525-543. Tokyo: Springer-Verlag.

[Feiner and Seligmann 1992] Feiner, S. and Seligmann, D. 1992. Cutaways and Ghosting: Satisfying Visibility Constraints in Dynamic 3D Illustrations. *The Visual Computer* 8(5-6):292-302.

[Feiner et al. 1992] Feiner, S.; MacIntyre, B.; and Seligmann, D. 1992. Annotating the Real World with Knowledge-Based Graphics on a See-Through Head Mounted Display. In *Proceedings of Graphics Interface 1992*, 78-85. Vancouver, Canada.

[Feiner et al., this volume] Feiner, S. K.; Litman D. J.; McKeown, K. R.; Passonneau, R. J. 1993. Towards Coordinated Temporal Multimedia Presentations. In this volume.

[Ferguson 1985] Ferguson, C. A. 1985. Special Language Registers. Editor's Note. *Discourse Processes* 8(4):392-394. (special issue)

[Finkler and Neumann 1988] Finkler, W., and Neumann, G. 1988. MORPHIX: A Fast Realization of a Classification-Based Approach to Morphology. In *Proceedings of the Workshop 'Wissensbasierte Sprachverarbeitung'*, 11-19. Berlin, Germany. Springer-Verlag, August 1988.

[Finkler and Schauder 1992] Finkler, W. and Schauder, A. 1992. Effects of Incremental Output on Incremental Natural Language Generation. In *Proceedings of the 10th ECAI*, 505-507. Vienna, Austria: ECAI, August.

[Fikes and Kehler 1985] Fikes, R., and Kehler, T. 1985. The Role of Frame-Based Representation in Reasoning. *Communications of the ACM* 28(9):904-920.

[Fisher et al. 1986] Fisher, S.; McGreevy, M.; Humphries, J.; and Robinett, W. 1986. Virtual Environment Display System. In *Proceedings of the 1986 Workshop on Interactive 3D Graphics*, 77-87. October 23-24, 1986. Chapel Hill, NC. New York: ACM, 1987.

[Fleming and Levie 1978] Fleming, M., and Levie, H. W. 1978. *Instructional Message Design: Principles from the Behavioral Sciences*. New Jersey: Educational Technology Publications.

[Flemming et al. 1989] Flemming, U.; Coyne, R.; Glavin, T.; Hsi, H.; and Rychener, M. D. 1989. A Generative Expert System for the Design of Building Layouts. Technical Report EDRC-48-15-89, Engineering Design Research Center, Carnegie Mellon University.

[Foley et al. 1988] Foley, J.; Gibbs, C.; Kim, W.; and Kovacevic, S. 1988. A Knowledge-Based User Interface Management System. In *Proceedings of the 1988 Conference on Human Factors in Computer Systems*, 67–72. Washington, DC. New York: ACM.

[Forbus and Stevens 1981] Forbus, K., and Stevens, A. L. 1981. Using Qualitative Simulation to Generate Explanations. BBN Report 4490, Bolt Beranek and Newman.

[Fox 1991] Fox, E. A. 1991. Advances in Interactive Digital Multimedia Systems. *IEEE Computer* 24(10):9-21.

[Franconi 1990] Franconi, E. 1990. The YAK Manual: Yet Another KRAPFEN. IRST Manual No. 9003-01, Instituto per la Ricerca Scientifica e Tecnologica.

[Freeman-Benson 1990] Freeman-Benson, B.; Maloney, J.; and Borning, A. 1990. An Incremental Constraint Solver. *Communications of the ACM,* 33(1):54-63.

[Friedell 1983] Friedell, M. 1983. Automatic Graphics Environment Synthesis. Ph.D. thesis, Case Western Reserve University.

[Furnas et al. 1984] Furnas, G. W.; Gomez, L. M.; Landauer, T. K.; Dumais, S. T. 1984. Statistical Semantics: Analysis of the Potential Performance of Keyword Information Systems. In *Human Factors in Computer Systems*, eds. J. C. Thomas, and M. L. Schneider, 187-242. Norwood, NJ: Ablex. Reprinted from *Bell System Technical Journal*, 1983, AT&T.

[Gargan et al. 1988] Gargan, R. A., Jr.; Sullivan, J. W.; and Tyler, S. W. 1988. Multimodal Response Planning: An Adaptive Rule Based Approach. In *Proceedings CHI '88 Human Factors in Computing Systems*, eds. E. Soloway; D. Frye; and S. Sheppard, 229-234. New York: ACM.

[Gerlinger et al. 1991] Gerlinger G.; Zhang J.; Lefort N.; Morizet-Mahoudeaux P.; and Sayettat C. 1991. An Integrated Real-time Multi-expert, Multi-task, On-board Diagnosis System. In *Proceedings of the PROMETHEUS Workshop on Intelligent Co-Pilot*, 273-284. Grenoble, France.

[Georgeoff 1987] Georgeoff, M. P. 1987. Planning. In *Annual Review of Computer Science,* eds. J. F. Traub, G. J. Grosz, B. W. Lampson, and N. G. Nilsson, 359-400. Palo Alto: Annual Reviews, Inc.

[Gnanamgari 1981] Gnanamgari, S. 1981. Information Presentation Through Default Display. Ph.D. thesis, University of Pennsylvania.

[Goldberg and Robson 1985] Goldberg, A., and Robson, D. 1985. *Smalltalk-80: The Language and its Implementation*. Reading: Addison-Wesley.

[Goodman 1986] Goodman, B. A. 1986. Reference Identification and Reference Identification Failures. *Computational Linguistics*, 12(4):273-305.

[Goodman 1991] Goodman, B. A. 1991. Multimedia Explanations for Intelligent Training Systems. In *Proceedings of the 1991 Conference on Intelligent Computer-Aided Training (ICAT-91),* ed. B. Loftin, 139-153. November 20. Houston, TX: NASA.

[Goodman and Litman 1992] Goodman, B. A., and Litman, D. L. 1992. On the Interaction Between Plan Recognition and Intelligent Interfaces. *Journal of User Modeling and User-Adapted Interaction*, 2(1-2):83-115.

[Goodman, this volume] Goodman, B. A. 1993. Multimedia Explanations for Intelligent Training Systems. In this volume.

[Gott and Pokorny 1987] Gott, S. P., and Pokorny, R. 1987. The Traning of Experts for High-Tech Work Environments. Paper presented at 9th Interservice/Industry Training Systems Conference, Washington, DC.

[Gott 1989] Gott, S. P. 1989. Apprenticeship Instruction for Real-World Tasks: The Coordination of Procedures, Mental Models, and Strategies. In *Review of Research in Education*, ed. E. A. Rothkopf, 15:97-169. Washington, DC: American Educational Research Association.

[Graf and Maaß 1991] Graf, W., and Maaß, W. 1991. Constraint-basierte Verarbeitung graphischen Wissens. In *Proceedings of 4 Internationaler GI-Kongreß Wissensbasierte Systeme - Verteilte KI und kooperatives,* eds. W. Arbeiten, D. Brauer, and D. Hernández, 243-253. Berlin: Springer-Verlag. Also DFKI Research Report RR-91-35.

[Graf 1992] Graf, W. 1992. Constraint-Based Graphical Layout of Multimodal Presentations. To appear in *Proceedings of AVI'92 (Advanced Visual Interfaces)*. Rome, Italy. Also DFKI Research Report RR-92-15.

[Gray 1991] Gray, P. D. 1991. Representation and Relationships in Iconic Interfaces. In *Current Human-Computer Interaction Research: An Anthology of Recent Papers – Volume II.*, ed. K. W. Waite. Also Research Report GIST-91-1, Glasgow Interactive Systems Centre, Department of Computing Science, University of Glasgow.

[Gray et al. 1993] Gray, W. D.; Hefley, W. E.; and Murray, D. (eds.) 1993. *Proceedings of the 1993 International Workshop on Intelligent User Interfaces*, Orlando, FL January, 1993. New York: ACM.

[Green 1985] Green, M. 1985. Report on Dialogue Specification Tools. In *User Interface Management Systems*, ed. G. E. Pfaff, 9-20. Berlin: Springer-Verlag.

[Grimes 1975] Grimes, J. E. 1975. *The Thread of Discourse*. Mouton: The Hague, Paris.

[Grishman 1986] Grishman, R. 1986. *Computational Linguistics. An Introduction*. Cambridge: Cambridge University Press.

[Grosz 1977] Grosz, B. J. 1977. The Representation and Use of Focus in Dialogue Understanding. Tech. Note 151. SRI Project 5844, SRI.

[Grosz and Sidner 1986] Grosz, B. J., and Sidner, C. L. 1986. Attention, Intentions, and the Structure of Discourse. *Computational Linguistics* 12(3):175-204.

[Grosz and Sidner 1990] Grosz, B. J., and Sidner, C. L. 1990. Plans for Discourse. In *Intentions in Communication*, eds. P. Cohen, J. Morgan, and M. Pollack, 417-444. Cambridge, MA: MIT Press.

[Guastello and Traut 1989] Guastello, S. J., and Traut, M. 1989. Verbal Versus Pictorial Representations of Objects in a Human-Computer Interface. *International Journal of Man-Machine Studies* 31:99-120.

[Guzdial and Soloway 1991] Guzdial, M., and Soloway, E. 1991. Design of an Educational Multimedia Compositon Environment. In [Maybury 1991c], 93-98.

[Hajicovà 1987] Hajicovà, E. 1987. Focusing: A Meeting Point of Linguistics and Artificial Intelligence. In *Artificial Intelligence II "Methodology, Systems, Applications"*, eds. P. Jorrand and V. Sgurev, 311-321. North Holland: Elsevier Science Publishers.

[Halasz 1988] Halasz, F. G. 1988. Reflections on NoteCards, Seven Issues for the Next Generation of Hypermedia Systems, *Communications of the ACM*, 31(7):836-852.

[Halasz et al. 1992] Halasz, M. S.; Davidson, P. L.; Abu-Hakima, S.; and Phan, S. 1992. JETA: A Knowledge-Based Approach to Aircraft Gas Turbine Engine Maintenance. In *Applied Intelligence: The International Journal of AI, Neural Networks and Complex Problem Solving Technology*.2(1):25-46.

[Halliday 1967] Halliday, M. A. K. 1967. *Explorations in the Functions of Language*. London: Arnold.

[Halliday 1985] Halliday, M. A. K. 1985. *An Introduction to Functional Grammar*. Baltimore: Edward Arnold Press.

[Harbusch 1991] Harbusch, K.; Finkler, W.; and Schauder, A. 1991. Incremental Syntax Generation with Tree Adjoining Grammars. In *Proceedings of 4. Internationaler GI-Kongreß Wissensbasierte Systeme - Verteilte KI und kooperatives Arbeiten (Proceedings Fourth International GI Congress*, eds. W. Brauer and D. Hernández, 363-374. Berlin: Springer-Verlag,

[Hallen et al. 1989] Hallen, A.; Franzén, S.; and Alm, H. 1989. Show Me the Way to Go Home. PROMETHEUS Report RI-IRG-02.

[Harel and Papert 1990] Harel, I., and Papert, S. 1990. Software Design as a Learning Environment. *Interactive Learning Environments*, 1(1):1-32.

[Hartley 1985] Hartley, J. 1985. *Designing Instructional Text*. (2nd edition). Great Britain: Kogan Page Ltd.

[Hawkins 1988] Hawkins, D. T. 1988. Applications of Artificial Intelligence (AI) and Expert Systems for Online Searching. *ONLINE* 12(1):31-43.

[Hauptman 1989] Hauptman, A. G. 1989. Speech and Gestures for Graphic Image Manipulation. In *Proceedings of SIGCHI '89*. 241-245. New York: ACM Press. Austin, TX, April 30- May 4.

[Hefley 1990] Hefley, W. E. 1990. Architectures for Adaptable Human-Machine Interface. In *Ergonomics of Hybrid Automated Systems II*, eds. W. Karwowski and M. Rahmimi, 575-585. Amsterdam: Elsevier Science Publishers.

[Hefley and Murray 1993] Hefley, W. E., and Murray, D. 1993. Intelligent User Interfaces. In [Gray et al. 1993], 3-10.

[Heinsohn et al. 1992] Heinsohn, J.; Kudenko, D.; Nebel, B; and Profitlich, H. J. 1992. *RAT - Representation of Actions using Terminological Logics*. Forthcoming DFKI Report. Saarbrücken, Germany.

[Hentenryck 1989] Hentenryck, P. Van (ed.). 1989. *Constraint Satisfaction in Logic Programming*. Cambridge: MIT Press.

[Heyer and Kese 1991] Heyer, G., and Kese, R. 1991. A Highly Efficient Situation Dependent Natural Language Help System for the Domain of Text Processing. In *Proceedings HCI '91*, ed. H. J. Bullinger, 910-914. New York: Elsevier Science Publishers.

[Heyer 1992] Heyer, G. 1992. Elements of a Natural Language Processing Technology. Working paper. Research Center TA-Triumph-Adler AG. Nürnberg.

[Hill et al. 1992] Hill, W.; Wroblewski, D.; McCandless, T.; and Cohen, R. 1992. Architectural Qualities and Principles for Multimodal and Multimedia Interfaces. In *Multimedia Interface Design*, ed. M. M. Blattner and R. B. Dannenberg, 311-318. New York: ACM Press.

[Hilton and Anken 1990] Hilton, M. L., and Anken, C. S. 1990. Map Display System: An Object-Oriented Design and Implementation. Rome Air Development Center Technical Report 90-54.

[Hollan et al. 1984] Hollan, J. D.; Hutchins, E. L.; and Weitzman, L. 1984. STEAMER: An Interactive Inspectable Simulation-Based Training System. *AI Magazine*, 5(2):15-27.

[Honda 1990] Honda Accord: 1990 Owner's Manual. Japan: Honda Motor Co. Ltd.

[Hobbs 1978] Hobbs, J. 1978. Why is a Discourse Coherent? Technical Report 176, SRI, Menlo Park, CA.

[Hobbs and Shieber 1987] Hobbs, J. and Shieber, S. 1987. An Algorithm for Generating Quantifier Scopings, *Computational Linguistics* 13(1-2):47-63.

[Hovy 1987] Hovy, E. H. 1987. Generating Natural Language Under Pragmatic Constraints. Ph.D. thesis, Department of Computer Science, Yale University.

[Hovy 1988a] Hovy, E. H. 1988. Planning Coherent Multisentential Text. In *Proceedings of the 26th Conference of the ACL,* 163-169. Buffalo, NY.

[Hovy 1988b] Hovy, E. H. 1988. *Generating Natural Language under Pragmatic Constraints.* Hillsdale, NJ: Lawrence Erlbaum Associates.

[Hovy 1990a] Hovy, E. H. 1990. Natural Language Processing at ISI. *The Finite String* 16(4):37-42.

[Hovy 1990b] Hovy, E. H. 1990. Unresolved Issues in Paragraph Planning. In *Current Research in Natural Language Generation*, eds. R. Dale, C. Mellish and M. Zock, 17-41. New York: Academic Press.

[Hovy and Arens 1990] Hovy, E. H., and Arens, Y. 1990. When is a Picture Worth a Thousand Words? – Allocation of Modalities in Multimedia Communication. AAAI Spring Symposium on Human-Computer Interaction, Stanford University, CA, March, 1990.

[Hovy and Arens 1991] Hovy, E. H., and Arens, Y. 1991. Automatic Generation of Formatted Text. In *Proceedings of the 10th NCAI (AAAI-91)*, 92-97. Anaheim, CA: AAAI.

[Hovy et al. 1992] Hovy, E. H.; Lavid, J.; Maier, E.; Mittal, V.; Paris, C. L. 1992. Employing Knowledge Resources in a New Text Planner Architecture. In [Dale et al. 1992], 57-72.

[Hunter et al. 1987] Hunter, B.; Crismore, A.; and Pearson, P. D. 1987. Visual Displays in Basal Readers and Social Studies Textbooks. In *The Psychology of Illustration, Basic Research*, eds. D. M. Willows and H. A. Houghton, 2:116-135. New York: Springer.

[Jacob 1990] Jacob, R. J. K. 1990. What You Look at is What You Get: Eye Movement-Based Interaction Techniques. In *Proceedings of SIGCHI '90*, 11-18. New York: ACM Press. Seattle, April 1-5.

[Jarvenpaa and Dickson 1988] Jarvenpaa, S. L., and Dickson, G. W. 1988. Graphics and Managerial Decision Making: Research Based Guidelines. *Communications of the ACM* 31(6):764-774.

[Joseph 1991] Joseph, R. L. 1991. A Presentation System for an Intelligent Piano Tutor System. In [Maybury 1991c], 58-62.

[Joshi 1985] Joshi, A. 1985. An Introduction to TAGs. Technical Report, MS-CIS-86-64, LINC-LAB-31, Dept. of Computer and Information Science, Moore School, University of Pennsylvania.

[Kahneman 1973] Kahneman, D. 1973. *Attention and Effort*. New Jersey: Prentice-Hall.

[Kanngießer 1989] Kanngießer, S. 1989. Korrespondenzen zwischen KI und Linguistik. In: Luck, K. v. (Hrsg.), *Künstliche Intelligenz*. 7. Frühjahrsschule, KIFS-89, 270-282. Berlin: Springer.

[Karp and Feiner 1990] Karp, P., and Feiner, S. K. 1990. Issues in the Automated Generation of Animated Presentations. In *Proceedings Graphics Interface '90*, 39-48. Halifax, NS, Canada. Morgan Kaufmann Publishers.

[Kasper 1989] Kasper, R. T. 1989. Unification and Classification: An Experiment in Information-Based Parsing. In *Proceedings of the International Workshop on Parsing Technologies*, 15-22. Pittsburgh, PA.

[Kasper and Hovy 1990] Kasper, R. T., and Hovy, E. H. 1990. Integrated Semantic and Syntactic Parsing using Classification. In *Proceedings of the DARPA Speech and Natural Language Workshop*, 54-59. Pittsburgh, PA.

[Kass and Finin 1988] Kass, R., and Finin, T. 1988. Modeling the User in Natural Language Systems, *Computational Linguistics*, 14(3):5-22.

[Kautz 1987] Kautz, H. A. 1987. A Formal Theory of Plan Recognition. Ph.D. thesis, Department of Computer Science, University of Rochester. Available as Technical Report 215.

[Kay and Goldberg 1977] Kay, A., and Goldberg, A. 1977. Personal Dynamic Media. *IEEE Computer*, 10(3):31-41.

[Kay 1979] Kay, M. 1979. Functional Grammar. In *Proceedings of the 5th Meeting of the Berkeley Linguistics Society*. Berkeley Linguistics Society.

[Kay 1980] Kay, M. 1980. Algorithm Schemata and Data Structures in Syntactic Processing. Technical Report CSL-80, Xerox Palo Alto Research Centers. Palo Alto, CA.

[Kerpedjiev 1992] Kerpedjiev, S. M. 1992 Generation of Multimodal Weather Reports. In [Dale et al. 1992], 284-286. Also see Kerpedjiev, S. M. 1992. Automatic Generation of Multimodal Weather Reports from Datasets. In *Proceedings of the 3rd ACL Conference on Applied Natural Language Processing* (ANLP-92), 48-55. Trento, Italy.

[Kirch 1990] Kirch, F. 1990. Spontansprachliche Dialoge in der zwischenmenschlichen Kommunikation und Mensch-Computer-Interaktion. Aufbau eines Simulationsmodells und Auswertung. Magisterarbeit LIR, Regensburg.

[Kissmeyer and Tallant 1989] Kissmeyer, K. Y., and Tallant, A. M. 1989. MACPLAN: A Mixed-Initiative Approach to Airlift Planning. In *Innovative Applications of Artificial Intelligence*, eds. H. Schorr and A. Rappaport, 271-286. Cambridge: MIT Press.

[Kjorup 1978] Kjorup, S. 1978. Pictorial Speech Acts. *Erkenntnis* 12:55-71.

[Kleinke 1986] Kleinke, C. 1986. Gaze and Eye Contact: A Research Review. *Psychological Bulletin*, 100(1):78-100.

[Kobsa and Wahlster 1989] Kobsa, A., and Wahlster, W. (eds.) 1989. *User Models in Dialog Systems*. Berlin: Springer-Verlag.

[Kobsa et al. 1986] Kobsa, A.; Allagyer, J.; Reddig, C.; Reithinger, N.; Schmauks, D.; Harbusch, K.; and Wahlster, W. 1986. Combining Deictic Gestures and Natural Language for Referent Identification. In *Proceedings of the 11th Conference on Computational Linguistics*, Bonn RFT.

[Kochhar 1991] Kochhar, S. 1991. Cooperative Computer-Aided Design. Ph.D. dissertation, Harvard University, 1991.

[Koller 1992] Koller, F. 1992. Multimedia Interfaces. In *Methods and Tools in User-Centred Design for Information Technology*, eds. M. Galer, S. Harker, and J. Ziegler, 299-315. Amsterdam: Elsevier Science Publishers.

[Koons et al., this volume] Koons, D. B.; Sparrell, C. J.; and Thorisson, K. R. 1993. Integrating Simultaneous Output from Speech, Gaze, and Hand Gestures. In this volume.

[Kosslyn 1985] Kosslyn, S. M. 1985. Graphics and Human Information Processing - A Review of Five Books. *Journal of the American Statistical Association* 80(391):499-512.

[Kosslyn 1989] Kosslyn, S. M. 1989. Understanding Charts and Graphs. *Applied Cognitive Psychology* 3:185-226.

[Kovacevic 1992] Kovacevic, S. 1992. A Compositional Model of Human-Computer Dialogues. In *Multimedia Interface Design*, M. M. Blattner and R. B. Dannenberg, 373-404. New York: ACM Press.

[Krause 1982] Krause, J. 1982. Mensch-Maschine-Interaktion in natürlicher Sprache. Tübingen: Neimeyer.

[Krause 1990a] Krause, J. 1990a. The Concepts of Sublanguage and Language Register in Natural Language Processing. In *Linguistic Approaches to Artificial Intelligence*, eds. U. Schmitz,R. Schütz, and A. Kunz, 129-158. Frankfurt: Peter Lang Publishers.

[Krause 1990b]   Krause, J. 1990b. Zur Architektur von WING. Grundtypen des Retrieval-prozesses, Integration von Komponenten eines "Intelligenten Information Retrieval" und Modellaufbau einer multimedialen Dialogkomponente für Werkstoffinformationssysteme. WING-IIR Arbeitsbericht. LIR Regensburg.

[Krause 1992]   Krause, J. 1992. Intelligentes Information Retrieval. Rückblick, Bestandsauf-nahme und Realisierungschance. In *Experimentelles und praktisches Information Retrieval,* ed. R. Kuhlen, 9-34. festschrift für Gerhard Lustig, Konstanz.

[Krause, this volume] Krause, J. 1993. A Multilayered Empirical Approach to Multimodality: Towards Mixed Solutions of Natural Language and Graphical Interfaces. In this volume.

[Krause et al. 1990]   Krause, J.; Bauer, G.; Lutz, J.; Roppel, S.; Wolff, C.; Womser-Hacker, C. 1990. WING: The Research Prototype of a Multi-Modal Materials Information System, Comprising Natural Language, Graphical/Direct Manipulation, and Knowledge Based Com-ponents. In *Pragmatische Aspekte beim Entwurf und Betrieb von Informationssystemen. Proceedings des 1. Internationalen Symposiums für Informationswissenschaft*: eds. J. Herget and R. Kuhlen, 329-338. Konstanz.

[Krause and Hitzenberger 1992] Krause, J., and Hitzenberger, L. 1992. *Computer Talk.* Zurich, New York: Hildesheim.

[Kum-yew et al. 1988] Kum-yew, L.; Malone, T.; and Keh-chiang, Y. 1988. Object Lens: A "Spreadsheet" for Cooperative Work. *ACM Transactions on Office Information Systems,* 6(4):333-353.

[Lajoie and Lesgold 1989] Lajoie, S. P. and Lesgold, A. 1989. Apprenticeship Training in the Workplace: Computer-Coached Practice Environment as a New Form of Apprenticeship. *Machine-Mediated Learning*, 3(1):7-28.

[Larkin and Simon 1987] Larkin, J. H., and Simon, H. A. 1987. Why a Diagram is (Sometimes) Worth Ten Thousand Words. *Cognitive Science* 11(1):65-99.

[Lavelli and Stock 1990] Lavelli, A. and Stock, O. 1990. When Something is Missing: Ellipsis, Coordination and the Chart. In *Proceedings of the 13th International Conference on Compu-tational Linguistics, COLING 90*, 184-189. Helsinki, Finland.

[Lavelli et al. 1992] Lavelli, A.; Magnini, B.; Strapparava, C. 1992. An Approach to Multilevel Semantics for Applied Systems. In *Proceedings of the 3rd Conference on Applied Natural Language Processing*, 17-24. Trento, Italy: ACL.

[Lenat and Guha 1990] Lenat, D. B., and Guha, R. V. 1990. *Building Large Knowledge-Based Systems - Representation and Inference in the Cyc project.* Reading: Addison-Wesley.

[Levelt 1989] Levelt, W. (ed.) 1989. *Speaking: From Intention to Articulation.* Cambridge: MIT Press.

[Levin et al. 1987] Levin, J. R.; Anglin, G. J.; and Carney, R. N. 1987. On Empirically Validating Functions of Pictures in Prose. In *The Psychology of Illustration, Basic Research, Vol. 1,* eds. D. M. Willows and H. A. Houghton, 51-85. New York: Springer.

[Levinson 1983] Levinson, S. C. 1983. *Pragmatics.* Cambridge: Cambridge University Press.

[Litman and Allen 1987] Litman, D. J., and Allen, J. F. 1987. A Plan Recognition Model for Subdialogues in Conversations. *Cognitive Science*, 11(2):163-200.

[Lombardi 1989] Lombardi, C. 1989. *Experiments for Determining the Assignment of Information Media in COMET.* Technical Memo. New York: Columbia University.

[Lotus 1991] Lotus Development Corporation. 1991. *Referenzhandbuch AmiPro für Windows.* (Version 2). Atlanta: Lotus Development Corporation.

[Maaß 1992] Maaß, W. 1992. Constraint-basierte Plazierung in multimodalen Dokumenten am Beispiel des Layout-Managers in WIP. Master's thesis, Dept. of Computer Science, University of Saarbrücken.

[MacGregor and Bates 1987] MacGregor, R., and Bates, R. 1987. The LOOM Knowledge Representation Language. Technical Report ISI/RS-87-188. Information Sciences Institute, USC.

[Mackinlay 1986a] Mackinlay, J. 1986. Automatic Design of Graphical Presentations. Ph.D. diss., Stanford University.

[Mackinlay 1986b] Mackinlay, J. D. 1986. Automating the Design of Graphical Presentations of Relational Information. *ACM Transactions on Graphics* 5(2):110-141.

[Mackworth1977] Mackworth, A. 1977. Consistency in Networks of Relations. *Artificial Intelligence*, 8(1):99-118.

[MacLaughlin and Shaked 1989] MacLaughlin, D. M., and Shaked, V. 1989. Natural Language Text Generation in Semi-Automated Forces. Technical Report 7092, Bolt Beranek and Newman.

[Mann and Matthiessen 1983] Mann, W. C., and Matthiessen, C. M. I. M. 1983. Nigel: A Systemic Grammar for Text Generation. Research Report RR-83-105, USC/ISI.

[Mann 1983] Mann, W. C. 1983. An Overview of the PENMAN Text Generation System. In *Proceedings of AAAI-83*, 261-265. Washington, DC.

[Mann and Thompson 1987] Mann, W. C., and Thompson, S. A. 1987. Rhetorical Structure Theory: Description and Construction of Text Structures. In *Natural Language Generation: New Results in Artificial Intelligence, Psychology, and Linguistics*, ed. G. Kempen, 85-95. Dordrecht: Nijhoff.

[Mann and Thompson 1988] Mann, W. C. and Thompson, S. A. 1988. Rhetorical Structure Theory: Towards a Functional Theory of Text Organization. *Text*, 8(3):243-281.

[Marks and Reiter 1990] Marks, J., and Reiter, E. 1990. Avoiding Unwanted Conversational Implicatures in Text and Graphics. In *Proceedings of the Eighth NCAI (AAAI-90)*, 450-456. Boston: AAAI/MIT Press.

[Marks 1990] Marks, J. 1990. A Syntax and Semantics for Network Diagrams. In *Proceedings of IEEE Workshop on Visual Languages,* 104-110. Skokie, IL, October, 1990.

[Marks 1991a] Marks, J. W. 1991. Automating the Design of Network Diagrams. Ph.D. thesis, Harvard University.

[Marks 1991b] Marks, J. 1991. A Formal Specification Scheme for Network Diagrams That Facilitates Automated Design. *Journal of Visual Languages and Computing* 2(4):395-414.

[Marks 1991c] Marks, J. 1991. Discourse Coherence and the Consistent Design of Informational Graphics. In [Maybury 1991c], 29-36.

[Marx et al. 1992] Marx, J.; Roppel, S.; Wolff, C. 1992. Der erste multimodale Systementwurf für den WING-Prototyp. WING-Arbeitsbericht 21. LIR Regensburg.

[Maskery and Meads 1992] Maskery, H., and Meads, J. 1992. Context in the Eyes of Users and in Computer Systems. *SIGCHI Bulletin* 24(2):12-21.

[Maskery et al. 1992] Maskery, H., Hopkins, G.; and Dudley, T. 1992. Context: What Does it Mean to Application Design. *SIGCHI Bulletin* 24(2):22-30.

[Massey et al. 1986] Massey, L. D.; de Bruin, J., Roberts, B. 1986. A Training System for System Maintenance. In *Intelligent Tutoring Systems: Lessons Learned*, eds J. Psotka, L. Massey, and S. Mutter, 369-402. Hillsdale: Lawrence Erlbaum Associates

[Matthiessen 1984] Matthiessen, C. M. I. M. 1984. Systemic Grammar in Computation: The Nigel Case. In *Proceedings of 1st Conference of the EACL*, 33-38. Pisa, Italy. Also available as USC/ISI Research Report RR-84-121.

[Matthiessen 1985] Matthiessen, C. 1985. The Systemic Framework in Text Generation: Nigel. In Systemic Perspectives on Discourse, eds. J. Benson and W. Greaves, 1:110-135, Norwood: Ablex.

[Maybury 1990] Maybury, M. T. 1990. Planning Multisentential English Text using Communicative Acts. Ph.D. diss., University of Cambridge, England. Available as Rome Air Development Center TR 90-411, In-House Report, December 1990 or as Cambridge University Computer Laboratory TR-239, December, 1991.

[Maybury 1991a] Maybury, M. T. 1991a. Planning Multimedia Explanations Using Communicative Acts. In *Proceedings of the Ninth NCAI*, 61-66. Anaheim, CA: AAAI.

[Maybury 1991b] Maybury, M. T. 1991. Topical, Temporal and Spatial Constraints on Linguistic Realization, *Computational Intelligence: Special Issue on Natural Language Generation.* 7(4):266-275.

[Maybury 1991c] Maybury, M. T. (ed) 1991. *Working Notes from the AAAI Workshop on Intelligent Multimedia Interfaces,* Ninth NCAI. 15 July, Anaheim, CA. Menlo Park: AAAI.

[Maybury 1992a] Maybury, M. T. 1992. A Critique of Text Planning Architectures. In *Journal of the International Forum on Information and Documentation (IFID).* 17(2):7-12. Special issue on the Bijormi Text Generation Symposium, Bijormi, Georgia, USSR, 23-26 September, 1991.

[Maybury 1992b] Maybury, M. T. 1992. Communicative Acts for Explanation Generation. *International Journal of Man-Machine Studies.* 37(2), 135-172.

[Maybury, this volume] Maybury, M. T. 1993. Planning Multimedia Explanations Using Communicative Acts. In this volume.

[Maybury, in press] Maybury, M. T. In press. Knowledge Based Multimedia: The Future of Expert Systems and Multimedia. *International Journal of Expert Systems with Applications. Special issue on Expert Systems Integration with Multimedia Technologies*, ed. J. Ragusa. New York: Pergamon Press.

[Mayer 1989] Mayer, R. E. 1989. Systematic Thinking Fostered by Illustrations in Scientific Text. *Journal of Educational Psychology* 81(1):240-246.

[McDermott 1990] McDermott, J. 1990. Developing Software is Like Talking to Eskomos about Snow. In *Proceedings of the Eighth NCAI (AAAI-90)*, 1130-1134. Boston, MA: AAAI.

[McDonald and Pustejovsky 1985] McDonald, D. and J. Pustejovsky. 1985. Description-Directed Natural Language Generation. In *Proceedings of the Ninth IJCAI*, 799-805. Los Angeles, CA: IJCAI.

[McKeown 1985] McKeown, K. R. 1985. *Text Generation: Using Discourse Strategies and Focus Constraints to Generate Natural Language Text.* England: Cambridge University Press.

[McKeown et al. 1990] McKeown, K. R.; Elhadad, M.; Fukumoto, Y.; Lim, J; Lombardi, C.; Robin, J.; and Smadja, F. 1990. Language Generation in COMET. In *Current Research in Language Generation*, eds. C. Mellish, R. Dale, and M. Zock, 103-136. London: Academic Press.

[McKeown et al. 1992] McKeown, K. R.; Feiner, S.; Robin, J.; Seligmann, D.; and Tanenblatt, M. 1992. Generating Cross-References for Multimedia Explanation. In *Proceedings of AAAI-92,* 9-16. San Jose, CA. 12-17 July.

[Means and Gott 1988] Means, B., and Gott, S. P. 1988. Cognitive Task Analysis as a Basis for Tutor Development: Articulating Abstract Knowledge Representations. In *Intelligent Tutoring Systems: Lessons Learned,* eds. J. Psotka, L. Massey, and S. Mutter, 35-57. Hillsdale: Lawrence Erlbaum Associates.

[Mel et al. 1988] Mel, B.; Omohundro, S.; Robison, A.; Skiena, S.; Thearling, K.; Young, L.; and Wolfram, S. 1988. Tablet: Personal Computer of the Year 2000. Technical Report UIUCDCS-R-88-1406. Department of Computer Science, University of Illinois at Urbana-Champaign.

[Mezrich et al. 1984] Mezrich, J.; Frysinger, S; and Slivjanovski, R. 1984. Dynamic Representation of Multivariate Time Series Data. *Journal of the American Statistical Association*, 79(385):34-40.

[Michel 1989] Michel, S. 1989. *HyperCard: The Complete Reference.* Berkeley: Osborne McGraw-Hill.

[Microsoft 1992] Microsoft Corporation. 1992. *Microsoft Word für Windows.* Version 2. Benutzerhandbuch: Microsoft.

[Miller 1986] Miller, A. 1986. *Imagery in Scientific Thought.* Cambridge: MIT Press.

[Molitor 1989] Molitor, S; Ballstaedt, S-P.; and Mandl, H. 1989. Problems in Knowledge Acquisition from Text and Pictures. In *Knowledge Acquisition from Text and Pictures*, eds. H. Mandl and J. R. Levin, 3-35. New York: North Holland.

[Moore 1989] Moore, J. D. 1989. A Reactive Approach to Explanation in Expert and Advice-Giving Systems. Ph.D. diss., University of California at Los Angeles.

[Moore and Paris 1989] Moore, J. D., and Paris, C. L. 1989. Planning Text for Advisory Dialogues. In *Proceedings of the 27th Annual Meeting of the ACL*, 203-211. Vancouver, Canada.

[Moore and Swartout 1989] Moore, J. D., and Swartout, W. R. 1989. A Reactive Approach to Explanation. In *Proceedings of the 11th IJCAI*, 1504-1510. Detriot, MI.

[Moore and Swartout 1990] Moore, J. D., and Swartout, W. R. 1990. Pointing: A Way Toward Explanation Dialogue. In *Proceedings of the Eighth NCAI*, 457-464. Boston, MA.

[Muckenhaupt 1986] Muckenhaupt, M. 1986. *Text und Bild.* Tübingen: Gunter Narr.

[Müller-Brockmann 1981] Müller-Brockmann, J. (ed.). 1981. *Grid Systems in Graphic Design.* Niederteufen, Switzerland: Verlag Arthur Niggli.

[Myers and Rosson 1992] Myers, B. A., and Rosson, M. B. 1992. Survey on User Interface Programming. In *Proceedings of CHI '92 Human Factors in Computing Systems,* 195-202. New York, NY: ACM.

[Neal et al. 1989] Neal, J. G.; Thielman, C. Y.; Dobes, Z.; Haller, S. M.; and Shapiro, S. C. 1989. Natural Language with Integrated Deictic and Graphic Gestures. In *Proceedings of the 1989 DARPA Workshop on Speech and Natural Language*, 410-423. Harwich Port: Morgan Kaufmann.

[Neal 1990]　Neal, J. G. 1990. Intelligent Multi-Media Integrated Interface Project. SUNY Buffalo. RADC Technical Report TR-90-128.

[Neal and Shapiro 1991] Neal, J. G. and Shapiro, S. C. 1991. Intelligent Multi-Media Interface Technology. In [Sullivan and Tyler 1991], 11-43.

[Neches et al. 1985]　Neches, R.; Swartout, W. R.; and Moore, J. D. 1985. Enhanced Maintenance and Explanation of Expert Systems Through Explicit Models of their Development. In *IEEE Transactions on Software Engineering*, SE-11(11):1337-1351.

[Nelson 1980] Nelson, T. 1980. Replacing the Printed Word: A Complete Literary System. In *Information Processing 80. Proceedings of the IFIP Congress 80*, ed. S. Lavington, S., 1013-1023. Amsterdam: North-Holland.

[Nielsen 1990a] Nielsen, J. 1990. The Art of Navigating through Hypertext. In *Communications of the ACM*, 33(3):296-310.

[Nielsen 1990b] Nielsen, J. 1990. *Hypertext and Hypermedia*. San Diego: Academic Press, Inc.

[Norman 1991] Norman, D. A. 1991. Cognitive Artifacts. In *Designing Interaction*, ed. J. M. Carroll, 17-38. Cambridge: Cambridge University Press.

[Novitz 1977]　Novitz, D. 1977. *Pictures and Their Use in Communication: A Philosophical Essay*. The Hague: Martinus Nijhoff.

[Ortony et al. 1992] Ortony, A.; Slack, J.; and Stock, O. (eds.) 1992. *Communication from an Artificial Intelligence Perspective: Theoretical and Applied Issues*. Berlin, Germany: Springer-Verlag, 121-144.

[Ostler 1989] Ostler, N. D. M. 1989. LOQUI: How Flexible Can a Formal Prototype Be? In *The Structure of Multimodal Dialogue*, eds. M. M. Taylor, F. Néel, and D. G. Bouwhuis, 407-416. Amsterdam: North Holland.

[Oviatt and Cohen 1989] Oviatt, S. L., and Cohen, P. R. 1989. The Effects of Interaction on Spoken Discourse. In *Proceedings of the 27th Meeting of the ACL*, 126-134. Vancouver, Canada: University of British Columbia.

[Paap 1988]　Paap, K. R. 1988. Design of Menus. In *Handbook of Human-Computer Interaction*, ed. M. Helander, 205-235. Amsterdam: Elsevier Science Publishers.

[Papert 1980] Papert, S. 1980. *Mindstorms: Children, Computers, and Powerful Ideas*. New York: Basic Books, Inc.

[Paris 1987a] Paris, C. L. 1987. The Use of Explicit User Models in Text Generation: Tailoring to a User's Level of Expertise. Ph.D. diss., New York: Columbia University.

[Paris 1987b] Paris, C. L. 1987. Combining Discourse Strategies to Generate Descriptions to Users Along a Naive/Expert Spectrum. In *Proceedings of IJCAI 87*, 626-632, Milan, Italy: IJCAI.

[Paris 1990] Paris, C. L. 1990. Generation and Explanation: Building an Explanation Facility for the Explainable Expert Systems Framework. In *Natural Language Generation in Artificial Intelligence and Computational Linguistics*, eds. C. L. Paris, W. R. Swartout, and W. C. Mann, 49-82. Norwell: Kluwer Academic.

[Paris and Bateman 1990] Paris, C. L., and Bateman, J. A. 1990. User Modeling and Register Theory: A Congruence of Concerns. Technical Report RR-307. Information Sciences Institute, Marina del Rey, CA.

[Passonneau 1988] Passonneau, R. J. 1988. A Computational Model of the Semantics of Tense and Aspect. *Computational Linguistics*, (14)2: 44-60.

[Pea et al.1990] Pea, R.; Boyle, E.; and Vogel, R. 1990. Design Spaces for Multimedia Composing Tools. In *Design for Learning,* 37-42. Cupertino: Apple Computer.

[Penman 1988] The Penman project. 1988. *The Penman Primer, User Guide, and Reference Manual.* Unpublished USC/ISI documentation.

[Petre and Green 1990] Petre, M., and Green, T. R. G. 1990. Is Graphical Notation Really Superior to Text, or Just Different? Some Claims by Logic Designers about Graphics in Notation. In *Proceedings of the ECCE-5*, 92-101. Urbino, Italy.

[Pianesi 1992] Pianesi, F. 1992. Head Driven Bottom Up Generation and Government and Binding: A Unified Perspective. In Proceedings of the 3rd European Workshop on Natural Language Generation, Pinter, London. Forthcoming.

[Pleczon and Kessaci 1991] Pleczon, P., and Kessaci, A. 1991. The Pro-LabI Man-Machine Interface. In *Proceedings of the PROMETHEUS Workshop on Intelligent Co-Pilot*, 71-82. Grenoble, France.

[Prevost and Banda 1990] Prevost, M., and Banda, C. P. 1990. A Visualization Tool for Human-Machine Interface Designers. Working Paper; NASA Ames Research Center.

[Psotka et al. 1988] Psotka, J.; Massey, L. D.; and Mutter, S. A. (eds) 1988. Intelligent Instructional Design. In *Intelligent Tutoring Systems: Lessons Learned,* 113-118. Hillsdale: Lawrence Erlbaum Associates

[Reddy et al. 1973] Reddy, R.; Erman, L.; Fennell, R.; and Neely, R. 1973. The HEARSAY Speech Understanding System: An Example of the Recognition Process. In *Proceedings of IJCAI 73*, 185-193. Stanford, CA, August 20-23, 1973.

[Reichman 1981] Reichman, R. 1981. Plain Speaking: A Theory and Grammar of Spontaneous Discourse. Ph.D. diss., Harvard University.

[Reichman 1989] Reichman, R. 1989. Integrated Interfaces Based on a Theory of Context and Goal Tracking. In *The Structure of Multimodal Dialogue,* eds. M. M. Taylor, F. Néel, and D. G. Bouwhuis, 209-227. Amsterdam: North Holland.

[Reiter et al. 1992] Reiter, E.; Mellish, C.; and Levine, J. 1992. Automatic Generation of On-Line Documentation in the IDAS Project. In *Proceedings of the 3rd Conference on Applied Natural Language Processing*, 64-71. Trento, Italy: Assocation for Computational Linguistics.

[Reithinger 1991] N. Reithinger. 1991. POPEL - An Incremental and Parallel Natural Language Generation System. In *Natural Language Generation in Artificial Intelligence and Computational Linguistics*, eds. C. L. Paris, W. R. Swartout, and W. C. Mann, 179-200. Norwell: Kluwer Academic.

[Rimé and Schiaratura 1991] Rimé, B., and Schiaratura, L. 1991. Gesture and Speech. In *Fundamentals of Nonverbal Behavior*, eds. R. S. Feldman and B. Rim, 239-281. New York: Press Syndicate of the University of Cambridge.

[Rist and André 1992a] Rist, T., and André, E. 1992. From Presentation Tasks to Pictures: Towards a Computational Approach to Automatic Graphics Design. In *Proceedings of the 10th ECAI*, 764-768. Vienna, Austria.

[Rist and André 1992b] Rist, T., and André, E. 1992. Incorporating Graphics Design and Realization into the Multimodal Presentation System WIP. To appear in *Proceedings of AVI'92 (Advanced Visual Interfaces)*, Rome, Italy. Also DFKI Research Report RR-92-44.

[Roth and Mattis 1990a] Roth, S. F., and Mattis, J. 1990. Data Characterization for Intelligent Graphics Presentation. In *Proceedings of the 1990 Conference on Human Factors in Computing Systems*, 193–200. New Orleans, Louisiana. ACM/SIGCHI.

[Roth and Mattis 1990b] Roth, S. F., and Mattis, J. 1990. Automatic Graphics Presentation for Production and Operations Management Systems. In *Proceedings of the Fourth International Conference on Expert systems for Production and Operations Management,* 493-509. Hilton Head, SC: AAAI/OMA/TIMS.

[Roth and Mattis 1991] Roth, S. F., and Mattis, J. 1991. Automating the Presentation of Information. In *Proceedings of the IEEE Conference on AI Applications*, 90-97. Miami Beach, FL.

[Roth et al. 1991] Roth, S. F.; Mattis, J.; and Mesnard, X. 1991. Graphics and Natural Language Generation as Components of Automatic Explanation. In [Sullivan and Tyler 1991], 207-239.

[Roth and Hefley, this volume] Roth, S., and Hefley, W. 1993. Intelligent Multimedia Presentation Systems: Research and Principles. In this volume.

[Roth and Hendrickson 1991] Roth, S. F., and Hendrickson, C. T. 1991. Computer Generated Explanations in Project Management Systems. *Journal of Computing in Civil Engineering,* 5(2):231-244.

[Sacerdoti 1977] Sacerdoti, E. D. 1977. *A Structure for Plans and Behavior*. New York: Elsevier North-Holland.

[Samek-Lodovici and Strapparava 1990] Samek-Lodovici, V., and Strapparava, C. 1990. Identifying Noun Phrase References, The Topic Module of the Al Fresco System. In *Proceedings of ECAI 90*, 573-578. Stockholm, Sweden.

[Scha 1983] Scha, R. 1983. Logic Foundation for Question Answering. Technical Report MS 12.331, Philips Research Laboratories.

[Schaffer Sider 1990] Schaffer Sider, J. 1990. Free Presumption Checking in KING KONG. In *Proceedings of the Ninth ECAI*, 591–593. Stockholm, Sweden: ECAI.

[Schaffer Sider and Burger 1992] Schaffer Sider, J., and Burger, J. D. 1992. Intention Structure and Extended Responses in a Portable Natural Language Interface. In *User Modeling and User-Adapted Interaction*, 2(1):155-179.

[Schauder 1992] Schauder, A. 1992. Incremental Syntactic Generation of Natural Language with Tree Adjoining Grammars. DFKI Technical Document D-92-21.

[Schmauks and Reithinger 1988] Schmauks, D., and Reithinger, N. 1988. Generierung multimodaler Ausgabe in NL Dialogsystemen - Voraussetzungen, Vorteile und Probleme. SFB 314 (XTRA), Memo Nr. 24, Universität des Saarlandes.

[Schmauks 1991a] Schmauks, D. 1991. Deixis in der Mensch-Maschine-Interaktion. Multimediale Referenzidentifikation durch natürliche und simulierte Zeigegesten. Tübingen: Niemeyer Verlag.

[Schmauks 1991b] Schmauks, D. 1991. Verbale und nonverbale Zeichen in der Mensch-Maschine-Interaktion. XTRA-Arbeitsbericht 81, SFB 314, Universität Saarbrücken.

[SDK 1990] SDK. 1990. Microsoft Windows Application Style Guide of the Software Development Kit. Microsoft Corporation.

[Searle 1969] Searle, J. R. 1969. *Speech Acts: An Essay in the Philosophy of Language*. London: Cambridge University Press.

[Seligmann and Feiner 1989] Seligmann, D., and Feiner, S. 1989. Specifying Composite Illustrations with Communicative Goals. In *Proceedings of the ACM SIGGRAPH Symposium on User Interface Software and Technology (UIST '89)*, 1-9. November 13-15, 1989. Williamsburg, VA: ACM.

[Seligmann and Feiner 1991] Seligmann, D., and Feiner, S. 1991. Automated Generation of Intent-Based 3D Illustrations. In *Computer Graphics* 25(4). Also in *Proceedings of the ACM SIGGRAPH '91*, 123-132. July 28-August 2, 1991. Las Vegas, NV: ACM.

[Senay 1991] Senay, H. and Ignatius, E. 1991. Compositional Analysis and Synthesis of Scientific Data Visualization Techniques. In *Scientific Visualization of Physical Phenomena (Proceedings of Computer Graphics International '91)*, ed. N. Patrikalakis, 269-281. Tokyo: Springer Verlag.

[Sheridan 1992] Sheridan, T. B. 1992. *Teleoperation, Automation and Human Supervisory Control*. Cambridge: MIT Press.

[Shneidermann 1983] Shneidermann, B. 1983. Direct Manipulation: A Step Beyond Programming Languages. In *IEEE Computer* 16(8):57-69.

[Sidner et al. 1984] Sidner, C.; Bobrow, R.; Bates, L.; Goodman, B.; Haas, A.; Schmolze, J.; and Vilain, M. 1984. Knowledge Representation for Natural Language and Planning Assistance. Unpublished manuscript, Cambridge: BBN Laboratories.

[Siemens 1991] Siemens A. G. 1991. COMFOTEX Version 4.0. Referenzhandbuch. München.

[Slack and Conati 1991] Slack, J. M., and Conati, C. 1991. Modeling Interest: Exploration of an Information Space. To appear in *Acta Psychologica on Cognitive Ergonomics*.

[Slack 1984] Slack, J. M. 1984. Cognitive Science Research. In *Artificial Intelligence. Tools, Techniques, and Applications*, eds. T. OShea, and M. Eisenstadt, 155-177. New York: Harper & Row.

[Smith et al. 1992] Smith, S.; Grinstein, G. G.; and Bergeron, R. D. 1992. Sterophonic and Surface Sound Generation for Exploratory Data Analysis. In *Multimedia Interface Design*, eds. M. M. Blattner, and R. B. Dannenberg, 173-182. New York: ACM Press.

[Smith and Smith 1966] Smith, K. U., and Smith, M. F. 1966. *Cybernetic Principles of Learning and Educational Design*. New York: Holt, Rinehart and Winston.

[Stafford 1990] Stafford, J. Y. 1990. Effects of Active Learning with Computer Assisted or Interactive Video Instruction. Ph.D. diss., Wayne State University.

[Stallard 1986] Stallard D. 1986. A Terminological Simplification Transformation for a Natural Language Question Answering System. In *Proceedings of 24th Meeting of the ACL*, 241-248. New York: ACL.

[Starker and Bolt 1990] Starker, I., and Bolt, R. A. 1990. A Gaze-Responsive Self-Disclosing Display. In *Proceedings of SIGCHI '90*. 3-9. New York: ACM Press. Seattle, April 1-5.

[Stein et al. 1991] Stein, A.; Thiel, U.; and Tißen, A. 1991. Towards Coherent Hypermedia Navigation by Pragmatic Dialogue Modeling. Arbeitspapiere der GMD 580, GMD, Darmstadt, Germany.

[Stevens and Roberts 1983] Stevens, A. L., and Roberts, B. 1983. Quantitative and Qualitative Simulation in Computer-Based Training. *Journal of Computer-Based Instruction*, 10(1):16-19.

[Steiner and Moher 1992] Steiner, K. E., and Moher, T. G. 1992. Graphic StoryWriter: An Interactive Environment for Emergent Storytelling. In *Proceedings of CHI '92,* 357-364. New York: ACM.

[Stock 1989] Stock, O. 1989. Parsing with Flexibility, Dynamic Strategies and Idioms in Mind. *Computational Linguistics* 15(1):1-18.

[Stock 1991] Stock, O. 1991. Natural Language and Exploration of an Information Space: The ALFresco Interactive System. In *Proceedings of IJCAI-91,* 972-978. Sydney, Australia.

[Stock 1992] Stock, O. 1992. A Third Modality of Natural Language?. In *Proceedings of ECAI-92, 10th ECAI,* 853-862. Vienna, Austria.

[Stock et al., this volume] Stock, O. and the AlFresco Project Team. 1993. AlFresco: Enjoying the Combination of Natural Language Processing and Hypermedia for Information Exploration. In this volume.

[Strapparava 1991] Strapparava, C. 1991. From Scopings to Interpretation: The Semantic Interpretation within the ALFRESCO System. In *Lecture Notes in Artificial Intelligence 549,* eds. E. Ardizzone, S. Gaglio, and F. Sorbello, 281-290. New York: Springer-Verlag.

[Streeter et al. 1985] Streeter, L. A.; Vitello, D.; and Wonsievicz, S. A. 1985. How to Tell People Where to Go: Comparing Navigational Aids. *International Journal of Man-Machine Studies,* 22(5):549-562.

[Strothotte and Schmid 1990] Strothotte, T., and Schmid, C. 1990. Semiformale Darstellungen in wissensbasierten Systemen. In *Graphik und KI, GI-Fachgespräch,* eds. K. Kansy and P. Wißkirchen, 1-9. Berlin, Heidelberg: Springer.

[Sturman 1992] Sturman, D. J. 1992. Whole-Hand Input. Ph.D. thesis, The Media Laboratory, Massachusetts Institute of Technology.

[Sukaviriya and Foley 1990] Sukaviriya, P., and Foley, J. 1990. Coupling a UI Framework with Automatic Generation of Context-sensitive Help. In *UIST '90: Proceedings of the 1990 ACM SIGGRAPH Symposium on User Interface Software and Technology,* 152-166. New York: ACM.

[Sukaviriya et al. 1992] Sukaviriya, P.; Isaacs, E.; and Bharat, K. 1992. Multimedia Help: A Prototype and an Experiment. In *Proceedings CHI '92 (ACM Conference on Human Factors in Computing Systems,* 433-434. New York: ACM.

[Sullivan and Tyler 1991] Sullivan, J. W., and Tyler, S. W. (eds.) 1991. *Intelligent User Interfaces.* Frontier Series. New York: ACM Press.

[Suthers 1991] Suthers, D. 1991. A Task Approporiate Hybrid Architecture for Explanation. *Computational Intelligence* 7(4):315-333.

[Suthers 1993] Suthers, D. 1993. An Analysis of Explanation and Implications for the Design of Explanation Planners, Ph.D. diss., Department of Computer Science, University of Massachusetts.

[Suthers et al. 1992] Suthers, D.; Woolf, B.; and Cornell, M. 1992. Steps from Explanation Planning to Model Construction Dialogues. In *Proceedings of the 10th NCAI (AAAI-92)*, 24-30. San Jose, CA: AAAI.

[Tauber 1990] Tauber, M. J. 1990. ETAG: Extended Task Action Grammar – A Language for the Description of the User's Task Language. In *Human-Computer Interaction - Interact '90*, eds. D. Diaper, et al., 163-168. Amsterdam: North-Holland.

[Taylor and Bouwhuis 1989] Taylor, M., and Bouwhuis, D. G. (eds). 1989. *The Structure of Multimodal Dialogue*. B. U.: Elsevier Science Publishers.

[Taylor 1991] Taylor, M. 1991. Multiplexing, Diviplexing, and the Control of Multimodal Dialogue. In Pre-proceedings of the Second Venaco Workshop on the Structure of Multimodal Dialogue. September 16-20, Acquafredda di Maratea, Italy. ISSN 1018-4554.

[Thimbleby 1990] Thimbleby, H. 1990. *User Interface Design*. Reading: ACM Press Addison Wesley.

[Thorisson et al. 1992] Thorisson, K. R.; Koons, D. B.; and Bolt, R. A. 1992. Multi-Modal Natural Dialogue. In *SIGCHI Proceedings '92*, 653-654. New York, NY: ACM Press.

[Trigg et al. 1987] Trigg, R. H.; Moran, T. P.; and Halasz, F. G. 1987. Tailorability in Note-Cards. In *Proceedings of Interact 87 2nd IFIP Conference on Human-Computer Interaction*, 723-728, Stuttgart.

[Tufte 1983] Tufte, E. R. 1983. *The Visual Display of Quantitative Information*. Cheshire: Graphics Press.

[Tufte 1990] Tufte, E. R. 1990. *Envisioning Information*. Cheshire, CT: Graphics Press.

[Tyler et al. 1991a] Tyler, S. W.; Schlossberg, J. L.; Gargan, R. A.; Cook, L. K.; and Sullivan, J. 1991. An Intelligent Interface Architecture for Adaptive Interaction. In [Sullivan and Tyler 1991], 85-109.

[Tyler et al. 1991b] Tyler, S. W.; Schlossberg, J. L.; and Cook, L. K. 1991. CHORIS: An Intelligent Interface Architecture for Multimodal Interaction. In [Maybury 1991c], 99-106.

[Twyman 1985] Twyman, M. 1985. Using Pictorial Language: A Discussion of the Dimensions of the Problem. In *Designing Usable Texts*, eds. T. M. Duffy, and R. Waller, R., 245-312. Florida: Academic Press.

[van Dijk 1980] van Dijk, T. A. 1980. *Textwissenschaft*. München: dtv.

[van Hoff 1991] van Hoff, A. A. 1991. HyperNeWS 1.4 Manual. Turing Institute. Glasgow, Scotland.

[van Luck et al. 1987] van Luck, K.; Nebel, B.; Peltason, C.; and Schmiedel, A. 1987. The Anatomy of the BACK System. Technical Report KIT 41, Department of Computer Science, Technical University of Berlin.

[Vilain 1985] Vilain, M. 1985. The Restricted Language Architecture of a Hybrid Representation System. In *Proceedings of the Ninth IJCAI*, 547–551. Los Angeles: IJCAI.

[Vilain 1991] Vilain, M. 1991. Private conversation about the use of animation in multimedia explanations.

[Vossers 1991] Vossers, M. 1991. Automatic Generation of Formatted Text and Line Drawings. Master's thesis, University of Nijmegen, The Netherlands.

[Wahlster 1988a] Wahlster, W. 1988. One Word Says More Than a Thousand Pictures: On the Automatic Verbalization of the Results of Image Sequence Analysis System. SFB 314, Report #25, Universität des Saarlandes.

[Wahlster 1988b] Wahlster, W. 1988. An Intelligent Multimodal Interface. In *Methodologies for Intelligent Systems,* eds. Z. W. Raz, and L. Saitta, 3:101-111. New York: North-Holland.

[Wahlster 1989] Wahlster, W.; André, E.; Hecking, M.; and Rist, T. 1989. WIP: Knowledge-based Presentation of Information, Project Overview. Technical Report, DFKI - German Research Center for Artificial Intelligence.

[Wahlster 1991] Wahlster, W. 1991. User and Discourse Models for Multimodal Communication. In [Sullivan and Tyler 1991], 45-67.

[Wahlster et al. 1991a] Wahlster, W.; André, E.; Graf, W.; and Rist, T. 1991a. Designing Illustrated Texts: How Language Production Is Influenced by Graphics Generation. In *Proceedings of the 5th Conference of the EACL*, 8-14. Berlin: Springer-Verlag. Also DFKI Research Report RR-91-05. Reprinted in [Maybury 1991c], 9-20.

[Wahlster et al. 1991b] Wahlster, W.; André, E.; Bandyopadhyay, S.; Graf, W.; and Rist, T. 1991. WIP: The Coordinated Generation of Multimodal Presentations from a Common Representation. In *Computational Theories of Communication and their Applications*, eds. A. Ortony, J. Slack, and O. Stock, 190-213. Berlin: Springer Verlag. Also appeared as DFKI Research Report RR-91-08, Saarbrücken, Germany.

[Wahlster et al. 1992] Wahlster, W.; André, E.; Finkler, W.; Profitlich, H. J.; and Rist, T. 1992. Plan-Based Integration of Natural Language and Graphic Generation. German Research Center for Artificial Intelligence, DFKI Research Report. To appear in *Artificial Intelligence.*

[Walker 1991] Walker, Maj. 1991. 4400 MTF Overview. Hills Air Force Base, Utah. October 8, 1991.

[Wazinski 1992] Wazinski, P. 1992. Generating Spatial Descriptions for Cross-modal References. In *Proceedings of the 3rd Conference on Applied Natural Language Processing (ANLP-92)*, 56-63. Trento, Italy, April, 1992.

[Webber 1988] Webber, B. L. 1988. Tense as Discourse Anaphor. *Computational Linguistics*, (14)2:61-73.

[Weicha and Boies 1990] Weicha, C., and Boies, S. 1990. Generating User Interfaces: Principles and Use of ITS Style Rules. In *Proceedings of the Third Annual Symposium on User Interface Software and Technology*, 21-30. Snowbird, Utah.

[Weimer and Ganapathy 1989] Weimer, D., and Ganapathy, S. K. 1989. A Synthetic Visual Environment with Hand Gesturing and Voice Input. *In SIGCHI '89 Proceedings*, 235-40. New York, NY: ACM Press.

[Wenger 1987] Wenger, E. 1987. *Artificial Intelligence and Tutoring Systems: Computational and Cognitive Approaches to the Communication of Knowledge*. Los Altos: Morgan Kaufmann Publishers, Inc.

[Westerstahl 1986] Westerstahl, D. 1986. Quantifiers in Formal and Natural Language. Center for the Study of Language and Information, Report No. CSLI-86-55, Stanford University, Palo Alto, CA.

[Westfold et al. 1990] Westfold, S.; Green, C.; and Zimmerman, D. 1990. Automated Design of Displays for Technical Data. AFHRL Technical Paper AFHRL-TP-90-66, AD-A226 729. Brooks AFB, TX: Air Force Human Resources Laboratory.

[Whittaker and Stenton 1989] Whittaker, S., and Stenton, P. 1989. User Studies and the Design of Natural Language Systems. In *Proceedings of the 4th Conference of the EACL*, 115-123. Manchester, UK.

[Whittaker and Walker 1991] Whittaker, S., and Walker, M. A. 1991. Toward a Theory of Multimodal Interaction. In [Maybury 1991c], 78-85.

[Wolff 1991] Wolff, C. 1991. Die graphische Benutzeroberflache des Forschungsprototypen WING und der kognitiv-graphische Zugangsweg WING-KOGRA. WING-IIR Arbeitsbericht 5. LIR Regensburg.

[Woolf and Cunningham 1987] Woolf, B., and Cunningham, P. 1987. Multiple Knowledge Sources in Intelligent Tutoring Systems. In *IEEE Expert*, 2(2):41-54.

[Woolf 1988] Woolf, B. 1988. Intelligent Tutoring Systems. In *Exploring Artificial Intelligence*, eds. H. Shrobe and AAAI, 1-44. Los Altos, CA: Morgan Kaufmann Publishers.

[Woolf 1991] Woolf, B. 1991. Training Technologies for 2000 and Beyond. Invited talk given at *1991 Conference on Intelligent Computer-Aided Training (ICAT-91),* November 20, Houston, TX: NASA.

[Young 1987] Young, R. L. 1987. An Object-Oriented Framework for Interactive Data Graphics. In *Proceedings OOPSLA '87* (SIGPLAN Notices 22(12)), ed. N. Meyrowitz, 78-90. New York: ACM.

[Yourdon 1978] Yourdon, E., and Constantine, L. L. 1978. *Structured Design.* New York: Yourdon Press.

[Zimmermann et al. 1987] Zimmermann, T.G; Lanier, J.; Blanchard, C.; Bryson, S; and Harvill, Y. 1987. A Hand Gesture Interface Device. In *Proceedings CHI-87 Human Factors in Computing Systems*, 189-192. New York: ACM.

[Zoeppritz 1988] Zoeppritz, M. 1988. 'Kommunikation mit der Maschine'. In *Technisierte Kommunikation*, eds. R. Weingarten, and R. Fiehler. Opladen: Westdeutscher Verlag.

Index